Legal Studies in International, European and Comparative Criminal Law

Volume 6

The main purpose of this book series is to provide sound analyses of major developments in national, EU and international law and case law, as well as insights into court practice and legislative proposals in the areas concerned. The analyses address a broad readership, such as lawyers and practitioners, while also providing guidance for courts. In terms of scope, the series encompasses four main areas, the first of which concerns international criminal law and especially international case law in relevant criminal law subjects. The second addresses international human rights law with a particular focus on the impact of international jurisprudences on national criminal law and criminal justice systems, as well as their interrelations. In turn the third area focuses on European criminal law and case law. Here, particular weight will be attached to studies on European criminal law conducted from a comparative perspective. The fourth and final area presents surveys of comparative criminal law inside and outside Europe. By combining these various aspects, the series especially highlights research aimed at proposing new legal solutions, while focusing on the new challenges of a European area based on high standards of human rights protection.

As a rule, book proposals are subject to peer review, which is carried out by two members of the editorial board in anonymous form.

Eduardo Demetrio Crespo • Alfonso García Figueroa • Gema Marcilla Córdoba
Editors

Crisis of the Criminal Law in the Democratic Constitutional State

Manifestations and Trends

Springer

Editors
Eduardo Demetrio Crespo
Faculty of Legal and Social Sciences
University of Castilla-La Mancha
Toledo, Spain

Alfonso García Figueroa
Faculty of Legal and Social Sciences
University of Castilla-La Mancha
Toledo, Spain

Gema Marcilla Córdoba
Faculty of Law
University of Castilla-La Mancha
Albacete, Spain

ISSN 2524-8049 ISSN 2524-8057 (electronic)
Legal Studies in International, European and Comparative Criminal Law
ISBN 978-3-031-13412-8 ISBN 978-3-031-13413-5 (eBook)
https://doi.org/10.1007/978-3-031-13413-5

This Springer imprint is published by the registered company Springer Nature Switzerland AG
The registered company address is: Gewerbestrasse 11, 6330 Cham, Switzerland

Foreword

It is a great pleasure for me to welcome in the Book Series *Legal Studies in International, European and Comparative Criminal Law* this excellent volume, coordinated by Eduardo Demetrio Crespo, Alfonso García Figueroa, and Gema Marcilla Córdoba. Again, our Series provides readers with a topic that cuts across various areas of criminal law and clearly reveals the benefits of an interdisciplinary approach to face the difficult challenges with which criminal law studies are more and more confronted. But the kind request of my friend and colleague Eduardo Demetrio Crespo, who asked me to write this foreword, filled me with particular joy and satisfaction. This book, indeed, provides an extraordinary synthesis of several key issues that highlight the tremendous developments which criminal law has undergone due to the deep changes that occurred in current societies, but also the not less remarkable developments that have taken place in democratic constitutional models as a result of new legislative policies and jurisprudential arrangements.

Therefore, building bridges with philosophy of law (as was emblematically indicated in the last meeting of the research project that led to this book) is not only an added value but furthermore indicates the best methodology to fully understand the connections between such complex phenomena which characterise the evolution of modern states and legal orders. These bridges, indeed, set the foundations for new theoretical and practical approaches, which must remain coherent with the main principles of a criminal law oriented towards constitutional law, while dealing with the huge problems arising from unprecedented criminal situations. This in turn shows another unquestionable merit of this research, which unifies the selected manifestations of the crisis of criminal law and democratic states in a multilevel framework that calls for in-depth reflection on the classical pillars of criminal law, such as the *ultima ratio* principle and the aims of punishment. By this means, the viewpoint of the crisis of criminal law systems leads to a critical examination of the rule of law and democracy. There is a clear *file rouge* that links together the four main parts of this book, since hate speech crimes, punitive feminism, and so on, reveal the rising tendency of criminal law to broaden its scope of application. One of the most worrisome results of this expansive tendency is surely the anticipation of criminal law intervention, which is often accompanied by the fragmentation of the factual components of several offences in which often neutral behaviours gain criminal law relevance that is often dependent on subjective elements; a tendency that in various situations entails the serious risk of a shift back towards dangerous forms of *Täterstrafrecht*.

There is little doubt that a proper understanding of such problematic areas presupposes clear theoretical coordinates, which in turn play an essential role to redefine the functions of criminal law in post-modern societies within democratic systems. Moreover, the insight into the causes of a widespread crisis of criminal law also provides the opportunity for a "crisis" in its original Greek meaning, that is, for a critical assessment of new manifestations and trends with a view to identifying the limits within which criminal law intervention finds its justification in constitutional systems today. The integrated approach of this study, therefore, allows criminal law to be confronted with itself and to find the boundaries that it must impose upon itself to maintain its legitimacy in democratic states. These demanding goals call upon lawmakers and practitioners to carry out their respective tasks by fulfilling the difficult challenges set by the growing inter-legality, particularly in regional areas, such as the EU area of freedom security and justice, in which intricated legislative tangle webs and the multiple forms of interaction between domestic jurisprudences, and supranational and international case-law, have strongly contributed to the evolution of criminal law systems but also to their crisis.

But this excellent research goes even beyond this level, thus proposing a reconstruction of the role of criminal law in democratic constitutional states by way of examining further essential problems with increasingly interfere with the proper functioning of criminal law in its inevitable relationships with other social factors. The analysis of highly critical phenomena, such as forced disappearances, conflictual situations, and contentious politics, reveals enormous difficulties which inevitably lead criminal law to stretch its own boundaries while showing the need for solution models that cannot solely be reduced to punitive responses. Moreover, a proper assessment of the factors of crisis would probably be impossible without an insight into the interaction between criminal law and communicative processes, which can give rise to problematic relationships between criminal trials and other mechanisms of fact-finding, but also play a key role to allow criminal law to satisfy its own aims of social orientation of human behaviours, particularly in the digital era.

I am therefore very grateful to the editors of this book and all contributors for enriching our Series with this stimulating study, which will certainly be of the utmost interest for both academics and practitioners, and I hope the readers will enjoy this book as much as I did.

Dipartamento di Giurisprudenza
"S. Pugliatti", Universitá di Messina,
Messina, Italy
4 August 2022

Stefano Ruggeri

Preface

Introduction: About the Research Project Crisis of the Criminal Law of Constitutional State of Law (CRESTA)

We are very pleased to publish this volume, which is the result of the research project *Criminal Law Crisis of the Rule of Law: Manifestations and Trends*, in which criminal lawyers and legal philosophers have joined forces to address some key issues that need to be approached from both sides. This cooperation and closeness, which we believe to be essential, has a long tradition in both the Anglo-American and continental European spheres, but has been losing strength over time in favor of a misunderstood specialization. From the outset, our objective was to make a cross-cutting analysis of the factors behind the crisis of what can be called the "criminal law of the rule of law," understood in turn as the most visible symptom of the "crisis of democracy," something about which there is growing evidence. To this end, it was essential to make an in-depth study of whether it was possible to speak about a *paradigm shift* in the foundations of punitive intervention, without losing sight of four major areas of legal knowledge, namely, epistemic, axiological, theoretical, and phenomenological.

The reasoning, apparently simple, involved dealing with an extraordinarily complex and changing object of study, since it requires a retrospective look at the historical-conceptual bases of *ius puniendi* from the perspective of the constitutional state, but also the analysis of everything that has been transforming the "good old liberal criminal law" until it became what we now know, which can be defined as a strange set of elements that have little to do with each other. Relevant authors such as Ulrich Beck (*The Metamorphosis of the World*), Harmut Rosa (*Resonance. A Sociology of the Relationship with the World*), or Yuval Noa Harari (*Homo Deus. A Brief History of Tomorrow*) give an account from the perspective of sociology or history of the immense difficulty of understanding the dangers facing liberal democracy in these times by virtue of another image of human beings ("Menschenbild"), another image of the world ("Weltbild") and the difficult dichotomy that arises between doctrines ("Glaubenssätze") and spaces for action ("Handlungsräume").

Indeed, if democratic criminal law is based internally on a series of guarantees derived from Fundamental Rights—which means that, *per definitionem*, not just any criminal law is possible in a state governed by the rule of law—this means that some deviations cannot be admitted in principle, which does not mean remaining indifferent to the challenges posed by the new phenomena of criminality. Although there are many possible classifications of the study sub-areas, in this project we proceeded to group them around four axes: (a) the theory of the goals of punishment as a framework theory of criminal law regarding the legitimization of punishment and, within this, the rise of retributive justice and its link to certain phenomena that are clearly present in the "spirit of our time" or *Zeitgeist* that inevitably marks an era; (b) second, and in close connection with the advances in the Theory and Philosophy of Law, the parallel transformations that are taking place in the very concept of the Rule of Law; (c) third, the permanent expansion of Criminal Law, both in terms of the field of action (legal assets protected and classification techniques used), as well as the punitive rigor and relativization of guarantees, where it is essential to proceed to establish areas of action; and, (d) finally, it was necessary not to lose sight of how the variable of dangerousness has been undermining the criminal law of the act based on the seriousness of the behavior and the perpetrator's guilty as defined by the principle of proportionality.

Therefore, the four parts of the table of contents of this volume respond to that initial structure and contain articles that we are convinced will generate maximum interest. Throughout this time, we have had the opportunity to meet on several occasions to celebrate seminars with the participation of colleagues of the highest level who have not been able to send a written contribution, but to whom we are grateful for their valuable insights. In the first of these meetings (2019), we presented the first drafts of the papers and benefited from the synergies arising among all of us; in the second one (2020), which had to be held in virtual mode due to the pandemic that has affected the planet, the level of the lectures and discussions was such that all those who attended could realize that it was impossible not to be enriched and learn a lot from such an "intellectual climate"; in the third and last one (2021), entitled *Building Bridges between Criminal Law and the Philosophy of Law*, we wanted to record the spirit that has moved us all this time and which we would like to see continued in the future.

But we do not want to end without expressing our deep appreciation to the Prof. Stefano Ruggeri for accepting to write a short introduction of the book and to Mónica de la Cuerda Martín and Faustino García de la Torre García, without whose enormous effort at the head of all the organizational tasks we would hardly have been able to achieve these results.

Toledo, Spain — Eduardo Demetrio Crespo
Toledo, Spain — Alfonso García Figueroa
Albacete, Spain — Gema Marcilla Córdoba
4 August 2022

Contents

Abbreviations

Art.	Article
Art.	Art. Código Penal (Article Criminal Code)
CEDH	European Convention on Human Rights
EH-Carpizo	Estado constitucional, derechos humanos, justicia y vida universitaria Estudios en homenaje a Jorge Carpizo (Constitutional State, Human Rights, Justice and University Life Studies in Tribute to Jorge Carpizo)
EH-Mir	Estudios de Derecho penal. Homenaje al profesor Santiago Mir Puig (Criminal Law Studies. Tribute to Professor Santiago Mir Puig)
EH-Terradillos	Liber amicorum. Estudios Jurídicos en Homenaje al Prof. Dr. Dr. h. c. Juan Mª Terradillos Basoco (Liber amicorum. Legal Studies in Tribute to Prof. Dr. Dr. h. c. Juan Mª Terradillos Basoco)
FGE	State Attorney General's Office
GA	Goltdammer's Archiv für Strafrecht
InDret	Journal of Law Analysis
JZ	Juristen Zeitung
KritV	Kritische Vierteljahresschrift für Gesetzgebung und Rechtswissenschaft
LCrim	Criminal Procedure Law
LH-Cerezo	Libro Homenaje al Prof. Dr. D. José Cerezo Mir (Tribute Book to Prof. Dr. José Cerezo Mir)
LH-Jorge	Libro Homenaje al Profesor Dr. Agustín Jorge Barreiro (Tribute Book to Prof. Dr. Agustín Jorge Barreiro)
LH-Luzón	Libro Homenaje al Profesor Diego-Manuel Luzón Peña con motivo de su 70° aniversario (Tribute Book to Prof. Diego-Manuel Luzón Peña on the occasion of his 70th birthday)

LH-Torío	El nuevo Código Penal. Presupuestos y fundamentos. Libro Homenaje al Prof. Dr. D. Ángel Torío López (The new Criminal Code. Assumptions and fundamentals. Tribute Book to Prof. Dr. Ángel Torío López)
Libertas	Libertas. Revista de la Fundación Internacional de Ciencias Penales
NFP	Nuevo Foro Penal
p., pp.	Page, Pages
RDPCrim	Revista de Derecho Penal y Criminología
RECPC	Revista Electrónica de Ciencia Penal y CriminologÚa
RP	Revista Penal
STS	Supreme Court Ruling
TC	Constitutional Court
TEDH	European Court of Human Rights
TS	Supreme Court
ZIS	Zeitschrift für Internationale Strafrechtsdogmatik
ZStW	Zeitschrift für die gesamte Strafrechtswissenschaft

Part I
Legitimacy of Punishment in the Democratic Constitutional State

Is It Possible to Limit the Penal Intervention in the Twenty-First Century?

Mirentxu Corcoy Bidasolo

Abstract In the face of the unstoppable expansion of criminal law that has taken place since the 1990s, criticism, is not enough, although essential. It is necessary to propose strategies that make it possible to limit the intervention of criminal law. In this direction, it is essential to apply the limiting principles of criminal law, particularly those of *ultima ratio*, subsidiarity, and proportionality (necessity, suitability, and proportionality, in the strict sense). Likewise, it is essential to conceive punishment with a preventive rather than a retributive purpose to avoid populism and revenge. I consider that it is essential to respect liability for the act, excluding liability for the character, and strict liability. Finally, the teleological interpretation of criminal types is essential, based on the role of exclusive protection of criminal-legal assets.

1 Introduction

Considering the phenomenon of the globally unstoppable expansion of criminal law since the end of the twentieth century, as well as its administrative nature, it seems infeasible to reconcile this situation with the principles of *ultima ratio*, subsidiarity and fragmentation. It is well known, and generally criticized, that the "creation" of offenses that punish behaviors are identical to those sanctioned in administrative, commercial, labor or civil proceedings. Even some behaviors that are lawful outside the criminal law are characterized, as is the case, for example, with the so-called corruption in business or private corruption, in which it is claimed that free competition is protected by sanctioning the unfair competition, although the commercial legislation (Law on Unfair Competition) does not contemplate such behaviors as unlawful. Likewise, the use of open criminal offenses ("or in any other way" "analogous"...) has been generalized, as well as the equivalence of preparatory and completed acts or authorship and participation.

M. Corcoy Bidasolo (✉)
Faculty of Law, University of Barcelona, Barcelona, Spain

E. Demetrio Crespo et al. (eds.), *Crisis of the Criminal Law in the Democratic Constitutional State*, Legal Studies in International, European and Comparative Criminal Law 6, https://doi.org/10.1007/978-3-031-13413-5_1

In order not to limit this work into a critic of the situation, I will try to propose possible solutions that, at least, reduce the expansion and improve the application of the types. In this sense, it is feasible to elaborate some proposals that limit, in practice, the current situation of criminal law, highly criticized by the doctrine, but which is profitable for politicians and, apparently, supported by most of the society. It is a matter of considering, both in legislation and in judicial application, the purpose attributed to criminal law and, most especially, the limiting principles. At the legislative stage, a prior analysis of the reform's necessity is essential, providing criminological data that support the existence of this deficit and the usefulness that this new type or aggravating circumstance may have, to protect a relevant interest—criminal legal asset—for society, at that historical and cultural moment. Therefore, their efficiency in resolving or reducing the conflict must be evaluated beforehand, and an in-depth study of the existing types should be carried out to avoid the increasing number of repetitions and contradictions which, regardless of their inaccuracy from the perspective of legislative technique, lead to practical difficulties in their application.

In most legislative reforms it would be enough to modify the wording of a certain type instead of creating a new one that, in whole or in part, partially overlaps with the previous one. This also explains the difficulties faced by legal operators when dealing with insolvency matters, which are often impossible to resolve. Among the many cases that we find in the Penal Code with this problem could be mentioned, for example, illicit associations and criminal organization, or the amalgamation of criminal offenses in crimes against the market and consumers, without any of them really serving what is theoretically intended, the protection of free competition and consumers. In short, new criminal offenses are created instead of improving and/or adapting existing offenses to current problems or, as the case may be, at least eliminating the previous one when a new one is created that contemplates a similar situation.

In a second stage, legal operators, especially judges, but also prosecutors and lawyers, require a teleological interpretation of the types, which, in turn, involves the link between the Theory of Crime (General Part), and the Special Part of Criminal Law (systematic interpretation), and the proof that, in the specific case, the protected criminal legal asset has been affected (teleological interpretation). That is to say, respect for the principle of harmfulness (material unlawfulness), being not enough that formally the typical elements concur, but it is necessary to prove that, taking into consideration the concurrent circumstances *ex ante*, *ex post* the protected criminal legal asset has been affected—legal result—which must concur both in the attempt and in the completion, both in offenses of mere activity and of result and both in offenses against individual and supra-individual legal assets.

From a different perspective, given the enormous influence that victimology and victims' associations currently have, their scope should be reasonably limited, preventing revenge from being a criterion in the determination of punishment, both at the legislative and judicial levels. The retributive justice positions, express or tacit, are increasing and promote a vision of a just criminal law, as if the victims will cease to be victims just because a greater penalty is imposed on the perpetrator.

Being a "victim" should not be a status, but the emphasis should be placed on their protection and, in that direction, on trying to get them out of that situation. In short, victims should not determine the political-criminal agenda, with total disregard for experts and with casuistic solutions, given that certain offenses have "names and surnames." It is a different case that the so-called secondary victimization should be avoided and that they should be compensated and psychologically helped, when necessary.

Finally, the proposal is as simple as a return to dogmatics—General Part—and to the essential interpretation of the types in the light of the limits of criminal law, particularly the exclusive protection of legal assets, avoiding a formal application, to a certain extent favored by specific functionalist positions related to the validity of the rule and also by the administrative nature of criminal law. Formal application and administration disregard the principle of harmfulness, linked to the material unlawfulness, basing the criminality on the infringement of certain extra-criminal regulations, through *iuris et de iure* presumptions. Consequently, the principles of *ultima ratio, subsidiarity and fragmentation*, closely linked to the principle of harmfulness, must be respected both at the legislative and judicial levels, when interpreting the types of law for their application.

In short, the expansion of criminal law is not exclusively due to the inflation of criminal types, but also to the abandonment of the Theory of Crime, especially by the legislator, but also by those who apply it, as well as to certain theories about it and to the neglect of the limiting principles of criminal law. These include, among others, the *ultima ratio*, subsidiarity and fragmentation principles, the infringement of which has its origin, essentially, in the administrative nature of criminal law, in the breach of the principle of proportionality, in its three aspects (necessity, suitability and proportionality in the strict sense) and of the principle of harmfulness, thus ignoring the essential function of protection of criminal-legal assets.

2 Limits to Punishment: Principles of *Ultima Ratio*, Subsidiarity, and Fragmentation

As has been pointed out, criticisms of the legal asset, together with some theories about the function of criminal law, lead to a crisis of the principles of *ultima ratio*, subsidiarity, and fragmentation. The problem posed by all retributive theories cannot be solved, as they claim, especially the neo-retributive theorists, by establishing limits, because the failure lies in the very foundation, since, denying the preventive effects of punishment, they try to attribute to it functions that are unrelated to retribution. A social and democratic state governed by the rule of law and secularism should not consider that the function of criminal law is to punish, but exclusively to prevent harm to criminal legal assets to the essential values of a given community. According to retributive theories, for the sake of justice, the criminal responsibility of the offender is defined by moral philosophers.[1] The purpose of the penalty as punishment is a feature of religions, especially those of Judeo-Christian roots, and of absolute states, but it cannot be the same in a modern state.[2] To inflict suffering on a citizen, holder of fundamental rights, does not represent a function of the state and this is not solved when, from neo-retributive philosophy, in a line very close to Kant,[3] it is stated that the infliction of suffering is a requirement of justice. In this sense, *Lesch* has defined the penalty as "an evil that is caused to a person in a public-general procedure, carried out by the state, formal and intended, insofar as the injury of a legal rule has occurred, if this harm is to be attributed to that person by way of accusation."[4] While it is true that the penalty conceptually is and should be a punishment, as Santiago Mir Puig[5] rightly stated, this does not imply that punishing a citizen is the function that a social and democratic state governed by the rule of law should exercise.

This idea of justice in certain neo-retributive theorists, closer to *Hegel*, is similar to the theories of penalty understood as confirmation of the validity of the rule or the reestablishment of the right. Although the latter are generally considered to defend positive general prevention, Welzel, for example, associates retributive theory with the validity of the rule, reaching what would be a form of retribution,[6] a similarity that can also be seen in the neo-retributive theorists. In Germany, in the last century, especially based on Jakobs, the theories related to the reestablishment of the validity of the rule acquired great relevance. In this sense, Frisch is very critical regarding the traditional theories of penalty and understands that the only legitimate purpose of penalty is to guarantee a certain rule of law, its validity, and its unbreakable nature.[7] Conceiving the purpose of the penalty as an affirmation of the validity of the rule is a formal theory that could only be legitimate and constitutional if it could be presumed that the rule responds to the essential values of a given society and is respectful of the principles of *ultima ratio* and proportionality.[8] Certainly, if we assume that, in a democratic state, the rules issued by the legislative power respond to the priority interests of the citizens, that the aforementioned principles have been respected and that a correct legislative technique has been followed, it could be logically deduced that this rule is legitimate and constitutional. However, even from this starting point, this cannot imply that the rule must be formally applied, without the need to be interpreted, according to the criminal legal asset that it is intended to protect and/or the constitutional principles, in accordance with the positions that directly derive the criminal law from the Constitution. As has been stated, the affirmation of the rule's

[1] Robinson (2014), pp. 54–57.

[2] Robinson (2014), pp. 10–11.

[3] Die Metaphysik der Sitten, págs. 227–230.

[4] Lesch (1999), p. 4.

[5] Mir Puig (2016), p. 102.

[6] Welzel (1969), p. 240.

[7] Frisch (2014), pp. 11–12.

[8] Robinson (2014), pp. 32–46.

validity as the purpose of the penalty, basing its legitimacy, even when it is situated in positive general prevention, leads us to retribution, if it is not limited with material contents. Frisch supports the theory of the rule's validity as the only valid one, but, as we shall see, he complements it by introducing requirements close to the deservedness and necessity of penalty.[9] Hörnle and von Hirsch consider that the consequences are identical to those that would be reached by defending a retributive theory and express their misgivings that society's sense of justice can be influenced by criminal law, emphasizing that this theory is based on the premises of the theory of retribution.[10] It is true that in the theory of the rule's validity the express reference to "inflicting an evil" is removed, however, this is replaced by the idea that regarding any rule that is violated, one must respond with a penalty, which implies an "evil." Materially it is another way of realizing or demanding justice. In contrast to the retributive theories, preventive theories are utilitarian, as is the *ultima ratio* principle, in the sense that the greatest welfare should be sought at the lowest individual and social cost.

The principles of *ultima ratio*, subsidiarity, and fragmentation, based on the concept of penalty as punishment,[11] should be respected not only in the creation of the types, but also in the amount and kind of penalty foreseen for the different offenses, that is, the penalty in the abstract, and, especially, in its concrete determination.[12] The penalty must be set in accordance with its preventive purposes, but without forgetting that, specifically in order to fulfill these purposes, it must effectively entail a punishment, taking into consideration the type of crime and the criminological profile of its perpetrators, always respecting the principle of proportionality, in the broad sense—necessity, suitability, and proportionality, in the strict sense. Thus, for example, in socioeconomic offenses the penalty consisting of a fine, in many cases, may not be suitable as it does not imply a punishment, especially when, at least in Spain, the principle of personal responsibility is forgotten and the payment is assumed by third parties or by the company, which have the possibility of passing it on in prices or losses, reducing profits and thus the corporate income tax. This means that the alleged perpetrators are in a position to perform a cost-benefit analysis to conclude whether it "pays" for them to run the risk of being punished. Therefore, it cannot be a solution to limit the expansion of criminal law and to respect, apparently, the principle of *ultima ratio*, to provide for the deprivation of liberty penalty only with respect to the so-called nuclear criminal law. In the other direction, some authors, to limit the expansion of criminal law, propose that socioeconomic crimes should not be punishable by imprisonment.[13]

Based on the utilitarian foundation of the *ultima ratio* principle, criminal law must intervene when strictly necessary in terms of general social utility and this

[9] Frisch (2014), p. 12.

[10] Hörnle and von Hirsch (1995), pp. 261–265.

[11] Mir Puig (2016), p. 43.

[12] *Vid;* Demetrio Crespo (2016); Besio Hernández (2011).

[13] Silva Sánchez (2011), pp. 50–55.

cannot be achieved, at least in today's complex society, by limiting criminal law to the protection of subjective rights,[14] in the sense proposed by the advocates of the so-called "minimum criminal law," since this position implies, for example, that any theft is punished and that tax fraud, however high it may be, constitutes only an administrative offense. The replacement of criminal law by an administrative sanctioning law, with less penalty, but also with fewer guarantees, as they propose, does not respond to the needs of the so-called risk society and, even if they intend to "punish less," the reduction of constitutional guarantees, typical of criminal law, can be very harmful to those involved.[15]

To determine when intervention is strictly necessary, it must therefore be assumed that we are in a social and democratic state governed by the rule of law and, in this sense, the Constitution will be an essential element in determining what must be protected. However, it does not mean replacing the legal asset with the Constitution, since the latter does not offer specific criteria as to what and, especially, how the rights and principles established therein should be protected, but only a general framework. Thus, for example, when Art. 15 states that "Everyone has the right to life," it is not specified whether only independent human life is protected (the problem of abortion) or whether this right excludes the possibility of regulating euthanasia and how. Or when, in section 45 CE, it is stated that "Everyone has the right to an environment appropriate for the development of the person, as well as the duty to preserve it," it provides little information on how the environment should be protected and to what extent it should be protected criminally or administratively, and it does not even offer a clear criterion of what the protected legal asset is, that is to say, it advocates an anthropocentric or ecocentric vision.

3 Limited Prevention

Preventive theories remain valid as long as they respect the limits of criminal law and are not used to legitimize its intervention. None of the theories of penalty offers a complete answer, but they are complementary, and it is necessary to relate them to the core of the question: the obligation of the state to protect criminal-legal assets, as the ultimate purpose of the penalty and the function of criminal law. Pérez Manzano correctly makes a distinction between the protection of legal assets as the ultimate purpose of the penalty and the mediate or intermediate purposes that correspond to the purposes of the penalty, and the necessary legitimacy for its imposition, in the specific case, based on the unjustness as a basis and personal responsibility as a limit.[16] The idea of the legal asset, with whatever terminology it may be used and

[14] VVAA (1999).

[15] Corcoy Bidasolo (2011).

[16] Pérez Manzano (1999), pp. 221 y ss.

despite the criticisms that have been made against it,[17] is indispensable for a non-authoritarian criminal law, for a criminal law proper to a democratic society and respectful of the principles of *ultima ratio*, subsidiarity and fragmentation. These criticisms focus on the fact that the legal asset does not have the capacity to limit the intervention of criminal law, basing this objection on its current expansion. However, these same authors criticize certain offenses because they do not protect any legal asset, thus implicitly accepting their usefulness. While the expansion is inevitable and open to criticism, it cannot be attributed solely to the concept of legal asset, but, on the contrary, to the fact that it is not considered by the legislator, especially if it is conceived as a criminal legal asset,[18] to the infringement of the principles of *ultima ratio* and subsidiarity and to a legislative technique that ignores the existence of the General Part of Criminal Law and makes use of case law, making criminal law administrative in nature. The so-called administrative nature of criminal law is not due, or at least not exclusively due to the intervention in new areas, but rather to the failure to introduce criteria in the types of offenses that qualitatively and quantitatively delimit administrative, commercial, tax, labor, etc., from criminal offenses. When there is a duplicity of punishments, it is essential that the criminal law be limited to intervene regarding those modalities of conduct that are particularly harmful, respecting the principle of proportionality, *ad extram* and *ad intra*.

For this reason, the principles of *ultima ratio* and subsidiarity are particularly relevant in the new areas in which criminal law intervenes. Without the need to defend a minimum criminal law, it is possible to have a criminal law that punishes particularly serious conduct in areas where there is already administrative, civil, commercial, labor and employment regulation. And this is not as new as it is claimed, since this duplicity of penalties already existed, and still exists, in offenses against the Public Administration or Justice and, especially, in matters of public order. Therefore, in both new and traditional types of offenses, the solution is not that criminal law should not intervene, but that it should be limited to a greater extent in the new offenses, respecting the aforementioned principles, together with the fragmentation principle. In other words, only the most serious behaviors are sanctioned, also considering that, since this area is regulated and sanctioned in other areas of the legal system, there will be no punishability gaps.

The omission of the limiting principles determines that offenses are being created in relation to which it is difficult to detect their harmfulness, not only because of the absence, in some cases, of an alleged legal asset (animal abuse), but also because they also violate the criminal law of the fact, as a requirement of the principle of criminal guilt, by punishing ideas (hate crimes) (Gómez Martín 2020). It is very serious that first the TEDH and then the TC and the TS have legitimized the criminal relevance of hate speech without the need to establish its suitability, in the specific case, to incite violence or affect dignity, applying the "guillotine effect" of Art. 17 CEDH which prevents hate speech from being covered by Art. 10 CEDH. A clear

[17] *Vid*; Appel (1999), pp. 297 y ss; Feijoo Sánchez (2010), pp. 163–230.

[18] Mir Puig (2016), pp. 171–176.

example of this position is provided by STS 4283/2020, of December 11, which, in line with established case law, states that the crime of hate: "*the only elements required for its determination are, one objective, such as the issuance of the provocative, discriminatory, hateful, violent message, to the effects contemplated therein, and another subjective, such as the will to issue it, despite being aware of that content, for whose consummation, being a crime of abstract danger, the potential danger entailed by the message issued is sufficient.*" That is to say, the principle of harmlessness is clearly ignored, since this "potential danger" is enough, in which neither the specific circumstances nor exactly what danger is referred to is considered.

Likewise, behaviors are classified as inappropriate to harm the legal asset to be protected (possession of virtual pornography of minors) or behaviors are punished based on—presumed—statistical danger (road safety) or merely formal infractions such as driving without a license (an offense that had previously been removed from the Criminal Code because the Constitutional Court considered that no legal asset was protected), without the need to prove that the protected criminal legal asset was affected in the specific case. This unacceptable situation not only does not demonstrate the ineffectiveness of the legal asset to limit criminal intervention, both at the legislative and judicial levels, but on the contrary, its necessity, highlighting the relevance of respecting the limiting principles when it is intended to introduce new criminal offenses or to aggravate existing ones.

4 Theory of Offense As a Limiting Instrument of Criminal Intervention

The abandonment of the theories of retribution and the adoption of preventive theories led to the abandonment of the factual-objective concept of offense so that, regardless of the theory of penalty that is adopted, the criminal conviction will only be legitimate when two conditions are fulfilled. The first is that the fact, as a typical wrongful act, involves a relevant interference by affecting criminal-legal assets, i.e., especially relevant—objective type—provided that the rule must have motivated the subject—subjective type—(typical wrongful act) and there are no causes of justification (unlawfulness). The second condition is that, in the specific case, the penalty is determined according to the personal circumstances of the subject (guilty). The penalty is not legitimized by the confirmation of the rule's validity or the reestablishment of the right, but by the possibility of motivating citizens not to harm criminal-legal assets. The basic differences between the confirmation of the rule's validity and the function of protecting criminal-legal assets lie in the fact that the rule must respond to the need and suitability of its creation to protect a specific criminal-legal asset and, furthermore, that rule must be interpreted teleologically in such a way as to prove, in the specific case, that the facts are suitable *ex ante* and *ex post* to damage/affect the criminal-legal assets that the rule seeks to protect, even in the so-called offenses of danger or in those of mere activity. In short, the rule's validity favors a formal conception of unlawfulness, while the express reference to the criminal—legal asset respects material unlawfulness—the principle of harmfulness.

The logical consequence of the above is that punishment should be based on the behavior, not on the result. It is not a matter of punishing to reestablish the situation prior to the harm caused to a person's subjective right, or to repair the "damage," but of punishing behaviors that are suitable, *ex ante-post facto*, to affect criminal-legal assets, whether individual or supra-individual. The reparation of the subjective right or of the "damage" is specific to civil law and, in that direction, our Criminal Code provides for civil liability arising from an offense. The purpose of the rule is to motivate the citizen not to engage in such harmful behaviors, regardless of whether or not an injurious result has occurred. The typical wrongful act is completed when *ex post*, taking into account all the existing circumstances *ex ante*, it is proven that the behavior was suitable for injuring/affecting the protected criminal-legal asset in that specific case. This approach does not preclude that, for political-criminal reasons and the need for a penalty, less punishment may be imposed when a result objectively attributable to such behavior has not been produced, or that in such cases no punishment may be imposed, due to the lower motivation capacity of the rule, as in the case of reckless offenses. What is inadmissible is to increase or base the penalty exclusively on the seriousness of the result, something that could be justified based on retribution or "damage" and that, in short, implies qualification by the result as a kind of strict liability.

The above approach reinforces the importance of continuing the defense of preventive rather than retributive theories. The social rooting of the retributive vision, to which is currently added the rise of Victimology, not only leads citizens to understand punishment as a fair response to a harmful result, but also leads the legislator to punish according to the extent of the harm. After decades of the rise of preventive theories, materially, there are still offenses qualified by the result, some as relevant as the offenses of injury, and it is still being discussed whether the punishment of the attempt and the so-called offense of danger is justified, even if there is room for the attempt in the offenses of injury. In short, if there is no direct victim, it seems that the intervention of criminal law is no longer necessary when the behavior may be particularly serious because it is harmful to society as a whole (corruption, tax crime, environmental crime...). A similar problem arises concerning subjective responsibility, since there is a tendency to make the offense objective, which, in practice, implies a presumption of the participation of willful misconduct or recklessness. The objective liability, de facto, cannot be mixed up with the objectivization of willful misconduct, understanding that it is a fact and that it must be proved based on objective evidence. A normative conception of willful misconduct, which excludes psychologistic evaluations in the proof of knowledge, is not the same as obviating the existence of willful misconduct, considering enough, at least for the initiation of criminal proceedings, to cause a result. Likewise, the existence of willful misconduct should not be presumed based on the character/profile of the perpetrator.

Although the *ultima ratio* principle is closely connected to the principle of minimum intervention, it cannot be confused with the latter, especially if minimum intervention is conceived according to the standards of the so-called minimum criminal law. Respect for the *ultima ratio* principle does not suppose affirming that criminal law should only protect subjective rights (life, health, freedom and private property) but implies a weighing of the harmfulness associated with the conduct to be criminalized. To affirm that socioeconomic crime, in a broad sense, should not be part of criminal law is not justified, since it is being forgotten that its harmfulness to society is greater than a large part of classic property crime. In the same line, the criticism that they are cumulative offenses, because with a single behavior the protected legal asset is not harmed, implies a questionable understanding of what the harm to the legal asset is, since, just as a tax offense does not "destroy" the Public Finance, a theft does not "destroy" a person's patrimony. This does not exclude the existence in the Criminal Code of many redundant offenses that are contrary to the *ultima ratio* principle. Thus, for example, in the area of road safety, there is an inflation of unnecessary types that are contrary to the principle of harmfulness—such as the presumption *iuris et de iure* of the criminal relevance of driving at a certain speed or with a certain degree of alcoholic impregnation (Art. 379)—or to the principle of exclusive protection of criminal-legal assets such as driving without a license (Art. 384) or the so-called "offense of absconding" (Art. 382 bis), introduced in the "penultimate" reform. In short, it is not a matter of excluding from criminal law the so-called risk or "cumulative" offenses, but of criminalizing only those behaviors that are particularly harmful.

Likewise, the criticism of the symbolic nature of these offenses is only acceptable when they have an exclusively symbolic function; on the contrary, when they concur with the protection of criminal-legal assets, not only is it not rejectable, but it is adequate—positive general prevention. The symbolic function is especially relevant in cases in which at least part of society is not fully aware of the importance of the protected criminal-legal asset, in short, of the harmfulness of these behaviors. This is (or was) the case, for example, with the tax offense (Art. 305) or the environmental offense (Art. 325). Therefore, intervention in these cases is legitimate as long as only the most serious acts are punished and that they are not sufficiently punished outside the scope of criminal law route, which is the case, for example, in the tax field with the accounting offense (Art. 310) or in the environmental field with the type of deposits and wastes (Art. 326).

When criminalizing a particular behavior, it is essential to consider its harmfulness, as well as the regulation that may exist in other areas of the legal system and the effectiveness of this new offense, as opposed to that outside the scope of criminal law route regulations. However, the assessment regarding effectiveness cannot be made in exclusively economic terms but must also considering other parameters related to harmfulness. Likewise, effectiveness cannot be evaluated exclusively based on, for example, that the case law in this area only punishes petty crimes, as has been stated in the case of offenses against the environment, or that they are not applied, as was the case years ago with tax offenses. The correct application or non-application of certain types is not a valid explanation, by itself, of the ineffectiveness of this offense, since it depends to a large extent on the political will to provide the means to prosecute these criminal modalities in an appropriate manner. Thus, for example, the opening of specialized prosecutors' offices, with the resources to investigate, could be a step in the right direction, as would be the existence of courts specializing in socioeconomic offenses.

The principle of subsidiarity, closely related to that of *ultima ratio*, must be interpreted in the sense that the behavior with criminal relevance must be more serious than that foreseen outside the scope of criminal law route. Similarly, the criminal sanction should be more severe than the extra-criminal sanction, which is not always the case, especially in the case of fines, since administrative fines are usually much higher. On the other hand, the fragmentation principle, as a sub-principle of the *ultima ratio* principle, has its scope of application when assessing which behaviors, from among those that are suitable to affect a certain criminal-legal asset, need to be punished. Thus, for example, to analyze whether, regarding a given offense, in view of the relevance of the legal right and/or the existence of extraordinary sanctions, it is appropriate to also punish attempt, recklessness, or complicity. These principles must also be considered by the judge at the time of application, particularly respecting the *non bis in idem* principle, since the legislator in his/her punitivist effort doubles, triples the aggravating circumstances. Aggravating circumstances that have the same basis or even have the same basic type. In this regard, from a procedural perspective, it is necessary to regulate, in the Criminal Procedure Act, the principle of opportunity and to improve the regulation of compliance.

At this point, it should be stated that, although not always, case law is sometimes more respectful than the legislator with the principles of *ultima ratio*, subsidiarity and fragmentation. This statement is clearly described in STS 434/2014 of June 3,[19] in relation to a crime of misappropriation, delimiting what would be a conduct with

[19] It has been consistently said by case law and doctrine, to the point of becoming dogma that the appeal to criminal law as an instrument to solve conflicts, is the last reason to be resorted to by the legislator who has to act, at all times, inspired by the principle of minimum intervention of punitive instruments. Principle of minimum intervention that is part of the principle of proportionality or prohibition of excess, the requirement of which is based on the dual nature of criminal law:

a) As it is a fragmentary right in that it does not protect all legal assets, but only those that are most important for social coexistence, limiting, moreover, this protection to those conducts that most intensely attack those assets.
b) As it is a subsidiary right that as ultima ratio, operating only when the legal order cannot be effectively preserved and restored by means of other less drastic solutions than criminal sanction.

However, reducing the intervention of criminal law, as ultima ratio, to the minimum necessary for social control, is a reasonable postulate of criminal policy that must be taken into consideration primarily by the legislator, but in judicial practice, although it can serve as a guide, it irremediably runs up against the requirements of the principle of legality, since it is not the judge but the legislator who must decide, by setting the types and penalties, what the limits of the intervention of criminal law should be.

criminal relevance and a mercantile one. In the same regard, there are two very relevant examples in which case law has significantly restricted the scope of application of the offenses: drug trafficking, where it is understood that the quantity should be assessed in relation to the active ingredient or that shared consumption is not punished, and illegal weapons possession, in the sense that this offense should not be punished when, in view of the circumstances, there is no danger to public order (Corcoy Bidasolo 2007, pp. 155–197). In virtual child pornography offenses, even the FGE Circular 2/2015, attempts to limit the scope of the type.[20]

5 Conclusions

The preventive purposes attributed to the penalty must be limited by the different principles of criminal law, essential in a democratic state governed by the rule of law, and indispensable to respect the fundamental rights of individuals. However, these principles, and especially the *ultima ratio* principle, are usually violated, both at the legislative and judicial levels and, in some cases, even by the doctrine that develops theories that, although coherent and even brilliant, the consequences of their application are contrary to a criminal law that respects the principle of minimum intervention. Prior to this, and in addition to the limits established by the principles, it is essential that criminal policy be supported by criminological studies and a cost-benefit analysis, which should not be interpreted in purely economic terms. This implies that we should not legislate in an irrational manner every time a case comes to the attention of public opinion. In the Criminal Code we have too many offenses and aggravating factors with "name and surname," some of which have never been applied, such as, for example, among many others, Art. 350, which was introduced, decades ago, on the occasion of the Tous dam breakage.

Since the expansion of criminal law is undeniable and difficult to manage, to respect the principles of *ultima ratio*, subsidiarity, and fragmentation, in addition of proposing legislative reforms that reduce criminally relevant behaviors, other measures should be adopted, such as the substitution of custodial sanctions for community service or mediation in minor offenses, allowing for less intervention in the sphere of freedom of citizens. In this regard, at the time of application—judicial field—it is essential to consider the function of protection of criminal-legal assets to carry out a teleological interpretation of the types. The purpose of this is to deny the

---

On the other hand, the principle of minimum intervention can only be fully understood if it is integrated in a context of social change in which there is a trend towards decriminalization of certain acts - the so-called "petty crimes" or behaviors that have ceased to receive significant social reproach - but also a trend in the opposite direction that criminalizes attacks against legal assets that the transformation that has occurred in the axiological plane makes particularly valuable.

[20]In the same line, the TS ruling dated October 27, 2009, requires that access to P2P file sharing software not be automatically applied, always requiring the concurrence of willful misconduct.

criminal relevance of a behavior when, although it formally fulfills the literal nature of the type, it is not suitable *ex post* to affect/injure the protected criminal-legal asset. In this way, the requirement of material unlawfulness—the principle of harmfulness—makes it possible to reduce criminal intervention and, consequently, to respect the principle of *ultima ratio*. Presumptions—presumed, hypothetical danger, etc.—or the precautionary principle—valid in the administrative field—should be excluded from criminal law.

In both the legislative and judicial aspects, the theory of offense plays an important role in providing legal certainty and, especially, in ensuring respect for the principle of criminal guilt, in its three aspects of liability for the act, subjective liability and guilt in the strict sense of the term. The theory of offense is also useful in facilitating respect for the principles of proportionality and the sub-principles of the *ultima ratio* principle: subsidiarity and fragmentation, in that it establishes categories that make it possible to establish a distinction between perpetration and participation, between preparatory acts, attempts and completion, and between willful intent and recklessness... Distinctions that, with the current legislative technique, disappear, given the fact that in many of the new precepts many behaviors are typified (promote, encourage, directly or indirectly incite—Art. 510—or directly or indirectly provoke or carry out—Art. 325), which implies that completion, attempt and preparatory acts or authorship and participation are punished with the same penalty. The legislator, by forgetting the existence of the General Part, not only makes behavior of a different value equivalent, but also introduces several specific aggravating factors which, in many cases, also give rise to serious conflicts in relation to the principle of *non bis in idem*.

Likewise, the *ex-ante* perspective in the analysis of the facts, which responds to the preventive function of criminal law, makes it possible for the legal operator not to be conditioned by the result and to attend to the seriousness of the behavior. It is true that the theory of offense does not provide solutions as to what behaviors should be punished and with what penalty, but it is no less true that without it the legislative technique followed in the Special Part is disproportionate and irrational and, consequently, the solutions in the specific case tend to be arbitrary.

Finally, two essential aspects should not be forgotten for the proper operation of criminal law and to prevent the legislator from being so pressured by public opinion to increase penalties and/or introduce new criminal offenses. It is a matter of justice being effective and for this, first, it requires a criminal process that combines speed—efficiency—with guarantees and legal operators, judges, and prosecutors, who are good jurists and are equipped with the means and are not influenced by politics. Second, it is necessary to ensure the effective execution of penalties and that their enforcement is focused on reintegration. If, as has been stated, the preventive effectiveness of the penalty does not depend so much on the harshness of the penalties as on the security in which they are to be applied, the process and enforcement play an essential role in the legitimization of criminal law.

References

Appel I (1999) Rechtsgüterschutz durch Strafrecht? Anmerkungen aus vefassungsrechtlicher Sicht. KritV 82(2):278–311
Besio Hernández M (2011) Los criterios legales y jurisprudenciales de individualización de la pena. Tirant lo Blanch, Valencia
Corcoy Bidasolo M (2007) Repercusiones de la doctrina del Tribunal Supremo en la doctrina penal, en Jurisprudencia penal (2005-2007). Análisis crítico. Estudios de Derecho Judicial 120:155–197
Corcoy Bidasolo M (2011) La legitimidad de la protección penal de bienes jurídicos supraindividuales. CENIPEC 30:89–120
Demetrio Crespo E (2016) Prevención general e individualización judicial de la pena. B de F, Montevideo
Feijoo Sánchez B (2010) Funcionalismo y teoría del bien jurídico. En: Jiménez MP (Dir.) Constitución y principios del derecho penal. Algunas bases constitucionales. Tirant lo Blanch, Valencia, pp 163–230
Frisch W (2014) Pena, delito y sistema del delito en transformación. InDret 3:1–12
Gómez Martín V (2020) Daño, ofensa y discurso del odio. Iustel, Madrid
Hörnle T, von Hirsch A (1995) Positive Generalprävention und Tadel. Goltdammer's Archiv für Strafrecht 142:261–282
Kant I (1798) Die Metaphysik der Sitten (2ª ed. Ausg.). Köninsberg
Lesch H (1999) La función de la pena. Dykinson, Madrid
Mir Puig S (2016) Derecho penal Parte General. Reppertor, Barcelona
Pérez Manzano M (1999) Culpabilidad y prevención: las teorías de la prevención general positiva en la fundamentación de la imputación subjetiva y de la pena. UAM, Madrid
Robinson P (2014) The proper role of the community in determining criminal liability and punishment. Univ Pa Law School:1–75
Silva Sánchez JM (2011) La expansión del Derecho penal. Edisofer, Buenos Aires
VVAA (1999) La insostenible situación del derecho penal. Comares, Madrid
Welzel H (1969) Das Deutsche Strafrecht (11 Ausg.). Walter de Gruyter, Berlin

Review on Retribution as Punishment Purpose

Eduardo Demetrio Crespo

Abstract The aim of the work is to critically reflect on retributionism as the end of punishment in the constitutional state of law. Taking German idealism (Kant and Hegel) as a starting point, the most recent reformulations of this apparently outdated current of thought are analyzed. A first approach to the methodological distinction between the term's retribution, reprobation, and revenge is proposed to defend a secularized theory of punishment.

1 Retributionism in German Idealism and Its (Premature?) Farewell

As is well known, retributionism is linked in origin to the thought of Kant (1724–1804) and Hegel (1770–1831), to whom the two main philosophical formulations of retributionism are attributed.[1] Despite much that has been written on the subject, speculation continues about the truly specific and concrete scope of the "absolute" in retributionist theories, while seeking a "restoration" of this legitimizing thought of punishment[2] or giving it a consequentialist dimension as a punitive

This work is part of the Research Project *Crisis of the Criminal Law of the Rule of Law: Manifestations and Trends* (SBPLY/17/18501/000223) granted by the Junta de Comunidades de Castilla - La Mancha and co-financed by the European Regional Development Fund (ERDF), under the direction of Prof. Drs. Eduardo Demetrio Crespo, Alfonso J. García Figueroa and Gema Mª Marcilla Córdoba [https://blog.uclm.es/proyectocresta/].

[1] Demetrio Crespo (1999), pp. 58 et seq.; Zaibert (2006), pp. 69 et seq.; Feijoo Sánchez 2007, pp. 63 y ss; Escamilla Castillo (2010), pp. 460 et seq.; White (2011), *passim*; Donna (2019), *passim*.
[2] Pérez del Valle (2020).

E. Demetrio Crespo (✉)
Faculty of Legal and Social Sciences University of Castilla-La Mancha, Toledo, Spain
e-mail: Eduardo.Demetrio@uclm.es

E. Demetrio Crespo et al. (eds.), *Crisis of the Criminal Law in the Democratic Constitutional State*, Legal Studies in International, European and Comparative Criminal Law 6, https://doi.org/10.1007/978-3-031-13413-5_2

"ideology" program.[3] According to some interpretations, the famous "farewell" to Kant and Hegel anticipated by Klug in a well-known article,[4] would have turned out to be not only unfortunate, but also unsuccessful,[5] which has been argued with particular vehemence by Hruschka.[6] But let us go in a little more detail to the arguments put forward by both of them.

Klug's essay, quoted here in an English translation,[7] begins by noting that German criminal courts express almost daily their conception of punishment when justifying why the punishment imposed seems to them to be adequate in the sense that it would "compensate for the harm caused by the crime." Such a theory would be based on the philosophical theses of Kant and Hegel, which are invoked in such a way that a taboo seems to be violated every time it is claimed that their arguments are insufficient or wrong. In Klug's opinion, however, what had to be done was to "bid farewell to Kant and Hegel in the field of penal theory." Particularly regarding Kant's theory of punishment, he claims that his reflections on it in the *Metaphysics of Morals* (1797) "constitute a hopeless prelude, resigned and conditioned by the spirit of the age."[8] Of the various passages in this work, Klug highlights those in which Kant defines the criminal law as a categorical imperative and refers to the *ius talionis* as a principle and criterion for determining the amount and type of punishment.[9]

---

[3] Mañalich (2015).

[4] Klug (1968), pp. 36 et seq.

[5] Mañalich (2015), p. 3; Teixeira (2018), p. 37; Bruckmann (2019), pp. 105 et seq.

[6] Hruschka (2010), pp. 493 et seq.

[7] Klug (2002), pp. 31 et seq.

[8] Ibíd., p. 32.

[9] It is worth reproducing them here (Kant 1989, pp. 165 et):

> *Criminal law* is the right which the sovereign has, with respect to him who is subject to him, to impose a penalty for his crime. (. . .) The *judicial penalty* (*poena forensis*), distinct from the *natural penalty* (*poena naturalis*), by which the vice punishes itself and which the legislator does not take into account at all, can never serve simply as a means to promote another good, either for the offender himself or for civil society, but must be imposed on him only *because he has committed a crime* (. . .). Before any thought can be given to deriving any benefit from this penalty for himself or for his fellow citizens, he must have been judged *worthy of punishment*. The criminal law is a categorical imperative and woe betide him who crawls through the sinuosities of the doctrine of happiness to find something that will exempt him from punishment, or even only from a degree of it, for the advantage it promises, following the Pharisaic motto "it is better that one man die than that the whole people perish". For if justice perishes, it is of no value that men should live on Earth. (. . .).
>
> But what is the type and degree of punishment that public justice adopts as a principle and as a pattern? None other than the principle of equality (in the position of the faithfulness) of the scales of justice): not to lean more to one side than to the other. Therefore, whatever undeserved harm you inflict on another in a town, you do to yourself (. . .). Only the law of talion (*ius talionis*) can safely offer the quality and quantity of punishment, but well understood that in the bosom of the tribunal (not in your private trial); all others fluctuate

With respect to Hegel, it should be noted that his theory of punishment set forth in his *Philosophy of Right*, published in 1821 ten years after his death, is also based on retribution. The famous consideration of punishment as "negation of negation," however, would rather have been transmitted through his disciple Eduard Gans in the *Additional Notes to Hegel's Lectures*. In this version of retributionism, typical of German idealism, the offender is honored as a rational being, which would not be the case if the measure of punishment were not drawn from their own act but from considerations of a different nature, such as intimidation or improvement.[10]

Klug rightly warned that these models of thought could be criticized at least from the following points of view.[11] The first has to do with the *theory of knowledge*, since at no time is it demonstrated, but only postulated, that the meaning of punishment is retaliation, which would be nothing more than a conviction that no one is obliged to

---

> from one side to the other and cannot be adequate to the opinion of pure and strict justice, because other considerations intrude (. . .). But if he has committed murder, he must *die* (. . .).
>
> This equality of penalties, which is only possible by the sentence of death by the judge, according to the strict law of talion, is manifested in the fact that only in this way the death sentence is pronounced on all in proportion to the *internal wickedness* of the criminals (even if it was not a murder, but another crime of State that only death can erase).

[10] Klug (2002), p. 34.
Also (Hegel 1968, pp. 107 et seq.):

> In the positive legal science of modern times, the theory of punishment is one of the subjects that has been the worst delved into, since in it the intellect is not sufficient, since it is essentially about the concept.
>
> If crime and its overcoming, as what is subsequently determined as punishment, is generally considered only as evil, it can certainly be judged as irrational to want an evil merely because another evil already exists.
>
> In the various theories of punishment, this superficial character of evil is presupposed as the main element: the theory of prevention, intimidation, punishment, correction, etc., and what, on the contrary, must result as good, is determined precisely in a superficial way. (. . .).
>
> In this discussion what is of interest is only that the crime must be denied not as the production of an evil, but as the violation of Law as Law, and then, what is the existence that the crime has, and what must be annulled; that is the true evil that must be uprooted and the essential point is where this existence is. As long as the concepts on this point are not strictly recognized, disorder must dominate in the consideration of punishment.
>
> The violation that affects the offender is not only just in itself - as just is, at the same time, his will, which is in itself and the existence of his freedom, the Right - but it is also a Right imposed on the offender himself, that is, in his existing will, in his action. Because in his action, as the action of a rational entity, a universal is implicit: (. . .)
>
> The overcoming of crime is punishment, because according to the concept it is the violation of the violation and according to the existence, crime has a qualitatively and quantitatively determined extension; therefore, its negation, as existence, has another existence. However, this identity that is based on the concept is not equality in the specific, external nature of the violation, but in what it is in itself according to the value of the same.

[11] Klug (2002), pp. 34 et seq.

share. The second points out that the *concept of equality* that is used lacks a basis, since the criminal act and the penalty are not comparable magnitudes. The third, derived from the previous one, places it in the *field of logic*, since the categorical imperative would be nothing but an empty formula, from which it would not be possible to infer any conclusion with content. The same criticism would be valid with respect to the Hegelian "pseudological" consisting in the *application of a concept to itself.* As Klug rightly says, "it is by no means necessary that 'coercion be overcome by coercion'" and it could equally be said that coercion increases coercion. To all this he adds that the argument against a functional and utilitarian rationale is simply a fallacy. Last but not least, this renowned philosopher of law points to the possibility of a *moral critique*, since (pure) retaliation that does not pursue any end, whether for the offender or for society, harms the dignity of the individual; and not only in the sense of recognized moral norms, but also of the constitution. Finally, he concludes, "it is time to bid farewell definitively to the criminal theories of Kant and Hegel, with all their lyrical and irrational excesses and all that is dubious in them from the epistemic, logical and moral point of view."[12]

Well, Joachim Hruschka reacts more than four decades later[13] in a rather abrupt way. He acknowledges that Klug's article has had a great influence, but immediately begins to criticize it, starting with formal aspects such as the lack of footnotes. His first reflection focuses on the interpretation of the formula *because they have offended* in Kant and Klug's inaccurate transcription of it.

Specifically, Kant points out:[14]

> The *judicial penalty* (*poena forensis*), as distinct from the *natural penalty* (*poena naturalis*), by which the crime punishes itself and which the legislator does not take into account at all, can never serve merely as a means to promote another good, either for the offender themselves or for civil society, but must be imposed on them only *because they have offended*; for the individual can never be handled as a means to the purposes of another nor confused among the objects of real law (*Sachenrecht*).

Klug reproduces this passage in the following way:[15]

> According to Kant, punishment can never be used simply as a means of promoting some other good, either for the offender themselves or for society. Rather, in any case, 'it may be imposed on them, because they have offended'. For the individual can never be treated as a means to the ends of another. When a penalty is imposed, it can never be considered whether any advantage is to be gained by it for the condemned person or for any of their fellow citizens.

According to Hruschka, Klug misrepresents almost everything Kant says, beginning with the fact that Kant speaks of *judicial punishment*, imposed by a judge, while

---

[12] Ibíd., p. 36.

[13] Hruschka (2010), pp. 494 et seq.

[14] Kant (1989), p. 165.

[15] Klug (1981), p. 150.

We deviate here slightly from the translation by which the article has been cited, which is why the passage is taken from the German version that appeared in 1981.

Klug leaves this aspect out of consideration, which would completely change the meaning insofar as it is a prerequisite for punishment in a state governed by the *Rechtsstaat* that a judge must do it. To this Hruschka adds that Klug does not really provide any argument as to why Kant should be considered a theorist of retribution.[16] Of course, this argument of Hruschka's in a short article that aims to completely disqualify Klug's is surprising, since it seems unlikely that the latter would want to overlook something so obvious, but rather to emphasize that the purpose of punishment in Kant is exhausted in that the basis of punishment is exclusively due to the fact that the perpetrator has committed a crime, without preventive purposes playing any role. This is the reason, moreover, why both Ulrich Klug and a large part of the doctrine saw in him, then as now, a prototypical theorist of retributionism.

Hruschka (2010) continues along this interpretative path when analyzing other points such as the principle according to which the judge can only impose the penalty established by law, etc., to conclude that Klug's arrogant handling of Kant's texts turns his famous article into a pamphlet that falls far short of the minimum requirements of a scientific article. Beyond the value that either text may have in itself, it is interesting to note that from the ranks of retributionism the article by Hruschka is used to disavow Klug, especially since the arguments he uses are not, as we have seen, convincing.

2 The Rise of Retributionism

2.1 Introduction

There are many and varied new "faces" that retributionism is adopting, although not all of them can be considered retributive in the strict sense insofar as they indirectly or mediately seek to obtain some kind of utility. Feijoo alludes to this upturn by distinguishing between an Anglo-Saxon liberal line and a more communitarian one with Hegelian roots.[17] Within *liberal neo-retributionism*, he mentions *the theory of unjustified or unjust advantage*, according to which the penalty would come to compensate the situation of unjust advantage produced by the crime, not based on a strict criterion of justice in the Kantian style, but of equity. For its part, *communitarian neo-retributionism* would be represented, in his opinion, by authors such as Günther Jakobs—who would have ended up maintaining a theory of punishment that combines retributive elements of punishment as a communicative contradiction of crime with effects of social psychology—and Michael Pawlik.[18] Feijoo's critical reflections on those retributive theories that do not present a satisfactory response to

[16]Hruschka (2010), p. 495.

[17]Feijoo Sánchez (2014), pp. 110 et seq.

[18]Cf. Duff (2015), pp. 151 et seq. on the "communitarian dream or Macintyre's nightmare."

the objections from which it follows, with good reason, that punishment is not only a question of moral philosophy, but a strategy for the survival of society, are extremely interesting. Neither retributive theories nor their variants could have adequately resolved the question of why the state should renounce punishment because it is not necessary although it is deserved.[19] In any case, he warns, the contributions of these new versions of retributionism are best channeled through positive general prevention in accordance with a modern rationality.[20]

2.2 *The Theory of the Duty to Collaborate in the Maintenance of the Common Good*

Paradoxical in this respect is Michael Pawlik, who, taking as his starting point the *ideal of human self-determination* linked to the development of modern societies between the seventeenth and nineteenth centuries and the protection of freedom as a task of criminal law, speaks *of cooperation in the maintenance of a Rule of Law (in terms of Rechtsstaat) of freedom* as a duty of the citizen.[21] He argues that "the coercive costs of a legal system can only be maintained within a framework acceptable from the point of view of the theory of freedoms on the assumption that, as a rule, behavior faithful to the law is self-evident for the subjects of Law."[22] This leads him to consider that the recognition of this co-responsibility is, in the final analysis, a mandate of fairness. He openly admits, in turn, that the interpretation he outlines is broadly consistent in its conclusions with the Hegelian characterization of crime as an injury to law as law.[23] However, his strategy of foundation would be rather *philosophical-transcendental* and, in this sense, with more Kantian than Hegelian traits.[24]

As far as the justification of punishment itself is concerned, Pawlik understands that it is not possible to deduce a convincing justification for retributive punishment from Kant's sparse considerations,[25] citing at this point Schopenhauer's decisive criticism: "all retribution through causation of pain, with no purpose for the future, is revenge, and can have no other purpose than to console oneself for the suffering that one traverses by seeing the suffering of others that one has caused oneself. This is evil and cruelty and cannot be justified from an ethical point of view." According to Pawlik, the retributive foundations of punishment are only acceptable if they manage to ascribe to punishment a *positive* sense compatible with the prior definition of tasks

[19] Feijoo Sánchez (2014), p. 117.

[20] Feijoo Sánchez (2014), p. 118.

[21] Pawlik (2016), pp. 33 et seq.

[22] Ibíd., p. 43.

[23] Ibíd., p. 46.

[24] Ibíd., p. 50.

[25] Ibíd., p. 51.

that allows everyone to enjoy their right and without having to resort to the arsenal of the traditional theories of prevention, something that Kant would not have achieved.[26] For this author, it would rather be a matter of transferring to the field of punishment the idea from tort law of the duty to restore the destroyed state, so that "because the offender has contravened the fundamental axiom of all legality [*Rechtlichkeit*] -the principle that freedom is only assured at the price of the fulfillment of duty- they have to endure that the indissolubility of the link between enjoyment of freedom and fulfillment of the duty of cooperation be confirmed at their expense."[27] Pawlik also recognizes the proximity between his approach and positive general prevention, given that a theory of punishment in the literal sense, detached from human and social ends, would certainly be unbearable from the legal-constitutional and everyday moral point of view, as Hassemer pointed out at the time.[28]

2.3 Expressive Theories of Punishment

The so-called expressive theories focus on the communicative aspect of punishment, which generates difficulties in offering a justification to the perpetrator of the crime.[29] According to Hörnle,[30] expressive theories share with preventive theories the search for an end based on the legitimate interests of individuals, with the particularity that for them what is relevant is not to influence the frequency of future crimes, but an adequate treatment of past behavior. In his opinion, a distinction can be made between three types of expressive theories of punishment: (a) norm-oriented, which seek, e.g., the reinforcement of moral values and requirements or the restoration of the validity of the norm; (b) person-oriented in the broad sense (all those who have had knowledge of the crime), which seek to mitigate feelings of indignation; (c) person-oriented in the strict sense, this time in relation to the interests of the victim in the punishment of the perpetrator.

Punishment would be composed of a "descriptive element" or of *disapproval* and, together with it, of a normative or *deserving* element. Now, according to Pérez Barberá,[31] the first element is part of the *concept of punishment*, while the second belongs rather to its *justification*; so that, if the latter is missing, retribution would be characterized as revenge. After making this distinction, this author points out, however, that both elements belong to the concept of punishment, which would be

[26] Ibíd., p. 52.

[27] Ibíd., pp. 56–57.

[28] Ibíd., p. 57.

[29] Demko (2017), pp. 227 et seq.

[30] Hörnle (2015), pp. 33 et seq.

[31] Pérez Barberá (2014), p. 3.

defined as an *institutionalized response that manifests itself disapprovingly through the infliction of harm*.

As we shall see, all this really leaves intact the basic problem, the *purpose of punishment*, which in this type of reasoning seeks to legitimize itself through a return to retribution as an end; since *one thing is what punishment is conceptually and another what it serves for*. It is not by chance that retributionism ends up presenting itself as a *mixed theory of the justification of state punishment* due to the moral correctness of both principles, retributive and preventive, based on the distinction between *deontological reasons* (punishment as an individual act) and consequentialist reasons (punishment as a general institution),[32] since both would come into play for the moral justification of punishment in relation to the perpetrator and society.[33]

Pérez Barberá is right when he warns about the acceptability in general terms of the deontological principle when limiting prevention, in the sense that only *when* a crime is committed can the state react with a penalty in accordance with the seriousness of the harmful act; which does not imply, in my opinion, any assumption of the retributive principle according to which "it is simply *just* -and therefore correct- that only he who deserves to be punished receives a penalty and that this corresponds to the measure of his deservedness."[34] It is clear that the Rule of Law (in terms of Rechtsstat) does not punish, as a matter of principle, if a crime has not been committed, nor should it do so beyond the gravity of the act. But this does not particularly mean that the punishment is deserved—at least in the sense of the moral theory underlying retributionism—without prejudice to the statistically undeniable possibility of convictions of the innocent. For this reason, despite the many criticisms that have traditionally been made of the limiting rather than foundational nature of guilt, it is clear that this distinction has a reason for being, beyond the attempts to deprive it of meaning to defend retributionist points of view under the cloak of mixed theories of punishment, invoking, on the other hand, in a confusing manner at least, the model defended by Roxin.[35]

Pérez Barberá[36] opts for the retributive principle for the deontological justification of punishment as a particular act—that is, against the perpetrator of the crime—

---

[32]On the distinction in Rawls' now classic article (Rawls 1955, pp. 3 ff.), vid. among other references, Demetrio Crespo (1999), pp. 48–50; Grosse-Wilde (2017), pp. 21–31; Teixeira (2018), pp. 44 et seq.

[33]Pérez Barberá (2014), p. 6.

[34]Ibíd., p. 6.

Cf., among other references, Robinson (2012), pp. 40–41 on the terms "deontological deservedness" and "empirical deservedness"; von Hirsch (1998), pp. 31 et seq. on the relationship between "censorship and proportionality"; and Sánchez Lázaro (2016), pp. 48 et seq. on the "normative structure of proportionality."

[35]Thus, Pérez Barberá (2014), p. 5, citing Pawlik. For details on the relationship between culpability and the purposes of punishment in the thought of Claus Roxin, see: Demetrio Crespo (2011), pp. 689 et seq.

[36]Pérez Barberá (2014), p. 10.

understood "completely independently of assessments related to the consequences of the punishment." In fact, he criticizes Pawlik, to whom he attributes the [dubious] "great merit of having brought the retributive principle back to the forefront of German discussion," due to his consideration that retribution has an extrinsic purpose consisting of the "maintenance of social order." In other words, Pérez Barberá consistently maintains a deontological basis for retribution—one could say, in a somewhat convoluted expression, a purely retributionist conception of retribution—as opposed to the attempts to seek a consequentialist anchorage for it.

2.4 *Retribution As the Satisfaction of Psychosocial Needs for Punishment*

As far as I can see, no attempt to place retribution at the center of the theories of the purposes of punishment has so far gone as far as Walter has done.[37] We must be grateful, in any case, that he has put on the table, without being shy, that the principle of retribution underlies, in the first place, "the human need to do justice," nothing more and nothing less. It is very significant that he begins his essay with the case of Oskar Gröning, sentenced in 2015 to four years imprisonment for complicity in the murder of 300,000 people as an accountant at Auschwitz, despite being 94 years old, having led a quiet life since the end of the war and having testified the cruelty of that place in the face of the denialists. The plaintiffs were not willing to pardon him but instead, demanded justice. Walter understands that the reason the trial took place more than 70 years after the events is none other than the need for retribution of human beings, with the exception of a few who have either learned to get rid of their desires in this regard at the time of their appearance or are able to forgive.

Walter[38] attributes the position paradigmatically represented by Claus Roxin—according to which retribution does not enter into consideration as an end of punishment and that the theory of retribution is not scientifically sustainable today—to a tremendous misunderstanding. Based on the analysis of the classic conflict or antinomies about the ends of punishment[39] and the alleged errors of the opponents of retribution—such as that retribution requires harsh and inhumane punishment, the belief that retribution requires punishment as the only possible reaction in any case and that it always requires "full" retribution, and that it can only be founded metaphysically and not through a legitimate benefit to society—he proposes a *purely empirically based* theory of retribution that should in any case be distinguished from the idea of vengeance.

---

[37] Walter (2016), pp. 7 et seq.

[38] Ibíd., pp. 8 et seq.

[39] In detail, as a scientific and ideological problem, see Demetrio Crespo (1999), pp. 73 et seq. [2016, pp. 70 et seq.].

The key question, however, is *what makes it possible to consider retribution as a purpose of punishmen*t. Well, although Walter recognizes that this question can be approached from two different approaches, namely, the philosophical-legal and the empirical-sociological, in his essay he only deals with the latter, a fact to which he downplays by saying that the former would in any case only complement it.[40] This, in my opinion, is a first critical point, since one can doubt the reliability of a theory of punishment formulated based on empirical considerations, leaving the underlying philosophical-legal aspect for a better occasion.

According to this author, the concept of punishment entails the infliction of a harm that the offender can and must suffer, so that the starting point of an empirical theory of retribution is the finding that in every human being there is a need for retribution: if this basic social need were not satisfied, it would generate instability, giving rise to private revenge. To support his argument he adduces, on the one hand, behavioral psychology studies according to which human beings determine the punishment in the concrete case, not only primarily and in the first moment, but in the long term and exclusively, according to their need for retribution. Against this it can be said preliminarily that what matters, however, is not that these feelings are humanly understandable, but what is the valuation and scope of the same from the legal-criminal point of view.[41] On the other hand, he adds that the positive law itself—since, in his opinion, § 46 (1) sub 1. StGB according to which "*Die Schuld des Täters ist die Grundlage für die Zumessung der Strafe*" is to be interpreted as "compensation for guilt," i.e., as just retribution—and the praxis of the criminal courts would support his conclusions.[42] But this argument does not appear to be decisive either, since neither the literal wording of a rule can be considered an empirical "finding" without further ado, nor is the interpretation that has been made of the cited precept uniform in its scope and consequences.[43]

In turn, the theoretical attempt to consider retribution as the essence of punishment, but not its end, despite being correct from the logical-conceptual point of view, would not be convincing according to Walter, since it makes no sense that the essence of punishment is not consequently related to its end.[44] To explain this, he resorts to the following coarse example; namely, it would be as if one were to place a milk cow in front of the house as a watchdog and say: yes, its essence is to give milk, but perhaps it can be used for entirely different purposes. It happens here, however, that the argumentation of this author is still not consistent; as he rightly points out, it is a correct distinction at the logical-conceptual level, which is essential for reasons of even constitutional order. To continue with his comparison, no one would put a

[40] In detail, as a scientific and ideological problem, Vid. Demetrio Crespo (1999), pp. 73 ff. [2016, pp. 70 et seq].

[41] On feelings and punishment, see, for example, Rodríguez Horcajo (2016), pp. 134 et seq.

[42] Walter (2016), p. 12.

[43] Vid. in this regard, with multiple references, Demetrio Crespo (1999), pp. 187 et seq.; 215 et seq. (2016), pp. 225 et seq., 273 et seq.

[44] Walter (2016), p. 12.

dairy cow to watch over the house, since it would be completely absurd and therefore it makes no sense to consider it, but rather, once the need has been established (to watch over the house; in our case, to make coexistence possible), it would be a matter of choosing the most appropriate and at the same time least harmful means (principle of necessity) in view of the end to be achieved (in our case, to avoid criminal acts in the future). The discussion would then focus on which dog can best fulfill this function, but it so happens that for a consistent retributive theory there is no end to be achieved beyond the punishment itself. That is, the question of the ends of punishment, although it may seem, is really alien to retribution, unless it is denaturalized. That is why we understand that Walter's construction is very weak even from this angle, because his theory does propose to achieve an end, that of satisfying the needs of retribution, which, despite its radical nature, does not place him so far from some versions of positive general prevention.

Even less consistent and clearly rejectable appears his argument about the naturalistic fallacy according to which one cannot make the leap to the plane of "should be" (*sollen*) directly from the plane of "is" (*sein*). Although he recognizes that this paralogism is true, he believes that it would not be correct to deduce the "should be" from the "should be" either, if one does not want to incur in the problem of the return to infinity. He indicates in turn that, although jurisprudence cannot violate the logical rules of deduction, neither is it allowed to dwell on them, as it already does, so that the choice of premises from which it starts is not guided by the rules of logic, but by the pretensions of a public that longs to see them satisfied. Thus, Walter concludes, the premises of an empirical-sociological theory of retribution are given by the existential value (*Daseinswert*) of our society.[45]

Walter's text truly exposes the worst of the modern upsurge of the retributionist conception; not only does it make an empirical presumption about what really matters to society and foreshadows what would happen if that starting point were not accepted—reminiscent of the way in which the ill-fated "criminal law of the enemy" has been defended as a descriptive and not prescriptive formulation[46]—but it is granted an absolute scope, free *ex ante* of any philosophical or logical-legal reproach. It is not difficult to imagine the scenario to which such an argument leads, which is unacceptable from the premises that inform the theory of law in the democratic and constitutional state.[47]

---

[45] Ibíd., p. 13.

[46] In this regard, with multiple references, Demetrio Crespo (2020), pp. 65 et seq.

[47] In this direction, e.g., Roxin/Greco: "Am deutlichsten werden diese Gefahren bei *Walter*: Geht es bei der Vergeltung um ein Urbedürfnis des Menschen, das deshalb, weil "die wenigsten die Kraft haben, ihren Drang nach Vergeltung aufzulösen (unterdrücken nützt nichts)", von der Gesellschaft abgefangen und kontrolliert werden muss, gibt es keinen Grund, weshalb einen Schuldunfähigen in gewissen Sonderfällen von Strafe verschonen sollte" (Roxin and Greco 2020, pp. 133–134).

3 Plea for a "Secularized Theory of Punishment"

3.1 Subordination of the Purposes of Punishment

Neither the modern "lectures" of retributionist theories, nor the reformulations that have been made of them by the so-called "neo-retributionists," and much less the proposal to confer on retributionism the status of the only valid end of punishment, are convincing from the perspective of a *secularized theory of punishment*. This is understood as one that is conditioned by the model of the constitutional state, in which the principles and guarantees that are proper to it (such as legality, proportionality and culpability) constitute the framework in which it develops both in terms of political philosophy and dogmatics.[48] The purposes of punishment thus appear subordinated, at a second level, to a higher purpose that limits them, *to protect legal assets in order to make coexistence possible*, which leaves out of play any overreaching of a preventive nature.[49] The state reaction through punishment only comes into consideration when a conduct typified as criminal has been committed and always in proportion to the seriousness of the crime.[50]

Schünemann has expressed the same idea in a lucid way; it would be about something basic, but buried for thousands of years under the ideological rubble of various theories of retribution: "Namely, the knowledge that punishment, in the vast majority of cases, is by no means mere retribution, but represents an excess or abuse (overkill) that cannot be justified by a -philosophically pretentious, but in reality primitive- theory of the restoration of the law, but only according to rules of necessity, precisely as an ultima ratio for the protection of legal assets."[51]

Roxin/Greco understand, in turn, that it is necessary to differentiate between the function of criminal law and the purpose of punishment, since the subsidiary protection of legal goods and, with it, the free development of the individual and the maintenance of a social order based on this principle, only entails the determination of what behaviors the state can threaten with punishment to achieve this ultimate goal. However, it is not yet clear how the state should try to achieve this end, an aspect that concerns the theory of the ends of punishment, which has been discussed since antiquity basically around three major points of view, which in very different combinations dominate the discussion to this day.[52]

---

[48] Demetrio Crespo (2020), esp. pp. 109 et seq., 187 et seq.

[49] Greco (2009), pp. 303 et seq.

[50] On the criticisms of such a consideration in the framework of mixed theories and the distinction between positive retributionism (in favor of the perpetrator as limiting) and negative (grounding punishment), Vid. Teixeira (2018), pp. 43 et seq; Chiesa (2020), p. 120.

[51] Schünemann (2019), p. 15.

[52] Roxin and Greco (2020), p. 128.

3.2 Concept, Function, and Ends of Punishment

State penalty is a punishment, a harm, which certainly expresses *disapproval* of the act committed, but which is not imposed to reestablish material justice or the validity of the legal system and, much less, to satisfy instincts of revenge, but by a bitter need of a purely earthly order, which consists in the protection of legal assets through the legitimate aspiration in any advanced society that in the future such acts do not occur again. One thing is, therefore, what the penalty is (*concept of state punishment*), another what it expresses (*functions it fulfills or is assigned*) and another what its imposition is legitimately intended to achieve (the*ory of the purposes of punishment as a framework theory of criminal law*). Such a distinction, beyond leveling and prosaic reductionisms, is possible and necessary in the criminal law of the democratic and constitutional state, that is, in a secularized and non-theocratic criminal law.

Regarding the concept of penalty, which is not a simple matter, a distinction must be made between a formal and a material concept. In the first sense, punishment is everything that the legislator designates as such. However, the decisive question refers to the material concept of punishment, which refers to the properties or characteristics by virtue of which it can only be imposed under certain conditions. In this sense, Roxin/Greco argue that the consideration of punishment as an evil that is imposed as a consequence of wrongful behavior (*malum passionis propter malum actionis*) has the advantage of not bagatelletizing the seriousness of the punishment, but it is not enough, since any other state reaction can meet this characteristic. Therefore, they rather appeal to the "special severity of the harm," which does not seem to help much either, since other types of sanctions can also be considered by those affected as extraordinarily harsh.[53] In Roxin/Greco's view, therefore, it is necessary to use the communicative rather than the "corporal" element of "disapproval" in addition, so that the concept of punishment would result from the corresponding link between the infliction of a harm and disapproval.[54]

The end purposes of punishment, on the other hand, become relevant at the level of justification, which according to Roxin/Greco can be approached as a dialogue in which it is necessary to offer reasons: on the one hand before society and, on the other hand, before the directly affected, the former appearing with a consequentialist character—so that the advantages for society of supporting the current criminal justice system can be appreciated, and the latter more of a deontological type—so that it is possible to argue why it is not unfair that society benefits at the expense of the affected person.[55]

---

[53] Ibíd., pp. 21–22.

[54] Ibíd., pp. 22–23.

On the problem of the "defitional barrier" in the philosophical discussion according to which any pre-theoretical definition of the concept of punishment entails the risk of prejudging the spectrum of relevant justificatory theories, see Mañalich (2015), p. 8 and note 25.

[55] Roxin and Greco (2020), pp. 128–129.

3.3 Explanatory Levels

It is necessary to resort to at least three explanatory levels. That of the theory of the state, which requires establishing certain convergences with criminal law in coherence with the historical moment in which they are formulated.[56] That of the theory of the state, in which the key methodological distinction between is and should be, which Ferrajoli has made fruitful to explain very clearly what questions are answered in each case,[57] cannot be ignored. And finally, in that of dogmatics (theory of the norm and theory of crime) to achieve an application of criminal law in accordance with certain logical premises based on the design of a rational criminal policy.[58]

As for the *theory of the state*, it is clear that the justifying model of criminal law and punishment in the constitutional Rule of Law has to conform to a purely earthly mission, and this is none other than that of making coexistence possible through the subsidiary protection of legal assets. In historical terms, this means grasping the transition from a theocratic criminal law to a secular criminal law conceived through the connection between state theory and criminal law. If we ask ourselves about the purposes of punishment, these must necessarily be framed in their historical-political context, since they depend to a large extent on the model of the state and the function that criminal law has within it. It can be said, with Frisch, that the *earthly state* is not called, nor is it authorized from today's perspective, to sanction the attack on God's authority or the violation of the divine will or commands, but that its task is earthly delimited and consists in making possible the peaceful and prosperous coexistence of its citizens.[59]

As far as the *theory of law* is concerned, the separation between law and morality, something that is so often lost sight of nowadays, is key in this matter. In fact, it is now commonplace to invoke reasons of a moralizing nature wrapped in programs of pure punitive ideology (in the worst sense of the word) of one or another sign in accordance with the populist maxims that govern the destiny of contemporary societies.[60] In the face of this evolution, the separation between law and morality must continue to govern, which has served, according to Ferrajoli, to promote the development of an iuspositivist penal science based on the principle of legality and the elaboration of a large part of the guarantees of freedom of the citizen and of the forms of government of the modern "democratic and constitutional state" as a political system subject to rules, limits and controls.[61] In contrast, the absolute or

---

[56]Frisch (2017), pp. 575 et seq.; Blom (2010), pp. 265 et seq.

[57]Ferrajoli (1995), pp. 27, 354 et seq.

[58]Corcoy Bidasolo (2017), pp. 297 et seq.

[59]Frisch (2017), p. 580.

[60]See, for example, Rosanvallon, who explains that populism is a phenomenon that revolutionizes the politics of the twenty-first century, although we have not yet fully appreciated the transformation to which it has given rise and we do not have a theory of the phenomenon (Rosanvallon 2020, Introduction).

[61]Ferrajoli (1995), p. 225.

retributionist doctrines of punishment are based on the maxim, whose origin goes back to the ancient "blood vengeance," that it is just to "repay harm with harm." As the Italian philosopher explains, this idea, present in the form of a divine precept in the Hebraic tradition, was transmitted, despite the evangelical precept of forgiveness, to the Christian and Catholic tradition, and revolves around three elementary ideas of a religious nature: revenge, expiation and the rebalancing of punishment and crime.[62]

Third, we have pointed out the existence of a discursive level at which preventive theories make sense in the face of a retributionist vision, and this refers to the internal dynamics of the *theory of the norm and the theory of crime* associated with it. In fact, according to the approach once expounded by Callies, the function of punishment can only be a consequence of the function of positive criminal law without incurring in the methodical inversion consisting of seeking the meaning of punishment outside positive law based on "metaphysical or speculative," "meta- or extra-legal" pre-suppositions.[63] In this respect, the statements made by Mir Puig, according to whom the analysis of positive law from the point of view of the preventive function of punishment to protect legal assets "leads to the conclusion that the function assigned to punishment in Spanish criminal law is not the realization of justice," can still be valid today, and this because "the retributionist approach could not explain that criminal law renounces to do justice beyond the facts punished by law" and, above all, because "the content *expressly* assigned to it by the current regulations on the execution of custodial sentences is absolutely opposed to the retributive function of punishment."[64]

---

[62] Ibíd., p. 254.

Puig also explained in his famous *Introduction to the Bases* (published in 1976) the following: "The fact that absolute theories have not found a place in criminal law, and instead in Christian ethics, is perfectly appropriate to the different *functions* of both orders. Criminal law, like every sector of law, cannot claim to establish absolute justice on earth, and the contrary would be to confuse its boundaries with those of morality" (Mir Puig 2003, p. 52).

[63] Callies (1974), pp. 35 et seq.

[64] Mir Puig (2003), pp. 80 et seq.

More details on the connection between the function of criminal law and norm theory on which it is not possible to elaborate in this short article in Demetrio Crespo (2017), pp. 55 et seq.

4 Conclusions

1. In my opinion, the old or modern retributive theories have still not overcome most of the criticisms that, with good reasons, were formulated some time ago by Roxin[65] and other authors:[66]

   (a) It can be said, primarily, that they presuppose the necessity of the punishment they are supposed to justify, and thus curiously lack the possibility of imposing a limit to the penal power of the state, which they generally attribute to themselves, as can be seen, for example, from the Kantian perspective, in the attempt to introduce relativizations to the *ius talionis* when it comes to the death penalty.[67] In Kant's thesis, which must certainly be examined in its context, we find the paradigm of absolute theories of punishment, since the meaning of the latter is exhausted in the sanction as an end in itself (*quia peccatum est*), according to a measure of equivalence with the crime.[68] This is the opinion of Pérez del Valle, who has emphasized, on the other hand, that the alleged "exceptions" to punishment as retribution in Kant, such as the assumptions of *ius necessitatis*, both in the famous case of the castaway and in that of a multitude of authors faced with the risk of the situation becoming a "state of nature lacking in external justice," are completely irrelevant and do not reconcile well with Kant's thought interpreted as a whole.[69]

   (b) Second, their ultimate philosophical foundation based on indeterminism or the possibility of acting otherwise (so-called alternativism) is unprovable. Moreover, at present, they are completely outside what scientific knowledge coming from brain research seems to indicate,[70] which has even led to suggest changes of considerable importance in the current configuration of the theory of crime and criminal law.[71] The suggestion to dispense with culpability seems to me, however, completely misguided because of the fundamental role it plays in democratic criminal law[72] and which is fully suitable for a compatibilist vision between determinism and freedom, which

---

[65] Roxin (1976), pp. 12 et seq.

[66] On this, Demetrio Crespo (1999), pp. 61 et seq.

[67] Thus, e.g., Mañalich clarifies the following: "to that extent, the categorical character of the criminal law by virtue of whose application the penalty is judicially imposed determines that it must necessarily be executed, without this practical necessity being relativized by prudential considerations of utility" (Mañalich 2018, p. 512). In the same sense pronounce Byrd and Hruschka: "Kant accepts no utilitarian calculus when it comes to the criminal law as a categorial imperative" (Byrd and Hruschka 2010, p. 268).

[68] Pérez del Valle (2020), pp. 220 et seq.

[69] Ibíd., pp. 224 et seq.

[70] Demetrio Crespo (2017), pp. 19 et seq.

[71] Hörnle (2013), pp. 49 et seq.

[72] Demetrio Crespo (2011), pp. 694 et seq.

is concerned, at the same time, by human dignity as an inalienable value.[73] What retributionism calls "deservedness" is, according to what I have defended in other works, personal imputation of the unjust to its author in accordance with a non-free-arbitrary syllogism, which has important implications from the point of view of the burden of proof of liberty.[74]

(c) Finally, the very idea of retribution requires an act of faith, since it is not possible to rationally understand how to make some harm disappear by adding a second equivalent harm; at the same time, it has been said that the doctrines that support it are suitable for justifying authoritarian models of maximum criminal law.[75] In this sense, the effort used to argue that retribution is not equivalent to revenge is striking,[76] although it seems to serve, apparently, to prevent the latter from occurring, which fuels the suspicion that the two are closely related to each other.[77]

2. It is true that the so-called "mixed theories" or "union theories" have not exactly contributed to clarify the debate, but rather the opposite. So much so, that at times one has the feeling that they incur in the defect of affirming one thing and the opposite at the same time in such a way that one could be in perfect agreement or/and disagreement with them depending on the passage, which, in my opinion, is caused by not adequately distinguishing the different discursive planes that are involved, something that can already be perceived in the very definition of punishment as retributive-preventive.[78] But what is presented in the "theories of union" (which are the majoritarian type of theory), in principle, as a methodological problem, in the renewed defenses of retributionism appears clearly as a mere "program of punitive ideology" or, even worse, as a "sociological interpretation" devoid of any philosophical or humanist basis.[79]
3. Due to the subordination of the purposes of punishment as a framework theory of criminal law to the function that the latter is called upon to fulfill in the constitutional Rule of Law and, therefore, to its subjection to the principles and guarantees proper to it, retribution can remain, as such, outside the *purposes* of punishment.[80] This is reflected both in the explanatory level of the theory of the

[73] Demetrio Crespo (2017), pp. 75 et seq.

[74] Ibíd., pp. 90–91.

[75] Ferrajoli (1995), pp. 257–258.

[76] García Amado (2018), pp. 323 et seq.

[77] Of "institutionalized revenge," even if it is called "justice," he speaks, e.g., Corcoy Bidasolo (2017), p. 285.

[78] Alonso Álamo (2019), pp. 1302 et seq.; Chiesa (2020), pp. 119 et seq.

[79] This argument, in the present text only sketched due to space limitations, should, however, be the subject of further development, due to the complexity of this type of theories, ranging from the so-called retributive theories of bonding, through the new approaches of the expressive theories mentioned above, to the preventive theories of bonding. (Vid. Roxin and Greco 2020, pp. 145–160).

[80] *Vid.* however, among many other references, Stratenwerth (1995), p. 20.

state itself and the convergences that must be established with the model of criminal law that corresponds to it at a given historical moment, as well as in the theory of law and, finally, in dogmatics.

4. In accordance with the above, it is necessary to differentiate between retribution, reprobation and revenge. *State penalty is a punishment*, a harm, and on this there is no room for "half-measures." If it is said that punishment is a harm, but that it does not necessarily have to be, because if retribution is defended as the purpose of punishment without bearing its disadvantages, one incurs in a flagrant contradiction. With it, the state expresses a *reprobation* of those behaviors that, due to their damaging capacity for the most important legal assets, have been previously foreseen as criminal. But, as we have tried to argue, the purpose of punishment is quite different, and this is of a preventive nature. Of course, the state punishment is neither revenge nor a substitute for revenge, but rather comes precisely to cut it off. Rather, it is imposed to achieve a *twofold practical purpose*, both of which are entirely understandable: to prevent the recurrence of such acts as far as possible and to avoid private revenge. Insofar as this is done because there is no other choice and in accordance with the principles, guarantees and limits that make up general and special prevention in the different phases of criminal intervention (and, within each of them, always in accordance with certain axiological, methodological and dogmatic guidelines), it can hardly be said that human dignity is thereby violated.

References

Alonso Álamo M (2019) Polisemia del término retribución y pena retributivo-preventiva. In: Cancio Meliá M et al (eds) Libro Homenaje al Profesor Dr. Agustín Jorge Barreiro. Servicio de Publicaciones UAM, Madrid, pp 1291–1307

Blom P (2010) Böse Philosophen. Carl Hanser, München

Bruckmann P (2019) Sinn und Unsinn gegenwärtiger Vergeltungstheorien – überholt, hilfreich oder notwendig zur Legitimation staatlicher Strafe? KriPoZ 2:105–118

Byrd S, Hruschka J (2010) Kant's doctrine of right. A commentary. Cambridge University Press, Cambridge

Callies RP (1974) Theorie der Strafe im demokratischen und sozialen Rechtsstaat. Ein Beitrag zur strafrechtsdogmatischen Grundlagendiskussion. Fischer Taschenbuch, Frankfurt am Main

Chiesa LE (2020) Selective incompatibilism, free will, and the (limited) role of retribution in punishment theory. RULR 71(4):101–125

Corcoy Bidasolo M (2017) Prevención limitada vs. neoretribucionismo. In: Silva Sánchez JMª et al (Coord.) Estudios de Derecho Penal. Homenaje al profesor Santiago Mir Puig BdeF, Montevideo – Buenos Aires, pp 285–297

Demetrio Crespo E (1999) Prevención general e individualización judicial de la pena, 1ª ed. Ediciones USAL, Salamanca [(2016), 2ª ed. BdeF, Buenos Aires-Montevideo]

Demetrio Crespo E (2011) Schuld und Strafzwecke. In: Heinrich M et al (Hg.) Strafrecht als Scientia Universalis. Festschrift für Claus Roxin zum 80. Geburtstag. Walter de Gruyter, Berlin/New York, pp 689–703

Demetrio Crespo E (2017) Fragmentos sobre Neurociencias y Derecho Penal. BdeF, Montevideo-Buenos Aires

Demetrio Crespo E (2020) El Derecho penal del Estado de Derecho entre el espíritu de nuestro tiempo y la Constitución. Reus, Madrid
Demko D (2017) Hegels Straftheorie im Lichte gegenwärtiger expressiver Straftheorien. In: Kubiciel M et al (Hg.) Hegel's Erben?. Mohr Siebeck, Tübingen, pp 277–300
Donna EA (2019) Persona y Derecho. Rubinzal - Culzoni, Buenos Aires
Duff A (2015) Sobre el castigo. Por una justicia penal que hable el lenguaje de la comunidad. Siglo XXI Editores, Buenos Aires
Escamilla Castillo M (2010) The purposes of legal punishment. Ratio Juris 23(4):460–478
Feijoo Sánchez B (2007) Retribución y prevención general. Un estudio sobre la teoría de la pena y las funciones del Derecho penal. BdeF, Montevideo-Buenos Aires
Feijoo Sánchez B (2014) La legitimidad de la pena estatal. Un breve recorrido por las teorías de la pena estatal. Iustel, Madrid
Ferrajoli L (1995) Derecho y Razón. Teoría del garantismo penal. Trotta, Madrid
Frisch W (2017) Von theokratischem zu säkularem Strafrecht. Zum Zusammenhang von Staatstheorie und Strafrecht. In: Saliger F et al (Hg.) Rechtsstaatliches Strafrecht. Festschrift für Ulfrid Neumann zum 70. Geburtstag. C.F. Müller, Heidelberg, pp 575–586
García Amado JA (2018) Retribución y justificación del castigo. In: Portilla Contreras G et al (Dir.) Un juez para la democracia: Libro Homenaje a Perfecto Andrés Ibáñez. Dykinson, Madrid, pp 323–340
Greco L (2009) Lebendiges und Totes in Feuerbachs Straftheorie. Ein Beitrag zur gegenwärtigen strafrechtlichen Grundlagendiskussion. Duncker & Humblot, Berlín
Grosse-Wilde T (2017) Erfolgszurechnung in der Strafzumessung. Mohr Siebeck, Tübingen
Hegel GF (1968) Filosofía del Derecho, Prólogo de Carlos Marx, 5ª ed. Editorial Claridad, Buenos Aires
Hörnle T (2013) Kriminalstrafe ohne Schuldvorwurf. Ein Plädoyer für Änderungen in der strafrechtlichen Verbrechenslehre. Nomos, Baden-Baden
Hörnle T (2015) Teorías de la pena. Universidad Externado de Colombia, Bogotá
Hruschka J (2010) Die "Verabschiedung" Kants durch Ulrich Klug im Jahre 1968: Einige Korrekturen. ZStW 122(3):494–503
Kant I (1989) La Metafísica de las Costumbres, traducción y notas de A. Cortina Orts y J. Conill Sancho. Tecnos, Madrid
Klug U (1968) "Abschied von Kant und Hegel". In: Baurmann J (Hg.) Programm für ein neues Strafgesetzbuch. Fischer, Frankfurt am Main, pp 36–41 [también en: Id. (1981), Skeptische Rechtsphilosophie und humanes Strafrecht, Band 2. Materielle und formelle Strafrechtsprobleme. Springer-Verlag, Berlin. Heidelberg. New York, pp 149–154 [≥ (2002), "Despedida de Kant y Hegel (Una crítica jusfilosófica básica)", en Id., Problemas de la Filosofía y de la Pragmática del Derecho, 2ª reimp. Fontamara, México D.F, pp 31–36 (trad. Jorge Mª Seña)]
Mañalich JP (2015) Retribucionismo consecuencialista como programa de ideología punitiva. InDret 2:1–32
Mañalich JP (2018) Respeto y retribución: la pena jurídica en La metafísica de las costumbres. Revista de Ciencia Política 38(3):507–526
Mir Puig S (2003) Introducción a las bases del Derecho penal. BdeF, Montevideo-Buenos Aires
Pawlik M (2016) Ciudadanía y Derecho penal. Fundamentos de la teoría de la pena y del delito en un Estado de libertades. Atelier, Barcelona
Pérez Barberá G (2014) Problemas y perspectivas de las teorías expresivas de la pena. Una justificación deontológica de la pena como institución. InDret 4:1–43
Pérez del Valle C (2020) Poena forensis y retribución. Propuesta para la restauración de una teoría. InDret 3:214–259
Rawls J (1955) Two concepts of rules. Philos Rev 64(1):3–32
Robinson PH (2012) Principios distributivos del Derecho penal: a quién debe sancionarse y en qué medida. Marcial Pons, Madrid-Barcelona-Buenos Aires-São Paulo

Rodríguez Horcajo D (2016) Comportamiento humano y pena estatal: disuasión, cooperación y equidad. Marcial Pons, Madrid-Barcelona-Buenos Aires-São Paulo
Rosanvallon P (2020) El siglo del populismo. Galaxia Gutemberg, Barcelona
Roxin C (1976) Sentido y límites de la pena estatal. En Id., Problemas básicos del Derecho penal. Reus, Madrid, pp 11–36
Roxin C, Greco L (2020) Strafrecht. Allgemeiner Teil. Band I. Grundlagen. Der Aufbau der Verbrechenslehre, 5. Auflage. C.H. Beck, München
Sánchez Lázaro FG (2016) Una teoría principialista de la pena. Marcial Pons, Madrid-Barcelona-Buenos Aires-São Paulo
Schünemann B (2019) El Derecho penal en el Estado democrático de Derecho y el irrenunciable nivel de su dogmática. BdeF, Madrid: Reus/Montevideo-Buenos Aires
Stratenwerth G (1995) Was leistet die Lehre von den Strafzwecken? Walter de Gruyter, Berlin-New York
Teixeira A (2018) Las teorías retributivas en el pensamiento angloamericano contemporáneo. Letra: Derecho Penal, Año IV 7:35–77
von Hirsch A (1998) Censurar y castigar. Trotta, Madrid
Walter T (2016) Strafe und Vergeltung – Rehabilitation und Grenzen eines Prinzips. Nomos, Baden-Baden
White MD (ed) (2011) Retributivism. Essays on theory and policy. Oxford University Press, Oxford
Zaibert L (2006) Punishment and retribution. Ashgate, Aldershot

Crises of the *Ultima Ratio* Principle: Shall We Resume the Constitutional Criminal Law Guidance?

Faustino García de la Torre García

Abstract The criminal law doctrine invokes *the ultima ratio principle* to minimize the arbitrary use of penal instruments. The principle submits, through the condition of necessity, the legitimacy of the criminal law to the axiological and empirical condition of the lack of another legal remedies to solve the social conflict which causes the punitive instrumental appeal. Notwithstanding, an expansion of penal law, which in principle has shown itself to be required, has degenerated to a punitive drift where it has casted doubt on the real ability of the *ultima ratio principle* for detracting the arbitrary use of criminal law, specially due to its limited linkage to public powers. Far from this case, from the latest developments of the constitutional law theory, we might claim nowadays that the real significance of the *ultima ratio principle* in a constitutional state implies that the minimum penal law demanded by constitution is at the same time the highest one to be allowed.

1 Introduction

Theoretically, the use of criminal law should be the most problematic decision to adopt in the *Constitutional State* due to the interference that it entails in the sphere of citizen's freedoms, the most serious one that the state can carry out. The presence of the criminal law in interpersonal relationships control causes so much tension between public power and private freedom, that is only desirable its restriction

This paper has been developed within the framework of the Research Project, Criminal Law Crisis of the Rule of Law: Manifestations and Trends, co-financed by the Castilla La Mancha Regional Government and FEDER Funds (SBPLY/17/180501/000223).

F. G. de la Torre García (✉)
Faculty of Legal and Social Sciences, University of Castilla-La Mancha, Toledo, Spain
e-mail: Faustino.GarciaTorre@uclm.es

E. Demetrio Crespo et al. (eds.), *Crisis of the Criminal Law in the Democratic Constitutional State*, Legal Studies in International, European and Comparative Criminal Law 6, https://doi.org/10.1007/978-3-031-13413-5_3

within the framework of a peaceful society. [1] Even when it really appears that there is no other effective or adequate legal instrument to ensure the enjoyment of fundamental and human rights, the legitimate punitive claim of the public powers comes face to face with the subjective right of all citizens not to suffer the threat or imposition of a penalty that is not strictly necessary.[2] Thus in theory, the idea (*Gedanke*) that criminal law is the last resort in the legislator's "toolbox" is considered by the doctrine as a common heritage (*Allgemeingut*).[3]

But in practice, the political option of using criminal law does not appear to be so problematic or costly in terms of freedoms after the 30 amendments were made on the so-called "Penal Code of democracy" since its promulgation in 1995 until it was transformed (reform after reform) into the "Penal Code of security," neither the loyalty shown by politicians to the idea of ultima ratio as it has been traditionally understood. The current scenario in Spain, and in the rest of our closest legal or political environment countries, is one in which a historical maximum of behaviors classified has been reached by penal code, a fact that often responds to national security policies or transnational criminal law claims.[4] Some examples from our own country are the 2015 and 2019 Penal Code reforms, where the political (and constitutional) power "wasted" the opportunity to conduct to the administrative order a number of minor crimes by means of the supression policy for misdemeanors, that the reform would supposedly implements, even taking the opportunity to penalize more. Later, the lawmakers entered through the window of the 2019 reform the bit that was taken out through the door of the 2015 reform.[5]

To this untenable situation of criminal law caused by the differences between the principles of the academic culture and the political praxis, is added a social atmosphere where the traditional claims for defending the man against the public power have been turned into legal requirements to protect the man by means of the state against non-state actors injuries, who have (supposedly) the same capacity to put in a real danger the existence of human rights or the constitutional freedoms guaranties. Consequently, if it does not so fear the risk of tyranny nowadays as the time when *the principle of ultima ratio* was developed, deep transformations on the common heritage, which is *the idea of ultima ratio*, are raised.[6] Because of lack of absolute certainly holding that criminal law is the most serious interference in the sphere of the individual from the state, and in the absence of consideration about the capacity of non-criminal sanction instruments, it is no longer clear whether we should consider that criminal law is the final instrument in the hands of public power, or another *ratio* such as the *prima*, *sola* or *unica* ratio.[7]

---

[1] Demetrio Crespo (2020), p. 16.

[2] Ferrajoli (2014), p. 209.

[3] Seher (2012a, b), p. 129.

[4] See, in Italy and Germany, respectively: Marra (2018), p. 2; Weigend (2016), p. 1.

[5] Quintero Olivares (2019), p. 15; González Cussac (2015), p. 19.

[6] Bernuz Beneitez and González Ordovás (2006), p. 24.

[7] Palazzo (2001), p. 441; Prittwitz (2017), p. 390.

There has recently been an intense debate from two points of view about the character of the ultima ratio principle between who hold that it implies a constitutional regulative limit (*Grenzen*) for the punitive desires of public power, and who only hope to be considering in the "careful" mind of public powers.[8] In this context, we defend the first mentioned position, and through this work we hold that *the principle of ultima ratio* implies in the constitutional & democratic state a real regulatory and binding limit for the *ius puniendi* that implies in substantial terms, that the penal sanctions required by constitutional law as the necessary measures (in terms of must/have to or *müssen*) to protect properly and ensure human rights, are in turn the highest allow interference on constitutional freedoms. This means that the so-called "minimum criminal law" *demanded* by constitutional law through duties to protect and ensure fundamental rights (*Grundrechtliche Schutzpflichten* or positive state obligations) involves the "maximum criminal law" that is finally *allowed* (in terms of *dürfen nicht*) from the perspective of the set of freedoms against punishment on which the human personality is based (*Abwehrrechten von Sanktionierung*).

2 The Ultima Ratio Principle in the History of Ideals

2.1 How the Criminal Law Was Moved to the Ultima Ratio in the Transition from the Absolute Towards the Liberal State

Criminal law could not be *the ultima ratio instrument* in the absolute state thinking of the earliest modernity, because in that ideal type of political coexistence, "whoever has the right to the end has the right to the means" and acts as judge both for the means of peace and defense, and to do whatever is considered necessary for the preservation of peace and security.[9] In fact, the absolute state has been described as a mere "ordo poenalis."[10] However, at the time that the state took the control of each and every sphere of social life enforcing civil peace by neutralizing the fears of the citizens among themselves, it itself becomes the object of fear.[11] Therefore, from the middle of the 18th century onwards, the discretionary use of criminal law entered into a serious crisis due to the fast expansion of the idea that the existence of the state (or sovereign) also could imply insecurity where there is no possibility of rejecting its claims.[12]

---

[8] Check these positions: Gärditz (2016) and Jahn and Brodowski (2016).

[9] Hobbes (1980), p. 384.

[10] Schmitt (2008), p. 151.

[11] Isensee (2014), p. 21.

[12] Bacigalupo (2005), p. 12.

From these claims raised the Doctrine of "(liberties) Defence against State" (also so-called *Staatsabwehrdoktrin*) within the framework of Enlightenment political philosophy where also the pillars of the criminal law as social science were built, not to eliminate the so-called Leviathan, but to tame it in its facet of "Magnus homo."[13] The first formulation of *the ultima ratio idea* appears systematically in the work of Beccaria, who points out that "every punishment, says the great Montesquieu, which does not derive from absolute necessity, is tyrannical; a proposition which can be made more general in this way: every act of authority from man to man which does not derive from absolute necessity, is tyrannical. Here therefore is the basis of the sovereign's right to punish crimes: the need to defend the deposit of public health from encroachments; and the more just are the penalties, the more sacred and inviolable is the security and the greater the liberty that the sovereign preserves for its subjects."[14]

2.2 *How the Criminal Law Became the Extrema Ratio in the Transition from the Liberal to the Welfare State*

But the Doctrine of (liberties) defence against the state (or *Staatsabwehrdoktrin*) was also involved in a process of self-denial since the end of the 19th century due to the inability of *bourgeois society* to (self-)regulate the huge proliferation of risks arising from the process of industrialization and the consequent mass migration from the countryside to the city.[15] Under the slogan that the state should be able to act with all its means when necessary to protect freedom against *the new risks* of work, unemployment, and the loss of the basic conditions for material subsistence, the public powers have been progressively encouraged to abandon its position as a simple "night keeper" of the juridical order under which it had been conceived by bourgeois society. In the mind of the new industrial class society, the boundaries between the state and the individuals are blurred.[16] From that time on, it began to be considered that the state may be required by a group of citizens to design the social organization by political means, among which criminal law is an instrument to fight against crime.[17]

After the collapse of the "wall" that separated the state from the individual in liberal society, the demands of social economy, which try to reach the greatest benefit at the lowest cost, are the main reasons for desiring the minimum intervention of the state through the exercise of violence.[18] The idea that criminal law should be

[13] Schmitt (2008), p. 106.

[14] Beccaria (1990), p. 86.

[15] Grimm (1991), p. 187 y ss.

[16] Forsthoff (1975), p. 123.

[17] Mir Puig (2003), p. 104.

[18] Mir Puig (1999), p. 151.

the *ultima ratio* of the political options does not move back in the transition from the liberal state to the welfare state, despite the social state tends to be reflected in the expansion of public powers action, both in terms of its objectives of protection and its rigor,[19] but even is reasserted by the increasing of the new interventions through social policies for the distribution of wealth, shifting the necessity of punitive sanctions to the *extrema ratio*.[20]

2.3 How Is Being Conducted (One Again) the Criminal Law to the Prima Ratio in the Transition from the Welfare to the Current Model of State

The penal code expansion is practically an inevitable fact in our times,[21] since it is assumed, with ever increasing rigor, that the state's regulatory intervention in areas that have traditionally remained free from political action could be positive.[22] The current "risk Society" coexist among inevitable dangers and risks that constantly threaten the security of the citizens, their lives, and physical integrity, which not only or are always due to the technification, industrialization, and globalization processes, but because of another traditional reasons where criminal law is often used with a symbolic value without examining how efficient and necessary it may be in relation to the existence of other techniques of protection and social control.[23]

Under these parameters, it has already been argued that the current model of the state may well be called a "security State."[24] Following the analysts, we can submit that the reform of the penal code made in 2015 has meant a whole "Apocalypse" for the "last European Penal Code," and many of the changes in penal legislation do not correspond to reasons of a strict need to protect legal interests, but exclusively to a repressive ideology whose opportunity lies in purely populist reasons.[25] It has even been said that the reform made in 2019 "has succeeded in narrowing, to the point of being inane, the ideological spectrum of criminal policy options."[26]

[19] Mir Puig (2003), p. 110.
[20] Mir Puig (2015), pp. 127, 129.
[21] Corcoy (2012), p. 46.
[22] Beck (1998), p. 14.
[23] Silva Sánchez (2011); Carnevali Rodríguez (2009), pp. 17, 18.
[24] Martínez de Pisón (2006), p. 53.
[25] González Cussac (2015), pp. 17, 18, 34.
[26] Quintero Olivares (2019), p. 11.

3 The Meaning of Ultima Ratio Principle in Criminal Law Doctrine

3.1 The Ultima Ratio Principle As Functional Limits of the Criminal Policy

The modern science of criminal law is currently guided by the classical principles of the political philosophy of the Enlightenment according to the fundaments of criminal law must be reduced to the strict protection of the most important legal interests of society,[27] adopting a critical position as counterweight to the public powers by examining the divergences between imperatives *de lege data* and *de lege ferenda* to subtract legitimacy from any public intervention that is not strictly necessary.[28] Among the functional limits of criminal law to which criminal science appeals to achieve its aims, such as the principle of exclusive protection of legal assets; the principle of subsidiarity; and the fragmentation principle, *the ultima ratio* occupies a prominent place, as it is the oldest and most univocal of them all and refers to the concept of limit in a clearer way.[29]

The ultima ratio principle describes the Enlightenment idea that criminal law can never be legitimate when exist other possibilities neutralizing social conflicts that are equally adequate for the intended purpose and less drastic than crime and punishment.[30] The embodiment of this ideology through law principles or categories appears frequently (only) in academic literature to deny the use of punitive tools when the other legal resources for social protection and control, such as civil law, administrative law, social policy, or the capacity for self-protection,[31] may offer any guarantee of effectiveness in achieving the public purpose or objective for which their use is proposed.[32]

3.2 The Ultima Ratio Principle Among the Dogmatic Categories of Criminal Science

In despite of the fact that the ultima ratio idea permeates the entire Dogmatics of Criminal Law Doctrine, it gains dogmatic meaning at the traditional categories of

---

[27] Sánchez Martínez (2004), p. 57.

[28] Schünemann (2012), p. 68.

[29] Prittwitz (2000), p. 432.

[30] Raised by Montesquieu (1987), p. 209; Beccaria (1990), p. 86; Bentham (1981), p. 308.

[31] Regarding the impact of private self-protection techniques on the ultima ratio principle: Schünemann (2012), p. 78 ff; Hörnle (2012), p. 88 ff.

[32] Muñoz Conde and García Arán (2019), p. 64; Zugaldía Espinar (2016), p. 49. From a constitutional perspective: Arroyo Zapatero (2016), p. 147. Orts Berenguer and González Cussac (2020), p. 74.

merit and necessity because there exhibits its greatest limiting potential.[33] The first category (so-called *Strafwürdigkeit*) expresses the need to carry out an evaluative judgment based on the importance of the legal interest and the social reprobation of the behavior that disturbs it, to verify that the personality of the person who suffers it can bear the burden that criminal law sanctions entail.[34] The second one (so-called *Strafbedürftigkeit*) deny the criminal law legitimacy to protect interests that may be adequately protected by using mechanisms other than punitive means, which are less harmful to the citizen and frequently much more effective for the protection of society.[35]According to Mir Puig, "in the presence of other means, a more serious recourse is not justified when the same or better results can be expected from other milder means, and only when none of them is sufficient will the use of punishment be legitimate."[36]

However, although the meaning of the categories of merit and necessity in comparative legal-criminal experiences is generally univocal (at least in Germany, Italy, Portugal, and Spain), these categories are rarely mentioned as independent models of limitation of criminal law, but as a rule they are confused with each other because their application requirements have not been specified, referring to each other to determine their contours.[37] In this sense, *the idea of Criminal Law as ultima ratio* is directly linked to the doctrinal category of *necessity*, because it clearly expresses its meaning as a judgment that delegitimizes criminal intervention in areas of social life where there are other alternative means to neutralize the adverse effects of behaviors deserving of prohibition.[38]

3.3 *Crisis of a Criminal Law Basic Principle?*

As we have already pointed out, public powers are no longer seen as a potential disruptor of freedoms, but rather as a vigorous guarantor and protector of individuals against the immense dangers and risks that threaten the current society and its citizens.[39] It is therefore not surprising that the call for a criminal law that neutralizes the high uncertainties and instabilities of the social environment is sounding louder and louder.[40] Given the lack of clarity regarding the issues of effectiveness and the real harmfulness of criminal law in relation to other means of control and especially in view of the lack of care that public powers show following the basic principles

---

[33] Silva Sánchez (1992), p. 247.

[34] Sax (1959), p. 914 y ss.

[35] Orts Berenguer and González Cussac (2020), p. 74.

[36] Mir Puig (2003), p. 110.

[37] Appel (1998), p. 391.

[38] Sax (1959), p. 923 y ss; Demuro (2013), p. 12; Mir Puig (2003), p. 110.

[39] Streuer (2003), p. 49.

[40] Lagodny (1996), p. 2.

developed by the Criminal Law Doctrine, we must decide between throwing these articulated programs overboard or polishing them to face the overflowing praxis of criminal law.[41]

Regarding that, Demetrio Crespo has noticed about the *Crisis and metamorphosis of the (Enlightenment) Criminal Law*, in the sense of witnessing the complete "pulverization," by means of reform and reduction to absurdity through populist instrumentalism, political demagogy and media spectacle the framework of guarantees developed by the criminal doctrine under the postulates of the Enlightenment, a program that seemed to be identified with the original wording of the Spanish Criminal Code of 1995.[42] According to this author, some of the criminal law borders may well be considered "a cliché devoid of concrete content," not only due to the phenomenon of the criminal law expansion that is inevitably taking place today, on which it recognizes certain advantages, especially when it comes to prosecuting the criminality of the powerful against the weakest, but more because the discourse of guarantees is beginning to be considered "the fruit of lack of solidarity, lack of vision or, in the best of cases, of the academic naivety of those who support this discourse."[43]

4 The Constitutional Dimension of Ultima Ratio Principle

4.1 The Constitutional Received of the Ultima Ratio Principle As Criminal Policy Limit

Constitutionalism is a trend of thought aimed to limit public powers activity, and to enhance the liberties of the individuals,[44] in such a way that the system constitutional guarantees must be more sophisticated and developed the greater the possibilities for public power to intervene in the individual's private sphere.[45] In this sense, *the Constitutional orientation of Criminal Law* offers the advantage, compared to the classic formulation of classical theories, of having the political capacity to bind the legislator and the criminal judge in a more intense way.[46] In the context of constitutional state, criminal law limits should only be addressed at the highest regulatory level, where effective constitutional and conventional control over material criminal norms is possible.[47]

---

[41] Prittwitz (2000), p. 428.

[42] Demetrio Crespo (2020), pp. 20 y ss.

[43] Demetrio Crespo (2020), p. 20 y ss.

[44] Fioravanti (2014), p. 17.

[45] Appel (1998), p. 26.

[46] Greco (2013), pp. 17, 18.

[47] Appel (1998), p. 328 y ss.

Under the framework of the so-called (in Spain) *constitutional Criminal Law* or its *constitutional orientation* (as is in Italy known), it has been said that "if *the ultima ratio principle* is not only an outline of the social contract, but also a component arising from the Constitutional State, it becomes an authentic barrier/limit (*Grenzen*) of law that participates in the regulatory power of the Constitution."[48] However, it should be noted that, although criminal and constitutional law often use the same terms, the concepts may have different content, and due to the high degree of abstraction of constitutional law, criminal lawyers will only be able to find a very rudimentary answer to their concerns.[49] Regarding that, it has been denounced that *the principle of ultima ratio* has not been correctly translated into the language of constitutional law, which has incorporated it into the second test of the principle of proportionality (*Erforderlichkeit*) in the wide sense, moving away somewhat from its classic understanding.[50]

4.2 *The Deferential Position of the Constitutional Jurisdiction*

In the process of *the ultima ratio idea* translation into constitutional jurisprudence, it has been stated that the resulting principle has lost its functional character of political limit inherent to the public powers exercise of the monopoly of force, vanishing the opportunity to generate authentic imperative effects from constitutional law, and being disqualified from a constitutional derivation.[51] Constitutional courts (at least from Italy, Germany, and Spain) have been pointed as main liable of allowing the subtraction of large part of the limiting potential that criminal science has always expected from the constitutional principle (of *ultima ratio*), due to the complexity involved in carrying out a comparative empirical trial to verify that there really is no other equally adequate means for the protection of legal assets. Constitutional courts resorting to the "miracle cure" that entails leaving the choice about the legal options to the experience of the Parliament members (by means of democratic principle) due to the complexity involved in carrying out a comparative empirical trial to verify that there really is no other equally adequate means for the protection of legal assets.[52]

Donini points out that in practice "no one can challenge a law that violates *the ultima ratio principle*."[53] Nevertheless, the criticism concerning the incompatibility of the principle of ultima ratio with the breadth of the legislator's prerogative in criminal matters is by no means new (it was formulated by Appel more than 20 years

[48] Greco (2013), p. 20.

[49] Greco (2013), p. 26 y ss.

[50] Correa Aguado (1999), pp. 240, 241.

[51] Jahn and Brodowski (2017), p. 969.

[52] Vid. STC 55/1996 FFJJ 7° y 8°.

[53] Donini (2010), p. 13.

ago) nor is it unknown among us, thanks to the famous work of Lascuraín regarding the restrictive and the deferential in constitutional jurisprudence in criminal matters.[54] In this regard, both the German and Spanish authors have pointed out that the deference shown by the *Bundesverfassungsgericht* (*BverfG*) and the Spanish Constitutional Court in the material control of criminal rules leads to a jurisprudence full of inconsistencies regarding the treatment of the ultima ratio principle. Such deference does not allow us to maintain the limiting capacity traditionally attributed to it, especially when the criminal legislator is granted a margin of maneuver as broad as the difficulty of determining the real effects of punitive norms.[55]

4.3 Metamorphosis of the Ultima Ratio Principle in Terms of Constitutional Law?

As evidenced by the above, only in obvious cases, where there are clearly other non-penal sanctions to adequately ensure the use of freedoms against third-party injuries, could *the "constitutional" principle of ultima ratio* (through the principle of proportionality) be involved, so that the constitutional limitations of *the ultima ratio principle* are circumscribed to the limits of irrational criminal policy verified through an evidentiary trial (so-called *Evidenzkontrolle*).[56] In turn, the foregoing means while there is no real obstacle to invalid a certain penal rule by the constitutional court if a logical reasoning exists or an empirical evidence emerges, about the penal sanction is (in the case) more harmful than other(s) of the correlatively suitable ones for the achievement of the specific purpose proposed by its use.[57]

Regarding that, the most eye-catching fact of the "constitutionally" making use of the principle by constitutional court is that it is normally carried out in cases of *duties of the State to ensure and protect Human Rights* (so-called *grundrechtliche Schutzpflichten*) which demands a *positive State obligation*.[58] Theoretically, the constitutional control over rules does not reach the specific means selected by the legislator, but at most, the achievement of a certain level or standard of protection of a given legal interest. However, when there is evidence that the other legal remedies do not offer guarantees of effectiveness in relation to the fulfilment of a state objective of protection, constitutional justice does address the legislative selection of means.[59] Accordingly, in the presence of a *duty of the State to ensure and protect*, the public authorities may even be obliged to use criminal law, because its recourse really works as *the ultima ratio* in terms of the appropriate legal remedies. But this

[54] Lascuraín Sánchez (2012, 2020).

[55] Appel (1998), pp. 99, 100, 142, 143, 178, 182, 407, 409, 415, 416, 540.

[56] Correa Aguado (1999), p. 241; Donini (2001), p. 30.

[57] Correa Aguado (1999), p. 241.

[58] See: STC 55/1996 FJ 7°; *BVerfGE* 39, 1, 45.

[59] Isensee (2011), p. 542.

kind of "positive" approach of the criminal law principles has been paradoxically understood as an "inversion"[60] of the principle or directly, the "annulment" of its meaning.[61] Regarding this, Prittwitz has been particularly emphatic, describing the "positive" point of view as a true "hypertrophy" of *the classic idea of ultima ratio*, since he states that such a position would only serve "to gamble everything on one card" and assume the risk of failure, when the other means of control and social protection do not provide sufficient guarantees of effectiveness.[62]

5 Should Gain the Ultima Ratio Principle a Constitutional Dimension?

5.1 Lights and Shadows of "Constitutionalizing" Criminal Law Principles

As Greco has highlighted, it seems that over the last decade, more efforts have been made to examine criminal rules from the dogmatic categories and principles of constitutional law without abandoning the hope that constitutional freedoms effectively put real borders the activity of the legislator.[63] So much so, that during the last ten years has appeared in German literature the term *constitutional Criminal Law* (*Strafverfassungsrecht*),[64] developed in Spain by the disciples of Barbero Santos at the beginning of the 1990s. [65] However, and even in our country, *constitutional Criminal law* is currently only a term that criminal doctrine uses in an informal way, which lacks deep reflections and only describes the expectations that a small group of criminal lawyers and philosophers of law have in the potential limitation of constitutional freedoms.[66]

But a constitutional criminal law doctrine primarily demands to break old objections that are well established in the mindset of criminal lawyers, such, the so-called "democratic and evaluative objections" over which is granted a wide margin of freedom for the organization of the legal system to the legislator, must be overcome.[67] Until then, penal students will continue to fear exposing its self-sufficient territory to the omnipotence of constitutional principles, because constitutional law could make the dogmatic differentiation between categories turns into a waste of

---

[60] Gärditz (2016), p. 643.

[61] Appel (1998), p. 144.

[62] Prittwitz (2000), p. 433.

[63] Greco (2013), pp. 17, 18.

[64] See: Jahn (2016) and Burchard (2016).

[65] See: Arroyo Zapatero and Berdugo Gómez de la Torre (1994), p. 43; Arroyo Zapatero (2016); Demetrio Crespo (2020); Quintero Olivares (2015); Mir Puig (2011).

[66] Jahn (2016), p. 65.

[67] Tiedemann (1991), pp. 4, 5.

time in the name of the specific case, and thus ruin the differentiations coined for more than 200 years.[68]

5.2 *Should the Principle of Ultima Ratio Remain in the Minds of the Careful Politicians?*

In the current discussion regarding the method and foundations of criminal law, two types of proposals are being debated: those who are in favor of the major "democratization" of criminal law (in terms of *majority principle*),[69] and those who see a certain light and hope in *the constitutionalizing Criminal Law process*, that had already begun.[70] In this context, the controversy regarding the current state of *the principle of ultima ratio* has arisen, and is important to remark that it has taken place using concepts of constitutional law, as is not usual. In this connection, Gärditz, who recognizes that the *constitutional Criminal Law* is currently an omnipresent topic, rejects the idea that the *Grundgesetz* should serve as a basis (*Schranken*) for criminal prosecution beyond its limiting function (*Grenzen*), since, according to him, democratic structures already legitimize criminal law within the constitution.[71] Consequently, criminal law is also "political law" and cannot be replaced by constitutional "dogma."[72]

Gärditz points out that *the principle of ultima ratio* should remain as an external category in the careful mind of the politicians, which they may or not consider it.[73] Furthermore, he agrees that *the principle of proportionality structure* would not support a perfect anchoring of *the ultima ratio idea*, first because the question of the legitimate aim (*Legitimes Zweck*) can hardly be solved by the controversial theories of punishment, on which *the ultima ratio principle* depends to a large extent; secondly, because the determination of what is merely to be punished (*Geeignetheit*) is the exclusive competence of politicians, and thirdly, because too many aspects of the actual effectiveness and degree of harmfulness of criminal law are unknown to make the necessity of penal protection (*Erforderlichkeit*) depend on *the classical idea of the ultima ratio*.[74] In conclusion, for Gärditz, *the ultimate ratio principle's crisis* is not due to the *BVerfG's* deference in criminal matters or to politicians who have gone completely off the rails, but to a doctrine that is excessively overloaded with unrealistic expectations.[75]

---

[68] Appel (1998), p. 46 y ss; Greco (2013), p. 33.

[69] Gärditz (2015).

[70] Demetrio Crespo (2020).

[71] Gärditz (2015), pp. 11–13, 24–25, 30–32, 39–47.

[72] Gärditz (2016), p. 641.

[73] Gärditz (2016), pp. 641, 646, 647, 649.

[74] Gärditz (2016), p. 649.

[75] Gärditz (2016), p. 649.

5.3 Should the Ultima Ratio Principle Be Placed at the Hands of Constitutional Court?

Jahn & Brodowski have remained skeptical facing Gärditz's thesis remarking that it would mean setting that the constitutional consequences of *the ultima ratio principle* at zero.[76] In this sense, Gärditz's approach has also been questioned by Prittwitz, who has pointed out, without adhering to Jahn & Brodowski's thesis either, that it is totally unreasonable and dangerous, in particular for the integrity of constitutional freedoms, to let politicians free from the "sword" of constitutional jurisdiction, because in the framework of the constitutional state, the "(constitutional-) knowledge" must be conveyed by constitutional courts and not by politicians.[77] Instead, the starting point of Jahn & Brodowski's reasoning lies in accepting that criminal law principles can only be addressed at the highest level of the hierarchy of rules, from *the dogmatic-constitutional concepts*.[78]

Without denying the scope of discretion that constitutionally belongs to the legislative power, the authors claims that it would be necessary to consider that human personality right (Art. 1. 1 GG) contains a free sphere of sanctions (*Freiheit von Sanktionierung*), which involves the special need for justification in the proportionality test of penal rules, expanding the constitutional powers of review concerning the material assumptions of the sanctioning rule.[79] To reach this conclusion, the starting point is to assume that criminal law is a communicative action by which the state communicates to citizens a series of unacceptable behaviors that inevitably entails state interference in the private sphere of personality.[80] According to the authors, only when is demanded a more restrictive material justification of criminal regulations, for example, by introducing into the judgment of constitutional necessity (*Erforderlichkeit*) the obviousness concept that requires greater detail to state that the punishment is necessary given the insufficiency of other equally suitable but less harmful measures for the achievement of an objective, may recover *the principle of ultima ratio* its character of functional limit, being then absolutely necessary for constitutional justice to abandon part of its deferential position before the legislative prerogative in criminal matters.[81]

---

[76] Jahn and Brodowski (2016), p. 971.

[77] Prittwitz (2017), pp. 392, 295.

[78] Jahn and Brodowski (2017), pp. 367, 378.

[79] Jahn and Brodowski (2016), pp. 969, 976.

[80] Jahn and Brodowski (2016), p. 976; Jahn and Brodowski (2017), pp. 378, 379.

[81] Jahn and Brodowski (2016), p. 977 y ss.

6 Proposal of Meaning for the Ultima Ratio Principle in the Constitutional State

6.1 *The Positive Approach of the Ultima Ratio Principle in Constitutional Law Doctrine*

As we have already mentioned, constitutional courts only invoke *the ultima ratio principle* when the framework character of the constitution for political decision making (*Schranken*) is at stake, while whenever its limiting character (*Grenzen*) is endangered, the Courts apply the "miracle cure" of entrusting to the majority principle the choice according to its institutional experience, since the constitution does not require in these cases the use of specific means, but the achievement of a standard of protection.[82] Drawing from the premise of the constitution performs the two functions regarding criminal law matters, it could point out the existence of *two constitutional important or relevant areas*: the reduced *space of behaviors that must be (or have to be) punished*, in which the effectiveness or adequacy of other legal resources is doubtful from the beginning; and *another broader area of behaviors where it is not allowed to do it*. Both describe the (*positive* and *negative*) perimeter boundaries of what is constitutionally unreasonable or absurd.[83]

But in a freedom-oriented constitutional order, which exhibits the same degree of certainty as to when criminal law intervention is required and how far it is permitted, would not *the ultima ratio principle* mean a requirement to reduce *constitutional permissions* regarding the use of criminal law to the strict *constitutional obligations of criminal protection*? If we depart of the fact that there is the same lack of learning over the specific behavior that form the "*constitutional calls for penal protection*" than those integrated into the "*no-go area,*" does it mean *the ultima ratio principle* a constitutional requirement to reduce the "*allowed area" of the constitutional permissions* regarding the use of criminal law to the strict constitutional obligations of criminal protection? We know very little concerning the doctrine of duties of the state to ensure and protect human rights and its relationship with criminal matters, but one thing is clear in our lack of knowledge: *(positive) State obligations in Criminal Law are not absolute constitutional requirements, but relative and accidental* to the insufficiency of other less drastic legal remedies, since criminal law cannot be an aim (in itself).[84] Then, could *the (constitutional) principle of ultima ratio* be located halfway between the prohibition of under- (or below-) protection (so-called *Untermassverbot*) and the classical prohibition of overprotection (so-called *Übermassverbot*)?

---

[82] Kaspar (2014), p. 246.

[83] Isensee (2011), pp. 525 y ss.

[84] Greco (2017), p. 123.

6.2 The Negative Approach of the Ultima Ratio Principle in Constitutional Law Doctrine

It is also clear in our limited knowledge about duties of the state to ensure and protect human rights that the resulting (positive) state obligations in criminal matters cannot be determined without the help of the defensive function of human rights.[85] The real existence of a "protection or positive" approach into human rights warranty claims against non-state agent's injuries, cannot invalidate, or detract the obliged respect the freedoms of citizens by public powers and its (negative) guarantees. Consequently, although it is certain that the duties of the state to ensure and protect human rights can create, as criteria of affirmation, a material legitimacy for criminal law, such grounds cannot under any circumstances degenerate into custodianship.[86] Thus, by *the ultima ratio principle*, public powers should be (constitutionally) compelled to achieve the greatest possible optimization of private freedom without major costs in terms of public security, restricting the political *"allowed (constitutional) area" sphere in criminal matters* to the strictest real needs of protection.

The duty of the state to ensure and protect human rights (*grundrechtliche Schutzpflicht* or *positive State obligations*) cannot access to the content or substance of human rights protected by guarantees of the defense against the state (*Abwehrrechten* or *negative state obligations*),[87] which Jahn & Brodowski now try to specify more rigorously through the relationship of the "*Freiheit von Sanktionierung*" with *the (constitutional) principle of ultima ratio*. In this sense, we think that it could be considered that the "positive approach" of the ultima ratio principle, expressed in the prohibition of under- or below- protection could be combined or complemented with the "negative approach," which arising of the defensive element of constitutional freedom against punishment, in such a way that *the constitutional grounds of Criminal Law are in turn the same (constitutional) limits to its recourse, without the existence of any "corridor" between those grounds and that limits of constitutional Criminal Law.*

6.3 Human Rights Minimum Criminal Law

As we have suggested along this paper, we think that the dogmatic of constitutional freedoms contains good opportunities by means of *the (constitutional) prohibition of under- or below- protection* (*Untermassverbot*) to approximate an answer to the question of the crimes and penalties required by the constitution. Such a formula, which is completely unknown to academic doctrine and lawyers, is used by German

[85] Appel (1998), pp. 307, 314.

[86] Vid. Isensee (2014); Isensee (2011), p. 551.

[87] See: Isensee (2011), p. 552; Isensee (2014), p. 85.

public law, and implicitly by European law, to measure the degree of compliance with the duties of the state to ensure and protect human rights, by assessing the adequacy of the measures adopted by the public authorities.[88] But can the constitutional prohibition of under- or below- protection be related adequately to *the ultima ratio principle*?

We think on the possibility to reach to an affirmative answer to the question by the fact that both institutions (*prohibition of under- or below- protection* and *the ultima ratio principle*) are referred to the *Human Rights minimum Criminal Law*, but a minimum criminal law, *that is at the same time the maximum one*, cannot be stated without considering the other aspect of the proportionality principle: the prohibition of overprotection or *Übermassverbot*, which would also be integrated in *the ultima ratio principle* according to its genuine meaning in academic doctrine. In this way, the constitutional principle of ultima ratio concerns a constitutional "*limiting-ground*" for the public powers activity, which arises from the global content (objective and subjective) of fundamental rights and represents the point of connection between protection and defense of human rights in the proportionality test.

7 Conclusions

The ultima ratio principle is a common heritage of academic-penal science and of all public law doctrine in general, which has been adopted from the Enlightenment approaches on which the modern constitutional state is also based. However, if we closely look at criminal law rules, rather than a functional limit that the constitutional state imposes on the public powers activity, *it seems to be a pragmatic proposition that lives "in the collective imagination of the most guarantee-minded scholars,"* which the legislator can ignore with impunity.

Without the help of the constitution and constitutional law, the ultima ratio principle cannot reach a sufficient degree of maturity to effectively bind the legislator to choose the least drastic means for the fulfillment of public purposes. In this context, the application of the ultima ratio principle in the first two tests that make up the principle of proportionality in the broad sense, keeps alive the hope of binding the legislator to the requirements of the fundamental rights of the constitutional state. *This keeps alive the genuine constitutional orientation* proposed by the theses of Bricola, Arroyo Zapatero and Sax, among others, which today offers us good opportunities to reduce the arbitrariness of criminal law. Within this doctrine and regarding *the ultima ratio principle*, the thesis of Jahn & Brodowski appears to have good limiting potential, while that of Gärditz must be rejected because of its inconsistency with the postulates of the constitutional rule of law for the reasons explained by Prittwitz.

---

[88] Streuer (2003), p. 143.

Following to the doctrine of constitutional state, *the ultima ratio principle* could mean in the framework of constitutional state that the minimum criminal law resulting from the duties of the state to ensure and protect human rights, which is made clear by the prohibition of under- or below-protection (*Untermassverbot*), is in turn the maximum criminal law allowed by constitutional freedoms by means of the prohibition of overprotection (*Übermassverbot*), with no corridor between the minimum punitive intervention required and the maximum permitted by the constitution. There is no absolute basis in the constitution for using the criminal law, but all of them are related to the lack of other equally effective means. Moreover, even in these cases where the constitutional law seems to require state intervention by punitive means, the Criminal instruments are subordinate to constitutional freedoms, so that if one squeezes the gap between the prohibition of under- or below- protection and the prohibition of overprotection within the framework of the proportionality test, one easily arrives at the conclusion held here: *The minimum Criminal Law required by Human Rights is, according to the constitutional Criminal law, the maximum permissible one.*

References

Appel I (1998) Verfassung und Strafe. Zu den verfassungsrechtlichen Grenzen staatlichen Strafrechts. Dunker & Humblot, Berín

Arroyo Zapatero LA (2016) Derecho penal y Constitución (II). En AAVV Curso de Derecho penal. Parte General 3ª Edición. Ediciones Experiencia, pp 143–162

Arroyo Zapatero LA, Berdugo Gómez de la Torre I (1994) Manual de Derecho penal. Parte General I. Instrumentos y principios básicos del Derecho penal. Editorial Praxis

Bacigalupo E (2005) Derecho penal y Estado de Derecho. Editorial Jurídica de Chile, Santiago

Beccaria C (1990) De los Delitos y de las Penas. Traducción de Juan Antonio de las Casas. Alianza, Madrid

Beck U (1998) La sociedad del riesgo. Hacia una nueva modernidad. Traducción de Jorge Navarro & Daniel Jiménez & M° Rosa Borrás. Ediciones Paidós bérica, Barcelona

Bentham J (1981) Tratados de legislación civil y penal. Edición preparada por Magdalena Rodríguez Gil. Editora Nacional, Madrid

Bernuz Beneitez MJ, González Ordovás MJ (2006) La levedad de la seguridad frente al caos. In: La tensión entre libertad y seguridad. Una aproximación sociojuriídica. Servicio de publicaciones de la Universidad de la Rioja, La Rioja

Burchard C (2016) Strafverfassungsrecht – Vorüberlegungen zu einem Schlüsselbegriff. En Tiedemann (Hrsg.) Die Verfassung moderner Strafrechtspflege Erinnerung an Joachim Vogel. Nomos, Baden-Baden, pp 25–62

Carnevali Rodríguez R (2009) Derecho penal como ultima ratio. Hacia una política criminal racional. Ius et Praxis 1–14:13–48

Corcoy M (2012) Expansión del Derecho penal y garantías constitucionales. Revista de Derechos Fundamentales 8

Correa Aguado T (1999) El principio de proporcionalidad penal. Edersa, Madrid

Demetrio Crespo E (2020) El Derecho penal del Estado de Derecho entre el espíritu de nuestro tiempo y la Constitución. Reus, Barcelona

Demuro GP (2013) Ultima ratio: alla ricerca di limiti all'espansione del diritto penale. Diritto@Storia. Rivista Internazionale di Scienze Giuridiche e Tradizione Romana 11

Donini M (2001) Un Derecho penal fundado en la carta constitucional: razones y límites: La experiencia italiana. Revista Penal 8:24–38
Donini M (2010) Principios constitucionales y sistema penal. Revista General de Derecho penal n° 13
Ferrajoli L (2014) Derecho y razón. Teoría del garantismo penal. Trotta. Madrid
Fioravanti M (2014) Constitucionalismo. Experiencias históricas y tendencias actuales. Trotta, Madrid
Forsthoff E (1975) El Estado de la sociedad industrial. Traducción de Luis López Guerra y Jaime Nicolás Muñiz. Institutos de Estudios Políticos, Madrid
Gärditz KF (2015) Staat und Strafrechtspflege. Braucht die Verfassungstheorie einen Begriff von Strafe? Ferdinand Schönig, Paderborn
Gärditz KF (2016) Demokratizität des Strafrechts und Ultima Ratio-Grundgesetz. Juristen Zeitung 13:641–650
González Cussac JL (2015) Prefacio. In: Comentarios a la reforma del Código Penal de 2015. Tirant lo Blanch, Valencia
Greco L (2013) Verfassungskonformes oder legitimer Strafrecht? Zu den Grenzen einer verfassungsrechtlichen Orientierung der Strafrechtswissenshaft. En AAVV Strafrecht und Verfassung. Nomos, Baden-Baden, pp 13–36
Greco L (2017) Por que inexistem deveres absolutos de punir. Católica Law Review 1–17:115–126
Grimm D (1991) Constitucionalismo y Derechos Fundamentales. Traducción de Raúl Sanz Burgos y José Luis Muñoz de Baena Simón. Trotta, Madrid
Hobbes T (1980) Leviatán. 2ª Edición preparada por Carlos Moya y Antonio Escohotado. Editora Naciona, Madrid
Hörnle T (2012) Subsidiariedad como principio limitador. Autoprotección. En Hefendeln (Dir.) Límites al Derecho penal. Principios operativos en la fundamentación del castigo. Atelier, Barcelona, pp 87–99
Isensee J (2011) Das Grundrecht als Abwehrrecht und als Staatliche Schutzpflicht. En AAVV Handbuch des Staatsrechts. Band IX. Allgemeine Grundrechtslehre.C. F. Müller, Heidelberg, pp 413–568
Isensee J (2014) El Derecho constitucional a la seguridad. Sobre los deberes de protección del Estado constitucional liberal, Traducción de Juan Carlos Gemignani y Teresa Manso Porto. Buenos Aires, Rubinzal-Culzoni Editores
Jahn M (2016) Strafverfassungsrecht: Das Grundgesetz als Herausforderung. Erinnerung an Joachim Vogel. En Tiedemann (Hrsg.) Die Verfassung moderner Strafrechtspflege. Nomos, Baden-Baden, pp 63–86
Jahn M, Brodowski D (2016) Krise und Neuaufbau eines strafverfassungsrechtlichen Ultima Ratio-Prinzips. Juristen Zeitung 20:969–980
Jahn M, Brodowski D (2017) Das Ultima Ratio-Prinzip als strafverfassungsrechtliche Vorgabe zur Frage der Entbehrlichkeit von Straftatbeständen. ZStW 129(2):363–381
Kaspar J (2014) Verhältnismässigkeit und Grundrechtsschutz im Präventionstrafrecht. Nomos, Baden-Baden
Lagodny O (1996) Strafrecht von der Schranken der Grundrechte. Die Ermächtigung zum strafrechtlichen Vorwurf im Lichte der Grundrechtsdogmatik dargestellt am Beispiel der Vorfeldkriminalisierung. Mohr Siebeck GmbH & Co, Tübingen
Lascuraín Sánchez JA (2012) ¿Restrictivo o deferente? El control de la ley penal por parte del Tribunal Constitucional. InDret 3:1–34
Lascuraín Sánchez JA (2020) El principio de proporcionalidad penal. Cinco retos (I y II). Almacén de Derecho
Marra G (2018) Extrema ratio ed ordini sociali spontanei. Un criterio di sindicato sulle fattispecie penali eccessive. G. Giappichelli, Torino
Martínez de Pisón J (2006) Las transformaciones del Estado. Del Estado protector al Estado de la seguridad. En AAVV La tensión entre la libertad y seguridad. Una aproximación sociojurídica. Ediciones de la Universidad de la Rioja, La Rioja

Mir Puig S (1999) El Derecho penal en el Estado social y democrático de derecho. Buenos Aires, Ariel
Mir Puig S (2003) Introducción a las bases del Derecho penal. BdeF, Montevideo
Mir Puig S (2011) Bases constitucionales del Derecho penal. Iustel, Madrid
Mir Puig S (2015) Manual de Derecho penal. Parte General 10ª Edición. Reppertor, Barcelona
Montesquieu (1987) Del espíritu de las leyes, Introducción de Enrique Tierno Galván y traducción de Mercedes Blázquez y Pedro de Vega. Tecnos, Madrid
Muñoz Conde F, García Arán M (2019) Derecho penal. Parte General 10ª Edición. Tirant lo Blanch, Valencia
Orts Berenguer E, González Cussac JL (2020) Introducción al Derecho penal. Tirant lo Blanch, Valencia
Palazzo F (2001) Principio de ultima ratio e hipertrofia del Derecho penal. In: Homenaje al Dr. Marino Barbero Santos in memoriam. Ediciones de la Universidad de Castilla- La Mancha & Ediciones Universidad de Salamanca, Cuenca, pp 433–441
Prittwitz C (2000) El Derecho penal alemán: ¿Fragmentario? ¿Subsidiario? ¿Última ratio? Reflexiones sobre la razón y límites de los principios limitadores del Derecho penal. En AAVV La insostenible situación del Derecho penal. Comares, Barcelona
Prittwitz C (2017) Das Strafrecht: Ultima ratio, propria ratio oder schlicht strafrechtliche Prohibition? Zugleich ein Kommentar zu den Beiträgen von Klaus F. Gärditz und Matthias Jahn. ZStW 129(2):390–400
Quintero Olivares G (2015) Derecho penal constitucional. Tirant lo Blanch, Valencia
Quintero Olivares G (2019) "Presentación". En Quintero Olivares (Dir.) Las reformas penales de 2019. Aranzadi, Navarra
Sánchez Martínez O (2004) Los principios en el Derecho y la Dogmática penal. Dykinson, Madrid
Sax W (1959) Grundsätze der Strafrechtspflege. In: Die Grundrechte. Handbuch der Theorie und Praxis der Grundrechte. Band III-2. Dunker & Humblot, Berlín, pp 907–1014
Schmitt C (2008) El Leviatán en la doctrina del Estado de Thomas Hobbes. Distribuciones Fontamara, México D. F.
Schünemann B (2012) Protección de bienes jurídicos, ultima ratio y victimodogmática. Sobre los límites inviolables del Derecho penal en un Estado de Derecho liberal. En AAVV Límites al Derecho penal. Principios operativos en la fundamentación del castigo. Atelier, Barcelona, pp 63–86
Seher G (2012a) ¿Puede ser subsidiario el Derecho penal? Aporías de un principio jurídico indiscutido. En AAVV Límites al Derecho penal. Principios operativos en la fundamentación del castigo. Atelier, Barcelona, pp 129–144
Seher G (2012b) ¿Puede ser subsidiario el Derecho penal? Aporías de un principio jurídico indiscutido. In: Límites al Derecho penal. Principios operativos en la fundamentación del castigo. Barcelona, Atelier, p 129
Silva Sánchez JM (1992) Aproximación al Derecho penal contemporáneo. J.M Bosch Editor, Barcelona
Silva Sánchez JM (2011) La expansión del Derecho penal. Aspectos de la política criminal de las sociedades industriales, 3ª Edición. Edisofer & BdeF, Madrid/ Montevideo & Buenos Aires
Streuer W (2003) Die positiven verpflichtungen des Staates. Nomos, Baden-Baden
Tiedemann K (1991) Verfassungs und Strafrecht. C. F. Müller, Heidelberg
Weigend T (2016) Mehr Strafrecht - und alles wird gut? StV 10-Editorial:1
Zugaldía Espinar JM (2016) Lecciones de Derecho penal. Parte General. Tirant lo Blanch, Valencia

Enforced Disappearance: A Precedent of the Enemy Criminal Law

Fernando Rovetta Klyver

Abstract World Trade Center attacks implied that Enemy Criminal Law (ECL) shifted from being a descriptive theory (Jacobs, 1985) to prescribing how to punish, in Abu Ghraib (2003) or Guantanamo (2004). We pose that this *ius puniendi* power is directly related to the preceding Terrorism of State (Garzón Valdés), in which enforced disappearance (ED) of persons practices in Latin America stand as its main antecedent. Our intention is to analyse the ECL metamorphosis and the relevant elements it shares with ED in the case of Tucumán (Argentina, 1975–1983) as well as the theories pretending to legitimise the ED and the ECL. In addition, given the fact that necrophilia was a practice with ED, we find it pertinent to complete the concept of bio-politics (Foucault) with that of necropolitics (Mbembé), which, as a normative regulation, would result in a necro-law.

1 Introduction

This paper analyses experiences that can be understood as the double denial of justice and communication implied by the maximum criminal law, or ECL, which was first described and subsequently proposed as a legitimising theory by Günther Jakobs (2003). In a previous work, we analysed the experiences in two Spanish prisons (Villabona and Nanclares de Oca) between 1992 and 2018, as expressions of restorative justice and communication. We then postulated that the theoretical framework of said experiences in these Asturian and Basque prisons could be the minimum criminal law or guarantee criminal law (GCL) proposed by Luigi Ferrajoli (1995). Both criminal doctrines, ECL and GCL, are diametrically opposed when attempting to answer the following two questions: is it legal for the state to punish?, and if so, how should it do so?

F. R. Klyver (✉)
Faculty of Social Sciences at the University of Castilla-La Mancha, Talavera de la Reina, Spain
e-mail: fernando.rovetta@uclm.es

E. Demetrio Crespo et al. (eds.), *Crisis of the Criminal Law in the Democratic Constitutional State*, Legal Studies in International, European and Comparative Criminal Law 6, https://doi.org/10.1007/978-3-031-13413-5_4

1.1 *Is It Legal for the State to Punish?*

On the legality of state punishment, when confronted with the negative responses of abolitionists, two classical responses were provided: Kant's retributivism and Bentham's consequentialism. The former required the state to punish those who broke the law in the same form as the offence that they had committed, after employing procedures that respected their dignity to ensure that they were the culprit. The latter, meanwhile, proposed that the state should apply the penalties whose consequences most favoured society and also the person who had broken the law, even if this meant that those penalties might sometimes be paid by an innocent person in the interests of satisfying social demands.

Confronted with this dilemma, and using the theories of jurist theologians from Tomás de Aquino (1956, T. VIII, p. 468)[1] to Suárez[2] (1967) (whose doctrine inspired the humanitarianism of Beccaría, who was educated in a Jesuit school) as a basis, we find a synthesis that in a way in which the minimum criminal law, or GCL, is currently viewed:

> According to the great Montesquieu, every penalty that is not derived from absolute necessity, is tyrannical: a proposition that can, therefore, be made more general: every act of authority from man to man, which does not derive from absolute necessity is tyrannical (Beccaría 2015, pp. 133–134).

The guarantee synthesis between the retributionist thesis and the consequentialist antithesis considers that punishment is lawful only: (a) if it is applied to those who could be proved guilty, whilst reliably and respecting due process, and (b) if the end of the punishment is the re-education and social reintegration of the prisoner, which will be beneficial for society.

The synthesis of the thesis and antithesis proposed by the maximum criminal law, or ECL, are, however, the opposite: (a) it is lawful to punish the crime that has allegedly been committed or may be committed by the enemy; (b) the inflexible harshness of the punishment seeks to assure society that these kinds of crimes will never be committed by the defendants again. These people are, therefore, deprived of the condition of citizens and even of persons, leading them to become individuals without any rights.

From this perspective, and returning to the initial question, the minimum or guarantee criminal law is in the middle ground between those who defend abolitionism and those who propose the maximum or enemy criminal law.

---

[1] "... imprisoning someone or detaining that person in any way is illegal if it is not done in accordance with the order of justice, either by punishment, or by prevention in order to avoid any harm" (ST. II-II.q.65, a.3). On judicial procedure, it also describes the functions and duties of the judge (q.67), the victim (q.68), the witnesses and the evidence (q. 70).

[2] Treatise on Laws, Book V. Different human laws, and especially those of a hateful nature. This admits the legality of the escape of a person sentenced to death, or of someone who is imprisoned in unsanitary conditions.

1.2 How Can the State Punish?

The types of punishment are already anticipated in the answers to the previous question, and since "the tree is known by its fruit", they will help to differentiate between the rule of law in a broad and strict sense. In a broad sense, this concept is applied to all states, even those that are dictatorial or totalitarian, because they create laws. On the contrary, in a strict sense, the rule of law is only that which guarantees the division of powers and fundamental rights.

(a) Regarding the GCL doctrine, a penalty can be applied only if at least the following four basic principles are respected: legality, proportionality, culpability and resocialisation, whose explanation we consider to be negative. This means of exercising *ius puniendi* is typical of a rule of law in the strict sense.
(b) The ECL, on the contrary, proposes the infliction of punishments in violation of the four basic principles of Beccaría. This is typical of a rule of law in a broad sense, and it does not admit the division of powers or defend the fundamental rights of its citizens; it is for this reason, and with regard to previous legislation, that it is also termed as the de facto state to distinguish it from the de jure state in a strict sense. It is, therefore, necessary to analyse how these regimes invert the principles that humanised criminal law by imposing their own means of punishment: illegality, the disproportion between punishment and crime, the discretion by which an innocent person can be punished, the dehumanisation of the accused and the destruction of the foundations of society that it claims to defend. Furthermore, these anti-principles remove the government's legitimacy to the extent that, as will be shown later, they lead to its practices being classified as state terrorism, the highest expression of which is enforced disappearance (ED).

We propose that when confronted with the insufficiencies of Enlightenment, it might be possible to discover a guaranteeist *philum* that would foreshadow an alternative modernity, characterised by its internationalism, its circumstantialism and its anamnestic culture. Theorists from Tomás de Aquino to Suárez have proposed the need: (1) to place more relevance on the law of nations (currently known as the international human rights law) than on the internal law of each country, which was proposed by Vitoria and resumed by Kant, Kelsen and Ferrajoli himself; (2) to consider the circumstances under which a rule had been violated and (3) to weigh those cases in which it would be possible to restore to individuals or people the rights that have been denied to them. It is now worth mentioning the orientations of an anti-guarantee theory:

b.1. Its "realistic" statism. The modern state surpassed medieval polyarchies and arose to claims the monopoly as regards the use of force for itself, as described by Weber. This idea led Hobbes to present a Leviathan-State that, to guarantee peaceful coexistence within a territory, assumes all political powers and also controls religious power, thus reducing the range of citizens' rights to those matters on which the state neglected to legislate.

It is now necessary to relate, as Ferrajoli does when discussing Jakobs, a descriptive account of how government was carried out at that time, using a prescriptive theory which proposes that the means of governing is a paradigm for the future. The exercise of sovereign power without limits, as *potestas soluta*, that can be imposed by means of terror, has been adopted by dictatorial regimes to various degrees, the most severe being that adopted by totalitarian regimes. In her study of Hobbes in The Origins of Totalitarianism, Hannah Arendt states that:

> Hobbes is one of the few authors, perhaps the only one, who makes no distinction between prince and tyrant . . . because there is no possibility of distinguishing between good government and bad government (Bobbio 2003, p. 204).

Bobbio's admiration for the realism of the author of Leviathan is fully explained by the descriptive character of the anominalist imprint: "True and false are attributes of words, not of things". But this mere description of "things that are the way they are", without making any reference to what they should be like to guarantee human dignity, passes through an almost imperceptible metamorphosis and begins to legitimise them: they are like that, ergo they must be like that, or there is no reason whatsoever for them to be otherwise; it makes the contingent necessary.

The epistemological paradigm that Hobbes adopted was somewhere between the physics of Newton and the geometry of Euclid, signifying that his conception of the political cannot admit the distinction between good and bad government. It can similarly be said that the following are neither good nor bad: gravity, inertia, or the fact that the sum of the interior angles of a triangle is equal to two right angles.

This way of theorising between mechanical and formal makes it possible to inadvertently go from admitting inequality as an unquestionable fact to tolerating it, both in states and in their citizens. The UN Charter (Art. 2.1) is based on the principle of the sovereign equality of all states, but, as Orwell would say, some are, in fact, more equal than others. Before exercising the enemy criminal law in territories of their administration, such as Guantánamo, the hegemonic powers tested the scope of this exercise of *ius puniendi* in states whose armies had acted as occupation forces against their own citizens. We shall now analyse two cases of the implementation of the enemy criminal law: first the ED, which was promoted by a military government under the orders of the United States, and second, two prisons managed by that same hegemonic power.

b.2. Obedient and safe citizenship. The ECL is different from the citizen criminal law. The citizen identifies himself by fully complying with the normative order, although he may eventually violate its norms. These citizens include executioners, who use the maximum criminal law to the extreme of committing state terrorism. When brought before international tribunals, their main argument was that they had only been obeying the orders of their superiors. Those from Adolf Eichman to the Italian or Argentine officials wished the criterion of "due obedience" to act as a means of mitigating or exonerating their crimes.

The dilemma raised by Gustav Radbruch as regards the difference between justice and legal security always leans towards the latter for ECL agents. There is no red line for them regarding unbearably unfair standards, simply because they cannot distinguish between fair and unfair:

> For Hobbes, subjects lack the right to judge what is just or unjust since that right refers only to the sovereign, and to hold that the subject has the right to judge what is just or unjust is considered a seditious theory (Bobbio 2003, p. 204).

These automata appear to confirm Hannah Arendt's thesis on the "banality of evil" that is in some respects described and simultaneously prescribed by Hobbes. ". . . in Hobbes we find for the first time a philosophy that has no use for philosophy, but rather seeks to develop from what common sense takes for granted" (Arendt 2008, p. 174).

This type of obedient citizen is the prototype of the worker serving those who benefit from the current growth in inequality, inequality that explains the self-preference principle proposed by Bentham in his *Psychology of homo oeconomicus* (1965). If liberalism and the laws of supply and demand in the market initially served to stimulate production and trade, then neoliberalism has now given rise to savage capitalism (Ferrajoli) or disaster capitalism (Klein), which manages to radicalise the difference between the sovereign wealth funds of the global class (Dahrendorf) and that which is superfluous (S. George). The ECL id functional for this stage of capitalism.

On the contrary, among the authors of the guarantor *philum*, we find a modern defender of conscientious objection in Francisco de Vitoria (1981, p. 223). In principle, soldiers can trust that the prince's decision is fair, but: "If there is certainty that the war is unjust . . . they cannot fight even if they are forced to do so by the prince".

b.3. Its counterfactual nature. This is the direct opposite of a self-critical attitude, which can assume that in the growing inequality promoted by central states and multinational corporations, punitive actions are proposed against those who question the system. This concerns punishing not only those who have committed crimes but also those who represent a potential threat merely for denouncing the regime, as a preventative measure.

2 Scenarios of Application of the Enemy Criminal Law

2.1 Enforced Disappearance in Tucumán (1975–1983)

In the 1960s and 1970s, Latin American military personnel at the School of the Americas (Panama) and the Conferences of American Armies (USA) were instructed to carry out coups in accordance with the National Security Doctrine.[3] An analysis of

[3]"In recent years, the so-called 'National Security Doctrine' has taken hold on our continent, which is in fact more of an ideology than a doctrine. It is linked to a certain economic-political model, with elitist and top-down characteristics, that suppresses the broad participation of the people in political

what occurred in Tucumán, Argentina, will, therefore, be provided as a reference case, including references to analogous regional scenarios.[4] The facts will be presented in the light of the four principles of criminal law: legality, proportionality, culpability and resocialisation. These principles were systematically ignored by those who perpetrated the enforced disappearance.

In 1998, Jakobs described some differences between the citizen criminal law and the enemy criminal law (ECL). He sought to legitimise the ECL after the attacks of 09/11/2001. We intend to prove that the antecedents of the ECL can essentially be found in the Doctrine of National Security, State Terrorism and the ED.

2.1.1 Illegality

On March 24, 1976, the Armed Forces staged a coup in Argentina; a similar phenomenon promoted by the US Embassies had occurred in other neighbouring countries, such as Chile on September 11, 1973.[5]It is significant that the attack on the World Trade Center took place 28 years later, perhaps to commemorate that date, and some hints of its suspicious authorship are provided by Michael Moore in Fahrenheit 9/11 (2008).

The ED was an illegal form of detention, preceded by a kidnapping on the public highway or at the victim's home, workplace or study, after a search without a warrant. This illegality then continued during the interrogation, during which cruel tortures were carried out. This frequently ended with the death of the victim, whose body was then hidden.

> From this central element of the repressive methodology (kidnapping), the rest follows: the subsequent disappearance of the victims (usually permanently; sometimes, temporarily); their transfer to unknown and clandestine detention centres: the participation of repressive units made up of elements that concealed their identity… (ICBDH 1991, p. 39).

These crimes were perpetrated by "task forces" made up of soldiers, police officers or civilians radicalised in their aversion to communism, liberation theology

---

decisions. It even tries to justify itself in certain Latin American countries as a doctrine in defence of Western and Christian civilization. It develops repressive systems in accordance with its concept of 'permanent war'. In some cases, it expresses a clear intention of political leadership" CELAM (1979): Puebla Document #547 (Rovetta 1991, p. 16).

[4]For a more detailed analysis of these events, I refer the reader to the Bicameral Commission Report that investigated human rights in Tucumán province (1974–1983), henceforth (ICBDH), whose edition I coordinated. I also refer the reader to the complaint that I presented before the Federal Court of Tucumán Province on February 20, 1987, regarding all those who were detained and disappeared from the National University of Tucumán (UNT), as Coordinator of the Human Rights Commission of its High Council. This was published on the UNT website as the "Informe Rovetta" from 2005 to September 28, 2017; henceforth: (IRUNT).

[5]Briefly, the coups d'état in the Southern Cone occurred in: Paraguay (1954), Brazil (1964), Bolivia (1971), Chile and Uruguay (1973) and Argentina (1976).

or other doctrines that preferentially attended to the needs of the less favoured classes (ICBDH 1991, pp. 331–334).[6]

The perpetrators were hooded with ski masks that covered their faces; they travelled in cars without license plates, generally assaulted at night and preferred open spaces or those in which there were no witnesses. The dual objective of total impunity for the perpetrators was, therefore, pursued, and facilitated the subsequent refusal to report on the place of detention. These centres were often military or police units, schools or homes converted into prison and extermination camps. The habeas corpus presented by relatives or friends of the victims were, accordingly, systematically rejected.[7]

This means of proceeding, which was diametrically opposed to the Kantian exigency for the publicity and transparency of the state's action, has been highlighted by Ernesto Garzón Valdés, who stated that:

> The clandestine nature of the activities of State terrorism . . . makes it possible to distinguish the regime of totalitarian States that practise it and nothing more, from that of governments that practise State terrorism, whether totalitarian or not (Garzón Valdés 2001, p. 140).

2.1.2 Disproportion

The proportionality between crime and punishment demanded by Beccaría was, in this case, violated not only by the facts, but also by its performers. Enforced disappearance involved physically and mentally torturing those abducted, sometimes in front of their relatives, subjecting them to electroshock, among other practices (ICBDH, pp. 164–168). This method of torture had been practised in North America by Dr. Ewen Cameron on his patients, and provoked a generalised perception of terror (Klein 2007, p. 50).[8]

Regarding its participants, Ferrajoli points out in the case of the ECL that in a rule of law in a strict sense, criminals are persecuted by the police, not the Army, whose function is to defend the sovereign territory from external enemies. The behaviour of the Army as an occupation force in its own territory turns its fellow citizens into enemies.

Another fallacy of those who attempted to legitimise state terrorism evidenced by Garzón Valdés is the equivalence of means when confronted with an urban or rural guerrilla who kidnapped or killed soldiers, businessmen and even a trade unionist.

---

[6] ICBDH, Annex X, entitled Most named individuals, refers to the perpetrators: Provincial Police, Armed Forces and Civilians.

[7] ICBDH, Annex I. Repressive methodology (pp. 37–93), which includes as subtitles: Kidnapping, looting, transfer to clandestine detention and torture camps, subsequent proceedings, coordination between security organisations . . . confusion, misinformation and terror.

[8] E. Cameron, an American physician, whose treatment for chronic paranoid-schizoid patients was published in the Canadian Medical Association Journal. vol. 78, 15. He proposed the advisability of giving them electric shocks in their frontal lobes to convert their minds into clean slates on which one could re-write from scratch.

The Army, the National Gendarmerie, the Provincial Police and the Federal Police were involved in their repression, receiving international advice and information within the framework of "Operation Condor".[9]

2.1.3 Criminal Discretion

If, in a rule of law in the strict sense, there is a presumption of innocence, a government that practises state terrorism presumes guilt. Another argument of those who seek to legitimise this is the alleged difficulty in identifying the enemy. This is unlikely in a society in which political parties, unions and social movements have been infiltrated by intelligence agents before being outlawed, not only from the state security forces and bodies, but also from the hegemonic state. This alleged difficulty was used as an excuse to torture those kidnapped to demand the names of future victims. Enforced disappearance was almost exclusively used against people who were not only not members of the guerrillas, but who even questioned the guerrillas' actions.[10]

The cases in which the attack against innocents is most evident are those that affect children born during their mothers' captivity or kidnapped with them (ICBDH, pp. 190–192). In accordance with a practice already used during the Spanish Civil War and Franco's regime, minors were handed over to the families of their kidnappers, or those related to the regime.

2.1.4 Social Disintegration

Those who kidnapped with impunity achieved a triple goal: they neutralised all possible actions of their victims, along with those who tried to claim the minimum procedural and criminal guarantees for them. Far from proposing the social reintegration of those who had been detained and had disappeared, the individual was generally murdered and the body was hidden.

The few people who, after their arrest-disappearance, were released, suffered post-traumatic consequences and the social stigma of having accused other people to obtain their release. Along with this suspicion regarding those who were released, rationalisations emerged that allowed society to cope with the impotence as regards changing that state of affairs, even regarding those who did not return, such as: "he

---

[9] Operation Condor, devised by Henry Kissinger, was put into action from Santiago de Chile on November 25, 1975 in a meeting between the head of the DINA (Chilean secret police), and the heads of Argentina's military intelligence services (SIDE), Bolivia, Chile, Paraguay and Uruguay. Robert Plummer (June 8, 2005). "The Condor Legacy Haunts South America". BBC. Consulted August 26, 2017.

[10] It is worth highlighting the work of the Abuelas de Plaza de Mayo (Grandmothers of May Square) in Argentina, who managed to create the world's first National Genetic Data Bank (BNDG, 1977), and who have already managed return the identity to 130 people, until May 2020.

must have done something", "we are children of severity/Spare the rod, spoil the child" or also "I, Argentine". The last expression is a curious definition that allowed each person to attend only to their self-interests, a typical native version of "the self-preference principle", present in Bentham's The Psychology of Economic Man (1965) mentioned previously.

The social effects of the ED, the main tool of de facto governments that applied state terrorism, have lasted for decades and up to the present. The destruction of generations of leaders who were able to develop alternatives to current neoliberalism resulted in the emergence of many opportunistic and corrupt leaders in the region, with some exceptions.[11]

2.2 *Torture in the Abu Ghraib and Guantanamo Prisons*

Three decades passed between the torture that was applied clandestinely in the detention camps in which those who were detained and disappeared were held in the 1970s and those presented as a spectacle thanks to the mass media. At that time, the cold war had ended, with the fall of the Berlin Wall in 1989, and there was a consequent need to generate a new war scene from the doctrine of Samuel Huntington (1996), The Clash of Civilizations. It was a question of giving way to the enormous production of the arms industry, and providing the private security corporations with work.

2.2.1 Illegality

The governments that practised state terrorism by virtue of the doctrine of national security principally violated their constitutional principles and also the international human rights law. The case of the second invasion of Iraq, which was decided in the Azores on March 20, 2003 by the US government, backed by the United Kingdom and Spain, was a kind of coup against the UN system itself and its Security Council. The alleged "weapons of mass destruction" that were intended to be deactivated did not exist; the democratic order that was intended to be imposed does not exist. It was an illegal war from the very beginning. This process of destroying a state, thus leaving its inhabitants in a Hobbesian state, was also perpetrated in Afghanistan and Libya, and continues today in Syria.

> The enemy criminal law scheme is nothing but the old 'enemy of the people' scheme of Stalin's time, along with the Nazi penal model of the 'normative type of author' (Tätertyp).... With the aggravating circumstance that it has been perfected ... it makes

[11] An example of resilience is found in José Mújica, who after 12 years of incommunicado captivity became president of Uruguay (2010–15), the only case of a ruler-philosopher who would agree with Plato in his Seventh Charter.

> the criminal and the terrorist an enemy to be suppressed and not to be judged. The result of this perversion is the model of criminal terrorism, or of terrorist criminal law. Considering 'criminal' as a feature not of the persecuted acts but of the 'right' itself . . . has allowed us to listen to what Fanchiotti said some time ago about the American Patriot Act and about the Guantanamo model: the cancellation of *habeas corpus* for non-American citizens (. . .) (Ferrajoli 2006, p. 17)

This is the same model of criminal terrorism, already carried out by the Latin American dictatorships of the sixties and seventies as a gift of the doctrine of 'national security', and currently practised by the United States" (Ferrajoli 2006, p. 19).

According to Baltasar Garzón, it is necessary for the state to remain within the framework of constitutional legality. Otherwise, "when confronted with the apparent impossibility of dealing with the terrorist phenomenon or when it overwhelms them, they justify or turn to illegal means, crossing the insurmountable limit of legality" (Garzón 2011, p. 40).[12]

2.2.2 Disproportion

Responding to acts of terrorist crime with one or more wars implies not distinguishing between the proper role of the police and that of the army. For Ferrajoli:

> It is clear that the attacks of September 11, 2001 were not an act of war. According to Alberico Gentilli's classical definition, an act of war consists of a '*publicorum armorum contentio*': a conflict between States, and, precisely, between public armies... while terrorism consists of violence aimed at spreading terror among innocent victims, certainly not because of a 'public' force, but because of hidden organisations which act clandestinely and are hidden from the beginning, as criminals always are (Ferrajoli 2006, p. 24).[13]
>
> During the Gulf War, the combined use of smart bombs and depleted uranium bombs, electronic detectors, laser-guided missiles, cluster and choke bombs, stealth technology, unmanned aerial vehicles, and cyber intelligence soon crippled the capabilities of the enemy (Mbembé 2011, p. 54).

The disproportion in the use of force leads the state to "not only lose its legitimacy, but also its effectiveness. Because it loses its asymmetry with crime".

---

[12] His argument continues: "Once that limit is crossed, everything is lost, and whatever happens is justified. It is the theory of the so-called 'areas with no rights', which has caused so much damage and pain, along with dictatorships, repression, death squads, the GAL, the Iraq war, and so on. It is the failure of democracy and ethics and the triumph of the irrationality of arbitrary power, without any limit other than the will of the person who exercises it". A similar criterion was expressed in 1986 by the deputies of Tucumán Alejandro Sangenis and Arturo Sassi: "Terrorism, whatever its political ideology, right or left, (. . .) must be brought down to its last consequences within what the law regulates. Otherwise, we will do what they want: use their own and aberrant methodologies" ICBDH, 34.

[13] This refers to A. Gentilli, *De iure belli libri III* (1588), ed. From J. Brown Scott, at de Claredon Press, Oxford, 1933, Lib. I, p. 12.

Perhaps in response to the participation of two governments in the Azores, the terrorist attacks that took place in Madrid on March 11, 2004, and in London on July 7 and 21, 2005 show that the war was not only ineffective but also counterproductive.

> Terrorism and war, in effect, feed on each other. Neither can war ever defeat terrorism, nor can terrorism ever defeat war (Ferrajoli 2006, p. 27).

However, Ewen Cameron's electroshock applied to the victims of ED "is being used with the prisoners of Guantanamo and Abu Ghraib" (Klein 2007, p. 56).

2.2.3 Criminal Discretion

The guarantee requirement to apply penalties only to the guilty vanishes in a war scenario. The percentage of civilian casualties in armed conflicts has not stopped growing since the Great War. Jakobs himself describes this fact without questioning it, although more recently:

> What can happen outside an orderly criminal proceeding has been known throughout the world since the events of September 11, 2001: in a procedure that, in the absence of a separation from the executive, with all certainty cannot be called an Administration of Justice process, but definitely can be called a war procedure. That State in whose territory those acts were committed attempts to destroy the sources of the terrorists, with the help of other States in whose territories nothing comparable has happened until now. Moreover, to get hold of them, or better yet, to kill them directly, also implies the murder of innocent human beings, which is known as collateral damage. The ambiguous position of the prisoners (criminals? war prisoners?) shows that this concerns the prosecution of crimes through war (Jakobs, 2003b, p. 46).[14]

The text above describes: the lack of division of powers between the executive and the judicial, the passage from a judicial process to another war, the ambiguous situation of the prisoner (already a warlike expression) or criminal, and the collateral damage and homicide of innocents. These constitute a cost that must be assumed by the state, which becomes a de facto state.

2.2.4 Social and Political Disintegration

There is no social reintegration for those who are detained and disappear, or for war prisoners or criminals dealt with by the ECL, because almost all of them are assassinated by the government that practises state terrorism; and those who survive suffer the consequences of clandestine torture or of being turned into humiliating spectacles. But in this case, as it is a hegemonic power and a permanent member of the United Nations Security Council, the damage takes on another dimension. It does not seek, as occurs with the GCL, the social reintegration of those who have broken

[14] Quoted by García Amado (2006, pp. 127–128).

the law but, by breaking it, the state itself breaks the social contract and returns to the state of nature of *homo homini lupus*.

When analysing, on a previous occasion, the cases of the Educational Therapeutic Unit (UTE) of Villabona or those of Nanclares de Oca, we highlighted the possibility and suitability of achieving high rates of social reintegration and self-criticism, even of those who have practised terrorism. On the contrary, at the entrance to Dante's inferno there was an inscription saying: "abandon hope all ye who enter here". This slogan would, according to those who systematically deny the principals of legality, proportionality and culpability, and lack interest in the social reintegration of the enemy, be equally appropriate for those who enter ECL prisons.

> By cancelling the asymmetry between public institutions and terrorist organisations, the response by means of illegal war and savage repression, both of which were terrorist in nature, have in turn deprived the former of their greatest political force, degrading them to the level of the latter. Or in other words, the terrorist organisations have been raised to the level of the public institutions (Ferrajoli 2006, p. 27).

3 Theories Whose Intention Is to Legitimise the Enemy Criminal Law

In his essay on State Terrorism (2001: 131–166), Ernesto Garzón Valdés begins by stating the problem of its legitimisation in the absence of legitimacy. This legitimisation resembles national socialism or apartheid, to the extent that those who hold power change what Hart called the "rule of recognition" of the other norms. They consequently get their closest collaborators to adopt an "internal point of view", which allows all reality to be interpreted according to this new rule. This factual legitimisation, which has no legal ethical normative legitimacy, is intended to be sustained by seven arguments put forward by regimes that practised and still practise state terrorism as a form of government. These are, in reality, fallacies, some of which have already been commented on when presenting the ED (Sect. 2.1) and the ECL prisons (Sect. 2.2), as regards the way in which they violate the principles of the GCL: the cult of efficiency that Ferrajoli qualifies as a realistic fallacy, the difficulty of identifying the enemy as an excuse for torture, and the equivalence of means by which the state identifies itself with its enemies through its actions.

We propose to analyse the other four alleged arguments: the difference between public and private morality, the double effect principle, the reference to tragic elections and moral absolutism. Although Garzón Valdés does not mention the ED in his criticism of state terrorism, it is, in our opinion, his principal hallmark. He does, however, appear to bear it in mind when indicating that secrecy is a modus operandi. He similarly does not refer to the ECL, simply because this doctrine had not yet been formulated by that date, and neither the Abu Ghraib nor the Guantanamo prisons existed to enforce it.

3.1 A Consequentialist Public Morality

The difference between public and private morality refers principally to the fact that the consequences of the former could benefit or damage more people than those of the latter. But this is simply its quantitative aspect. Qualitatively, it would appear to correspond to the distinction between the morality of responsibility and that of conviction proposed by M. Weber. While the first would admit a calculation of consequences inspired by Bentham, the second would conform to principles such as dignity or freedom defended by Kant. Although it is true that Max Weber shows this difference, he adds:

> One cannot prescribe to anyone whether he should follow an ethic of absolute ends or an ethic of responsibility, or when according to one and when to the other (Weber 1989, pp. 92–93).

In the Argentinean case analysed, the government that practised state terrorism by making people disappear attempted to hide behind the presumed effectiveness stated previously, and consequently avoided the quantitative increase in victims of the guerrillas. However, and as stated by Carlos S. Nino, this qualitatively destroyed the republic and democracy that is a substitute for morality (of conviction).

3.2 The Doctrine of Double Effect

The difference between the action to be taken and the collateral effects (which would conform to the doctrine of double effect assumed by Grotius in his defence of effectiveness during the war) would have been used in the twentieth century to justify the disappearances by stating: what we want is to save Western and Christian civilisation. If we have to kidnap and torture to accomplish this goal, we are sorry. It is not our end but only a means to achieve it. This is another way of presenting the aforementioned dilemma, ignoring that the choice of means anticipates or prefigures that of the end. This has been proved after the separation of ethics and politics proposed by Machiavelli, which he himself seems to question in Ch. VIII "Of those who became sovereign through wickedness" of The Prince.

3.3 The Tragic Decisions

Governments that practised state terrorism were allegedly doomed to commit crimes and adopt tactics similar to those of terrorists. This is a kind of connection fallacy: the seriousness of the insecurity generated by the guerrillas so as to perpetrate enforced disappearances is emphasised as a presumably inescapable consequence. In opposition to this, we can refer to myths, or even real events, which show that there were other alternatives. The so-called "Ulysses Argument" (Elster 1998) refers to the hero of the Odyssey who, in fear of being seduced by the song of the mermaids, had himself tied to the mast of his ship. In our case this could signify respect for the dignity of each person. He then gave orders that he was not to be unleashed until the singing had stopped. Confronted with this literary account, we find a tragic historical event: the case of Aldo Moro, who had been Prime Minister on two occasions. He was kidnapped by the Red Brigades in 1978; the chief of police received the suggestion of torturing a terrorist to oblige him to confess where the Prime Minister was being held. General Dalla Chiesa stated: "Italy can bear the loss of Aldo Moro, but not the practice of torture" (ICBDH 1986, p. 32) and (Garzón 2011, pp. 40–41).

3.4 Moral Absolutism

This is the unspoken premise in the aforementioned fallacies: invoking the defence of the Christian West against the communism of the East. The government could practise state terrorism or promote ED, believing that it has the legitimate right to do so. It is possible to suspect that this premise fed on Spanish national Catholicism in addition to being nourished by the doctrine of national security. Although it has more remote antecedents, it can be related to the Collective Letter of the Spanish bishops to the bishops of the world of July 1, 1937 regarding the war in Spain.

> This fight is a fight for the defence of morality, of the dignity of man; in short it is a fight in defence of God. (. . .) That is why I ask for divine protection in this 'dirty war' in which we are engaged, said Bishop Victorio Bonamín (Garzón Valdés 2001, p. 24).[15]

This statement was ratified by Marcial Castro Castillo:

> . . . our civilization is not contradictory like liberal democratic stupidity. . . We can annihilate subversion while remaining good Christians; (. . .) Those who deny those aims and principles of our splendid Catholic tradition, directly enlist with the enemy. . . (Garzón Valdés 2001, pp. 153–154).[16]

[15] Quote from the book by Emilio F. Mignone: Witness to the Truth: The Complicity of Church and Dictatorship in Argentina, Buenos Aires, 1986, p. 24.

[16] Quote taken from Marcial Castro Castillo's book: Armed Forces. Ethics and repression. Buenos Aires, 1979 (pp. 32–33), to whom he erroneously attributes the condition of military chaplain (p. 64), when he was in reality a professor at the Air Warfare School. His name was Edmundo Gelonch Villarino (1940-), and he used this pseudonym to publish this work in New Order in 1979. This rectification is found in Esteban Damián Pontoriero: Counterinsurgency and intransigent Catholicism. The sacralisation of the "war against subversion" in the work of Marcial Castro Castillo (1969–1976). National University of San Martín, Aletheia: Journal of the Master in History and Memory of the FaHCE, ISSN-e 1853-3701, Vol. 5, N°. 9, 2014. Pontoriero (2014, p. 4), contributes another ideological source of state terrorism: "Doctrine of the Revolutionary War" which was devised by the French military for their colonial wars in Indochina (1946–1954) and in Algeria (1954–1962) (Ranalletti 2009, p. 252).

These expressions of a moral absolutism allow us, on the one hand, to delimit by exclusion the "enemy" of the government that practises state terrorism, to which we shall again refer later. On the other hand, it shows the fusion between the Army and the Church in their common endeavour to maintain... a "dirty war".[17] And, finally, it shows how this attempts to justify itself in the Christian religion by denying the pluralism of the "liberal democratic stupidity", which is identified as contradictory.

From a moral absolutism stand, President George Bush (Jr) considered himself authorised to declare on September 14, 2001: "the infinite war to free the world from evil", or three days later: the preventive war "of indefinite duration". In 1976, J.R. Videla had similarly stated, "our government has objectives, not deadlines".

3.5 *Necrophilia, Irrationality and Nihilism*

As in the Spanish case, there was a necrophiliac cult among the intellectual authors that supported state terrorism.[18] Erich Fromm describes necrophilia as:

> The desire to kill, the worship of force; attraction to death, to suicide, to sadism; the desire to transform the organic into the inorganic (...).
>
> It is the most morbid and the most dangerous among the orientations to life of which man is capable. It is true perversion... (Fromm 1966, p. 20).

In his study of this pathology, Fromm reproduces a fragment of Unamuno's diagnosis of October 12, 1936:

> "... I have just heard the necrophiliac and insane cry, 'Long live death' (...) It torments me to think that General Millán Astray could dictate the norms of mass psychology ..." At that time, Millán Astray could not hold back and shouted: 'Down with intelligence! Long live death!'" (Fromm 1966, p. 16).

This second cry makes it clear that necrophilia is, simultaneously, a cult of irrationality; it is intended to end life, and particularly intelligent life. The principal enemies of state terrorism are those who think differently, who assume the enlightened ideal of "sapereaude". This is exemplified by the fact that it was the political and trade union leaders, and mainly university students, who, in proportion to their number, were the main victims of enforced disappearances (IRUNT 1987) and (ICBDH 1991, pp. XIV–XXII).

To this double psychological perversion against life, and especially against intelligence, we can add a third, of an ontological nature. It is not only about taking

---

[17] In the Spanish case, 5 bishops did not sign the Collective Charter of 1937; in Argentina, Bishops Enrique Angelelli and Carlos Ponce de León were assassinated by Task Forces. ICBDH, 33.

[18] The Francoist ideology was vindicated by Dr. Gaona, defender of Brigadier Orlando Agosti at the Trial of the Military Juntas once democracy was restored: "because the cry 'Long live death' of Millán Astray, whose ideology was here described as perverse, makes sense" (Garzón Valdés 2001, p. 160).

life, but something more radical: removing existence. The claim of General J.R. Videla regarding "annihilating subversion" uses a verb that, in his so-called Christianity, alludes to a properly divine action. According to the Book of Genesis, the *ex-nihilo* creation could be carried out only by God, who took the being from nothing (*nihil*), signifying that each entity will have its own attributes that can change or transform, but its essence is not lost: a living being can die, its body can decompose, but its materiality continues to be a reference to what it was, the skeletal remains of who it was.

Those who promoted the ED, in their eagerness to hide the bodies of their victims (they threw them into the sea, into mass graves or burned them), wished not only to end those people's lives, but something additional: to deny their existence. The government that practised state terrorism assumed an anti-Creator dimension by attempting to erase the memory of the people it made disappear; its intention was to commit a retroactive crime: to go back in time to avoid a situation in which whoever had intelligent life could not only not exercise their intelligence by being subjected to torture, and one in which they not only died in the most atrocious ways but had not even existed. The family members seeking them, including the police and the military, chaplains and judges, were recommended not to persist in their search because it could be detrimental to the person who had been detained and had disappeared.

If the denial of *habeas corpus* might initially damage the criminal guarantees of the victim, that second moment (of concealment of the body, even after death) supposed psychological damage for his or her family members. From a psychological perspective, the absence of the recumbent body hinders the grieving process to the point of making it impossible. In addition, there was perverse government propaganda according to which those who had been detained or had been disappeared were actually exiled in other countries. This gave many families the hope of finding them alive, even decades after their disappearance.

This nihilistic dimension of enforced disappearance as a practice that identifies state terrorism, became a kind of black hole, like that to which cosmologists refer: antimatter space, which consumes all kinds of energy. A society that has been subjected to state terrorism, and thus deprived of more than one generation of thoughtful leaders, promoters of human rights and their guarantees, cannot find its balance in subsequent decades. Moreover, the scope of the ECL progressively absorbs more criminals (real or imagined) whom it transforms into enemies.

3.6 Expanding Victims: From Persons-Citizens to Individual-Enemies

Having discussed the link between absolute morality and the ontological scope of the ECL's discourse, we now consider it appropriate to briefly digress and return to the classical debate between natural law and legal positivism. We shall, depending on the topic in hand, focus on the concept of person.

Just as for Antigone there was an unwritten law that governed her conscience, even when it contravened what was legally established, for Creon there was only one positive law. This law defined what was just and what was not. It can be considered that every human being (1) is naturally a person as long as they are endowed with a conscience, freedom and the capacity for rational communication. Legally, a person is a subject to rights and duties only if they are recognised as such by an ordinance.

This second definition of person is linked to the concept of subjective right, a key aspect of civil law which supposes that the state can grant or deny natural persons this character, but it is also linked to legal persons, from the Roman jurists[19] to the Napoleonic Code of 1804. Legal persons can be: from another state, a company, a union, a foundation or the same ecosystem, as stipulated in the 2008 Constitution of Ecuador in Art. 71.

The first definition of person, with its claim to universality, is developed as a contemporary version of the *ius gentium* as opposed to the *ius civili*, by the international human rights law in its preliminary document.[20] The second is predominant in the constitutional texts of each state, in which the concept of natural person tends to be linked to that of citizen.[21]

The modern state was presented as an ideal instrument with which to guarantee the rights of its citizens; However, the development of the aforementioned ECL signified that it does not concern defending all citizens, but rather only those who regularly obey laws; the others who habitually commit crimes or are presumed to be able to do so, will be considered enemies, even to the point of taking away their status as persons.

In fact, law as a historical and cultural construct could not suppress the personal nature of any human being; what could be removed was their status as a subject of rights because they did not know how to assume their obligations. But, if the status

[19] According to Roman law, a man was a person only if he complied with the following three statuses: *libertatis, civitatis* and *familiae*. The last was denied to women, to whom the term *capitis diminutio* was applied. On legal, civic or moral entities, they distinguished between: corporations (*civitates, universitates* ...), foundations (*pia causae*), public treasury (*fiscus*) and recumbent inheritance.

[20] The Universal Declaration of Human Rights uses the expression "person" in 18 of its 30 Articles (2, 8, 11, 13–15, 17, 18 and 20–29), as a synonym for "all human beings" (aa. 1, 6 and 7), individuals (aa. 13, 12 and 29) and in its negative version, nobody (aa. 4, 5 and 9), which is "*personne*" in French.

[21] The current Spanish Constitution, for example, refers to the dignity of the person (10.1) and to the international human rights law (10.2) in its Title I On fundamental rights and duties; and immediately distinguishes between Spaniards and foreigners in Chapter I (aa. 11–13). Chapter II begins with a.14, which guarantees equality before the law and non-discrimination only to its citizens. Perhaps because of this asymmetry in the treatment of citizens and foreigners in state constitutions, Ferrajoli maintains that citizenship (*status civitatis*) is the last privilege, since slavery (*status libertatis*) has already been prohibited and equality between men and women is advancing (*status familiae*).

as a person is removed, then that person is condemned to death, because if the right to life is the condition of possibility to exercise the other rights, and the enemy has no right, s/he is destined "to two deaths: physical , which is evident, and hermeneutical, which hides it".[22]

Of those who applied enforced disappearance, the Iberian General Saint Jean, with his moral absolutism and necrophiliac cult, made an exhaustive catalogue of enemies:

> First we shall kill the subversives, then their collaborators, then the supporters, later the indifferent, and finally the lukewarm (Garzón Valdés 2001, p. 145).

According to Jakobs, this shock wave anticipates the condition by which a person-citizen (including men) can lose their status as such, to become an individual-enemy (including women):

> What is still implied as regards the everyday criminal, that is, not treating him as a dangerous *individual*, but as a person who acts wrongly, is already difficult (. . .). In the case of the *perpetrator by tendency* or what is embedded in an organization, the need to react to the danger emanating from these people's repeatedly contrary conduct to the norm comes to the fore and they eventually become *terrorists*. A terrorist is one who rejects the legitimacy of the legal system on principle and, therefore, pursues the destruction of that order.[23]

As García Amado states, Jakobs' intention is to separate two groups of citizens: those who regularly abide by the law and only exceptionally and by mistake contravene it, and those who systematically and repeatedly contravene it, for which they will lose their citizenship and their status as persons, to become "dangerous individuals". The citizen criminal law must be applied to the former. Only the ECL can be applied to the latter. These wrongdoers have, to date, been classified as guerrillas or terrorists, but Jakobs himself broadens the spectrum to drug traffickers, paedophiles, the corrupt . . .:

> The enemy is an individual who, not only incidentally, in his behavior (sexual crimes. . . according to paragraph 20 of the German Penal Code) or in his professional occupation (economic crime, organised crime and also, especially, drug trafficking) or mainly through his association with an organisation (terrorism. . .). . . has abandoned the law.[24]

The variety of behaviour that is criminalised in this text makes it possible to infer that

> Jakobs can compare and put terrorism and sex crimes in the same category or, more spectacularly, drug trafficking. The entity of the protected good does not matter, because in reality there is no good more protected than the status quo, the norm by virtue of being a norm and totally independent of its rational foundations (García Amado 2006, p. 122).

As shown previously, in the scenarios in which the ECL is applied, a factual legitimisation is sought from which a normative change and a new legality are

---

[22] This double death is described by Walter Benjamin as regards the Holocaust. Quoted by Reyes Mate: 2011. pp. 10–11.

[23] Jakobs (2003a, b, pp. 19–46). Quoted by García Amado (2006, p. 4). Italics are ours.

[24] Jakobs (2003a, b, pp. 53, 59 and 63) Quoted by García Amado (2006, p. 120).

generated; This occurs in the total absence of legitimacy, while in violation of fundamental rights, human rights and even international humanitarian law, its norms are complied with only through terror (*summisio propter iram*) and not thanks to its rationality and universality (*submissio propter conscientiam*).

The exact opposite of the individual-enemy is the submissive and obedient citizen-person (out of fear and not out of conscience) who obeys the rules regardless of their degree of rationality, universality or coherence with fundamental rights. Jakobs does not appear to consider the conclusions of Stanley Milgram's experiment (1974), reflected in his work *The Perils of Obedience*. Nor does he appear to consider the limits stipulated by Gustav Radbruch regarding the possible conflict between the legal certainty and justice of a norm.

Consequently, "a person would only be the basically compliant individual. The person would be the sum of two elements: the normative one consisting of being the centre of imputation of obligations by the legal system, and the empirical-subjective one which is a certain attitude towards such imputed legal obligations" (García Amado 2006, p. 103). This is a reductionist or devalued view of the concept of person without rights in which what matters is to preserve order, although to do this, his freedom, his capacity for judgment, his *sapere aude*, his conscience and his ability to dissent are ignored, as in an inquisitorial setting.

As stated previously, those governments that practise the ECL lose their legitimacy and are reduced to a band of criminals, and, according to the criticism made by the pirate to Alexander the Great, "although on a different scale, both manage to subdue out of fear". Now we see that not only is the state devalued, but so is the concept of the person-citizen who submissively abides by all the rules, even the "unbearably unjust" (Radbruch) like those of the ECL.

3.7 ECL Between Biopolitics and Necropolitics

The prisons, territories and populations subjugated by those who monopolise the use of force are a reflection at the level of the state that administers them. The type of criminal law that is applied in them constitutes the test bed of the degree of its legitimacy. The Abu Ghraib and Guantánamo prisons, as the clandestine centres in which those who had been detained and disappeared were confined in Latin America, allow us to conclude that state terrorism, which was practised in peripheral countries at the request of the United States in the 1970s, was directly exercised by this hegemonic power from the beginning of the millennium.

Foucault (1975), in his work on the origin of prisons, analysed the emergence and evolution of this institution in the eighteenth and nineteenth centuries, describing how the torture and medieval dungeons were left behind and "the disappearance of the punitive spectacle... and of pain" was observed (Foucault 2002, pp. 16 and 19). At that time, he argued that states, and principally those that had most evolved, generated "biopolitics" through a "microphysics of power". Biopolitics is:

> The respect for life by power; (. . .) an exercise of power over man as a living being, as some kind of nationalisation of the biological or at least a tendency leading to what could be called the nationalisation of the biological (Foucault 2000, p. 217).[25]

This work by the aforementioned French political scientist is contemporary with state terrorism in Latin America and with its ED policy. In these twentieth century scenarios, the diagnosis of the "disappearance of the punitive spectacle" is confirmed, to the extreme of preferring clandestineness not at the time of the kidnapping and detention alone. What does not disappear, however, is the pain inflicted on those who were detained and disappeared and who underwent particularly sadistic torture. Three decades later, since the beginning of the twenty-first century, not only is similar torture practised in the prisons of Abu Ghraib and Guantánamo, but the spectacle of torture has also returned with the objective of humiliating the enemy in a kind of regression to inquisitorial scenarios.

The Cameroonian political scientist Achille Mbembé radicalises the reading of Foucault when analysing the history of Africa, slavery, racism and neo-colonialism, and asks: "Is the notion of biopower sufficient to account for the contemporary ways in which politics, under the guise of war, of resistance, or of the fight against terror, makes the murder of the enemy its primary and absolute objective?" (Mbembé 2011, p. 20).

This no longer simply concerns biopolitics that can be exercised within industrialised countries, but also necropolitics which is, from such decision centres, imposed on the peripheral countries. And this expression can also be applied to Iraq, Afghanistan, Libya and now Syria.

> More and more often, war does not take place between the armies of two sovereign states, but between armed groups which act under the state mask, against armed groups without a state but that control well-defined territories; the main objective of both sides is the civilian population, which is neither armed nor organised into militias (Mbembé 2011, p. 20).[26]

This description of a fragmentation or privatisation of the use of force was already present among those who practised ED, as described in the Inter-American Convention of 1994, or the later International Convention on Enforced Disappearance of 2006.[27]

---

[25] Anthological examples of biopolitics can be found in public policies in the current situation of a pandemic.

[26] Mbembé argues: "My approach is based on Michel Foucault's critique of the notion of sovereignty and its links with war and biopower in the course of the Collège de France, 1976, Akal, 2003".

[27] According to the Inter-American Convention on Enforced Disappearance, a.2, "Enforced disappearance is considered to be the arrest, detention, abduction or any other form of deprivation of liberty by agents of the State or by persons or groups of persons acting with the authorisation, support or acquiescence of the State, followed by a refusal to acknowledge the deprivation of liberty or by concealment of the fate or whereabouts of the disappeared person, which place such a person outside the protection of the law". It is defined in analogous terms by the 2006 International Convention.

3.8 Necrolaw, Solitary Confinement and Injustice

States that exercise necropolitics do so through a "necro-law", a normative and coercive order which, far from questioning the inequality as regards the property and privileges of a minority, protects it by denying the right to life or existence of others, especially if they express their dissent.

The aim is to apply different forms of solitary confinement: (1) that of those who have been detained/disappeared or that of separating isolated enemies from each other; (2) that of these people with respect to their next of kin, (3) those who deny their procedural guarantees in life, (4) or preventing the discovery of their remains. Finally, to these four factual issues, the necro-law adds a regulation: the isolation between the norms created by necropolitics and the international human rights law.

The deepening of the Euro-Foucauldian concept of biopolitics, towards the necropolitics of the African Mbembé, can be explained by a keen observation by Luis Villoro regarding the theories of justice, highlighted by M. Reyes Mate:

> "On the one hand, there is a type of theories that usually start from a rational consensus between equal subjects, which are related to each other in terms that produce the features that a well-ordered democracy would have" and, on the other, there is a type of theories that "instead of starting from consensus in order to found justice, start from its absence; instead of moving from the determination of universal principles of justice to their realization in a specific society, they start from the perception of real injustice and move to a project that could remedy it" (Villoro 2007, p. 15).[28]

One last issue which deserves a separate mention is the following: on the tragic situation of the survivors of enforced disappearance, along with the distinction between ECL and the citizen criminal law proposed by Jakobs: What conditions do asylum and refuge seekers find themselves in, when they are neither citizens nor enemies?; Why are they overcrowded in camps, as occurs in those in Moira on the island of Lesbos, which was described by one of the inmates as hell, if they did not commit a punishable offence but instead attempted to exercise their rights?

Providing refuge was understood to be a humanitarian action by states that had nothing to do with the conflict that caused the flight of thousands of innocent people. But, by agreements with the US or NATO, if the European states are responsible for the destruction of other states (Iraq, Afghanistan, Libya, Syria, Yemen . . .), should it not be mandatory for them to deal with the consequences of these military adventures? Can the latest decisions made by the European Union (to reinforce its borders, sponsor the return of refugees to their countries of origin and distribute them in resettlements without mandatory quotas) be considered rational consensus that is capable of universalising well-ordered democracies?

[28] Quoted by Reyes Mate (2011, p. 16).

4 Conclusion

The ED and the ECL have relevant elements in common: denying the personhood of certain citizens to conceive of them as enemies; applying torture outside of the law, which is a disproportionate use of force, even against possible criminals. There are also some differences: while the ED was applied in peripheral countries around the 1970s (Tucumán), the ECL was assumed by at least one hegemonic country at the beginning of the millennium (Abu Graib and Guantánamo); If the ED as the main tool of state terrorism made a cult of secrecy, the ECL recovered the "punitive spectacle".

Of the various discourses presented as theories that legitimise the ED and the ECL, we find necrophilia. This makes the description of necro-politics that makes use of a necro-law ideal, as it not only dehumanises people conceived of as enemies but also the states that practise it.

References

Aquino T (1956) "Treaty of justice" in Suma teológica <1265-74>, T. VIII. BAC, Madrid
Arendt H (2008) "Socrates" in the promise of politics. Paidós, Barcelona, Buenos Aires, México
Beccaría C (2015) Of crimes and punishments. <1764> http://hdl.handle.net/10016/20199, Creative Commons Madrid: UCIII
Bentham J (1965) Economic writings, selection and prologue W. Sark. FCE, Mexico
Bobbio N (2003) "II. Politics, morals, law" in general theory of politics. Trotta, Madrid
Elster J (1998) "Ulysses reviewed: Previous commitments and constitutionalism". Political analysis. Journals. Unal.edu.co
Ferrajoli L (2006) "The enemy's criminal law and the dissolution of criminal law", New Penal Forum. January June
Foucault M (2000) The punitive society: course at the Collège de France (1975-1976) (trans: Pons H). FCE, Buenos Aires
Foucault M (2002) Discipline and punish. The Birth of the Prison. (*Surveiller et punir)* <1975> (trans: Garzón del Camino A). Siglo XXI, Buenos Aires
Fromm E (1966) The heart of man (trans: Torner FM). FCE, México
García Amado A (2006) "The obedient, the enemy, criminal law and Jakobs", New Penal Forum, January-June
Garzón B (2011) The power of reason. Debate, Barcelona
Garzón Valdés E (2001) Philosophy, politics, law. Colec. *Honoris causae*. University of Valencia
ICBDH (1986) Informe de la Comisión Bicameral investigadora de las violaciones a los Derechos Humanos en la provincia de Tucumán. IEPALA, Madrid
ICBDH (1991) Informe de la Comisión Bicameral investigadora de las violaciones a los Derechos Humanos en la provincia de Tucumán. IEPALA, Madrid
Jakobs G (2003a) Enemy criminal law, (*Bürgerstrafrecht und Feindstrafrechc*) (trans: Cancio Imel M UAM). Civitas, Madrid
Jakobs G (2003b) Citizen criminal law and enemy criminal law. In: Jakobs G et al (eds) Enemy criminal law. Civitas, Madrid
Klein N (2007) The shock doctrine. The rise of disaster capitalism. Paidós, Barcelona, Buenos Aires, Mexico

Mbembé A (2011) Necropolitics (translation and editing by Archambault EF). Melusina, Santa Cruz de Tenerife

Pontoriero E (2014) Contrainsurgencia y catolicismo intransigente: La sacralización de la "guerra contra la subversión" en la obra de Marcial Castro Castillo [1969–1976]. Aletheia 5(9)

Ranalletti M (2009) Contrainsurgencia, catolicismo intransigente y extremismo de derecha en la formación military argentina. Influencias francesas en los orígenes del terrorismo de Estado (1955–1976). Terrorismo de Estado y genocidio en América Latina:249–480

Reyes Mate M (2011) Treatise of injustice. Anthropos, Barcelona

Rovetta F (1987) Rovetta report. https://ddhhtucuman.deigualaigual.net/category/documentos/informe-rovetta/

Rovetta F (Ed., 1991) Report of the Bicameral Commission investigating human rights in the province of Tucumán (1974-1983). Iepala, Madrid

Suárez F (1967) "Different human laws, especially the odious ones" in Treaty of laws and God legislator <1612>, L.V. IEP, Madrid

Villoro L (2007) The challenges of the coming society. FCE, Mexico

Vitoria F (1981) Relectio De iure belli or Dynamic Peace<1526-60>, CHP, VI. CSIC, Madrid

Weber M (1989) Politics and science. Leviathan, Buenos Aires

Part II
Crisis of Warranty Thinking in the Democratic Constitutional State and Criminal Law

Criminal Law and Legal Theory: Not Just Legal Dogmatics, but Never Without It

Miguel Díaz y García Conlledo

Abstract This paper reviews some of the common discussions and criticisms regarding criminal-law dogmatics, some of which are considered less important than their historical weight makes them seem (for example, the debate about their scientific nature) and others are valid in the face of an incorrect practice of dogmatics or, better, in the face of "bad" dogmatics (such as the criticism of the prevalence of the system over the law). A correctly developed dogmatics is claimed, without any pretensions of absolute objectivity, with the positive law as limit and reference, away from an exercise of "art for art's sake." A dogmatics that is not isolated from other knowledge nor above them, not hermetic, with respect for the Constitution and fundamental rights and, most especially, focused on the solution of real problems. This kind of solution often does not arise simply from the wording or the language of the positive law. Certain misuses of dogmatics in jurisprudence are reported and the advantages of its correct use for jurisprudence are highlighted. In short, dogmatics is claimed as an important guarantee (not a panacea), with others, of the citizen in avoiding arbitrariness and, therefore, as a limit to punitive power.

1 Introduction

When approaching a legal discipline, both in relation to what it rules and how it rules and how it should be ruled, especially one with as many particularities as criminal law (the "extreme branch" of law), it is, in my opinion, simplistic to pretend that all

This paper belongs to the research projects DER2016-76715-R and PID2019-108567RB-C21 (AEI), as well as to the research tasks of the UIC 166 of Castilla and León. The references related to the topic addressed are endless, so we do not claim to be exhaustive in the citation. In many of the works cited above, there are abundant further references.

M. Díaz y García Conlledo (✉)
Faculty of Law, University of León, León, Spain
e-mail: mdiag@unileon.es

E. Demetrio Crespo et al. (eds.), *Crisis of the Criminal Law in the Democratic Constitutional State*, Legal Studies in International, European and Comparative Criminal Law 6, https://doi.org/10.1007/978-3-031-13413-5_5

of this can be approached with a single "weapon" or from a single methodological point of view.

First, solving the reality or problem addressed by a criminal law is not, of course, the exclusive responsibility of the law itself: there is no better measure against petty property crime (and against other types of crime) than a fair social distribution of wealth, avoiding large social differences and groups of people living in poverty and marginalization. However, when events occur that could be criminal, a criminal policy must be established to deal with them. This will be nourished by sociological, criminalistic, and other data. And there is no need for further examples to explain the complexity of extra-legal and juridical crime prevention and the difficulties involved in creating and applying criminal laws.

Among the disciplines that address criminal matters, one of those that has received the most criticism or doubts is dogmatics (a definition will be included later), whose best-known result, although it is not the only one, is the theory of offense, of obvious Germanic origin and influence. It has often been criticized due to its "theoretical" character, pure art for art's sake, its abstraction to the point of separating itself from the real world and its problems, its lack of scientific accuracy and objectivity, contrary to what its defenders claim, its uselessness or limited usefulness, in short (if not even its harmful character for a correct application of criminal law).

In the following paragraphs, we will attempt to briefly respond to some of the criticisms to vindicate a criminal-law dogmatics that, without being a panacea or a unique or "uncontaminated" or infallible tool, is essential, especially in the interpretation and application of the law to guarantee the rights of citizens.

2 Scientific and Objective Nature of Dogmatics

In Germany, Spain and elsewhere, one of the most repeated criticisms of dogmatics is related to its lack of scientific character (von *Kirchmann*[1] is always cited, of course!) and the impossibility of being objective.[2]

In Spain, for example, *Vives Antón* and his followers attribute to the scientific pretension of dogmatics many of its problems: making the system take precedence over the law, forgetting its words, having a pretension of veracity, justifying any decision and even having an authoritarian pretension.[3]

[1] Von Kirchmann (1848), especially his well-known sentence "Three corrective words from the legislator and whole libraries become waste paper" (p. 23).

[2] It is enough to cite the quotation already made by v. Kirchmann (1848) in Germany; in Spain, to cite only one author and in a work (among many others in which he denies the scientificity of dogmatics) dedicated to the thought of v. Kirchmann, Vives Antón (2017), pp. 233 et seq. with further references.

[3] It is important to underline that the school of Vives Antón is integrated by relevant criminal lawyers with serious works (most of whom I have an excellent relationship with), who in my

Probably the accusation includes the repeated idea that we as dogmatists surround our work, better or worse carried out, with the word science to send a message of prestige and greater knowledge and thus hide the limits of our tasks and possibilities, even our miseries.[4]

There are authors on the defenders of dogmatics side who maintain the fully scientific and totally objective character of dogmatics. This is the case of *Gimbernat Ordeig*, in a very well-known and quoted work of years ago, in which he points out that the lack of certainty of the solutions is not enough to exclude the character of science of legal dogmatics and the objective character of this cannot be disputed by those who pretend to deny its scientific character.[5]

Other authors make more measured reflections, some without definitively denying the character of legal dogmatics as a science but highlighting the confusion of our own explanations. Thus, from Argentina, *Nino* warned: "Philosophers who deal with human action often wonder whether it is possible to do something without knowing what is being done. Regardless of the remarkable inaccuracy of the question, a positive example seems to be found in the activity of lawyers. Because although dogmatists perform a task that, as we have seen, is subject to some set of rules and has certain common assumptions, when they reflect on the nature of their

opinion often do dogmatics. For this reason, my mention to its representatives here should in no way be taken as disqualifications, but rather, on the contrary, as opinions to continue the debate. It would be impossible here to mention all the works in which Vives and his followers express criticisms and objections to dogmatics or to the way in which criminal lawyers do it. In some of the following sections, I will especially cite one of the works by Cuerda Arnau (2017) in which further references to others can be found. In any case, I wish to state here for the record that some works by this author [e.g., the most recent (2019), pp. 11 et seq., with very interesting application of her theses to specific problems] in which she insists on the criticisms and on the need (which I fully agree with) not to make dogmatics beyond the law, actually show that our positions are not so far apart and that a "good" dogmatics does not have to incur in the deficiencies that she reports (although it is not possible to demonstrate this here in detail, later on I will offer some example of coincidence). These criticisms are based on Vives Antón's view of meaningful action (see. the work in which he develops it in a general way: Vives Antón 2011). Vives' disciples have applied this conception of their teacher to the most diverse subjects in books and works [just to mention one among many, in which quite a few of them have recently written: González Cussac (coord.) (2019)], in many of whom at least misgivings towards dogmatics can be noticed, probably with the exception of Martínez-Buján Pérez, an important developer of Vives Antón's conception, but admitting the need for dogmatics (based on law), as he acknowledges, I believe, in the foreword to the very interesting book by Martínez-Buján Pérez (2019), foreword in which Vives once again criticizes dogmatics or the way of doing dogmatics and the pretension of its scientificity (pp. 13 et seq.), but he concludes by stating: "In the work of Carlos Martínez-Buján, all these requirements are combined with a special insight to analyze the concepts and a deep knowledge of the existing jurisprudence and dogmatics, so that the reader will find in it a dogmatics that has renounced its complexes and the pretensions of infallibility that arise from them, offering simply, an authentic lesson of Law" (pp. 14 et seq.).

[4] For many, summarized in this sense Vives Antón (2017), p. 233.

[5] Gimbernat Ordeig (1970), pp. 379 et seq. [1990, pp. 140 et seq.].

own activity, they very often incur in a set of superficial, imprecise and contradictory statements."[6]

And others, like *Atienza*, believe that dogmatics, more than a science, is a techno-praxis, a technique for solving practical problems, more related to engineering or architecture than to physics or chemistry, which is why he prefers the (old) designation of "jurisprudence" for dogmatics. However, he warns that there is no pejorative tone in this.[7]

Personally, I believe that the whole debate regarding the scientificity of dogmatics ends up being excessive, since it all depends on how we define what science is, something that is not exactly easy and frequently discussed. And perhaps the debate is overly influenced by the concept of science in the empirical sciences.[8]

Well, after his broad review of the debate on the scientificity of dogmatics, in another work *Nino* recognizes that the calm and unhurried work of the theoretician of law offers him more possibilities to argument and counterargument than the judge urged by the need to issue sentences, often in record time, who needs to rely on the reflections of the theoretician. Precisely, he points out, in *common law* countries, the judge must make that argumentative effort, which I am sure is more difficult.[9]

And *Schüneman* is absolutely right when he points out that the debate ends up being a matter of words (a "sterile controversy"[10]) and what is decisive is: (1) To sustain whether a conduct is ordered or forbidden, arbitrariness, caprice, should not decide, but rational foundations (reasons) should be offered that can be followed to a generally accepted assumption. (2) The resulting conceptual and argumentative system must be free of contradictions. (3) Through free speech, an ongoing, continuous verification, revision or review of the standard to be observed, to which it is

---

[6] Nino (1984), p. 103.

[7] Atienza (2015), pp. 169 et seq., 189 et seq.

[8] And I would even say, although this requires further verification, that some of the criticisms of criminal-law dogmatics [e.g., those of Vives Antón or his disciple Cuerda Arnau, in Spain; see. only Vives Antón (2011), p. 578; Cuerda Arnau (2017), p. 494] are influenced by the use of dogmatics made by a very definite current, that of ultra-normativism of Jakobsian tradition, which here it is not possible to evaluate, but which, in my opinion, differs to a large extent from what dogmatics and its most refined source, the theory of offense, should be, by dissolving the categories of this into others of allocation that are much more vague, general and even manipulable. In this sense, with clarity, among others, Demetrio Crespo (2010), p. 15: "In this way *Jakobs* has been deconstructing the systematic structure of the theory of offense at its very foundations through the formalism of the categories and the use of vague and imprecise concepts that lack the capacity of subsumption."

[9] Nino (1980), p. 14.

[10] Schünemann (2011), p. 447. This author, by the way, continues to vindicate the value of dogmatics and its service to the democratic rule of law. He has done so in multiple works and, recently, citing all of them and many more and in the face of critical positions such as especially those of Vogel (2012), pp. 25 et seq. or Ambos (2016), pp. 177 et seq., in Schünemann (2016), pp. 654 et seq. In these recent works Schünemann has argued that in a liberal constitutional state, criminal-law dogmatics is vital as a "fourth power" against totalitarian pretensions of criminal policy and has even introduced a new paradigm in the global science of criminal law: the paradigm of the *analytical-philosophicus mos civitatis iuris*, abbreviated as "*mapci*."

necessary to adhere, is established.[11] In addition, I would say that the categories must be contrasted in relation to the purposes assigned to them.

Not separated from the line just described, the functions attributed to it by *Alexy*[12] clearly seem to me to be indicative about the advantages of legal dogmatics in general:

(1) The stabilization function, by means of which certain solutions to practical questions, particular forms of decision, are fixed for long periods of time, avoiding the solution to the case that may be different each time. Naturally, this is in line with some of the advantages of the theory of offense, in fact almost all of them. Obviously, *Alexy* states that this does not mean that a dogmatic solution must be maintained indefinitely, but it does mean that it forces the one who is contradicting it to justify and argue. And even different dogmatic solutions will coexist, but, to put it in my own words, we will know what we are arguing about.
(2) The progress function, closely connected to the previous one. The progress in the dogmatic discussion, although influenced by many factors (among others, legislative changes), is easier to achieve (given the stabilization) than in the merely punctual discussion. This seems clear, as demonstrated by the evolution (at least not abruptly) of the theory of offense.
(3) The relief function, in the sense that it is possible to appeal to relatively firm dogmatic statements without carrying out an ex-novo verification each time, which relieves the interpretative task of the courts and doctrine and the application task of the courts. Naturally, this function will be enhanced the clearer the dogmatic statement in question is and the greater the consensus it generates. This effect can be limited to such an extent that, in extreme cases, it can even result in the opposite: an argumentative burden. But again, the theory of offense evolution shows that in normal cases, over long periods of time, there are elements with enough consensus that they do not need to be substantiated every time they are referred to in the interpretation and application of the law.
(4) The technical function is particularly relevant in relation to the theory of offense. The development of general basic concepts, statements, institutions, allows for quick information, facilitates legal teaching and learning (*Roxin* also emphasizes the importance of the theory of offense "for the training of students at the University; for as a rule in the examination the student is presented with a certain factual assumption, requiring her/him to make an opinion on whether and, if so, how the persons involved are responsible"[13]), and makes its communication easier. This didactic function, if we want to be didactic, I think it is also important in another sense: it also facilitates the discussion; thus, even if we do not entirely agree on the conception of willful intent, I think we all know what

[11] Schünemann (2011), p. 447.

[12] Alexy (1991), pp. 326 et seq. [(1997), pp. 255 et seq.]

[13] Roxin (2006), § 7 paragraph. 1 (pp. 194 et seq.) [1997, § 7 paragraph. 1, p. 192]. Igual Roxin and Greco (2020), § 7 paragraph. 1 (p. 288).

we are talking about and what we are discussing when we talk about willful intent. And likewise for attempt, unimputability, etc. It allows us an easier communication and discussion.

(5) The control or consistency control function, which automatically checks the logical compatibility of the dogmatic statements with each other and the general practical compatibility of the decisions to be based on the different dogmatic statements. This again contributes to the universalization and fairness of solutions.

(6) The heuristics function (as an art or technique of inquiry) assumes that dogmatics has at its disposal a series of solution models, distinctions and points of view that would not be available if it had to start from scratch each time. In short, dogmatic instruments, especially visible in the theory of offense, make it possible to investigate, to advance the discussion and to make it more productive. Its relationship with the technical (and other) function seems clear to me.

The contrary is arbitrariness, incompatible with the democratic rule of law. As *Schünemann*[14] emphasizes, it is not, contrary to *Kindhäuser*,[15] the question of whether the dogmatics possesses superior knowledge to other citizens, but the question of the objective criteria for the correctness of the dogmatics, whose observance is demanded and controlled in the institutionalized discourse.

Therefore, whether dogmatics is science or not, pure technique or legal argumentation, does not excessively concern me. It is, in any case, an organized way of doing (a method, a system), with rules such as coherence and non-contradiction, which is subject to constant reviews and which seeks a non-arbitrary application of the law.[16] Nothing more and nothing less!

3 Objectivity and Dogmatics Purity? Dogmatics Above the Law? Dogmatics As Panacea?

Regardless of its scientificity, is dogmatics completely objective? Is it pure? Does it allow reference to values? Is it above the law? Does it magically solve all problems?

In a very critical tone, *Cuerda Arnau* recently said:[17] "It is urgent for dogmatics to assume that the dogma role must be attributed to the constitutional principles that govern the entire legal system, so as to affirm the priority of fundamental rights and the claims of justice that are inherent to them over any pretended science." It is not possible to deny the importance of the Constitution, but I believe that we must be

---

[14] Schünemann (2011), p. 448.

[15] Kindhäuser (2009), pp. 963 et seq.

[16] Gimbernat Ordeig very clearly states (1970), p. 405 [(1990), p. 158].

[17] Cuerda Arnau (2017), p. 485.

more careful with the principles.[18] *Cuerda Arnau* does so, as I have already stated, from the idea of the meaningful action of her teacher *Vives Antón* and of the Habermassian dialogued consensus. She accuses all dogmatic conceptions of offense of having failed at reducing insecurity. Curiously, she accuses dogmatics in general of starting from a superior language that is imposed on what the law says, thus altering the law and drawing unpredictable consequences for the citizen.[19]

This dogmatic understanding also seems to me to be unfair and the appeal to constitutional principles rather than to the precepts of the Constitution and other laws (criminal laws) seems to me to contain the danger of precisely calling preferences, often even personal preferences, principles.

Of course, good dogmatics (not the one that uses contradictory arguments, that disregards the provisions of the law, etc.), by definition, takes the law very much into account. It is enough to cite the definition of dogmatics offered by *Luzón Peña*:[20] "Criminal law dogmatics is so called because it analyzes statutory criminal law as if it were a 'dogma' [n. 1: "However, as *Muñoz Conde* (1975) states, the expression 'dogma' should not be understood here as the uncritical acceptance of an absolute and unchangeable truth, but only as a postulate that can be used as a starting point, and nothing more, to a certain activity, in this case to the knowledge and applicability of the current law. Dogmatics in this sense does not, therefore, imply 'dogmatism'."] especially because of the due *respect for the principle of criminal legality*, but otherwise in the same way that legal dogmatics generally involves the interpretation, technical elaboration and systematization of statutory law—regardless of its critical evaluation, which corresponds fundamentally to criminal policy, although dogmatic work itself also allows, after the rigorous analysis of a legal regulation, the criticism of defective regulations from a technical point of view. The purpose of criminal law dogmatics is to *determine what rules in accordance with the statutory criminal law*: its mission is thus to identify and determine the content of criminal law. It therefore makes it possible to know and apply the provisions of the criminal law in force in a rigorous and systematic way, thus promoting legal certainty in this field, a function to which some add that of systematizing, stabilizing, and operationalizing the aims and objectives of criminal law (*Hassemer*) or that of reducing—although initially expanding—the complexity of the problems (*Luhmann*, *Hassemer*)."[21]

---

[18] I cannot discuss this idea here, which would require many aspects, but I would like to express that I do not reject the appeal to principles, but I notice that some references to them together with the idea of weighting hide personal preferences, far removed from the law and the Constitution itself.

[19] Cuerda Arnau (2017), pp. 486 et seq.

[20] Luzón Peña (2016), Cap. 3 paragraph 2 (p. 29).

[21] I personally wrote many years ago: "(. . .) the evaluations that I believe to be most important are those that can be extracted from the law, trying to make them compatible with those that seem more correct from the point of view of material justice, of political-criminal needs, but always within the maximum limit of the letter of the law itself, of the principle of legality" [Díaz y García Conlledo (1991), p. 35].

Or, as *Roxin*[22] states, "Criminal-law dogmatics is the discipline that deals with the interpretation, systematization, elaboration and development of the *legal provisions* and opinions of scientific doctrine in the field of criminal law... By its reference to *current law* and by its methods it differs from the history of criminal law and comparative criminal law, but also from criminal policy..."[23] Its high elaboration occurs "especially in its main field, precisely in the theory of the punishable offense, also called the general theory of offense, because through the abstraction of the concrete offenses of the Special Part it covers the general assumptions of the punishable action" and, regarding the formation and evolution of a system: "Thus, criminal law dogmatics is not content with jointly expounding and successively treating its dogmatic propositions, but attempts to structure the totality of the knowledge that makes up the theory of offense into an 'ordered whole' and thereby simultaneously make visible the internal connection of the specific dogmas".

It is true that criminal-law dogmatics, the theory of offense and its systematization, transcend a specific statutory law (hence the possibility of universalizing its categories to a large extent), but they are limited by the statutory law to which they are applied in each country.[24]

A full confidence in the theory of offense and dogmatics for the equal, predictable and reasoned solution of all cases would be a vain illusion, since there are discussions and, obviously, some of the proposed solutions will be wrong, sometimes even the majority and even the unanimous ones (as shown in the history of criminal thought), but, even in this way, it contributes to legal certainty: we will know what we are talking about and what we must abide by and, furthermore, we will even know what to counter-argue and what to criticize. This becomes more complicated if intuitive solutions are made in each case. Dogmatics is not a panacea, of course, but in another (not so distant) context, as the American author Geertz states: "I have never been impressed by the argument that, as complete objectivity is impossible in these matters (as, of course, it is), one might as well let one's sentiments run loose. As Robert Solow has remarked, that is like saying that as a perfectly aseptic environment is impossible, one might as well conduct surgery in a sewer".[25]

As a dogmatist, it is well known that I adopt (nuances aside, which are not possible here), in the matter and in the theory of offense, the Roxinian position. The particularity of *Roxin's* approach (which he himself calls rational-final or, in the terminology that has been most successful, teleological -functional-)[26] does not need to be explained here, as it is well known: from a focus on the political-criminal bases of the theory of the sentencing purposes, the political-criminal preventive

[22] Roxin (2006), § 7 paragraphs. 1, 3 (pp. 194, 195) [1997, § 7 paragraphs. 1, 2 (pp. 192, 193)]; Roxin and Greco (2020), § 7 paragraphs. 1, 3 (pp. 288, 289).

[23] Emphasis added.

[24] Very clearly and with multiple references, by many, Silva Sánchez (2004), especially pp. 680 et seq.

[25] Geertz (1973), p. 30 [(2003), p. 39].

[26] Stated by him in its general lines almost half a century ago: Roxin (1973).

considerations must guide all the elements of the theory of offense, without the system being able to prevail over the purposes, but rather being guided by them. All of this to safeguard legal assets.

It is possible that this "intrusion" of criminal policy[27] into the theory of offense and dogmatics breaks somewhat the "perfect" structure of offense. However, in my opinion, *Roxin* provides a breakthrough (beyond the discussion of the details regarding the actual purpose of each category and the like): the systematic and dogmatic structure cannot be a mere aseptic interpretation of the law (otherwise impossible) or just an exercise in internal coherence, a sort of "art for art's sake," thus correcting the defects of an excessively abstract dogmatics, detached from the concrete problems and purposes of criminal law. It may lose in purity, but it gains more realism and closeness to real life, more flexibility.

Therefore, the fact that dogmatics cannot operate independently of other sciences, techniques or, to use a more neutral word, knowledge (legal and non-legal), seems to me to be indisputable.[28] But, even more, that the evaluations (rationally founded and subordinated to the law) are not alien to it, it also seems to me, insofar as it works in a certain system, not in any ideal one, which is ruled by certain purposes, to which it aspires. Thus, the theory of offense would combine a teleological and a categorical aspect. The dogmatic approach can and should also consider the particularities of the social context in which it is developed,[29] without this preventing the universalization of its structures and systematization.[30]

---

[27] It is not possible here, unfortunately, to expose and reply to the relevant critical remarks of a specialist such as Díez Ripollés (2021), *passim*, on Roxin's way of understanding criminal policy (for him incorrect), whose influence would have had negative consequences for true criminal policy. It is enough to say here, provisionally and as far as this paper is concerned, that even if the German author were to extend, as Díez Ripollés argues, incorrectly the term criminal policy to all evaluation content used in criminal law, this would not contradict the idea that I hold in the text that dogmatic construction does not need to be "pure" and ignore evaluations. We cannot either evaluate here the important reflections that the mentioned author makes in the aforementioned work, pp. 14 et seq., under the heading "The fagocitate (or absorption) of criminal policy by the dogmatics of liability," which aims to demonstrate the dogmatic excesses (including "going beyond the legal interpretation" or "highlighting a criminal law in force according to a certain concession of society not necessarily coinciding with that of the legislator"), but, I understand, he does not discuss the need for it (in its, for him, fair terms) either.

[28] Interesting and with very extensive subsequent references are the recent considerations regarding the "encounters and misunderstandings" of criminal dogmatics and legal sociology offered by Gómez Martín (2019), pp. 165 et seq. Also, recently Miró Llinares (2020), pp. 279 et seq., avoiding the "old and unfruitful debate on the scientific nature of criminal-law dogmatics" (pp. 279 et seq.), extensively argues the need to open criminal law and dogmatics to other fields of knowledge and the risks of "isolationism."

[29] See only, for example, the considerations in this regard of Latin American criminal lawyers such as Sotomayor Acosta (2008), pp. 148 et seq., 164; Zaffaroni (2017), pp. 245 et seq.; Arias Holguín (2018), pp. 49 et seq.; Moreno Hernández (2018), pp. 82 et seq., 371 et seq., 392 et seq., entre otras; (2020), pp. 311 et seq.

[30] In the sense stated, for example, by Silva Sánchez (2004), pp. 679 et seq. It is not possible to explain or discuss here, however, the relationship of "universalization" with the criminal-law categories regarding the importance of the *a priori* categories that would shape criminal-law

In this way, I distance myself from an absolutely pure or uncontaminated dogmatics and theory of offense, in which only the abstraction of elements common to the norm is considered, with a refined objectivity.

In addition, respect for fundamental rights is undoubtedly above dogmatic considerations (and other methodological approaches), but it is not clear why a correct dogmatic approach should disregard them.[31] Rather, it reinforces them with its claim to legal certainty, equality and containment of the punitive power of the state.[32] It is true that there has been dogmatics in undemocratic systems and times,[33] but it has surely contributed to limit the excesses and insecurities of those systems (even if only minimally and without being able to defeat them). And it could also be argued as a counterexample that the moments in which the distance between dogmatics and the theory of offense has been greatest have been the least democratic (think of the defense on criminal offender types based on criminal law -*Täterstrafrecht*-).[34]

4 Solution-Oriented Approach to Practical Problems

It is important, however, not to forget that the theory of offense should not be a set of brilliant and useless structures that come out of nowhere, nor to forget the focus on the solution (as far as possible, predictable and well-founded) of concrete problems. Just a few examples, among many that could be given:

Discussions concerning error on prohibition (mistake of law, in a les correct terminology),[35] its distinction from that of the mistake of fact, its object, its avoid

---

knowledge (different from those of other branches of law, which would work in the same way in their field), categories that would not operate based on the positive norm, as García Amado (2020), particularly explains pp. 156 et seq.

[31] See regarding the importance of fundamental rights and their relationship with dogmatics, warning of certain "postmodern" risks, recently, Moccia (2020), pp. 289 et seq. In a critical work on different aspects of dogmatics (or its approach to certain problems), Parma (2020) arrives at a conclusion that is (to a large extent) comparable and that points to the importance of human rights [even for a "good" non-hermetic dogmatist, of course! Criminal law must move away from the arcane labyrinths of scholars, avoid the excessive pseudo-university artillery, the promiscuity of populist policies and renounce the media oracles that condemn without trial. It must offer solutions, hold on to the humanization of conflict, aspire to freedom equalizations" (p. 333)].

[32] It is enough to recall, among others, the reflections of Schünemann in his work referred to *above* at the end of n. 10.

[33] And it is very true that dogmatists, hiding behind the shield of their "science," of its "purity" or forgetting central aspects of it (contradicting themselves), have come to do much worse things than not criticizing non-democratic regimes. See only, with further references, the recent reflections of García Amado (2020), especially pp. 158 et seq.

[34] He critically warns about the conditions under which the theory of offense (remember: the most refined product of dogmatics) "could be linked in the same way to a conservative, progressive, liberal, social, fascist or communist system" Figueiredo Dias (2019), p. 155.

[35] Which also refers Greco (2008), pp. 180 et seq.

ability, etc. are not purely theoretical and classificatory structures, nor are they a mere gloss on what the legal precepts say about mistake, but respond to the need to determine, within the framework of the law (or advocating its change, if necessary), how much knowledge about the facts and the law (of the prohibition) can be demanded of an individual in today's society, or, more specifically, whether the person who doubts whether what he or she is going to do is prohibited or whether he or she cannot rely on what a lawyer tells him or her, or whether it is sufficient for him or her to investigate it on his/her own or whether he/she should seek the advice of more than one expert to ensure his/her lack of criminal liability (because his/her error of prohibition is invincible).[36] Almost no law or legal wording solves this for us without further explanation.[37] A dogmatic elaboration is necessary, without forgetting the corresponding considerations focused on problems and goals.

The law (certainly not the Spanish law) does not provide us with a solution either, to mention another example, as to how we should distinguish between possible intent or knowledge (dolus eventualis) and conscious recklesness or negligence.[38] And nevertheless, it is essential to establish it with the arsenal of dogmatics (without escaping from evaluative considerations, as I have been arguing[39]): it is a matter of deciding (and allow me in this case the caricatures) whether the person who, aware that the high speed with which he/she is driving implies a high possibility of running over the pedestrian he/she perceives a few meters away, continues driving and finally runs over him/her causing death acts with dolus eventualis (and has to receive the penalty of the intentional crime) (theory of probability) or whether he/she does not act with dolus eventualis anymore, but only with conscious recklessness, if he/she trusts that the pedestrian has the physical capacities of a high-level athlete and will manage to jump out of the car's reach or, even more, that an angel will lift him/her by his/ her armpits when he/she reaches his/her height and thus will not run over him/her (more or less broad versions of the theory of consent or acceptance) or trusts that, considering that his/her car is a high-end car and he/she is a formula one racer, he/she has enough chances to avoid the pedestrian (limited or restricted theory of consent or acceptance).[40]

[36] An example (among many possible ones by other authors) of my dogmatic treatment of these issues is given in Díaz y García Conlledo (1999), pp. 335 et seq.

[37] It is not possible to develop here the evident connection of this with the impossibility of automatic subsumption in the law by judges, today widely recognized. I will refer, just as a recent example, to the interesting work of Sánchez-Ostiz Gutiérrez (2019), pp. 325 et seq., warning, however, that I do not necessarily agree with all of his proposals (pp. 336 et seq.).

[38] In fact, our Penal Code (unlike others) does not even contain a definition of willful intent (and its classes) and recklessness (and I believe, by the way, that it does well).

[39] Among them, of course and inexcusably, those that derive from the positive law itself, such as the fact that, in this case, intentional homicide (even with dolus eventualis) is punished much more harshly than reckless or negligent homicide.

[40] Again, as a mere example of dogmatic treatment, this time not mine, of this issue: Luzón Peña (2016), Cap. 16 paragraphs. 54 et seq. (pp. 234 et seq.).

Or, as a final example, the dogmatics of participation will have to offer (in accordance with the guidelines it must respect and to which I have already referred) criteria to decide what it means to cooperate "to its [that is of the act] execution with an act without which it would not have been carried out", since this is far from being evident with the mere linguistic proposition of Art. 28, second paragraph, b) CP, which is of great practical importance, since the necessary cooperator is sentenced to the same penalty as the perpetrator, as opposed to the one reduced by one degree for the accomplice or non-necessary cooperator of Art. 29 CP. The law does not instruct the applicator whether, in this decision, he/she must adopt an abstract or concrete vision of necessity, whether there are auxiliary criteria to carry out a judgment that seems hypothetical, whether they must be exclusively objective or whether subjective elements may be introduced or even exclusively used, etc.[41] In practice, we cannot avoid deciding whether a person is a necessary cooperator or a simple accomplice (or, in some cases and according to some criteria, a co-perpetrator) who gives lock picks to a thief to enter a house under certain circumstances, or who watches for the police to come while others beat up a person, or who drives the perpetrator(s) to the crime scene, or who by his or her silent presence encourages (if he or she does so) the perpetrators of a rape during their act, or who lends his or her computer to an expert to carry out a computer scam, etc. It cannot simply rely on the letter of the law and should not be decided based on (subjective) intuitions on a case-by-case basis.

5 Dogmatics and Jurisprudence of Judges and Courts

Cuerda Arnau says that we must ask ourselves whether we have not turned the scenario into a marketplace of opinions, abandoning the context of use in which the words of the law make sense. This would produce a changing and unpredictable jurisprudence.[42]

Once again, I believe that this author's criticism is due to the existence of "bad" dogmatics, in other words, dogmatics that disregards the essential presuppositions of correct dogmatics. Not just any proposed solution has the characteristics of an admissible (although not the only) dogmatic solution. Thus, a solution that dispenses from dogmatics cannot truly be called that which dispenses with the law or that which implies an internal contradiction. Precisely from a correct dogmatic exercise we will be able to reject solutions that are incompatible with it and we will contribute to predictability. An argument with solid dogmatic backing is much more acceptable

[41] A new example of our own treatment can be found in Díaz y García Conlledo (2002), especially pp. 656 et seq.

[42] Cuerda Arnau (2017), p. 489. In the following, I do not dispute this author's assertion that case law is in fact becoming less and less predictable, but that this is due to (correct) dogmatics.

and, more importantly, controllable, than a decisionism that hides its reasons or surrounds them in "principles" that often have little connection with the law.

The problems of the focus on dogmatics by the courts are diverse and many were already highlighted by *Schünemann* in his polemic of some years ago with *Fischer*, which it is not possible to mention here.[43] *Schünemann* himself acknowledges in any case real difficulties of the courts to adequately access the contents of good dogmatics and apply them in their decisions, especially the number of cases that judges and courts must resolve.[44] If this is the case in Germany, the problem is amplified in Spain,[45] not to mention other countries, where the problem is much greater. In any case, (good) dogmatics is very positive for judges and courts and, thus, for citizens.[46]

But, as I must almost conclude, I would like to mention here a frequent misuse of "theories" by courts in different countries (probably less in Germany). Case law sometimes takes advantage, in an unacceptable manner, of "theories" or their authors (especially if they are very important) by using them as slogans or arguments of authority empty of content. This happens openly when, for example, the resolution is based on incompatible or even contradictory theories. Or, to give a couple of examples regarding a topic on which I have worked a lot, when the *Roxin's* thesis is used to support the perpetration-by-means of the leaders of an organized power system, but it is not proven or explained that the requirements for it are met (existence of a criminal apparatus, its management, fungibility of the perpetrators and their proclivity to commit the act).[47] But, also in my own country (and in others), when there is a need to affirm the co-perpetration of several subjects in an offense and it is often argued based on the idea of functional control of the act (which is correctly handled in other judgments), also by *Roxin*, without stating that there is a common decision to the act with sharing of tasks or accumulation of efforts, the importance of the contribution of each subject and the provision of the behavior in the executive phase[48] (often lacking some of them), thus concealing a decision that, at best, is based (veiled) on the old Spanish case law structure of prior agreement[49] or is taken intuitively (and, therefore, difficult to control). And it should be noted that I have given two examples in which I do not agree with the proposals of my German teacher.[50]

---

[43] Schünemann (2011), pp. 445 et seq.

[44] Schünemann (2011), p. 460.

[45] See Pantaleón Díaz (2018), p. 105. Different data on judicial statistics (not only criminal) can be obtained in "Justicia Dato a Dato," an annual publication offered by the General Council of the Judiciary: https://www.poderjudicial.es/cgpj/es/Temas/Estadistica-Judicial/Estudios-e-Informes/Justicia-Dato-a-Dato/. The latest available (2019), contains multiple statistical data, but it is sufficient to refer, for the criminal jurisdiction, to the indicators summary on p. 116.

[46] Illustrative, even in his title, and from the hand of a sadly famous case in Spain, the work of Pantaleón Díaz (2018), pp. 103 et seq.

[47] Roxin (2015), pp. 242 et seq., 736 et seq.

[48] Roxin (2015), pp. 275 et seq.

[49] Regarding it, with further references, Díaz y García Conlledo (1991), pp. 349 et seq.

[50] See Díaz y García Conlledo (2017), pp. 518 et seq., (2011), 274 et seq.

An author as critical of dogmatics as *Cuerda Arnau* denounces this same way of proceeding with absolute clarity,[51] which makes me think that we agree on many things and that her criticisms are not really directed or should not be directed at correctly developed dogmatics, but at "bad" dogmatics.

6 Conclusion

In short, and as many others before me have stated, criminal-law dogmatics and the theory of offense are, when properly developed, limits, by no means the only ones, to the punitive power of the state in the broad sense, especially of judges (although not only, also of the legislator), not eliminating the impossible to delete degree of discretion in their decisions, but limiting it, giving coherent and refutable arguments, not allowing the margin of discretion to become arbitrariness that is impossible to control. These are not absolute limits, but they are important insofar as they attempt to eradicate arbitrariness and *ad hoc* solutions. That is why it is better to defend dogmatics and strive to improve it.

References

Alexy R (1991) Theorie der juristischen Argumentation. Die Theorie des rationalen Diskurses als Theorie der juristischen Begründung, Nachwort. Antwort auf einige Kritiker, Suhrkamp, Frankfurt am Main [(1997) Teoría de la argumentación jurídica. La teoría del discurso racional como teoría de la fundamentación jurídica, trad. Atienza M/Espejo I, Centro de Estudios Constitucionales, Madrid]

Ambos K (2016) Zur Zukunft der deutschen Strafrechtwissenschaft: Offenheit und und diskursive Methodik statt selbsbewusster Provinzialität. GA, pp 177–194

Arias Holguín DP (2018) Contexto, interdisciplinariedad y dogmática penal en EH-Terradillos. Tirant lo Blanch, Valencia, pp 49–62

Atienza M (2015) La dogmática jurídica como tecno-praxis, en EH-Carpizo T. IV vol 1 Estado Constitucional, Universidad Nacional Autónoma de México. Instituto de Investigaciones Jurídicas, pp 169–196

Consejo General del Poder Judicial (2019) La Justicia Dato a Dato. Año 2019. Estadística Judicial, 2019 (https://www.poderjudicial.es/stfls/ESTADISTICA/FICHEROS/JusticaDatoaDato/Datos%20Anteriores/Justicia%20Dato%20a%20Dato%202019.pdf) (diversos años en https://www.poderjudicial.es/cgpj/es/Temas/Estadistica-Judicial/Estudios-e-Informes/Justicia-Dato-a-Dato/)

Cuerda Arnau ML (2017) La función de la dogmática (Una crítica desde la concepción significativa de la acción), en EH-Mir, B de F, Montevideo/Buenos Aires, pp 485–495

Cuerda Arnau ML (2019) La concepción significativa de la acción v. las pretensiones sistemáticas, en Vives Antón, T S (Cuerda Arnau M L, compiladora) Pensar la libertad. Últimas reflexiones sobre el Derecho y la Justicia, Tirant lo Blanch, Valencia, pp 11–46

Demetrio Crespo E (2010) Crítica al normativismo funcionalista. RDPCrim, 3ª época, 3, pp 13–26

Díaz y García Conlledo M (1991) La autoría en Derecho penal. PPU, Barcelona

[51] Cuerda Arnau (2019), p. 16.

Díaz y García Conlledo M (1999) El error de prohibición: pasado, presente y futuro, en LH-Torío, Comares, Granada, 1999, pp 335–368
Díaz y García Conlledo M (2002) ¿Es necesaria la cooperación necesaria?, en LH-Cerezo, Comares, Granada, 2002, pp 645–669
Díaz y García Conlledo M (2011) Der Einfluss der Roxinschen Taterschaftstheorie (insbesondere bretreffend die Mittateschaft) auf die spanische Rechtslehre und Rechtsprechung: kritische Betrachtungen. GA, pp 259–283 [(2011) La influencia de la teoría de la autoría (en especial de la coautoría) de Roxin en la doctrina y la jurisprudencia españolas. Consideraciones críticas. NFP (Colombia) 76, pp 15–48]
Díaz y García Conlledo M (2017) Actuación en el marco de un aparato organizado de poder: ¿autoría o participación?, en EH-Mir, pp 509–521 [(2017) Das Handeln im Rahmen eines organisatorischen Machtapparates: Täterschaft oder Teilnahme? GA, pp 711–719)
Díez Ripollés JL (2021) La política criminal en las ciencias penales: un análisis crítico de la contribución de Roxin. Revista Electrónica de Ciencia Penal y Criminología (RECPC) 23-02: 1–32
Figueiredo Dias J (2019) Sobre la crisis del paradigma penal, en LH-Jorge vol 1, Universidad Autónoma de Madrid. Servicio de Publicaciones, Madrid, pp 147–163
García Amado JA (2020) Neokantismo y derecho penal. Sobre el papel y el sentido de la dogmática penal y sobre el papel de los penalistas, en LH-Luzón vol I, Reus, Madrid, pp 153–166
Geertz C (1973) The interpretation of cultures. Selected essays. Basic Books, New York, 1973 [(2003) La interpretación de las culturas, trad. Bixio A L, 12ª reimpr., Gedisa, Barcelona]
Gimbernat Ordeig E (1970) Hat die Strafrechtsdogmatik eine Zukunft? ZStW 28:379–410 [(1990) ¿Tiene un futuro la dogmática jurídico-penal?, en: Estudios de Derecho Penal, 3ª ed., 1990, pp 140–161]
Gómez Martín V (2019) Dogmática penal y Sociología jurídica: encuentros y desencuentros, en LH-Jorge Barreiro vol 1, Universidad Autónoma de Madrid. Servicio de Publicaciones, Madrid, pp 165–180 [(2018) Diritto Penale Contemporaneo 2/2018: pp 149–161]
González Cussac JL (coord.) (2019) Lenguaje y dogmática penal. Actas del II Congreso Ibero-Americano de Derecho Penal y Filosofía del Lenguaje, Tiranto lo Blanch, Valencia
Greco L (2008) Dos formas de hacer dogmática jurídico-penal. Revista Discusiones 8:177–181
Kindhäuser U (2009) Die deutsche Strafrechtsdogmatik zwischen Anpassung und Selbstbehauptung. Grenzkontrolle der Kriminalpolitik durch die Dogmatik? ZStW 121:954–964
Kirchmann JH (1848) Die Werthlosigkeit der Jurisprudenz als Wissenschaft. Ein Vortrag gehalten in der juristischen Gesellschaft zu Berlin, Julius Springer, Berlin [(1961) La jurisprudencia no es ciencia, trad. y escrito preliminar de Truyol y Serra A, 2ª ed. con una nota adicional, Instituto de Estudios Políticos (Colección Civitas), Madrid –reimpr. 1963- (existen otras ediciones)]
Luzón Peña D-M (2016) Lecciones de Derecho Penal. Parte General, 3ª ed., Tirant lo Blanch, Valencia
Martínez-Buján Pérez C (2019) La autoría en Derecho penal. Un estudio a la luz de la concepción significativa de la acción. Tirant lo Blanch, Valencia
Miró Llinares F (2020) Cientismo, dogmatismo y Derecho penal, en LH-Luzón, vol I. Reus, Madrid, pp 279–288
Moccia S (2020) El rol de la dogmática penal ante la transformación de la política criminal, en LH-Luzón, vol I. Reus, Madrid, pp 289–300
Moreno Hernández M (2018) Dogmática Penal y Política Criminal. Ibáñez/Ubijus, México
Moreno Hernández M (2020) Hacia una dogmática penal latinoamericana más acorde a sus realidades, en LH-Luzón, vol I. Reus, Madrid, pp 311–326
Nino CS (1980) Los límites de la responsabilidad penal. Una teoría liberal del delito, Astrea, Buenos Aires
Nino CS (1984) Consideraciones sobre la dogmática jurídica (con referencia particular a la dogmática penal), Universidad Nacional Autónoma de México, México (1ª reimpr. 1989)

Pantaleón Díaz M (2018) La utilidad de una buena dogmática para una buena jurisprudencia (y viceversa). El ejemplo de la sentencia de la Sala Segunda del Tribunal Supremo 805/2017, de 11 de diciembre (caso «Madrid Arena»), en: Libertas 7:103–120

Parma C (2020) En busca del futuro del Derecho penal, en LH-Luzón, vol I. Reus, Madrid, pp 327–333

Roxin C (1973) Kriminalpolitik und Strafrechtssystem, 2. Aufl. (1., 1970), Walter de Gruyter, Berlin/New York [(1972) Política criminal y sistema del Derecho penal, trad. e introducción de Muñoz Conde F, Bosch, Barcelona]

Roxin C (2006) Strafrecht Allgemeiner Teil. Band I: Grundlagen. Der Aufbau der Verbrechenslehre, 4. Aufl., C. H. Beck, München [(1997) Derecho Penal. Parte General. Tomo I: Fundamentos. La estructura de la teoría del delito, trad. de la 2ª ed. alemana por Luzón Peña D-M/Díaz y García Conlledo M/de Vicente Remesal J, Civitas, Madrid]

Roxin C (2015) Täterschaft und Tatherrschaft, 9. Aufl., Water De Gruyter, Berlin/Boston [Autoría y dominio del hecho en Derecho penal, trad. de Cuello Contreras J/Serrano González de Murillo J L, Marcial Pons, Madrid]

Roxin C, Greco L (2020) Strafrecht Allgemeiner Teil. Band I: Grundlagen. Der Aufbau der Verbrechenslehre, 5. Aufl., C. H. Beck, München, 2020

Sánchez-Ostiz Gutiérrez P (2019) El mito de la mecánica aplicación judicial de la ley, en LH-Jorge vol 1, pp 325–338

Schünemann (2011) Was heiβt und zu welchem Ende betreibt man Strafrechtsdogmatik? Zu Fischer's These der "fremden seltsamen Welten" anhand aktueller BGH-Urteile zu Begriff und Funktion der "besonderen persönlichen Merkmale" im Strafrecht. GA, pp 445–461

Schünemann (2016) Über Strafrecht im demokratischen Rechtsstaat, das unverzichtbare Rationalitätsniveau seiner Dogmatik und die vorgeblich progressive Rückschrittspropaganda. ZIS, pp 654–671 (http://www.zis-online.com/dat/artikel/2016_10_1051.pdf) [(2019) El Derecho penal en el Estado democrático de Derecho y el irrenunciable nivel de racionalidad de su dogmática, trad. de Roso Cañadillas R/Pérez-Sauquillo Muñoz C, Reus/B de F, Madrid/Buenos Aires/Montevideo]

Silva Sánchez JM (2004) Straftatsystematik deutscher Prägung: Unzeitgemaβ? GA 2004, pp 679–690

Sotomayor Acosta JO (2008) ¿El Derecho penal garantista en retirada? RP 21:148–164

Vives Antón TS (2011) Fundamentos del Sistema Penal, 2ª ed., Acción Significativa y Derechos Constitucionales, Tirant lo Blanch, Valencia

Vives Antón TS (2017) Reivindicación del pensamiento de un fiscal prusiano, en: EH-Mir, B de F, Montevideo/Buenos Aires, pp 233–242

Vogel J (2012) Strafrecht und Strafrechtswissenschaft im internationalen und europäischen Rechtsraum. JZ 67:25–31

Zaffaroni ER (2017) ¿Hacia dónde irá la ciencia jurídico-penal?, en: EH-Mir, B de F, Montevideo/Buenos Aires, pp 243–250

The Populist Traces of Punitive Feminism

Alfonso García Figueroa

Abstract Worldwide, populism is transforming democracy and reinforcing the so-called "punitive turn" of criminal law. This is part of a three-pronged strategy that populist politicians perform as soon as they assume power: colonization of state structures, mass clientelism, and discriminatory legalism. The latter assumes the Schmittian split of the *demos* into friends (i.e., the *genuine* "people") and enemies. Now, the discrimination criterion to legislate has developed according to the very evolution of the class struggle and the ways to identify "friends" and "enemies": classical Marxist *"economicism"* (capitalists vs. proletarians), populist *metaclassism* (*"ordinary people" vs. "the elite"*) and current *hyperclassism* (which assigns to one and only one class or group, namely women, the leading role to unite the whole "people"). In terms of criminal law, punitive feminism is the consistent consequence of the influence of the class struggle evolution of punitive populism.

1 Introduction: "Counter-Enlightenment" and "Criminal Involution"

An "unstoppable evolution of punitive populism" (Demetrio Crespo 2020, p. 174) is recognizable in four worrying aspects of the current criminal law (id., pp. 38 ff., 195): the advancement of punishability (i.e., crimes are punished at an earlier stage), the adoption of a forward-looking perspective (e.g., crimes of danger), the increase

This work is part of the research project CRESTA, *Crisis del Derecho Penal del Estado de Derecho: Manifestaciones y Tendencias*, funded by the Junta de Comunidades de Castilla-La Mancha (SBPLY/17/180501/000223DER https://proyectocrestauclm.wixsite.com/proyectocresta). I am grateful to the two anonymous reviewers for their advice to improve this work and to Ms. Bridgith McQue for her advice on the use of English.

A. García Figueroa (✉)
Faculty of Legal and Social Sciences, University of Castilla-La Mancha, Toledo, Spain
e-mail: alfonsoj.gfigueroa@uclm.es

E. Demetrio Crespo et al. (eds.), *Crisis of the Criminal Law in the Democratic Constitutional State*, Legal Studies in International, European and Comparative Criminal Law 6, https://doi.org/10.1007/978-3-031-13413-5_6

of penalties, and the suppression of certain procedural guarantees (id., p. 17). Such a "punitive turn" is usually considered as a "modernization," despite the fact that it paradoxically brings us back to a pre-modern criminal law. From this standpoint, the evolution of the current criminal legislation (id., pp. 20 ff.) describes more of an "involution" (id., p. 15), which leads us to an "untenable situation." Famously, Günther Jakobs' "enemy criminal law" doctrine (*Feindstrafrecht*) tends to justify this involution. In political terms, the punitive turn seems to satisfy a conservative ideology rooted in the value of security.

However, nowadays the punitive turn surprisingly has been vindicated by left-wing thinkers and progressive political parties. Now, how is it possible that even a certain left-wing legal culture, which is often claimed to be the legitimate heir of the Enlightenment, has moved from prison abolition to the maximum expansion of criminal law? How is it possible that the same left-wing politicians and thinkers, who in the past had claimed prison abolition, today vindicate the punitive turn? My following reflections stem from this intriguing contradiction, which confronts left-wing legal culture within a broader context: "the reactionary drift of the left" (Ovejero 2018).

The most elementary explanation for this (so to speak) *antinomy of the penal involution* (from prison abolition to punitivism) could be a sign of the times. After all, punitive inflation seems a prudential response to the oxymoronic state of *permanent exceptionality*, caused by global terror, particularly since September 11, 2001 (hereafter 9/11). Indeed, such a punitive turn apparently is the nostalgic response to the yearning for security, which certain authoritarian, autarkic and anti-liberal (or "illiberal") policies are quick to satisfy at the cost of the restriction of individual rights and guarantees. However, verifying these growing reactionary appetites caused by global terror is not enough to explain the antinomy of the involution. One enigma persists even under this scenario: how is it possible that such a reactionary logic has been invoked for progressive and modernizing purposes alike, especially by self-proclaimed left thinkers and politicians?

Very probably, such a punitive turn is an "echo of the prison abolition movement, which vindicates giving conflicts back to their protagonists" (Demetrio Crespo 2020, pp. 30 ff.). In other words, by focusing on victims, such "victimology" has led to a victim-centered criminology. Specifically the so-called "*victidogmática*" (Demetrio Crespo 2020, p. 29) fosters the punitive turn, because "giving back" such criminal conflicts to their "protagonists" entails an extreme dilemma: either the abolitionist alternative, that dispenses with criminal law—which is unnecessary where bargaining among victims and perpetrators takes place (Demetrio Crespo 2020, pp. 31 ff., footnote 69)—or the populist approach, that appeases the vengeance instincts of such victims by means of the expansion of criminal law, even at the expense of the offender's rights and safeguards. Obviously, this second alternative leaves aside the general and special prevention aims of criminal law with the excuse of democracy (a "street democracy," a "twitter democracy," a "digital democracy"). No wonder that much of our perplexities stem from this populist transformation of democracy, as we will see later.

Furthermore, both strategies, namely, prison abolition and populist punitivism, result in a state receding, for both strategies lower the *institutionalization* of *"the political"* and somehow take us back to the state of nature, insofar as the state comes to give up its functions. Namely, the prison abolition movement rules out State Criminal Law, where general and special prevention require that; but so does punitive populism when it prompts the state to exercise its *jus puniendi* to satisfy the worst retributionist instincts of the citizens. After all, populism typically tends to *"disintermediate"* the state, to *de-institutionalize it;* that is, to advocate the boundless "direct representation" of the people by their representatives. As the assault at the Capitol in Washington D.C. on January 6, 2021 shows, such a delegation to the "people" is all the more dangerous, the emptier and more biased when the very concept of the *people* is in use among the populist theorists themselves.

To sum up, given that the current punitivism stems from the crisis of Modernity—"counter-enlightenment," as Dahrendorf puts it (2009, p. 210)—we may conclude that this *"punitive turn"* also leads us to a new perplexity: with the apparently enlightened purpose of saving us from the uncertainties of the state of nature in a context of global terror, this punitive turn resorts to anti-enlightenment and pre-modern instruments that plunge us into the barbarism it apparently intends to avoid. Obviously, we cannot aspire to the benefits of Modernity by neglecting the principles on which it was built and for this reason, as Eduardo Demetrio puts it, "the 'discourse of guarantees' is not a kind of luxury that can be renounced in times of crisis, and even less so a conservative thesis" (Demetrio Crespo 2020, p. 57). In other words, only our fidelity to classical liberal principles will allow us *all* to benefit from their best results. However, it is precisely such universality (that *"all")* that populism undermines by splitting every society into two categories: the true people and their enemies, i.e., first-class citizens and second-class citizens.

Once the involution of the criminal law theory is explained based on the rise of the victim-centered paradigm, it is possible to ask why the legal culture as a whole has neglected the abolitionist path—or, at least, the path of Ferrajoli's "garantismo penale"—and has taken the second—the dark path of punitive expansion. After all, the latter has fostered decisions that were simply unjustifiable (see, e.g., García Amado 2020; Lloria et al. 2019; Lascuraín 2019), often in violation of essential principles of our legal-political culture, such as the presumption of innocence, the *ultima ratio principle,* the rejection of the offender-based criminal law (*Täterstrafrecht*) and, in short, the great background of the Enlightenment (see, e.g., Prieto 2011). The examination of the "untenable situation" that criminal law is going through today leads us naturally to investigate such causes beyond the confines of criminal law theory and invites us to reflect on the transformations of our legal-political culture in the midst of the rise of populism.

Keeping these ideas in mind, I would like to deal with the legal-political background of the antinomy of involution as follows: first, I will refer to the general conditions of punitive populism, as a result of a global geopolitical context marked by insecurity, and then I will deal with the legal-political phenomenon of populism as a companion to this punitive turn. Finally, I will draw my conclusions by applying the results of my reflection to the significant continuity between punitive populism and punitive feminism. I will argue that this reveals the *hyperclassistic* phase into which populism has entered.

2 A Dichotomous Rhetoric in a World of Friends and Enemies

On 9/11, global terror plunged our "*liquid Modernity*" (Bauman 2007, 2010) into a new normal. *Out of the blue* (Bernstein et al. 2002) a growing feeling of insecurity and vulnerability took hold. Individuals had never been more aware of their rights and dignity and more aware of their own fragility and vulnerability (Bauman 2007, p. 85). Thus, this prompted a redefinition of the state's mission. Indeed, welfare policies declined in favor of security policies. As a result, citizens demanded increasing protection against a lurking enemy that is sometimes invisible, but sometimes merely imagined. Consistently, the welfare state transformed itself into a "preventive state" (Denninger, *apud* Demetrio Crespo 2020, p. 97) and then into a punitive state (Bauman 2007, p. 74).

As we know, the scenario of *permanent exceptionality* has never offered a morally good atmosphere. Unfortunately, exceptionality has often been used as an excuse to put aside our noblest principles, for it plunges us into a substitute for the state of nature, from which it is imperative to flee at any cost. After all, justice is only possible once the civil state has been (re)established. Thomas Hobbes' ideas support this Schmittian argument that tends to sacrifice fundamental principles of justice so as to ensure minimum security and save us from alleged barbarism: "Out of it [state of civil government], there is a Dominion of Passions, war, fear, poverty, slovinlinesse, solitude, barbarism, ignorance, cruelty. In it, the Dominion of reason, peace, security, riches, decency, society, elegancy, sciences, and benevolence," Hobbes stated in *De cive* (1993: 90; X.1 *in fine*). Under these premises, the following question seems rhetorical: how can we reject the measure, whatever its content, keeping us *in* the "dominion of reason" and *out of* the terrible state of nature? Bobbio (1991, p. 237) called this kind of reasoning, which threatens our most elementary moral principles by means of such dilemma, the "dichotomous argument" (i.e., either Leviathan or chaos).

This anthropological pessimism that has instilled in us a feeling of permanent exceptionality is a characteristic feature of the most reactionary policies. After all, if there is no hope of improving the world—and we are living in "the end times," in Slavoj Žižek's words (2011)—then we must cling at any cost to what we still have and keep it, no matter how good or bad it is. Hence progressivism can only thrive under a certain anthropological optimism.[1] So the antinomy of involution can be explained as a compromise with more reactionary thinking, as long as pessimism is

[1] On the psychological continuity of anthropological pessimism with conservatism and of anthropological optimism with progressivism see Kolakowski (1970).

an essential part of our *Zeitgeist.* 9/11 has provided progressives and conservatives alike with a common populist background, a single *concept of the political,* which allows punitivism to settle comfortably across the whole political spectrum.[2]

Indeed, neither right nor left wing has been immune to the reactionary temptations of the "dichotomous argument" and its implications. On the right, the classic liberal principles embodied in individual rights and constitutional guarantees have receded to unbearable restrictions (think of Guantánamo, maintained by the Obama and the Trump administrations, and the xenophobic policies of some countries of Central and Northern Europe). On the left, there is a punitive revival that has been forged in Latin-American populism, finding acceptance in Spain's populist, leftist party, Unidas Podemos. As a result, with the excuse of the insecurity and the *counter-enlightened* complicity of post-modernity every party is tempted by the punitive turn. However, in doing so, conservatives and progressives betray meta-principles superior to both political traditions, namely, the classical liberal principles on which our democracy is based. Therefore, if political power has succumbed to such punitivist temptations, then the cause must be sought in a broader crisis, namely: in the profound transformation of political discourse and democracy itself. Such a transition towards new *political styles* is usually identified in a very general way with the term "populism."

3 Populism, a "Slippery Political Animal"

When discussing populism, it is already commonplace to begin with a clause on the ambiguity of the term (Panizza 2009b, p. 9) and the problems to grasp the concept—"inasibilidad conceptual" (conceptual ungraspability) in Arias Maldonado's words (2019, p. 326). Isaiah Berlin referred to it as the "Cinderella syndrome" of populism, meaning that it is so hard for social scientists to fit populism into real politics, that they remind us of the prince searching for a foot that fits into Cinderella's shoe (*apud* Vallespín and Bascuñán 2017, p. 44). In fact, this "slippery political animal," as Fieschi (*apud* Cossarini 2019, p. 81) called "populism," is so hard to define that conceptual elusiveness seems to be its only indisputable trait.

Nevertheless, the "nodal point" (*point de capiton)* of the populist discourse is the *people,* a notion *which* is no clearer. "People" is an "empty signifier" (Laclau 2004), but for populism this is no drawback, but a perquisite. After all, the *intended* indetermination of the concept's properties (*intension)* allows it to admit within its *extension* practically any content (any configuration of the people, provided it is

[2]There is no need to deal with debates such as the continuity of Carl Schmitt's thought with that of Günther Jakobs' (see Portilla 2007, p. 36 and, against this, Muñoz and Tripolone 2018) or the discussion on the purely descriptive (García Amado 2000, p. 247) or prescriptive (Demetrio Crespo 2020, pp. 66, 89) nature of Jakobs' theory. Interestingly, despite the underlying reactionary logic of Schmitt's ideas, left-wing populist thinkers such as Chantal Mouffe proclaimed themselves "Schmittian against Schmitt".

convenient). From this perspective, the vagueness of "people" is at once *intensional, extensional*, and *intentional.* This is not surprising. In our societies the democratic demands of the various groups that make up the (*genuine*) *people* are so pluralistic (gender, race, poverty, immigration, etc.), that their reunion under *one* people *is* possible, if and only if the very concept of people is flexible enough to encompass them all. This explains the need for a certain *souplesse* in the concept of the *people,* that "absent fullness," as Ernesto Laclau puts it.

The flexibility (or emptiness) of "people" allows the striking versatility of the populist discourse. This can be not only revolutionary and subversive, but also opportunistic and pragmatic, when necessary. At this point, it is worth recalling the distinction made by F. Panizza (*apud* Arditi 2009, p. 108) between "populism in the streets," which is practiced *on the way to power*—e.g., Pablo Iglesia's "assault to Heaven" from Madrid working-class districts, such as Vallecas and Carabanchel [3]—and pragmatist "populism *in power*"—e.g., Pablo Iglesia's *Heaven* at his Moncloa Palace Vice-presidency. In this aspect, populism is essentially different from other movements such as communism or fascism. Populism seems to undermine the state structures, but it never does so completely. A substantial difference between populism and fascism is revealed here (see Eatwell and Goodwin 2018, pp. 50 ff. for national populism), since populism does not intend to destroy the democratic rule of law. Rather, it seeks, as we shall see, to *disfigure* or parasitize *it* and every parasite needs its *living* host to take advantage of it. Despite the "anti-system" manners of populism on street demonstrations, its anarchism is deceptive and merely cosmetic.

Some say populism is a pathology of our democracy. Others instead say that it is the therapy for our decaying democracy. But populism rather looks like the sign of the transformation of democracy itself, in the quest for new channels of development. In fact, the historical approach provides us with a somewhat less dramatic account, which should not obscure our criticism of populism when it threatens fundamental rights and guarantees. Multiple attitudes towards populism are possible here.

4 Pathology, Symptom, Therapy, or Episode?

Once the intensional and intentional vagueness of populism has been sketched, it should be added that the conceptual vagueness of an ideology or a social movement has never prevented human beings from holding categorical opinions about it. I now recall how two American authors began their old introduction to socialism as follows: "The only thing most Americans know about socialism is that they don't like it" (Huberman and Sweezy 1976, p. 15). Similarly, in spite of its conceptual vagueness, attitudes towards populism are very diverse, but can be very categorical

[3] *El País*, October 18, 2014 (https://elpais.com/politica/2014/10/18/actualidad/1413645294_999870.html).

at the same time. I believe that we can distinguish at least four basic attitudes towards populism, which respectively describe this phenomenon as: pathology, symptom, therapy and episode:

(a) *Pathology*. According to the first, *populism is a pathology of democracy*. In this sense, populism would be nothing more than a deviation. In Spain, José María Lassalle (2017) holds this view.
(b) *Symptom*. According to the second attitude, *populism is a symptom* that makes it possible for us to check the real quality of our democracy. Populism would be the shadow (Canovan *apud* Eatwell and Goodwin 2018, p. 50), the blind spot of our political system. It would be a sort of "mirror" (Panizza 2009a), reflecting the miseries of our societies. This is well illustrated by the famous analogy proposed by Benjamín Arditi (2009, p. 122) between populism and the "uncomfortable guest," who starts drinking immoderately during a dinner, up to the point of stirring up the rest of attendees. The uncomfortable guest is disturbing because of her impertinence and bad manners, but also because of her true opinions. After all, only drunkards would dare to air the truth so frankly.
(c) *Therapy*. The third attitude entails that populism is a *therapy* for those ills of democracy. Typically, the influential ideas of Ernesto Laclau (2004) would express this attitude, since his view on populism embodies *democracy* "in its best version" ("*al suo meglio*") (Urbinati 2020, p. 61). From this optimistic perspective, populism would be the remedy for an ailing democracy.
(d) *Episode*. The fourth attitude conceives *populism, beyond all criticism, as a normal physiological episode of democracy* in the course of its historical evolution. Somehow, populism could remind us of puberty, which, as detestable as it may seem to us, is the price (but also the announcement) of the forthcoming maturity that will one day be reached in a new phase of development.

5 Populism As a Transformation of Democracy

Paradigmatically, Nadia Urbinati's balanced point of view represents the latter attitude. Urbinati avoids "apocalyptic" temptations and seeks the objectivity that a broader historical perspective usually provides (Urbinati 2020, p. 39). Nadia Urbinati's approach can be stimulating since it is less normative and more dynamic.

First, Urbinati's approach is quite neutral in normative terms. By distinguishing populism from *true* deviations of a totalitarian nature, Urbinati emphasizes that populist phenomena often come along as a reaction to deep crises of the democratic system. Let us recall that Urbinati believes that "fascism *destroys* democracy after using its instruments to strengthen itself. Populism *disfigures* democracy, *transforming it without destroying it*" (Urbinati 2020, p. 45, my italics). Similarly, unlike original Marxism, populism does not seek to destroy the state, but to *occupy* it.

The second advantage of Urbinati's approach is that it frames the populist phenomenon in a broad and dynamic historical context and, since Polybius' *anacyclosis*, democracy has been a dynamic scenario, where multiple crises take place. For instance, the *People's Party* (the *grangers' party* that emerged at the end of the nineteenth century in the United States) was a reaction to a society that did not give them enough recognition; but the Latin American populism of the 1950s aimed at consolidating national states in unstructured societies, which were strongly divided between the indigenous people and well-off urban classes. Similarly, populism has also re-emerged today in a context of profound transformation of political *communication* since traditional channels have been totally overwhelmed in the era of social networks. After all, social networks allow people and their representatives to *bypass* the traditional political parties and media and "re-link" (quite in the sense of *religious "re-ligare"*) the leader directly to *the people*. No wonder that "the revolt against the intermediate bodies" (Urbinati 2020, p. 50) is so suitable for new messiahs.

In general terms, the evolution of modern democracy might be described as follows. After the rise of *English parliamentarianism* (from the 1830s to the 1860s) and the introduction of universal male suffrage in 1867, the *party democracy model* was dominant for a hundred years. However, in the 1970s the decline of traditional parties and the rise of the *mass media* and major political campaigns prompted an *audience democracy* (Arditi 2009, p. 112). Today, after the rule of *notables*, *parties* and *audiences* (Urbinati 2020, p. 49), we find ourselves at a turning point in representative democracy, in search of an oxymoronic "direct representation" (Urbinati 2020: cap. IV).One of its most unsettling manifestations is not only the current "street democracy" (Nieto 2018), but also the so-called "digital democracy" (Vallespín and Bascuñán 2017, p. 144). And by the way, this, so to speak, "*twitter democracy*" ("*Me Too*," "*Black Lives Matter" or "Hermana, yo te creo*") usually supports punitive demands (García Figueroa 2020, p. 121 ff.). Populism, in short, promotes a direct, polarized democracy in which the popular will is expressed immediately and spontaneously (Rosanvallon 2020, pp. 39 ff.).

To sum up, rather than *pathology, diagnosis* or *therapy* for democracy, we should consider populism as an *episode* of its *transformation,* something like a physiological crisis that bodies ordinarily face in their normal development. Populism would be something like the puberty of a new version of democracy still *in fieri*. Of course, we do not know very well where this "transformative phenomenon of democracy" (Urbinati 2020, p. 36) will lead us. However, we cannot neglect the very principles, rights and guarantees of our constitutional states. After all, puberty is also a critical phase in the development of the individual, which needs control. Like puberty, populism needs to be *overcome* and very probably it will be recalled not only as a necessary *passage*, but also as a sort of disease, an "*adolescence*." Hence, even when we accept the thesis that populism is nothing more than an episode within the normal crises of democracy on its way to a later phase of its development, this should not make us any less critical (after all, we, parents, do not renounce our duty to educate and correct our adolescent children, whose resulting maturity will depend to a large extent on our educational efforts during their teen years).

6 Populism in Power

Once power has been "assaulted" from the "street," populism is transformed into a new form of politics that usually follows a triple strategy, as Jan-Werner Müller (2016) has pointed out:

(a) The first strategy consists of "colonizing power" (Müller 2016, pp. 44 f.). It is a matter of placing "our own," "our people,"[4] in political positions and administrative posts; limiting judicial independence, modifying the civil servant recruitment system and controlling the media and the secret services, while stigmatizing any criticism of such measures with the argument that critics serve old *élites* or ancient regimes. This justifies (it should be added here) the establishment of a subtle "area of immunity" (Vecina 2020) in favor of the politicians, so that the populist leaders can act at their leisure. Müller illustrates this first strategy with the political action of Viktor Orbán in Hungary or the Kaczynskys in Poland, but they can also be found in the PSOE-Unidas Podemos Government measures in Spain.

(b) The second strategy is "mass clientelism" (Müller 2016, p. 46), that is, the large-scale *granting* of material or immaterial benefits in exchange for electoral support (see Rivas 2019, p. 45 ff.). Müller illustrates it again by looking at Central Europe, where the Austrian Jörg Haider went as far as handing out 100-euro bills on the streets of Carinthia to "his people." Müller also refers to the client dilapidation of the *oil boom* by Chávez in Venezuela, to which could be added *alleged*[5] "basic income" measures. Anticipating a response from those who recognize such clientelistic practices in any party (populist or not), Müller argues that the special hallmark of populist clientelism consists in the open, public and justified way in which the populist ruler uses this ruse as old as democracy.

(c) The third strategy is, finally, "discriminatory legalism" (Müller 2016, pp. 46 ff.). This entails a law-making process based on discrimination. Such discrimination is based on identity criteria, which allows for a clear distinction between members of *the people* (*friends*) and their *enemies*. Discriminatory legalism is an instrument of punitive populism.

---

[4]Interestingly, in Spanish, "our people" means "nuestra gente" (our guys) and "nuestro pueblo" (*demos*).

[5]"Alleged," because not every current transfer from the state to the citizen for social purposes is properly "basic income." Strictly speaking, the "basic income" is universal and not subject to conditions. This is why it has also been claimed by pragmatic neo-liberals who abhor the squandering of the enormous state apparatus that demands the administration and control of such social benefits (cf. Pacheco 2017, p. 73).

7 The *Legislative Technique* of Populism: Discriminatory Legalism

Discriminatory legalism is the legal translation of the Schmittian *concept of the political,* for this strategy of *populism in power* entails the split of the population into two antagonistic and irreconcilable groups. Obviously, discriminatory legalism can be extremely dangerous under the influence of punitivism.

Now it is important to make two points. The first one is that this *populist legislative drafting* (if I may say so) applies not only to Statutes, but also to the Constitution.[6] The second point is that, to be effective, discriminatory *legislation* needs to become a discriminatory *practice.* Thus, by controlling judges, education, mass media, culture, trade unions, streets and even a new interpretation of history ("memoria histórica"—historic memory), populist leaders take over the whole society. Unlike the *"economism"* of classic Marxist "neoconservatism," Gramsci's strategy (2017, pp. 218 ff.) assumed that injustice can have its origin in economic factors as much as in cultural factors. Therefore, both, economic and cultural factors, form a "historical bloc" (Gramsci 2017, pp. 202 ff.), but culture should be put at the very centre of the political struggle.

In short, the ultimate populist goal is controlling the entire legal-political consciousness by appropriating nothing less than the *common sense* (e.g., Gramsci 2017, pp. 272 ff.). The populist approach to law, therefore, tends to be *topic* and also realistic. It seeks to modify not only the "law in the books," but especially the real law, the living law, which has its origin in the judiciary in practice, i.e., "law in action." Thus, the holistic and totalitarian strategy of populism is based on the transformation of the *communis opinio* itself. Pressure on the judiciary is required to change their *legal loci communes*—say, legal *topoi* in the sense given by Viehweg (1964). No wonder that populism implicitly supports judicial activism in line with the proposals of the so-called *Uso Alternativo del Diritto* (see, e.g., Barcelona et al. 1977) and the well-known *Critical Legal Studies* in the English-speaking legal culture (see Pérez Lledó 1996).

The, so to speak, *populist legislative technique* is based on two principles that I will call respectively: "antagonism" (relating to groups) and "principle of identity" (relating to individuals). By virtue of *antagonism,* a permanent and cultural confrontation between friends and enemies must be maintained at all costs. By virtue of the *principle of identity* or the "irrevocability of exclusion" (Bauman 2007, p. 100) individuals should not be allowed to modify their identity at will. No one should be allowed to cross the line between friends and enemies. Therefore, the *antagonistic principle* assumes the severe division of the population, for the populist *concept of the political* is based on a cultural class struggle (not economic struggle, though). Populists think that struggle is the only way in politics because consensus means

---

[6] See, e.g., the "feminization of the Constitution" proposal by Gómez (2017, 2019). See my critical remarks in García Figueroa (2019) and general criticism of "feminist constitutionalism" in Álvarez (2020).

defeat. Significantly, both the political philosophy of Jürgen Habermas and that of John Rawls, flagships on either side of the Atlantic of a liberal egalitarianism based on *communication* and *consensus*, are vehemently rejected by populist theorists. Not by chance, the great *bête noire* of Spanish populism is precisely the foundational myth of Spanish democracy of 1978: the very word "*consensus*."

In an interview, when asked by James Martin about the Arab Spring and other democratic struggles, the populist theorist Chantal Mouffe shifts her attention significantly to the movement of the so-called "*indignados*" (*outraged*) of March 15, 2011 in Madrid, which she predicts will fail, precisely because of the desire for consensus and lack of leaders. These were her words: "Although I sympathize with the movement of the *indignados* in Spain, I am really concerned when I hear them calling for a participatory democracy without leaders or parties and that the objective of these forms of direct participation should be to reach an inclusive consensus" (*apud* Martin 2013, p. 235). For this populism, the "assault on heaven" admits neither compromises, nor agreements, nor consensus, and the confrontation must be continuously fostered by reinforcing the antagonism between the two parties in perpetual conflict until the achievement (merely utopian) of a perfect hegemony that defines the authentic people. For these movements, unanimity exists just as an "illusion" (Zanatta 2019) of something, lost or yet to come, that people are not able to reach spontaneously. After all, such an immanent Hegelian consciousness can only be revealed to the people by its leader.

This is how friends oppose enemies, "ordinary people" (*pueblo*, *gente*) oppose élite (*la casta*), and likewise (and this is especially relevant here) *victims oppose criminals*. This dialectic can follow multiple criteria. In Greece, Syriza's slogan during the 2012 political campaign was, despite its abstraction, very clear in the context of the intervention from the European Union: "They decided without us, we will go on without them" (see Siomos and Stavrakakis 2019, p. 142). In France, the *Lepenists* appeal to the "*français d'abord*," while the harangue of Mélenchon in Marseille invokes "*le peuple central*" (Vallespín and Bascuñán 2017, p. 81). In the United States, while "99%" demonstrate on Wall Street, others seek refuge in the essences of the "*heartland*" (Taggart), i.e., the spiritual reservoir of national essences (*apud* Vallespín and Bascuñán 2017, p. 73). In Spain, "good Basques" are opposed to the *Spanish "maketos"*[7] ("the scum of the European people,"[8] as suggested by the racist founding father of Basque nationalism, Sabino Arana). Similarly, the "*catalans de debò*" (genuine Catalonians, Catalan speakers) oppose Spanish speakers, "scavengers."[9] In short, the populist legislative technique is structured based on two antagonistic categories: first-class citizens (the genuine *people*) and second-class citizens (the rest, the enemies).

7 "*Maketo*" is the contemptuous word used by Basque nationalists to refer to the rest of Spaniards.

8 "La hez de los pueblos europeos" in Sabino Arana's words (*apud* De la Granja 2006, p. 196).

9 "*Bèsties carronyaires*" in the words of the former president of the Catalonian *government*, Quim Torra (2012). On the racist background of Iberian nationalisms, see Wulff (2003).

Once this antagonism between friends and enemies is clear, then the membership of the individuals in the group needs to be defined in terms of *identity*. Thus, the underlying anthropology of the populist friend/foe dialectic entails that membership is unchangeable and irrevocable. It has an essentialist and *quasi-religious* flavor. Apparently, in this *liquid* society of ours, where nothing is *solid*, only membership to a friend or enemy social group is permanent (Bauman 2007, p. 71). You may try to become a "good Catalonian" or a "good Basque," but lacking the necessary Catalonian or Basque surnames you will probably fail. Back in history, in the anti-Moorish literature of the seventeenth century the expulsion of the Moors was justified because these Muslims, formerly called "*mudéjares,*" were considered to be lying, irrational, lustful, or anti-Christian, and all of this by their very nature ("by nation"), i.e., in the conviction that not even baptism could ever change such a condition (see Bravo 2018, p. 206). To sum up, in the same way that evangelization could never redeem the Moor five centuries ago (nor today transform *charnegos* into *genuine Catalonians*, *maketos* into *genuine Basques*), neither penal and penitentiary legislation, nor educational measures could ever redeem certain criminals (i.e., redeem them from their *original sin*, that of *being* enemies). Significantly Eduardo Demetrio points out that when Günther Jakobs assimilates certain criminals to "wild animals" (Jakobs 2005, p. 843, *apud* Demetrio Crespo 2020, p. 61, footnote 38), he does not only deprive them of their status as moral agents, but does so irreversibly.

Something similar applies to men, who are stigmatized by our legal system with essentially violent properties and deprived under the so-called "State feminism" of any redemption of their cursed condition (see a general criticism in De Lora 2019). The enemy minority (e.g., 1%, oligarchy, EU-beaurocrats, *charnegos*, *maketos*, men) is not only singled out, but also *blamed* (Vallespín and Bascuñán 2017, p. 84) and, of course, deserves to be punished. Tamar Pitch (2018, p. 44) with the term "punitive feminism" refers to "the mobilizations that, claiming to be feminists and in defense of women, lead demands for criminalization (introduction of new crimes into the legal system and/or an increase in the penalties for already existing crimes)." However, such demands are much more than mere "mobilizations" (i.e., street populism) and have already been transformed into legislative initiatives of "populism in power," as demonstrated by the strength of "State feminism" (García Figueroa 2019).

This unambiguous and irreversible division of the population between first-class citizens (the real people, the people who deserve *recognition*) and second-class citizens—the elite, "la casta" (i.e., other politicians), criminals, immigrants, *maketos*, *charnegos*, men, *wet-backs*, liberals ("*derechona,*" "*fachas*"), i.e., the second-class citizens, who do not deserve *recognition*—is the first step in achieving discriminatory legislation that privileges first-class citizens at the expense of the punishment of second-class citizens. Furthermore, this strategy increases the legitimacy and encourages a new "street democracy" in the masses to exert social pressure on politicians and judges so that the antagonism between essentially irreconcilable enemies is kept. Now, how are the real people and their enemies kept apart and isolated?

8 The Bad Taste of Talking About Money

As I have already pointed out, the timeliness of Gramsci in understanding today's political reality lies in the correction he proposes of the classical Marxism, *"economism"*, and its replacement by a *cultural socialism*. According to Gramsci's approach, the quest for justice cannot be reduced to an economic redistribution of resources; it requires, above all, a cultural battle that transforms the very depths of society. In this spirit, the social struggle must adopt a certain religious air and embed itself in all spheres of culture. Otherwise, any transformation would be superficial, apparent and absorbable by the structures of capitalism. That is why some post-socialists are calling for a full "deconstruction" of society as a whole.

In this new context for the left, the defenders of the so-called "recognition paradigm"[10] have emphasized the Gramscian approach by clearly distinguishing between the *injustice of distribution* and the *injustice of recognition*. The former is caused by the economic imbalance between rich and poor and is solved by means of typical welfare state redistributive measures. The latter is caused by the lack of recognition of certain groups that prevents their members from having equal access to the same opportunities, no matter how redistributive the state might be in economic terms. When a group is the victim of injustice of distribution (it is poor), then that group must disappear. So Olof Palme was right in replying "we want to finish with the poor," when Otelo Saraiva de Carvahlo stated that the *Revolução dos Cravos* ("Carnation Revolution") would "finish with the rich." In other words, the welfare state's aim is that nobody should be poor, that the very category "poor" should vanish. On the contrary, when a group is the victim of injustice of recognition (e.g., Black people), then the group or class identity must be preserved and emphasized, not ignored. Under these premises, the dilemma arises when a group suffers both types of injustice (distribution and recognition) simultaneously. In this case, one might ask which part of, for example, the Black culture would require its elimination because of an economic factor and which part should be overemphasized to reinforce the recognition of its identity.

Should we rule out that class or overemphasize its relevance? This is not the time to address such post-socialist debates (e.g., Butler 2016 v. Fraser 2016). They simply help us to understand that in our current multicultural and fragmented society "the *people*" can no longer be determined merely on economic grounds, for disadvantaged classes are the ones that *must* disappear. Thus, after the post-socialist renunciation of a clear division rich/poor, capitalist/proletariat, the definition of the "people" can only resort to cultural and identity aspects, for these classes do need recognition and should be actively preserved by the state.

To sum up, the classical class struggle has thus been replaced by a struggle of *mentalities*, and this is also reproduced in the most reactionary conservative populism. For example, Chantall Delsol (2019, p. 341) illustrates the conflict of mentalities between Western and Eastern Europeans with the bitter complaint of a former

---

[10] On its historical origins in French, British, and German thought, see Honneth (2019).

President of Poland, Aleksander Kwaśniewski, against the *economic* policy of Brussels: "When we talk to you about justice, you tell us about EU funds." Behind these words, one can guess, there is in fact, a clash of mentalities between a multiculturalist, bureaucratic and *economicist* Western Europe and an identity-based, heroic and recognition-hungry Eastern Europe. In short, it is as if populism (left and right) had relegated the economy to a secondary plane. Against the *bad taste of talking about money,* all populists seem to rebel unanimously.

9 The Bernstein Party: An Impossible "*e pluribus unum*"?

Once the *more Gramscian* Left abandons *economism*, there arises the distinctive problem of its populism to redefine the limits of *the people* in the face of its enemies with the phenomenon of *intersectionality*. In effect, as a consequence of the infinite number of overlapping identities in our multicultural societies, each subject can be located at the same time within and outside the confines of *the people* structured by cultural criteria. Let us take an eye-catching example and imagine a cocktail party held in the 1970s by Leonard Bernstein and his wife in their New York City mansion. What does Mrs. Bernstein (an idle, white, rich, Jewish, wife) have to do with her guests that night, the *black panthers* (black, poor, working-class men)? In his story "*Radical chic*," novelist Tom Wolfe (2011) used this perplexity to write a hilarious reconstruction of that encounter between the most prominent members of New York's *radical chic* society and a few of Macolm-X's followers, who in another context might well be against the interests of their hosts. There was little affinity between the two groups, but rather considerable *antagonism*. Certainly, Mrs. Bernstein was at least a woman and could claim to be a secular victim of *heteropatriarchy*, as any member of the Black community would be of racism; but could Mrs. Bernstein and her friends really demonstrate hand in hand with black panthers? Could they share something more than those "little Roquefort cheese morsels rolled in crushed nuts" that memorable evening?

This problem has been confronted by populist theorists such as Ernesto Laclau or Chantal Mouffe, resorting to the idea that among the different "democratic demands" (those of women, blacks, poor, immigrants, the marginalized, slum dwellers, atheists, workers, etc.) an alliance can be established through "chains of equivalence," that is, reasons capable of unifying the plurality of "democratic demands" around a single "popular demand." These would be reasons capable of uniting the various members of society around a single and authentic people. However, as far as we can see, any serious "*e pluribus unum*" that is not liberal and/or economistic is extremely complicated and requires a nuanced balance. At this point the principle of antagonism comes into play, since, naturally, the best way to consolidate the unity of the people is to create an external frontier in the face of the common enemy of the otherwise irreducible *plures*. In such a way, the groups that make up the *people* (and only they) are then constituted as *unum* negatively, in the face of a common adversary, and the *people* can oppose (and unite in front of) the *caste* ("*the elite-la casta")*, as the *people do in the face* of their *enemies*. To give an example, this explains why the women of the liberal party, Ciudadanos (*Citizens),* were harassed in the Madrid *gay* pride demonstrations of 2019: Those *women* are not *really* part of the people (friends). [11]

As a result, the class struggle is transformed into a mentality struggle. This is the evolution of justice struggle:

(a) The (economy-based) *classic classism of* Marxism (rich/poor) maintains a traditional dualism (capitalist/proletarian) that vindicates the primarily economic nature of social demands and political struggle. This strategy of classical classism would have been *neutralized* by the welfare policies, by means of which capitalist liberalism would silence the left-wing demands.
(b) Laclau's (multi-identity-based) *metaclassism* that tries to join under one popular demand a heterogeneous and conflicting set of *democratic demands* with the explicit support of the paradigm of recognition. In our multicultural societies, where classes become indistinguishable in a categorical way for economic reasons and the *welfare state* obscures antagonisms, only *meta-classism,* which has its origin in Gramscian anti-economism and its support in the "recognition paradigm," would allow a reaction to the allegedly dissolving response of capitalism.
(c) The (one-identity-based) *Hyperclassism* (Aránguez 2019, p. 193) is the postmodern tendency to take as central *only one democratic demand*. Hyperclassism thus privileges a class that leads the rest. For example, in its current stage of development, *metaclassism* would have given way to a *hyperclassism* that assigns the leadership to one group in particular: women. Thus, their demand (feminism) unites and provides them with a structure, the multiple "democratic demands." Somehow, this is how feminism has become *the voice* of all the groups.

The hybridization of the feminist discourse in the economic, ecological or racial plane (let us recall, e.g., the so-called "ecofeminism") is an instance of the evolution from metaclassism to hyperclassism. Furthermore, feminism and women's demands have become the very centre of the hyperclassical populist strategy and almost all parties rely on it. In Spain, the very change of the populist "*Unidos* Podemos" party's name ("United We Can", with epicene *masculine*) to *Unidas* Podemos (exclusively *feminine*) is quite meaningful. It somehow describes the shift from metaclassism to hyperclassism. Consistently, punitive populism transforms itself into "punitive feminism," where "State feminism" has taken root. From this point of view, state feminism is the most complete consummation of the populist strategy of discriminatory legalism in its *hyperclassistic* phase.

---

[11] *ABC*, July 7, 2019 (https://www.abc.es/espana/madrid/abci-orgullo-2019-boicot-insultos-ciudadanos-acude-orgullo-escolta-policial-201907070126_noticia.html.Último accessed 30/11/2020).

10 Conclusion: From Punitive Populism to Punitive Feminism

This work has assumed that the paradoxical shift from prison abolition to punitivist doctrines is a special case of the "reactionary drift of the left." The fact that the prison abolition movement and punitivism share the very same victim-based criminal law approach mitigates somewhat such contradiction, but it does not justify the shift to punitivism. Thus, we have looked for an explanation in the rise of populism in general.

Certainly, under the current crisis of representative democracy, the rise of populism can be interpreted in various ways. As we have seen, populism has been considered as a *pathology*, but also as a *symptom*, and even as a *therapy*. However, populism is, above all, an *episode* defining a transformation of democracy in need of new forms of representation. This point of view allows us to understand that, beyond our attitudes towards populism, this expresses especially a crisis of the parties and the traditional media, which will never be the same again. This does not imply assuming other attitudes such as political pessimism or fatalism (say, "*fata volentes ducunt, nolentes trahunt*"). On the contrary we need to bear in mind the new political scenario so that we can look for new ways to ensure the protection of our individual rights and safeguards in the face of populist misuse of democracy. Particularly in the light of the evolution of post-socialism from metaclassicistic populism to hyperclassicistic populism, the fact that punitive populism has led to a vigorous punitive feminism is not accidental. Feminism has become the great equivalence chain for hyperclassicistic populism, while punitive feminism has coherently become the central and binding specification of punitive populism.

As we have seen, once in power populism typically follows three fundamental strategies so as to "disfigure democracy": "colonization" of power, mass clientelism, and discriminatory legalism. And, specifically, within discriminatory legislation, populist governments use the division of the population between friends and enemies to enact norms (in the broadest sense, including constitutional, administrative and judicial enactment) that distinguish between first-class citizens and second-class citizens. The *legislative technique of* punitive feminism is, in this sense, a specification of punitive populism and is based on the use of punitivism to sharpen the antagonism between the true people (whose representation feminism and women assume) and the critics of these policies. Furthermore, the essentialist principle based on identity entails a supreme advantage for the consolidation of feminism and populism, inasmuch as it is articulated on the *natural* dichotomy male/female.[12]

It is difficult to exaggerate the importance of this debate insofar as, at its core, it substantiates a cultural struggle on the validity of a liberal philosophy that has been

[12] Despite the "germ of Simone de Beauvoir" (De Lora 2019, p. 160) that replaced *sex* for *gender in the* feminist discourse, real discriminatory legislation responds to a strictly sexual distinction between men and women. This has generated new debates in feminism that cannot be examined here.

part of the *common sense of* jurists until now, and it is precisely that common sense (that "hegemony") that populism explicitly seeks to force and control. When Antonio Gramsci urged his comrades to abandon classical Marxist economism, he insisted on the need to replace the existing common sense with a new philosophy that should permeate everything as a religion—for "in the masses as such philosophy cannot be lived, but as a faith," Gramsci wrote (2017, p. 295).

Populist leaders and thinkers assume that the rule of law and judicial independence only serve a "*juridictatorship*" (see Rosanvallon 2020, p. 43). They are also well aware of the *enthymematic* nature of legal reasoning (i.e., that legal reasoning assumes commonplaces, unnecessary to make explicit, for they are taken for granted by the legal community beforehand). Therefore, populism aims to replace the most profound and valuable legal and political commonplaces, *loci communes* (the *topoi of* legal reasoning) with new ones. By modifying our "deep conventions" (Bayón 2002), populist leaders try to control the morality involved in legal reasoning, especially in hard cases requiring moral reasoning (García Figueroa 2018). As a result, the current politics is nothing but the impressive success of Gramsci's culturalist offensive, by altering what has usually been part of the common sense of jurists and which has been largely identified to date with the philosophy of the Enlightenment.

Bibliography

Álvarez I (2020) Crítica del constitucionalismo feminista. Atelier, Barcelona

Aránguez T (2019) De la clase social al pueblo y del pueblo a la clase social. ACFS 53:183–206

Arditi B (2009) El populismo como periferia interna de la política democrática. In Panizza 2009a, pp 97–132

Arias Maldonado M (2019) Claroscuros populistas. ACFS 53:325–335

Barcelona P et al (1977) La formación del jurista. Capitalismo monopolístico y cultura jurídica. Civitas, Madrid

Bauman Z (2007) Tiempos líquidos. Vivir en una época de incertidumbre. Spanish transl. C. Corral. Tusquets, Barcelona

Bauman Z (2010) Miedo líquido. La sociedad contemporánea y sus temores. Spanish transl. A. Santos Mosquera. Paidós, Barcelona

Bayón JC (2002) Derecho, convencionalismo y controversia. In: Navarro PE, Redondo MC (comps) La relevancia del derecho. Ensayos de filosofía jurídica, moral y política. Gedisa, Barcelona, pp 68 ff

Bernstein R et al (2002) Out of the Blue. The Story of September 11, 2001. From Jihad to Ground Zero. Times Books, New York

Bobbio N (1991) Thomas Hobbes, Spanish transl. M. Escrivá de Romaní. Plaza & Janés, Barcelona

Bravo F (2018) Brevísima historia de la islamofobia en España (siglos XVI–XXI). In: de La Cueva J, Hernando de Larramendi M, Planet A (eds) Encrucijadas del cambio religioso en España. Secularización, cristianismo e islam. Comares, Granada, pp 199–225

Butler J (2016) El marxismo y lo meramente cultural. In: Butler J, Fraser N (2016), pp 67–87

Butler J, Fraser N (2016) ¿Reconocimiento o redistribución? Un debate entre marxismo y feminismo. Traficantes de sueños, Madrid

Cossarini P (2019) Populismo, acción política y emociones. Líneas de intersección. ACFS 53:79–95

Dahrendorf R (2009) La libertad a prueba. Los intelectuales frente a la tentación totalitaria, Spanish transl. P. Madrigal Devesa. Trotta, Madrid
De la Granja JL (2006) El antimaketismo: la visión de Sabino Arana sobre España y los españoles. Norba 19:191–203
De Lora P (2019) Lo sexual es político (y jurídico). Alianza, Madrid
Delsol C (2019) Democracias iliberales. ACFS 53:339–343
Demetrio Crespo E (2020) El Derecho penal del Estado de Derecho entre el espíritu de nuestro tiempo y la Constitución. Reus, Madrid
Eatwell R, Goodwin M (2018) National populism. The revolt against liberal democracy. Pelican, London
Fraser N (2016) ¿De la redistribución al reconocimiento? Dilemas de la justicia en la era "postsocialista". In: Butler & Fraser, 2016, pp 23–66
García Amado JA (2000) ¿Dogmática penal sistémica? Sobre la influencia de Luhmann en la teoría penal. Doxa 23:233–264. https://rua.ua.es/dspace/bitstream/10045/10249/1/doxa23_09.pdf. Last accessed: 17/09/2020
García Amado JA (2020) Sobre la sentencia por agresión sexual a los jugadores de la Arandina. Almacén de Derecho, 03/01/2020. https://almacendederecho.org/sobre-la-sentencia-por-agresion-sexual-de-los-jugadores-de-la-arandina/. Last accessed 20/09/2020
García Figueroa A (2018) El convencionalismo jurídico o la irrelevancia del juspositivismo. Persona y Derecho 79(2):71–114. https://revistas.unav.edu/index.php/persona-y-derecho/article/view/34242/29820. Last accessed 20/09/2020
García Figueroa A (2019) Feminismo de Estado: fundamentalmente religioso y religiosamente fundamentalista. Eunomia. Revista en Cultura de la Legalidad 17:358–376. https://e-revistas.uc3m.es/index.php/EUNOM/article/view/5040. Last accessed: 20/09/2020
García Figueroa A (2020) Populismo universitario y crisis de la razón. Un homenaje a Luis Prieto. In: Andrés Ibáñez P et al (eds) El compromiso constitucional del iusfilósofo. Homenaje a Luis Prieto Sanchís. Palestra, Lima (Perú), pp 477–504
Gómez I (2017) Una Constituyente feminista. ¿Cómo reformar la Constitución con perspectiva de género? Marcial Pons, Madrid
Gómez I (2019) ¿Qué es eso de reformar la Constitución con perspectiva de género? Mitos caídos y mitos emergentes a partir del libro Una Constituyente feminista. Eunomía. Revista en Cultura de la Legalidad 16:312–329. https://e-revistas.uc3m.es/index.php/EUNOM/article/view/4708. Last accessed 20/09/2020
Gramsci A (2017) Escritos. Antología, ed. C. Rendueles. Alianza, Madrid
Hobbes Th (1993) El ciudadano, bilingual ed. Latin/Spanish J. Rodríguez Feo. Debate/CSIC, Madrid
Honneth A (2019) Reconocimiento. Una historia de las ideas europea, Spanish transl. S. Chaparro Martínez. Akal, Tres Cantos
Huberman L, Sweezy PM (1976) Introducción al socialismo, Spanish transl. A. Gallifa. Ediciones Martínez Roca, Barcelona
Jakobs G (2005) Terroristen als Personen im Recht? ZStW 117:839 ff
Kolakowski L (1970) El racionalismo como ideología y ética sin código, Spanish transl. J. Muñoz. Ariel, Barcelona
Laclau E (2004) La razón populista, trad. S. Laclau. FCE, México
Lascuraín JA (2019) La sentencia de La Manada: ¿todos contentos? Blog Público, 01/11/2019. https://blogs.publico.es/otrasmiradas/24970/la-sentencia-de-la-manada-todos-contentos/. Last accessed 30/11/2020
Lassalle JM (2017) Contra el populismo. Cartografía de un totalitarismo posmoderno. Debate, Madrid
Lloria P et al (2019) Los riesgos de una justicia expuesta. Agenda Pública. El País, 18/12/2019. http://agendapublica.elpais.com/los-riesgos-de-una-justicia-expuesta/. Last accessed 30/11/2020

Martin J (2013) An interview with Chantal Mouffe. In: Martin J (ed) C. Mouffe, Hegemony, radical democracy and the political. Routledge, London/New York, pp 228–236
Müller JW (2016) What is populism? University of Pennsylvania Press
Muñoz L, Tripolone G (2018) Una vez más sobre los "vínculos" entre Carl Schmitt y Günther Jakobs. Res Publica 21(1):47–62. https://revistas.ucm.es/index.php/RPUB/article/view/59696, Last accessed 14/09/2020
Nieto A (2018) "Democracia callejera" (intervención en la sesión de 30 de octubre de 2018). Anales de la Real Academia de Ciencias Morales y Políticas 96:59–71. www.racmyp.es/docs/anales/a96-5.pdf, Last accessed 10/02/2020
Ovejero F (2018) La deriva reaccionaria de la izquierda. Página indómita, Barcelona
Pacheco MÁ (2017) El estado del Estado social. Una culminación pendiente. Atelier, Barcelona
Panizza F (comp) (2009a) El populismo como espejo de la democracia. FCE, Buenos Aires
Panizza F (2009b) Introducción. El populismo como espejo de la democracia. In Panizza 2009a, pp 9–49
Pérez Lledó JM (1996) El movimiento Critical Legal Studies. Tecnos, Madrid
Pitch T (2018) Feminismo punitivo. Jueces para la democracia 92:44–47
Portilla G (2007) Bases teóricas del "nuevo" Derecho penal schmittiano: el Derecho penal y el Derecho procesal del "enemigo". Revista del Instituto de Ciencias Jurídicas de Puebla A.C. 17 (1):23–45. https://www.revistaius.com/index.php/ius/article/view/177/172. Last accessed 12/09/2020
Prieto L (2011) Garantismo y Derecho penal. Iustel, Madrid
Rivas P (2019) En los márgenes del Derecho y el poder. Crisis de la representación, clientelismo, populismo. Tirant Humanidades, Valencia
Rosanvallon P (2020) El siglo del populismo, Spanish trans I. Agoff. Galaxia Gutemberg, Barcelona
Siomos T, Stavrakakis Y (2019) El populismo de Syriza: Verificación y extensión de una perspectiva de la escuela de Essex, Spanish transl. A.M. Jara Gómez. ACFS 53:131–156
Torra Q (2012) La llengua i les bèsties. Tarragona Digital, 19 de diciembre de 2012. https://tarragonadigital.com/opinio/5052/la-llengua-i-les-besties. Last accessed: 30/11/2020
Urbinati N (2020) Io, il popolo, Italian transl. C. Bertolotti and revision by the author. Il Mulino, Bolonia
Vallespín F, Bascuñán MM (2017) Populismos. Alianza, Madrid
Vecina J (2020) Contra las inmunidades del poder: el caso español. In press. Manuscript available to me by courtesy of its author
Viehweg T (1964) Tópica y jurisprudencia, Spanish transl. L. Díez-Picazo. Taurus, Madrid
Wolfe T (2011) La Izquierda Exquisita & Mau-mauando al parachoques, Spanish transl. J.M. Álvarez Flores & Á. Pérez. Anagrama, Barcelona
Wulff F (2003) Las esencias patrias. Historiografía e historia antigua en la construcción de la identidad española (siglos XVI-XX). Crítica, Barcelona
Zanatta L (2019) El populismo latino y la nostalgia de la unanimidad. ACFS 53:15–28
Žižek S (2011) Living the end times. Verso, London

Harm, Offense, and Hate Speech

Victor Gomez Martin

Abstract According to the doctrine of "hate speech," any message qualifying as such will imply an abuse of the fundamental right to freedom of speech. This doctrine, elaborated in different stages by the European Court of Human Rights over the last decades, has been followed by Spanish jurisprudence as an interpretive guideline for the so-called "apologetic crimes." In keeping with this interpretative line, the ratio legis of this group of crimes would consist of the prohibition of hate speech. The vagueness of this idea has led a doctrinal sector to defend the distinction between damage (serious violation of individual interests) and offense (slight annoyance for collective interests). In this paper, the assumptions and effects of the doctrine of "hate speech" will be exposed and critically assessed and the practical efficacy of the "harm-offense" binomial will be relativized, to reach a common conclusion: both conceptions are tautological.

1 Approach

After the tragic experience of Nazism in Germany and fascism in Italy, the **European Convention for the Protection of Human Rights and Fundamental Freedoms** (ECHR) was born in 1950, as is well known. The Convention pursued the firm purpose of laying the foundations of a new model of liberal democracy that would succeed in completely eradicating the threat of totalitarianism. A fundamental part of this objective was the will to decisively limit the scope of discourses that, like the Nazi and the Fascist, or the then flourishing Stalinist communism, could seriously threaten the foundations of the newly recovered continental freedom (Landa 2018, p. 27). Based on the ECHR, the judicial body responsible for ensuring respect by the member states of the Convention for the rights and freedoms enshrined therein, the European Court of Human Rights (ECtHR), has been developing since

V. Gomez Martin (✉)
Faculty of Law, University of Barcelona, Barcelona, Spain
e-mail: victor.gomez@ub.edu

E. Demetrio Crespo et al. (eds.), *Crisis of the Criminal Law in the Democratic Constitutional State*, Legal Studies in International, European and Comparative Criminal Law 6, https://doi.org/10.1007/978-3-031-13413-5_7

then and for decades the line of jurisprudence of the so-called **"hate speech**." In accordance with this line, the right to freedom of expression, recognized in Article 10 of the ECHR, [1] is restricted in all cases where it is exercised in an abusive manner, under Article 17 of the ECHR.

The ECHR elaborated this doctrine through various stages. In the following lines, the main lines of development of each of these stages will be set out, and then submitted to critical evaluation.

2 About the Doctrine of "Hate Speech"

2.1 Exposure

In an initial phase of development of the concept, the ECHR relentlessly applied the so-called **"guillotine effect"** enshrined in Article 17 ECHR, according to which the possibility of the discourse analyzed being protected by the exercise of freedom of expression under Article 10 ECHR would be completely ruled out, particularly in cases of direct incitement to racist or xenophobic violence and historical revisionism of the Nazi holocaust (Landa 2018, p. 29). The latter is particularly understandable in view of the easy identification of the denialist message, by which extreme right-wing and neo-Nazi groups feed the image of the Jewish people as manipulators and liars, to the point of exaggerating or even inventing the holocaust for the sake of obtaining huge economic benefits (Landa 2018, pp. 76 f.). In this way, the ECHR would assume the logic of **"militant democracy"** for conducts of expression, according to which no message aimed at destroying the model of rights and freedoms enshrined in the Convention could be protected by Article 10 ECHR (Landa 2018, p. 52). Subsequently, the ECHR has extended the scope of its doctrine Kurdish people (Landa 2018, p. 27; Rodríguez Montañés 2012, pp. 240 f.), as well as to other groups, such as LGBTI (Landa 2018, p. 35). The turning point in this jurisprudential

[1] According to this precept: "1. Everyone has the right to freedom of expression. This right shall include freedom to hold opinions and to receive and impart information and ideas without interference by public authority and regardless of frontiers. This article does not prevent States from subjecting broadcasting, cinematographic or television enterprises to a system of prior authorization. The exercise of these freedoms, which entail duties and responsibilities, may be subject to certain formalities, conditions, restrictions, or sanctions, provided for by law, which constitute necessary measures, in a democratic society, for national security, territorial integrity or public safety, the defence of order and the prevention of crime, the protection of health or morals, the protection of reputation or of the rights of others, to prevent the disclosure of confidential information, or to ensure the authority and impartiality of the judiciary." For its part, the clause prohibiting the abusive exercise of Convention rights, provided for in Article 17 ECHR, reads: "Nothing in this Convention shall be interpreted as implying for any State, group or person any right to engage in any activity or to perform any act aimed at the destruction of any of the rights or freedoms set forth in this Convention or at their limitation to a greater extent than is provided for herein."

evolution was determined by STEDH 16-7-09 (*Féret v. Belgium* case), which dealt with an alleged case in which a political candidate (*Féret)* insulted and abused immigrants. Despite having three individual votes, the resolution ended up considering irrelevant the absence in the political discourse of threats or expressions of incitement to violence, to stop its attention on the nature of the victims of the message as susceptible to configure vulnerable groups or suspicious categories. [2]

In line with this idea, years later, judgments of the ECHR such as that of July 10, 2008 (*Soulas* case against France), May 7, 2010 (*Jean Marie Le Pen* case against France) and 17-12-13 (*Perinçek case* against Switzerland), qualified as "hate speech" any incitement to discrimination, hatred or racial violence, xenophobia, homophobia, etc., and recall in their legal grounds that political discourses inciting hatred based on religious, ethnic or cultural prejudice represent a danger to social peace and political stability in democratic states (Aguilar et al. 2015, pp. 42 ff.). This interpretation was finally consolidated by the ECHR on May 9, 2012 (*Vejdeland and Others vs. Sweden*), without any particular vote being taken at that time. Through this resolution, the ECHR recognized that the propaganda broadcast in a secondary school by several schoolchildren against homosexuals who were blamed for causing AIDS and HIV, contained unacceptable content. The resolution highlighted the need to protect a section of the population threatened as a result of hate speech by stating:

> Hate speech does not necessarily imply a call for violence and other criminal acts. Attacks on individuals committed by means of insults, exposing specific groups of the population to ridicule or defamation are sufficient reason for the authorities to combat racist discourse in the face of freedom of expression exercised in an irresponsible manner.

In the same vein, the European Union Agency for Fundamental Rights (FRA), the European Commission against Racism and Intolerance (ECRI) of the Council of Europe, and the Organization for Security and Cooperation in Europe (OSCE), through its Office for Democratic Institutions and Human Rights (ODIHR), in a joint statement issued on March 21, 2015, on the occasion of the International Day for the Elimination of Racial Discrimination, described hate speech as an extreme form of intolerance, which would contribute to hate crime and should be criminally prosecuted. Specifically, the ECRI of the Council of Europe, in its Recommendation R (97) 20 of the Committee of Ministers, defined hate speech as

[2] In the words of the aforementioned STEDH 16-7-09, "the language used by the plaintiff clearly incited discrimination and racial hatred, which cannot be camouflaged by the electoral process. Incitement to hatred does not necessarily require the calling of this or that act of violence or other criminal act. Attacks committed against individuals by insulting, ridiculing, or defaming certain parts of the population and their specific groups, or incitement to discrimination, as in this case, are sufficient for the authorities to privilege the fight against racist discourse over irresponsible freedom of expression that violates the dignity, even the security, of such parts or groups of the population. Political discourses that incite hatred based on religious, ethnic or cultural prejudice represent a danger to social peace and political stability in democratic States." For all these reasons, the ECHR considers the Belgian sentences against *Féret* to be in accordance with Article 10 ECHR. Particularly graphic in this regard is F.J. No. 46 of the ECHR 17-12-13 (case of *Perinçek v. Switzerland*).

> [...] all forms of expression which propagate, incite, promote or justify racial hatred, xenophobia, anti-Semitism and other forms of hatred based on intolerance, inter alia, intolerance expressed by aggressive nationalism and ethnocentrism, discrimination and hostility towards minorities, immigrants and persons of immigrant origin.[3]

Under this definition, what would be subject to punishment would not be represented by the mere expression of ideas, however abhorrent they may be, but by being carried out in such a way and under such circumstances as to provoke hatred, discrimination or violence, in violation of the constitutional values of human dignity and non-discrimination based on birth, racial origin, sex, religion, opinion or any other personal or social condition or circumstance contained in Articles 10 and 14 EC (Aguilar et al. 2015, p. 35; Dolz 2011). ECRI Recommendation No. 7 of 13 December 2002 is expressed in similar terms. This Recommendation identifies hate speech with those expressions that intentionally disseminate: (a) a public incitement to violence, hatred, discrimination; or (b) insult and publicly defame persons or groups of persons because of their race, color, language, religion, nationality or origin, nation or ethnicity. This recommendation is complemented by ECRI Recommendation No. 13 on anti-Gypsyism and Recommendation R (97) 20 of the Council of Europe on hate speech. The latter Recommendation defines hate speech as "*covering all forms of expression which spread, incite, promote or justify racial hatred, xenophobia, anti-Semitism or any other form of hatred based on intolerance.*" Furthermore, it expressly urges states to "*act against all forms of expression that propagate, incite or promote racial hatred, xenophobia, anti-Semitism or any other form of hatred based on intolerance.*"

Already in Spain, the concept of "hate speech" that has just been exposed has not been at all alien to the jurisprudence of the **Supreme Court** and the **Constitutional Court**. As for the former, it is worth noting, among others, STS 10-5-11 (*Blood & Honour* case) and, more recently, **STS 72/18, 9-2** points out that Article 510.1 CP

> ...sanctions those who promote discrimination, hatred or violence against groups or associations for **different reasons that are included in the precept.** The core element of the criminal act consists of the expression of epithets, qualifiers, or expressions that contain **a message of hate that is** transmitted in a generic way. This is a criminal offence structured in the form of a crime of danger, and all that is required to carry it out is the creation of a danger that is **embodied in the** message, which has a content specific to the 'discourse of hatred', and which **implies the danger referred to in the international conventions from which the crime arises**. These refer to the unlawfulness of the discourse of hate **without the need for a demand that goes beyond the very discourse that** contains the message of hate and that in itself is contrary to coexistence and therefore considered harmful. In order to be applied, the criminal law requires the confirmation of the commission of certain offenses included in the hate speech, since such inclusion already implies the commission of a conduct that directly or indirectly provokes feelings of hate, violence, or discrimination. In some way, **these are expressions that, because of their seriousness, and** because they hurt the common feelings of citizens, are included in the definition **of the crime** (STS 72/18, 9-2, F.J. 1).

[3] Decision adopted by the Committee of Ministers on October 30, 1997, at the 607th session of the Ministers' delegates.

With respect to the **Constitutional Court**, the aforementioned STC 176/95 (Makoki case) should be noted.[4]

2.2 Critical Assessment

As can be seen from the presentation just made, the most recent development of the doctrine on hate speech, particularly that which corresponds to the jurisprudence of the ECtHR, on the one hand, and in Spain to that of the Supreme Court and the Constitutional Court, on the other, highlights the fundamentally utilitarian vocation that explains the growing recourse to it. Such usefulness would essentially consist of the following: to constitute an instrument at the service of a considerable simplification of the always complex balancing act between the fundamental right to freedom of expression and the legal interests protected by means of the eventual restriction of that right in supposedly limited circumstances, such as those posed by the phenomenology of extreme political discourse. In accordance with the aforementioned jurisprudential logic of the concept, the discourse of hate would operate as a *topos* that would deploy, as has already been explained with respect to the interpretation of Article 17 of the ECHR, a sort of "guillotine effect." According to the ECHR, no expression that could be described as "hate speech" could be protected, as a matter of principle, on the grounds of justification of the legitimate exercise of the fundamental right to freedom of expression (Article 21.7 CP, in relation to Articles 10 ECHR and 20 EC), so that in such cases it would no longer be necessary to weigh up the alleged fundamental rights at stake (Alcácer 2016, p. 3).

When the unnecessary manifestation of an idea is particularly damaging to the honor and dignity of individuals (e.g., through serious insults) or to freedom (e.g., through threats), or does not limit itself to questioning the democratic system in theory, but rather puts it in material danger, it could prevail—as already mentioned above in relation to the limits of the right to freedom of expression honor, freedom, or human dignity over freedom of expression (Lascuraín 2010, p. 1). Such a conclusion logically requires an exercise in weighing the interests at stake, which, however, the concept of "hate speech" would make it possible to avoid. In accordance with the logic of hate speech, in the event that its underlying elements are understood to be concurrent in a given expression or manifestation of ideas, the applicability of Article 21(7) CP in relation to freedom of expression will be excluded as a matter of principle. This circumstance leads to what some authors have rightly called "*the use and abuse of the notion of hate speech,*" since it gives rise to an obvious request in principle: the weighing of rights is avoided, and the possibility that the fundamental right to freedom of expression may come into play in

[4]The doctrine of hate speech is also found in the jurisprudence of the Provincial Courts (SSAP Barcelona, 5ª, 27-4-18; Santa Cruz de Tenerife 7-3-14) and the Criminal Courts (SSJP n° 2 Manresa 307/11, 11-11; n° 2 Lleida 16-11-06; n° 2 Logroño 2-4-04).

cases of hate speech is flatly denied, when what is at issue is precisely whether or not the latter is possible by weighing freedom of expression against other interests that may conflict with it (Alcácer 2016, pp. 3 ff.).

This, however, is not the only pernicious effect of the concept of "hate speech." A second inconsistency in the concept, or at least in the content with which jurisprudence is endowing the notion at hand, relates to its **excessive degree of vagueness**. It can be shared, as has already been stated with respect to Recommendation R (97) 20 of the Committee of Ministers of the European Commission against Racism and Intolerance (ECRI) of the Council of Europe, that certain forms of expression that propagate, incite, promote or justify racial hatred, xenophobia, are not in accordance with the law, anti-Semitism and other forms of hatred based on intolerance expressed by aggressive nationalism and ethnocentrism, discrimination and hostility towards minorities, immigrants and people of immigrant origin may not be covered by the exercise of the fundamental right to freedom of expression (Alcácer 2016). This conclusion can be reached both from a constitutional perspective (Article 20 EC) and from the point of view of the European Convention on Human Rights (Article 10 ECHR). With regard to the latter, the aforementioned clause on the limitation of the application of the restrictions on rights set out in Article 18 of the ECHR would be perfectly applicable to the latter. However, it is equally clear that not every speech expressing an abusive exercise of the fundamental right to freedom of expression will automatically be relevant from a criminal perspective. As is logical, there must be a space reserved for the legitimate exercise of the fundamental right set out in Articles 10 ECHR and 20 EC, on the one hand; a second sphere, possibly, for those expressive manifestations that, in a more socially intolerable manner, endanger legal assets such as honor, freedom, or human dignity that may be jeopardized by freedom of expression; and, finally, a sphere somewhere in-between between these two extremes, in which there is room precisely for all those cases in which the abusive use of that right is not typically relevant (Alcácer 2016).

Not surprisingly, the lack of clarity regarding the objective assumptions of the concept of "hate speech" has led, almost inevitably, to the fact that jurisprudence has begun to resort to it to justify compliance with the fundamental right to freedom of expression of judicial decisions condemning crimes that bear little or no relation to the natural context of the doctrine, that is, Article 510 of the Criminal Code. This is the case, for example, with the crime of glorification of terrorism (Article 578 of the Criminal Code) and crimes against the crown (Article 490 of the Criminal Code). In relation to the latter group of cases, **STC 177/15, 22-7,** which echoes the concept that we are dealing with here, confirms in amparo the conviction handed down in a case involving the burning of photos of the king during an anti-monarchist demonstration (Alcácer 2016, p. 4). Along the same lines, **STEDH 13-3-18**, F. J. 3°, which condemned Spain in this case for violation of the fundamental right to freedom of expression, is also based on the argument that the conduct, since it did not involve incitement to violence, would not constitute expression of hate speech either. [5]

If some limiting virtuality of freedom of expression typically relevant to the notion of hate speech can be recognized, it probably goes through the analysis of how acceptable the use of such concept is for the sake of criminal protection of minorities, immigrants and other groups particularly in need of protection. As Landa Gorostiza points out, it is likely that when we refer to the ECtHR, we are not referring to a single concept of "hate speech," but to several, in keeping with the opening of this doctrine to contexts other than the historical revisionism of the National Socialist Holocaust or philo-Nazi incitement, such as those relating to anti-immigrant political discourse, homophobia or incitement to religious hatred (Landa 2018, pp. 33 and 37). It is clear, in this context, that neither the king, nor the members of the crown, nor the state security forces and corps form part of any of the so-called **"target groups"** referred to in Recommendation R (97) 20 of the Committee of Ministers of the European Commission against Racism and Intolerance (ECRI) of the Council of Europe, and therefore recourse to that doctrine in cases of threats or insults against any of those crimes is completely out of the question (Landa 2018, p. 46). [6]

In line with what has just been stated, Alcácer Guirao denounces the lack of clarity in the concept of hate speech, which is particularly clear and widely shared:

---

[5] Vid. also, on this subject, the SAN 5-12-08 and, in particular, its interesting particular vote. A similar reference is found, previously, in STEDH 8-3-11, which resolved the case of *Otegi* against Spain, F.J. 1: "Although some of the terms in the plaintiff's speech paint one of the most negative pictures of the King as an institution, thus acquiring a hostile connotation, they do not call for the use of violence nor is it hate speech, which in the Court's view is the essential element to be considered (see, a contrario, Sürek v. Turkey (No. 1) [GS], No. 26682/1995, para. 62, ECHR 1999-IV). On the other hand, it points out that neither the domestic courts nor the Government have justified the applicant's conviction by mentioning incitement to violence or hate speech."

[6] Along the same lines, and very graphically, the SAP Barcelona, 6ª, 12-12-18, F.J. 2°: "It is necessary to restrict the scope of the concept to its original core: the fight against inequality to protect groups that may be described as historically vulnerable in the framework of the production of the event, which does not allow for the inclusion of State institutions, which may be susceptible to protection by other means, where appropriate". The resolution continues: "(. . .) it seems a complete institutional contradiction to affirm (as do the ECtHR and the Constitutional Court) that freedom of expression has a particularly preferential position when it contributes to the public debate on matters of general relevance, in which subjects exercising public functions are involved, and then to point out that such subjects may form part of some of the groups susceptible to discrimination through the discourse of hate, since there is no doubt about the tremendous discouraging effect that this recognition has on the exercise of the right. Therefore, not any group or social group of persons can be subject to the protection provided by the prohibition of the so-called 'hate speech', which must be limited to vulnerable and historically discriminated groups in the specific context in which the speech is issued." In the same sense, the STEDH 28-8-18 has recently been pronounced, which in the case of *Savva Terentyev* against Russia considered that the police forces cannot be considered a group or collective that needs special protection under the umbrella of hate speech. On the contrary, it would be a public institution, which like others of its kind, must have a greater degree of tolerance for offensive words. In the same vein, but in a broader context in relation to freedom of expression and the crime of slander, STEDH 20-11-18 was issued, relating to the case of *Toranzo Gómez* against Spain.

> Certainly, the very vagueness and indetermination of the notion of 'hate speech', or of other formulas coined by our criminal legislator as 'direct or indirect incitement to hatred or discrimination' (Article 510 of the Criminal Code), allows for its application to a very broad framework of expressive behavior-with the consequent broadness in the restriction of freedom of expression. If the royal family considers itself to be a suitable victim of hate speech, there is no reason not to include any other person or group to whom messages of hate, discrimination, or repudiation are projected, whether they are performing public functions or are ordinary citizens. Thus, any insult, insult or public contempt could be considered 'hate speech', losing the meaning with which it had been coined (Alcácer 2016, pp. 3 ff.).[7]

3 Damage, Offense, and Glorification of Terrorism (Art. 578 CP)

3.1 Approach

The review of some of the most paradigmatic factual assumptions regarding the phenomenology of the glorification of terrorism through the use of social networks[8] highlights at least one of the main features of current Spanish jurisprudence on the subject: an **erratic interpretation of Article 578 of the Criminal Code**, which ends

---

[7]In a similar vein, Section 5 of the Barcelona Provincial Court handed down its ruling 787/12, 6-9, which revoked the sentence imposed in the case of the Plataforma per Catalunya pamphlet by the SJP no. 2 Manresa 11-11-11. It also warns of the risk of abuse of the regulatory model that we are dealing with in the Recommendation on General Policy No. 15, on the fight against hate speech, of 8 December 2015.

[8]Particularly revealing are the cases of Cassandra Vera and Cesar Strawberry. The facts of the Cassandra Vera case consisted of the continued publication on the social network Twitter of thirteen jokes about the so-called "Operation Ogre," that is, the attack perpetrated by ETA on December 20, 1973 against Admiral Luis Carrero Blanco, the then president of the government of Spain during Franco's dictatorship. The jokes alluded to the way in which the damaged vehicle flew over an adjacent wall as if it were some kind of space trip. The SAN, 4ª, 9/17, 29-3, condemned Cassandra Vera to a first instance sentence of 1 year in prison and 7 years of absolute disqualification for the commission of a continuous crime of exaltation of terrorism with humiliation of its victims. However, this decision was overturned by STS 95/18, 29-2, which held that the reference messages prosecuted could not be subsumed under Article 578 of the Criminal Code. For his part, Augusto Montaña Lehman, known artistically as "César Strawberry," was tried as the alleged perpetrator of a crime of glorification of terrorism for the publication on Facebook of six jokes with different content relating to certain terrorist attacks and their victims, as well as the Royal House. SAN 1, 20/16, 19-7, analyzed each of Strawberry's messages in detail, to conclude that none of them really praised terrorism in general, or the ETA terrorist organization in particular. Nor did the Audiencia Nacional observe in them any humiliation or discredit of the victims of terrorism. The National Court's decision was overturned by STS 4/17, 18-1, which therefore revoked the acquittal and sentenced César Strawberry to a year's imprisonment and six and a half years' absolute disqualification as the author of a continuing crime of glorifying terrorism with humiliation of its victims. This sentence was recently annulled by STC 25-2-2020, which considered that the convicted person's expressions would be covered by the fundamental right to freedom of expression.

up leading to judicial decisions of very different nature regarding similar or even identical factual assumptions. The fundamental reason for this lies in the almost absolute **lack of definition of the legal right** protected in the crime in question. The following lines are devoted to this extreme circumstance.

3.2 Lack of Concreteness of the Protected Legal Good

Under the doctrine set forth, among many others, by STS 812/11, 21-7, Art. 578 CP protects

> (...) the **interdiction** (...) of **hate speech, that is,** the praise or justification of terrorist actions, which cannot be included within the coverage granted by the right to freedom of speech or ideology insofar as terrorism constitutes the most serious violation of the human rights of that community which suffers it, because the discourse of terrorism is based on the extermination of the different, on the most absolute intolerance, on the loss of political pluralism and, in short, on collective terrorization (sic) as a means of achieving those ends.[9]

In view of this jurisprudential reference, one must ask what exactly, in the opinion of the High Court, is the interest protected by the precept. The fact that hate speech is not protected by freedom of expression and that, in one of its recent jurisprudential developments, Article 578 of the Criminal Code constitutes one of the mechanisms for the criminal punishment of this type of speech is something that—as discussed above—both the Supreme Court and the Constitutional Court have already emphasized on several occasions. When the doctrine of hate speech is invoked for the purpose of specifying the object of criminal protection under Article 578 of the Criminal Code, what is actually happening is, however, an irremediable request in principle. The issue is precisely to determine in what cases, and in the name of what interests deserve protection, the violation of the prohibition against hate speech should be criminally sanctioned. In this way, the jurisprudential doctrine in question would appear to be paving the way for the criminalization of behaviors that are fundamentally aimed at expressing internal attitudes of offense, humiliation, or discredit of certain groups, without a clearly determinable legal object of protection (Miró 2018, p. 39).

It is not surprising, in this context, that some voices have recently suggested a hermeneutic reformulation of the apologetic and discrediting crimes that concern us with support in the doctrine of the *offense principle,* fundamentally defended by Feinberg (1986, pp. 5 ff.). This principle would imply a reformulation of the well-known *harm principle*, according to which in a civilized society the state could only legitimately limit the will and actions of individuals to prevent harm to other individuals (Stuart Mill 1859, p. 128). According to the *harm principle,* freedom and the free development of personality would constitute two of the essential principles of individual welfare. The state should ensure the protection of individual

[9]This criterion is followed, for example, the most recent SAN 4ª, 9/17, 29-3.

freedom, so that when the exercise of the freedom of one subject limits that of another, thereby harming him, then the state, or even another individual, would be entitled to intervene by limiting the freedom of the disturber (Stuart Mill 1859, p. 127).

In accordance with the variant of the *harm principle* represented by the *offense principle,* the minimum limit of state intervention in the sphere of individual freedom would no longer be represented by damages to third parties, but by the disturbance of collective feelings (Feinberg 1986, pp. 5 ff.). Based on this principle, and on the *harm/offense* scheme that constitutes its fundamental pillar, Miró distinguishes between **harmful and offensive expressions** to conclude that the only behaviors that deserve to be punished with a prison sentence are those that could cause **harm,** understood as endangering or harming interests that are closely related to the essential freedom and personal autonomy of a specific citizen, that is, the interests that are essential to the development of the personality and dignity of specific individuals (Miró 2018, p. 29). For their part, those behaviors that do not cause serious harm or danger but do constitute **offenses** or *wrongdoing*, that is, unpleasant experiences, inconveniences, and nuisances that do not constitute harm, could only be punished under criminal law, at most, with a fine (Miró 2018, pp. 27 ff.). It would also be necessary for the offense to be serious and for the criminal law to be understood as not being disproportionate to it, "*both from an ethical perspective of proportionality with what has been done and from a consequentialist perspective in terms of deterrence*" (Miró 2018, p. 31). Finally, criminal law should not be concerned with the **mere nuisance** caused by behavior that might disturb the peace of the individuals (Feinberg 1986, p. 5; Miró 2018, p. 27).

With the support of this tripartite classification, Miró distinguishes between the two types of behavior typified in Article 578 of the Criminal Code, that of exaltation of terrorism, on the one hand, and that of humiliation and discredit of the victims, on the other. On paper, only the first "*would constitute the criminalization of a conduct because of its potential to cause harm,*" while the type of humiliation of the victims "*would rather imply the criminalization of an offensive conduct that would affect the honor of the victims, their relatives, or the community*" (Miró 2018, p. 37). Despite this supposed legislative distinction, the jurisprudence on glorification in social networks, by not requiring that such conduct endanger or harm interests that are closely related to the spheres of essential freedom and personal autonomy of citizens, would equate the glorification of terrorism with the humiliation of its victims, as if both cases were offenses against collective feelings, and not harm to individual interests (Miró 2018, p. 42). Based on this exegesis of Article 578 of the Criminal Code, since the provision provides for both a prison sentence and a fine as a legal consequence, the criminal intervention of the state in all the cases contemplated by the provision, whether they involve glorification or humiliation, should always be limited—to be legitimate, to the imposition of non-custodial sentences (Miró 2018, p. 43).

The distinction between harmful and offensive expressions proposed by Miró and, in general, the discussion on the minimum limits of criminal law intervention and, thus, on the eventual criminalization of offensive behavior, is undoubtedly highly suggestive. For the time being, the adoption of the so-called *offense principle* will probably provide the unquestionable advantage of its capacity to yield in normative areas, such as that of Article 578 of the Criminal Code, where the determination of the criminally protected legal right is far from uncontroversial. In the face of the uncertainty of the indetermination of exactly what is the legal object endangered by the conducts of exaltation of terrorism or humiliation of its victims, the distinguishing criterion between damages and offenses could serve to reduce to some extent the complexity of the question posed. Specifically, it would make it possible to discern in an apparently simple manner whether the corresponding typical behavior would endanger some individual interest linked to the freedom, dignity, or free development of the personality of specific individuals, or rather would be allegedly offensive to more or less ascertainable collective feelings. The application of the *offense principle* could thus contribute, in a reasonably well-founded way, to a restrictive interpretation of Article 578 of the Criminal Code, which is in essence tenable (Miró 2018, p. 28).

However, the alleged lack of definition of the concept of a legal good, which in some ways justifies recourse to the *offense principle, is* not entirely unrelated to the criterion that we are now considering. The difficulties involved in determining the legal right protected under Article 578 of the Criminal Code are perfectly comparable, if not identical, to those that would be involved in knowing when any of the acts listed in the aforementioned provision might harm an individual's very personal interest or disturb a collective feeling pursued by the *offense principle.* Moreover, if, as it would seem, the decisive delimitation for determining how criminal law should intervene, if it were to do so at all is based on the legal object of protection (interests that are intimately related to the spheres of essential freedom and personal autonomy of citizens *versus* collective feelings), it is not clear what capacity for concreteness the *offense principle* and its *harm-offense* binomial provides with respect to the principle of exclusive protection of legal assets.

In these terms, it would be perfectly possible to establish the corresponding parallelism between the *harm* and *offense principles,* on the one hand, and the continental principle of exclusive protection of legal assets, on the other. As we have seen, according to the *harm principle,* criminal intervention by the state would only be legitimate in cases of harm to very personal individual interests; and according to the *offense principle,* it would also be appropriate, although with legal consequences that are less restrictive of individual freedom in the face of disturbances of collective feelings. In terms of the continental European principle of exclusive protection of legal assets, according to the *harm principle,* criminal law should only intervene to protect individual legal assets, while the *offense principle* would admit criminal intervention for the protection of collective interests. Therefore, there is nothing to prevent the use of the term "legal asset" for all these interests and to focus the discussion, then, on which of them, in the face of which attacks, and with what legal consequences they should be criminally protected.

This conclusion is based, in turn, on the premise that nothing prevents the concept of a legal good from encompassing collective interests or feelings such as, for example, religious or security-related ones. Whether they are worthy of criminal protection or, if so, what should be the *intensity* and *extent* of the criminal response is a different matter. As is well known, the concept of legal property was born with Birnbaum (1834) in mid-nineteenth century liberal Germany. It is often asserted that the concept did not arise with the intention of limiting the *ius puniendi* of the state, but rather, on the contrary, with the desire to broaden it, thus allowing for the emergence of certain crimes that, because they consisted of the violation of supra-individual interests (such as religion or morality), could in no way fit into criminal law that was exclusively protective of individual rights (Mir 1976, p. 128). Thus, if we consider the purpose for which the notion of the legal good was originally conceived, not only did this concept not prevent the violation or endangerment of collective, not individual, interests from being characterized as a crime, but its historical birth was due to the desire to extend criminal protection to certain supra-individual interests as well. Not surprisingly, all of the liberal criminal laws of the nineteenth century already contained crimes that threatened or endangered collective or state-owned legal assets.

Certainly, it can be stated that at least one of the recognized fathers of the concept of legal good, Birnbaum did not attribute to that concept a particularly limiting capacity of *ius puniendi*. It can be, and indeed is, disputed whether the concept of legal property was born with such a vocation or whether it was born with a different or even opposite one. Thus, for example, while some authors are in favor of the second alternative, others, on the other hand, consider that, in Birnbaum, the concept under discussion, although on the one hand it came to legitimize an expansion of the legal-criminal order, on the other hand it contributed to increasing the degree of rationality and legal security that should govern its application. Thus, for example, authors such as Alcácer Guirao understand the transit operated by Birnbaum of the crime as an injury to individual subjective rights to the crime as an injury to a legal good, far from representing an ideological turn from liberalism to communitarian-ism, it actually sought to operate a dogmatic and methodological concretion of the concept of "subjective right." Specifically, what Birnbaum and his notion of the legal good would have sought was to provide the subjective right with a factual, tangible substratum, which in reality would be damaged by the commission of the crime, and all of this in the interest of legal security (Alcácer 2003, pp. 101 f. and 110).

Nonetheless, leaving aside the controversy over what Birnbaum's true intention was in the process of establishing the concept of legal property, the truth is that there are strong reasons, in my opinion, to understand that the concept we are now dealing with can be assumed without trauma from the perspective of a liberal criminal law. I believe that the concept of a legal right is fully capable of fulfilling the liberal political-criminal function that limits the punitive power normally entrusted to it within the framework of a liberal state. In my opinion, the historical implications of the concept do not justify the fact that the concept under analysis is not valid, but rather that it probably demonstrates that it is a notion that is still awaiting a higher level of development and concreteness in the doctrine (Alcácer 2003, p. 68). In my opinion, not only is it *possible* to shape the concept of legal good in this way, but there are ample reasons to understand that it is also *advisable*. The latter could be based, principally, on three ideas.

The first idea is of a historical nature, and aims to draw attention to the following fact. Perhaps it can be said that the concept of the legal good was coined by Birnbaum in a not necessarily liberal sense, and that, subsequently, placed in the hands of some neo-Kantian authors, it reached considerable levels of abstraction and spiritualization, not contributing, of course, to its understanding as a liberal concept. However, his concept of the legal good had little or nothing to do with the original meaning of it (Schwinge and Zimmerl 1937, p. 62). In fact, it is not at all difficult to find antecedents (not too far removed in time from the origin of the concept) of authors who would have used it in an unequivocally limiting sense of *ius puniendi*. It should be noted, moreover, that while it is true that the concept under consideration may not have originally appeared as a limiting instrument in the sense indicated, this sense has begun to be recognized by a sector of the doctrine in relatively recent times (Mir 2016, 4/58 ff.). As Roxin (1976) points out, an increasingly important segment of the literature is now suggesting a possible connection between the concept of the legal good and the enlightened notion of "social harm" (Mir 1976, p. 129; Rudolphi 1970, p. 154).

Finally, we must call attention to the fact that spiritualized conceptions of the juridical good (defended at the time, for example, by the so-called Marburg School: Schwinge and Zimmerl 1937, pp. 62 ff. and 77 ff.) should not be seen at all as a necessary or inevitable consequence of the very notion of the juridical good. On the contrary, it is not only a matter of the possible ways of shaping it, but certainly one of the ways that has most betrayed the essentially liberal spirit of the concept of the legal good. In fact, there is, for example, a possible material foundation of the concept that we are now interested in that is fully consistent with the illustrated political-criminal program. I am referring to the *personalist* conception of the juridical good. Indeed, if, from the perspective of a liberal state, criminal law could be viewed as an instrument of the state for the protection of the interests of the citizen, particularly his freedom, then a concept of legal good centered on the individual interests of the person would be perfectly adaptable to that perspective. In other words, a concept of a legal good that can be brought back to the individual, and that is resistant to any "communitization" and "etization" of criminal law (Alcácer 2003, p. 72). As opposed to "spiritualized" conceptions of the legal good, a personalist conception of the legal good presents unquestionable advantages in terms of legal security. This is due mainly to the fact that, from the standpoint of the criminalization of conduct, the aforementioned personalist perspective would obligate the legislator to provide a greater rationale and foundation for the creation of criminal norms by taking as a point of reference "objects" that are external to the logic of the norm itself and to the underlying "value of the object" (Alcácer 2003, pp. 73 and 77 et seq.).

Does this positioning in favor of a personalist concept of legal good, and the consequent rejection of its "spiritualized" conceptions, mean that there is no room for protecting supra-individual interests, that is, that any crime that attempts against collective legal goods can be automatically labeled as improper of the criminal law of a liberal state? The question that has just been asked must be answered in the negative. I share the position of those authors who defend the idea that the protection of the individual, particularly his freedom, through criminal law should not be articulated exclusively through the protection of individual legal assets, but also through the protection of certain supra-individual legal assets that are especially important for the individual in terms of the subject's participation in the social system. Paradigmatic in this respect would be, for example, the Public Treasury, the environment or the Administration of Justice (Alcácer 2003, pp. 96 f.).

Nor is there any justification, in my view, for the criticism that the concept of a legal good would be exclusively "causal," "naturalistic," or "materialistic" in nature (Werle 1989, p. 711). That is, it can only explain the content of material interests that are susceptible to legal protection, not, therefore, those of an "ideal" nature (Schwinge and Zimmerl 1937, p. 68; Sina 1962, p. 81). Both the Philosophy of Law and the Jurisprudence on Civil Law Interests, and finally, Criminal Law, have taken it upon themselves to show that the term "legal good" can also be used without trauma in a sense that encompasses not only strictly material interests, but also ideal or immaterial ones. Thus, for example, from the logic of legal and philosophical language itself, the affirmation of the ideal interest "honor" as a legal good deserving of civil or criminal protection is considered unproblematic (Schwinge and Zimmerl 1937, p. 68). Nevertheless, in this work it is considered preferable to uphold a concept of legal good in accordance with which the latter is viewed neither as a "thing," nor as a "value" or "interest" to be protected, but rather as something that participates in both the former and the latter. From the perspective adopted here, defended in Spain by Mir Puig, it is considered appropriate to define the legal asset that is criminally protected, therefore, as a dialectic relationship of reality and value. That is, as a "valuable thing" (Mir 2016, 6/40; Alcácer 2003, p. 90).

From the conception of criminal unlawfulness that is considered preferable here, criminal law must be contemplated as a means of social control whose function consists in the protection of society through the avoidance of crimes, that is, the injury or endangerment of legal-criminal assets. According to this approach, criminal law assets should be considered as conditions of social life that affect the possibilities of participation of individuals in the social system (Mir 2016, 4/55 and 6/41), as valuable social functional units necessary for the existence of our society in its concrete configuration (Rudolphi 1970, p. 167) or as development of possibilities in its evolution towards the achievement of the stage of emancipated subject of law (Otto 1971, p. 5). Understood in this way, the concept of legal-criminal good is not only legitimate for a social and democratic state governed by the rule of law, but it is even mandatory to punish the most dangerous attacks against legal assets with a penalty because they are socially harmful in terms of the individual's possibilities of participating in society. This being so, I believe it is possible to affirm that the notion of individual freedom lies at the very basis of this concept. For this reason, it can be understood that the social-preventive function of criminal law, that is, the protection of society through the prevention of crimes, seeks, in a certain way, to guarantee the freedom of individuals by ensuring the indemnity of their minimum living conditions (legal-criminal assets). Understood in this way, the individual freedom of citizens would become not only a limit to the *ius puniendi* of the state, but the very foundation of criminal intervention (Mir 2016, 4/47; Mendoza 1999, p. 312).

Based on all of the foregoing, and in light of the interpretation of Article 578 of the Criminal Code contained in the *above-mentioned* convictions, it is necessary, as suggested by one sector of the doctrine, to carry out a **constitutional review of the provision**, in line with the provisions of the decisive **STC 112/16, 20-6**. According to this resolution,

> [t]he criminal punishment of the acts of exaltation of terrorism punished in Article 578 ... entails a legitimate interference in the sphere of freedom of expression of its perpetrators insofar as they can be considered a manifestation of hate speech by fostering or encouraging, albeit indirectly, a situation of risk for persons or rights of third parties or for the system of freedoms itself (STC 112/16, 20-6, F.J. 4).[10]

This criterion was recently accepted by **STS 378/17, 25-5**. For this ruling, a criminal penalty is only constitutional if the denial and justification operates as an incitement, albeit an indirect one, to commit it, and there must be an objective risk to the persons or rights of third parties or to the system of freedoms covered by the author's malice. In the words of the resolution under review,

> the criminal punishment of the acts of exaltation of terrorism punishable under Article 578 constitutes a legitimate interference with the freedom of expression of its perpetrators insofar as they can be considered a **manifestation of the discourse of hatred because they propitiate or encourage, albeit indirectly, a situation of risk for the persons or rights of third parties or for the system of freedoms itself**. Hence the relevance, for the purposes of classification, as a matter of ordinary legality, but under constitutional requirements, of the accreditation of the purpose or motivation for which the acts of exaltation or humiliation are carried out. And of the assessment of the risk created by the act in question. Even though this risk must be understood in the abstract as "aptitude" inherent to the act in question, it does not refer to a specific crime of terrorism, but is limited in time and space by reference to the persons affected.

In similar terms, Judge Andrés Ibáñez pronounced a **private vote on the aforementioned STS 4/17, 18-1,** which revoked the acquittal and sentenced Cesar Strawberry to a year in prison and six and a half years of absolute disqualification as the author of a continuous crime of exaltation of terrorism with humiliation of its victims. According to this particular opinion,

> since what makes the aforementioned acts criminal is their ability to encourage the practice of the actions described in Articles 571 to 577 of the Criminal Code, legitimizing them in some way, it is necessary that they maintain a minimal contextual relationship and effective functionality with them, so that those who carry out acts of terrorism can benefit from them

[10] Through STC 112/16, the Constitutional Court extended the criteria set out in STC 235/07 for the denial and justification of genocide set out in the now-defunct Article 607.2 CP, integrated from LO 1/2015 into the current Article 510 CP, to cases of the exaltation of terrorism under Article 578 CP, in a manner that is fully compatible with the criteria set out *in that article*.

> or make them profitable in terms of support, consensus-building, or social prestige. And in the case of those relating to the victims, it should be a matter of formulations capable of making a hypothetical victim consider himself or herself directly concerned and feel vilified by them.[11]

A final element to be considered in cases of exaltation of terrorism and humiliation of its victims would be, in Miró's opinion, whether or not the person who commits the alleged offense has the right to carry it out. This would be the case, for example, in cases of **political criticism,** which "*cannot give the right to harm another, but must limit as much as possible the intervention of criminal law in the face of what it simply offends so as not to endanger the dispute*" (Miró 2018, p. 43). When the possible offense is carried out within the framework of political criticism, criminal law will not be legitimized to intervene, and civil law should do so, at most (Miró 2018, p. 43). While this view is certainly worthy of being widely shared, it is equally clear that it once again suffers from a high degree of circularity. It is not reasonably debatable that in a democratic state ideological debate and political disagreement constitute the basis of the system itself, to the extent that without them, the system itself could hardly continue to be called democratic (Rodríguez Montañés 2012). However, as the recent **STEDH 13-2-18 (Stern Taulats and Roura Capellera *vs.* Spain case)** recalls, also in cases of political criticism, the fundamental right to freedom of expression is subject to limits. Specifically, those already known to be in the interest of the honor and dignity of individuals (e.g., through serious insults), freedom (e.g., through threats), or those relating to discourses that do not merely theoretically question the democratic system, but rather put it in material danger (e.g., through acts of criminal promotion) (Lascuraín 2010, p. 1). When political discourse collides with such interests is precisely what must be determined.

References

Aguilar MA et al (2015) Manual práctico para la investigación y enjuiciamiento de delitos de odio y discriminación. CEJFE, Barcelona

Alcácer R (2003) ¿Lesión de bien jurídico o lesión de deber? Apuntes sobre el concepto material del delito. Atelier, Barcelona

Alcácer R (2016) Diversidad cultural, intolerancia y derecho penal. RECPC:18–11

Birnbaum JMF (1834) Sobre la necesidad de una lesión de derechos para el concepto de delito [trad: Guzmán JL 2010]. Edeval, Valparaíso

Dolz M (2011) Los delitos de odio en el código penal tras la modificación operada por LO 1/2015. Breve referencia a su relación con el delito del art. 173 CP. Diario La Ley 7721: 24-10-11

[11] This argument can also be found in another recent private vote issued by Judge Manuela Fernández Prado in relation to SAN 3/18, 2-3, in which Pablo Hasel was convicted of the crime set out in Article 578 of the Criminal Code for tweets extolling the terrorist group Grapo against the King and the Guardia Civil, among other institutions. In the same direction, see, STS 646/18, 14-12 and SAN 6/18, 1-3.

Feinberg J (1986) Offense to others. The moral limits of the criminal law, vol 2
Landa J-M (2018) Los delitos de odio. Tirant lo Blanch, Valencia
Lascuraín JA (2010) La libertad de expresión tenía un precio. RAD 6/2010, 24 septiembre 2010
Mendoza B (1999) Exigencias de la moderna política criminal y principios limitadores del Derecho penal. ADPCP, pp 279 ss
Mir S (1976) Introducción a las bases del Derecho penal. Concepto y Método. Bosch, Barcelona
Mir S (2016) Derecho penal. PG, 10ª edn, 2ª reimpr. Reppertor, Barcelona
Miró F (2018) Derecho penal y 140 caracteres. Hacia una exégesis restrictiva de los delitos de expresión, en el mismo (Dir) Cometer delitos en 140 caracteres. El Derecho penal ante el odio y la radicalización. Marcial Pons, Madrid
Otto H (1971) Rechtsgutsbegriff und Deliktstatbestand. In: Müller-Dietz H (Dir) Strafrechtsdogmatik und Kriminalpolitik. Carl Heymanns, Colonia, pp 1 ss
Rodríguez Montañés T (2012) Libertad de expresión, discurso extremo y delito. Una aproximación desde la Constitución a las fronteras del derecho penal. Tirant lo Blanch, Madrid
Roxin C (1976) Sentido y límites de la pena estatal, en el mismo, Problemas básicos del Derecho Penal [trad: Luzón Peña D-M]. Reus, Madrid
Rudolphi HJ (1970) Die verschiedenen Aspekte des Rechtsgutsbegriffs, FS-Honig. Otto Schwartz & Co, Göttingen
Schwinge E, Zimmerl L (1937) Wesensschau und konkretes Ordnungsdenken im Strafrecht. L. Röhrscheid, Bonn
Sina P (1962) Die Dogmengeschichte des strafrechtlichen Begriffs "Rechtsgut". Helbing & Lichtenhahn, Basel
Stuart Mill J (1859) Sobre la libertad [trad: Azkárate P, 1997]. Alianza Editorial, Madrid
Werle G (1989) Justiz-Strafrecht und polizeiliche Verbrechensbekämpfung im Dritten Reich

For a Feminist and Guarantism-Based Methodology in the Criminal Protection of Sexual Freedom

Gema Marcilla Córdoba

Abstract The purpose of this paper is the reflection on the criminal protection of sexual freedom from a double perspective: the criminal guarantism, as a model of law and criminal legal science for constitutional democracies, and feminism, as a political theory and social movement that demands the end of discrimination against women. The criminal guarantism protects the person liable to be punished in a criminal proceeding. Feminism considers it essential in the struggle for equality to combat all gender-based violence and, in particular, sexual violence, whose manifestations are not isolated events, but an expression of patriarchal social structures. Projection of the feminist struggle strategy in Spain is the current Organic Law of integral protection of sexual freedom (LO 10/2022, de 6 de septiembre, de garantía integral de la libertad sexual), whose main changes with respect to the previous regulation are two: (1) the end of the distinction between two types of sexual attack, abuse and assault, to include all attacks against sexual freedom under the serious crime of assault; (2) and the definition of consent, as the only aspect that can exclude the unjust, understanding as such an express, of will. As the article 178 says, "it will only be understood that there is consent when it has been freely expressed through acts that, in view of the circumstances of the case, clearly express the will of the person". These amendments, from the guarantism perspective, call for a prudent examination of their suitability and constitutional legitimacy, since they increase the penalties, especially for non-consensual sexual intercourses that, before the planned amendment, were included in the most permissible type of abuse, and that way weaken principles that must be considered in the production and application of the criminal law.

G. Marcilla Córdoba (✉)
Faculty of Law, University of Castilla-La Mancha, Albacete, Spain
e-mail: Gema.Marcilla@uclm.es

E. Demetrio Crespo et al. (eds.), *Crisis of the Criminal Law in the Democratic Constitutional State*, Legal Studies in International, European and Comparative Criminal Law 6, https://doi.org/10.1007/978-3-031-13413-5_8

1 Introduction

In the following pages we will analyze the criminal protection of sexual freedom, from the double perspective of the *guarantism* and *feminism*.[1] The *guarantism* defends the law of the weakest, which, in the criminal sphere, is always the offender.[2] Inherent in criminal law is the risk of judging and sentencing an innocent person in a disproportionate or even totally unfair process. *Feminism* claims the lack of protection of women against different forms of violence, which statistically affects women disproportionately more than men, being this gender violence one of the struggles against discrimination.[3]

The offender's vulnerability, which is dealt with by the guarantism, is structural for two additional reasons: first, because we inherited criminal codes that direct their punitive force at deviations in social behavior that have their genesis in social situations of marginalization and poverty; and, second, because criminal law, under the growing influence of populism, incriminates more than is strictly necessary, responding to the demands of a complex society that is persuaded to achieve security by means of criminal protection.[4] Ironically, this "oversized" criminal law appears "stunted" in certain cases to fulfill its function of social defense, for example, by failing to protect against criminality perpetrated by the political and economic, national and transnational elites.[5]

Feminism denounces a similar lack of social defense or protection associated with criminality whose origin is heteropatriarchy, which causes and promotes different forms of gender-based violence. One of the findings of current feminist theory is

---

[1] The work is developed within the framework of the project "Crisis of the Criminal Law of the Rule of Law: Manifestations and Trends" (SBPLY/17/18501/000223), granted by the Castilla-La Mancha Regional Communities Board and co-financed by the European Regional Development Fund (ERDF), its principal investigators being E. Demetrio Crespo, A. J. García Figueroa and myself, all professors at the University of Castilla-La Mancha.

[2] Ferrajoli (1997).

[3] Feminist theory has its genesis and develops in parallel to the subsequent historical movements of struggle for rights. In this way, there is talk of three or four feminist waves. The first of these is in line with the Enlightenment and criticizes the omission of women from the revolutionary program. The second, also known as the "suffragette movement," began in the early nineteenth century, turning feminism into a mass movement that claimed equal rights and, above all, political equality through active suffrage or the right to vote. Finally, the third wave will expand from the 1960s onwards and will diversify into different feminisms, such as equality, liberal, radical and that of difference. The fourth wave crystallizes in "postfeminism" or "transfeminism," which gives theoretical coverage to the struggle for the rights of transgender people, especially with regard to "self-identification" or a person's choice of gender even if it is not in accordance with the biological characteristics. Wolstonecraft (1792), Beauvoir (1949 [2005]), Amorós and De Miguel (2005), Valcárcel (2008), and Butler (2007).

[4] VVAA (2019).

[5] "The guarantism takes the class discrimination record [...] The real 'dangerous classes' are no longer the social outcasts, those who practice subsistence crime, but the ruling elites, who nevertheless almost always succeed in maintaining their impunity," Prieto (2011), pp. 131–132.

that, to combat such violence, including sexual violence, it cannot be assumed that it is a sum of isolated violent acts, but rather that they are acts linked to structures of male domination. Sexual violence is a type of gender-based violence. Traditionally, the legal right protected in sexual crimes was the woman's honesty, which did not even belong to her, because what was damaged was the honor of her father or husband.[6] In the Spanish legal system, there have been significant advances since the 1978 Constitution in terms of the protection of sexual freedom. But a criminal law with a gender perspective must critically review legislative and judicial practices concerning sexual assaults, which are still burdened by moral prejudices about female sexuality. For this reason, in the last few months a penal reform has been carried out (*Organic Law on the Comprehensive Protection of Sexual Freedom*[7,8])

[6]The 1989 Criminal Code is the one that changes the protected legal right in the Spanish legal system from honesty to sexual freedom. See, LO 3/1989, dated June 21, 1989.

[7]The bill, approved by the Council of Ministers on July 6, 2021, essentially replicates the draft law of the parliamentary group "Unidos Podemos-En Comú Podem-En Marea." See, Official Gazette of the Spanish Parliament. Congress of Deputies. XII legislature. Series B: Proposition of law, No. 297-1, dated July 20, 2018. The realization of this chapter took place before the final approval of the law (Organic Law 10/2022, of September 6). The considerations that are made in the paper still have value, since the definitive law has been approved with few changes with respect to the Bill. The enactment of the law has unleashed a severe political and social crisis due to the effect that the promoters of the law did not sufficiently explain: releases and reductions in the penalties of prisoners for sexual crimes as a consequence of the application of one of the Penal Law principles: the application of the "more favorable criminal law," that is to say, the one that, ones there is a regulatory change by a subsequent law, obliges the judge to choose the one that establishes the lower penalties. The consequence of this social and political crisis is the reform of the law with only a few months of implementation to pay attention to the populist social demand to raise sanctions.We can see that social criticism is due to the little pedagogy done with this law. LO 10/2022 is, as will be said later in this work, through a series of tables with the penalties corresponding to the crimes in the "Only yes is yes" legislation, guaranties better the criminally prosecuted rights than the previous regulation. However, at the same time, the new one protects better sexual freedom because it denies that there can be tacit consent or rejects a situation of paralysis of the victim who goes into shock due to fear, or even annulment of the victim's will to act, can be interpreted as consent, through a drug like the scopolamine. In other words, the political and social crisis little after the "Only yes is yes" law entered into force is not a matter of poor legislative technique, as most social media are saying, but a lack of explanation to citizens about the operation, purposes, and limits of criminal law.

[8]The explanatory memorandum of the bill we are discussing in this paper declares the purpose of making equality between men and women real and effective, through the prevention and eradication of the different forms of violence against women. Thus, the project includes non-criminal measures and criminal reforms. For example, criminal conducts are expanded, with the classification of "street harassment," "non-coercive procuring," that is, the obtaining of profit by exploiting the prostitution of others even without coercion of the prostituted person, or "third party renting," that is, the obtaining of profit by renting real estate for prostitution, regardless of the will of the prostituted persons. In the latter two cases, the consent of the victims does not exclude the crime due to their vulnerable nature. The reform has been in the making since mid-2018. In April of that year, the Provincial Court of Navarra ruled in the case known through the media as "La Manada": during the San Fermin celebrations, a group of young men had non-consensual sexual relations with a 19-year-old girl, recorded part of it and proudly boasted of the event on social networks. The judgment qualified the facts as constituting the minor type of abuse (relationship without consent)

that introduces two significant changes: first, the inclusion of sexual assaults without violence and intimidation, traditionally called "abuse," in the aggravated form of "assault," under the premise that such attacks were receiving an unjustifiably generous penal treatment; second, the definition of consent in sexual intercourse, as an express, unequivocal and conclusive manifestation of will. That the consent excluding sexual crime needs to be external and conclusive, would change macho attitudes, little concerned about obtaining it in sexual intercourses, and would avoid secondary victimization, i.e., the prosecution of the personality and sexual morality of the victim in the process.

As we shall see, both critical perspectives of criminal law, the feminist and guarantism, can come into conflict. From the feminist perspective, an effective protection against sexual crimes seems to require, on the one hand, the aggravation of some sexual assault behaviors. And, on the other hand, a definition of sexual assault as a non-consensual sexual intercourse. These two feminist claims, i.e., aggravation of penalties in non-consent sexual intercourses and looseness in the standards of proof for a commission of a sexual crime, as a consequence and as an exigence of a new concept of consent, is against the guarantism principles.

2 Criminal Guarantism

The guarantism is a philosophy of law with liberal and enlightened roots.[9] Its basic idea is that law is and must operate as a framework of rights and guarantees. Rights represent individuals' expectations of how political power should act, in its dual mission of respecting freedoms and removing obstacles against inequality. Guarantees are the legal techniques for enforcing rights, safeguarding "what is undecidable" (illegitimate actions) or "what is not undecidable" (illegitimate omissions), i.e.,

---

and not the aggravated assault (because violence or intimidation was not sufficiently proven). There was even issued a dissenting opinion advocating the innocence of the defendants. This resolution was, in fact, the trigger for the reform that is now included in the bill LO. The most controversial point of the judgment was that of consent: the need to turn from "no is no," to "only yes is yes," and the requirement of not making the proof of the crime depend on the effective resistance of the victim. The root cause of the reform is, therefore, an intense and passionate social movement of feminist protest in Spain, which found obvious links with the American protest known as "Me Too." #MeToo emerged in October 2017 to condemn the persistence of impunity for sexual assaults against women, and this following several complaints filed in this regard, some of them by celebrities, against the American film producer Harvey Weinstein. Socially and politically, the penal reform, especially regarding the increase of criminal reproach for any sexual intercourse not consented to by a woman, even if it took place without violence or intimidation, becomes a feminist campaign: the state must urgently fulfill its obligation to prevent or minimize behavior, but in a concrete way: not by focusing on particular events, but on the need to promote the rapid change of cultural and moral values and of course of judicial practices, which have obviated the gender perspective, the fact of violence of all kinds and also sexual, exercised on women for being women.

[9] Montesquieu (1748) and Beccaria (1764 [2008]).

enforcing the limits and links imposed by rights. They are, consequently, obligations to do or not to do, addressed to the lawmaker and also to the judge.[10]

From this perspective of the law as an instrument at the service of rights, the purpose of the guarantism, far from seeking the legitimacy of the law, is to serve as a critical point of reference. It warns that Law is an evil because of its unavoidable tendency to abuse. Thus, Law has an unyielding margin of illegitimacy, insofar as the human action in which power is materialized can only imperfectly conform to the model that justifies it.

The guarantism provides a paradigm of legal science and dogmatics, suitable to account for and fulfill the model of legal system predominant in the countries with the highest levels of civilization since the end of World War II, that is to say, the constitutional democracy or the constitutional rule of law.

The juridical method known as guarantism is projected in a legal science and dogmatics far removed from *legalism*, *positivism* and *neo-constitutionalism*. *Legalism* is formalist. It restricts the legal disciplines to the interpretation and systematization of the law, thus confusing the legal with the fair. In the face of this perspective, the guarantism advocates criticism, not only external or philosophical, as *positivism* does, but also internal or legal, drawing attention to the "gaps" (which in the terminology of guarantism is identified with the legislative omission of statutes for the development of constitutional mandates) and the "antinomies" (or legislative violations of constitutional limits). However, guarantism-based law also differs from neo-constitutionalist and post-positivist proposals,[11] because its critical perspective is not based on the morality of constitutional law, nor of law in general.

In terms of criminal law, guarantism is also a philosophy of criminal law, with legal-positive support within the framework of the constitutional rule of law, which allows for a model of criminal-legal science. The main idea of guarantism is that the risk of abuse and illegitimacy of those who are at the head of institutions is increased when the instrument of power is *ius puniendi*, since it is the most intense form of coercion. The risk is serious if criminal law moves away from the procedures and requirements of the idea of law as an instrument of rights and approaches *authoritarianism*, where, conversely, rights are implemented by a leader without limits or counterweights, or *populism*, which postpones rights in the name of majority

[10] "Therefore, criminal guarantism [...] clearly means contemplating and approaching criminal law necessarily from its limits, that is, from the basic rights established in the constitutions and the human rights enshrined in the different international conventions and treaties, which poses quite a few problems of constitutional-criminal hermeneutics that have yet to be developed in the context of the so-called *global law*, where the problem of overlapping different levels of protection arises. Ferrajoli has spoken in this framework of the critical, projective and constructive role of the paradigm of limited power as a shaper of the historical development of the rule of law," Demetrio Crespo (2020), p. 194.

[11] Atienza emphasizes that neo-constitutionalism and post-positivism are not equivalent conceptions of law. Neo-constitutionalism disregards the authoritative element of Law, its corollary being judicial activism. In contrast, post-positivism, which is represented in the conception of Law of Dworkin, Alexy or Nino, conceives "Law as a social practice guided by ends and by values, but which has to develop within certain authoritatively fixed limits," Atienza (2019) p. 492.

emotions, lacking the support of arguments and verification regarding facts. For this reason, the guarantism system moves the focus of attention of legal science towards the weakest once the machinery of *ius puniendi* has been set in motion: the defendant, who in subsequent phases will be charged, accused, prosecuted, convicted and/or imprisoned.

Thus, the guarantism demands a reduction of the scope of what is punishable, together with a utilitarian rationale for punishment, which is the deterrence of violent behavior. But, as opposed to other utilitarian theories, the guarantism pursues an additional utility: the minimization of the violence that results from punishment. Minimum offenses and minimum penalties are the core of the so-called minimum criminal law. The measure of institutional violence has a parameter: it has to be less than the informal or private violence that would be produced in the absence of punishment for the crime. In short, there are two purposes of criminal law based in the guarantism: crime prevention and proportionality of penalties. Together they constitute the scheme to delegitimize criminal institutions or norms.

For this last reason, although it cannot be confused with *abolitionist proposals* (denying the need for a criminal law), *guarantism* approaches them very closely when it delegitimizes criminal designations where it is empirically confirmed that remedies can be alternatives to penalties, that private violence is less serious than institutionalized criminal violence, or that criminal law provides little deterrence to the perpetration of offenses. On the other hand, the guarantism is placed at the antipodes of the "criminal law for the enemy" *(Feindstrafrecth)*, which, under the premise of confronting a citizen criminal law, unlimitedly expands the punitive powers of the state.[12]

3 Criminal Guarantees: Limits and Links in the *Creation* and *Application* of Criminal Law

Criminal guarantees are aimed at ensuring the effectiveness of the rights of those who are susceptible to punishment in criminal proceedings. They are a critical reference in the sense that, if they are not established, Criminal Law is delegitimized.[13]

[12]For example, terrorist actions (and terrorists are enemies) are not infringements of the law, but acts of war, removed from criminal guarantees. The term "Enemy Criminal Law," as opposed to "Citizen Criminal Law," was introduced by Günther Jakobs and is based on Carl Schmitt's friend-enemy distinction. Accordingly, a citizen is a person who does not deviate from the normative behavior as a matter of principle. On the other hand, an enemy is a dangerous individual who systematically commits offenses and to whom a criminal law different from that of the citizen is applicable, with a preventive function, not of criminal behavior, but of dangers that threaten the citizen's right to security. Jakobs and Cancio Meliá (2003), pp. 55 et seq. Guarantism arose in Italy in the 1970s specifically as a criticism of emergency criminal legislation, which put into practice the enemy criminal law. Demetrio Crespo (2004).

[13]Prieto (2011), p. 81. Regarding the distinction between *primary* guarantees (established by the constituent or the lawmaker) and *secondary* guarantees (applied by the judge when the primary guarantees are breached), See, Ferrajoli (1997, 2011).

Criminal guarantees may refer to the *creation* of law or to its *application*, although those relating to the creation of law have priority, since they create the conditions for a non-arbitrary jurisdiction.[14]

The guarantees relating to *creation* are, in turn, of two types: *formal*, or relating to *how to punish*, and *substantive*, relating to *the circumstances in which to punish*. The *formal* ones are identified with the formal aspects of the *rule of law* principle, and require exclusive competence of the *democratic lawmaker*,[15] *typification* or *written wording*, *taxation* and *non-retroactivity* in the case of unfavorable regulations.[16]

The *substantive ones* take the form of the principles of *harmfulness* (classification of behaviors that harm a criminal protected good o a fundamental right, causing damage to third parties), *materiality* (the prohibited actions must correspond to acts that can be empirically verified, without being able to prohibit the "immoral" condition or personality of the offender), *necessity* (the penalty must be the only social control mechanism available to prevent offense), *culpability* (only those who are responsible for the criminal action can be punished), *proportionality* (it is only legitimate to prohibit actions that seriously infringe fundamental legal rights and in any case there must be a correspondence between the seriousness of the criminal actions and the penal response).

The *guarantees referring to the application of criminal law*, which can be synthesized in the "due process" clause, include, in the first place, the principle of *strict jurisdiction*, so that, just as there is no offense or penalty without law, there is no offense or penalty without prosecution. Second, the organic or jurisdictional guarantees, which are identified in terms of the judge's *impartiality* regarding the parties, the *independence* of the judiciary from other powers and the *naturalness* or predetermination of the judge's competencies. And, in the third place, the *guarantees of the application process*, which include the *accusatory principle* and the *presumption of innocence* (which imply that the burden of proof falls on the accusation and that the requirements of such burden are high) and the principles of *contradiction*, *orality*, *publicity*, and *motivation*.

---

[14] Prieto (2011), p. 105. Beccaría has already emphasized this principle of legislative science, which links taxation and neutral application of the law: "A fixed codex of laws, which must be strictly observed to the letter, leaves no other power to the judge than that of examining and judging in the actions of citizens whether or not they are in conformity with the written law; when the rule of what is fair and or what is unfair, which must rule the actions of both the ignorant citizen and the philosopher citizen, is a matter of fact and not of controversy, then the subjects are not subject to the petty tyranny of the many." Beccaría (1764 [2008]), p. 37.

[15] Senese (2002)

[16] Ferrajoli (1997), pp. 382 et seq., develops the guarantees attached to the principle of criminal legality, distinguishing between those of *mere* legality (the *formal* guarantees of exclusive competence of the lawmaker, written character and non-retroactivity) and those of *strict* legality (taxativity and consistency with constitutional precepts). From my point of view, taxation can be included in the formal requirements. And consistency with constitutional principles is undoubtedly a fundamental requirement, and we believe that it is best understood if it is linked to the second group of guarantees relating to the *creation* of law, i.e., to the substantive guarantees.

The constitutions expressly recognize some of the aforementioned guarantees,[17] while others are implicit, as they represent the meaning of constitutional values, principles or rights, as well as the basis for judicial decisions.

4 The Effective Protection of Sexual Freedom Under the Framework of the Guarantism Principle in Criminal Law

From the watchtower of the guarantism, in tune with the currents that advocate a minimum criminal law, *ultima ratio* in social defense, the effective protection of criminal legal good or fundamental right must be balanced with respect for the weaker party, which is the one against whom criminal actions are directed. But this balance has specific questions *when the victim of the crime is a discriminated person*. Legal structures, including penal structures, have traditionally served the prevailing majorities. The feminist diagnosis is along these lines: legal structures at the service of the prevailing majority, men in a heteropatriarchal society, do not protect women from violence in general or from sexual violence in particular, thus contributing to maintaining a discriminatory situation.

Women's sexual freedom has traditionally been a legal right traditionally excluded or poorly protected by criminal law. Such lack of protection has been the consequence of legislative and judicial legal practices based on gender stereotypes, typical of societies of undisputed male dominance. The guarantism-based demands concerning the moderation of penalties for sexual offenses would be misleading if they were used to hide the persistence of a discriminatory legal culture that normalizes different forms of violence against women.

[17] Accordingly, the Spanish Constitution includes the principle of legality and the non-retroactivity of criminal laws (Articles 25.1 and 9.3); the prohibition of the Administration to impose penalties of deprivation of liberty (25.3); the prohibition of courts of honor (Article 26); the proscription, due to their disproportionate nature, of the death penalty, torture and inhuman or degrading punishment or treatment (Article 15); the attribution to penalties of a special positive preventive purpose, of re-education and social reintegration, as well as the express prohibition of forced labor (25.2); the right to effective judicial protection (24.1); the right to a natural judge, to defense and to the assistance of counsel, as well as to be informed regarding the accusation, to a public trial without undue delay and with all the guarantees, to use the means of evidence relevant to the defense, to not testify against oneself, to not declare oneself guilty and to the presumption of innocence (Article 24.2); the independence and irremovability of judges (117.1, 4, 5); the prohibition of extraordinary courts (117.6); the publicity and orality of trials and the motivation of judgments (120 CE).

Sexual violence is one of the manifestations of "gender violence."[18] This can be defined as that *directed at women for the fact of being*[19] women and is one of the most significant concepts of feminist thought,[20] as it is an irrefutable manifestation of female discrimination.[21] The fundamental idea behind the concept is that violence against women transcends individual cases. In the criminal sphere, gender-based violence does not consist of isolated episodes of criminal deviance. On the contrary, it is rooted in social and political structures of male domination and consequent subordination of women.[22] In short, *gender violence is that which takes place against women in the context of a patriarchal society*, and that is the methodological presupposition for legal analysis and for the reform proposals of feminist legal theory.[23] Legislative and judicial practices take place in a society in which gender stereotypes and political, economic and social conditions that place women in a subordinate position are still in force. Overcoming violence against women, which is linked to male domination, requires a deep transformation of all social structures, including the law.

This notion of gender violence as structural violence, key within current feminist theory, has inspired a broad repertoire of legal norms in Spain at the beginning of the millennium. Specifically, Organic Law 1/2004, *on Comprehensive Protection Measures against Gender Violence* and Organic Law 3/2007, *for the Effective Equality between Women and Men.*[24]

In terms of criminal law, it should be noted that the comprehensive legislation against gender violence made a penal reform consisting of aggravating the crimes of injury, abusive treatment, threats and intimidation[25] if "the victim was or had been a wife, or a woman who was or had been linked to the perpetrator by an analogous affective relationship, even without cohabitation, or if the victim was a particularly vulnerable person who lives with the perpetrator." *The reason for the aggravation of penalties is a social context of special vulnerability of women in general*, as well as

---

[18] This is the perspective of the so-called *Istanbul Convention*, within the Council of Europe, the most important European international organization for the protection of human rights. See, Ratification instrument of the *Council of Europe Convention on preventing and combating violence against women and domestic violence*, concluded in Istanbul, on May 11, 2011 (BOE of June 6, 2014).

[19] Poggi (2019), p. 303; De Lora (2019).

[20] See, Tubert (2003).

[21] Feminists denounce the fact that women's equality in the public sphere has been achieved at the cost of maintaining structures of discrimination in the private sphere.

[22] Turégano (2011) and Poggi (2019).

[23] One representative of this theory is, among others, MacKinnon (1982, 2001). In Spain, we highlight, among others, Añón (2008).

[24] These laws are intended to provide a comprehensive legal treatment of gender violence, including educational, labor, economic, political and welfare reforms to change the culture of women's subordination.

[25] See, Spanish CP Articles 148.4° and 148.5° (Injuries); 153.1 (Abusive Treatment); 171.4° (Threats and Intimidation).

the belief that the use of violence against partners is legitimate, and taking advantage of this situation by men, which, in turn, reinforces the violent and discriminatory social context.[26]

This aggravating circumstance, which could be called "structural gender violence," is reflected in the Bill Organic Law on the Comprehensive Guarantee of Sexual Freedom, as we shall see below. The guarantism theory is based on the attribution of *collective responsibility* to the man who is the perpetrator of an offense. In this sense, the aggravating circumstance is not in line with the requirements of the substantive legislative guarantee of culpability, which restricts penalties to the person responsible for the criminal action. Likewise, it contradicts the presumption of innocence and the accusatory principle if the aggravating circumstance establishes an *iuris et de iure* presumption of criminalization of power relations between men and women in the private sphere or in the sphere of affectivity.[27]

5 Spanish Regulation of Sexual Offenses Under the 1978 Constitution: The Distinction Between Sexual *Abuse* and Sexual *Assault*

Thus, the most important of the recent feminist criminal instruments against gender violence was the aggravating circumstance that criminalizes patriarchal relationships in the domestic sphere. But the penal reform forgot the adaptation of sexual offenses to the social perceptions of the twenty-first century. The prevention of sexual violence as a manifestation of gender-based violence is the purpose of the Istanbul Convention.[28] Its effective implementation is the aim of the aforementioned *Bill Organic Law on the Comprehensive Guarantee of Sexual Freedom*, which is awaiting amendments from the Parliament, and whose novelties will be analyzed later on.

The criminal regulation of sexual offenses in the framework of the 1978 Constitution places the legal right of "sexual freedom" at the center. It represents a major progress, since it overcomes a sifted legislation by the Catholic morality and by the most variegated patriarchal culture, in which honor and honesty are protected, which

[26] See, SSTC 59/2008, of May 14 and 45/2009, of February 19. According to the Constitutional Court, the aggravating circumstance punishes "a deep-rooted type of violence that is a manifestation of discrimination, a situation of inequality and power relations between men and women."

[27] This critical position was reflected in several separate opinions to the aforementioned judgment. The criticism would be mitigated if the aggravating circumstance establishes "to assess whether the basis for the aggravation of the penalty is found in a specific case of aggression perpetrated by a man against a man who is or has been his partner. It is not a matter of proving motive or intention, but of proving that the assault occurs in a context of domination" (Turégano 2011).

[28] See, Ratification instrument of the Council of Europe Convention on preventing and combating violence against women and domestic violence, concluded in Istanbul, on May 11, 2011. BOE of June 6, 2014.

does not even belong to the woman, but to her husband or father, as the case may be. However, feminists criticize the fact that the criminal legislation continues to make the classification of the crime depend on the woman being able to prove that she is honest; that her sexual conduct is adequate to those standards.[29] In the opinion of Bodelón: "the incrimination of rape did not originally or in its subsequent development respond to a concern for addressing the women's demands, but on the contrary, the legal form of the rape offense was more concerned with the protection of men's honor than with the harm to women, more with the creation of a model of feminine and masculine sexuality than with guaranteeing women's freedom."[30]

The feminist criticism regarding the regulation in force since 1995 lies in the fact that these assumptions about what are the correct sexual habits or behaviors of women survive, primarily, in a conception of consent, as an excluding element of injustice, which is presumed unless expressly denied, and which continues to consider women available for sexual relations, unless they clearly demonstrate that they oppose or resist.

The same assumptions also remain in the differentiation between two types of sexual assault:[31] a minor type (*abuse*) and a serious type (*assault*).[32] According to the aforementioned distinction between abuse and assault, and sexual freedom as a criterion for the systematization of offenses, sexual assaults are ranked, and the more intense the limitation of freedom, the more serious they are considered to be. Thus, the criminal reproach must be adjusted according to the means used to attack such freedom and it is considered more serious to act with *violence* (force enough to bend the will) or *intimidation* (threat of future harm, credible, that makes the victim not to resist). In contrast, it is considered to be less criminally reproachable to commit an offense by taking advantage of some defect in the victim's consent, i.e., to commit an offense by taking advantage of, deceiving or abusing victims who are senseless or mentally disturbed (current Article 181.2).

In addition to the distinction between two types of offenses, abuse or assault, depending on whether the consent is flawed by undue advantage or different forms of deception—in abuse—or by violence or intimidation—in assault—the lawmaker uses three other criteria to determine the degree of punishment: first, the *victim's age*, under or 16 years old, is considered. The legal right protected in persons over 16 years old is sexual freedom, while in minors under that age the protected legal asset is sexual indemnity, and abuses or aggressions against minors deserve a greater criminal reproach. Second, a distinction is established between whether or not the

[29] De Vicente (2018), p. 213: "Amendments to the Criminal Code will only have a positive effect when accompanied by substantial changes in the social, political and moral conceptions of those involved in its application, that is, when judging with a gender perspective which simply translates into requiring the Judiciary to reason with a logic different from that of past times, which is useful to remove the obstacles that hinder effective equality."

[30] Bodelón (1998), p. 185.

[31] See, Articles 178 et seq.

[32] Faraldo Cabana and Ribas (2018), pp. 289–290.

offense against sexual freedom *involves carnal access* through the vagina, anus or mouth, or the penetration of sexual organs or objects through the first two routes, with the offense involving carnal access or similar conduct being more criminally punishable. The term "rape," popularly used to refer to sexual assault with carnal access, is in fact used in relation to assaults against persons over 16 years old, which constitute assault (not abuse) and carnal access, or behavior assimilated to it. Third, it is important to consider whether the offenses against sexual freedom have been perpetrated under a series of *aggravating circumstances*. In relation to the *current aggravating circumstances*, the current legislation distinguishes between those corresponding to abuse,[33] and those corresponding to assault.[34]

Well, 25 years later, the criterion of distinguishing between abuse and assault is being challenged, first, because it contradicts international trends regarding the protection of women's rights, as set forth in the most important international instrument for this purpose, the Istanbul Convention,[35] and, second, because such a distinction results in inadequate protection for the victims for several reasons.

Thus, in the first place, the abuse offense leads one to think, without sufficient grounds, that the lack of consent with which the sexual relationship is maintained does not already involve some degree of intimidation or violence. It is disputable whether a greater degree of violence or intimidation requires an aggravation of the penalty, but the starting point is that any sexual act without express consent should be considered an offense of the same nature and severity.[36]

Second, the current legislation defines under the type of minor sexual assault as abuse behavior that it is reasonable to judge to be more serious, such as assaulting a woman who is unconscious or placing her in such a situation, or a woman who for any physical or psychological reason is unable to resist.[37]

Third, from a practical or evidentiary point of view, it is often difficult to distinguish between intimidation and undue advantage. In fact, the undue advantage of abuse has been interpreted as a kind of second-rate intimidation. It refers to an intimidating context in which no specific threats are made, but the victim does not resist because he/she is clearly under a disadvantage.[38] But, definitively, undue advantage is a type of intimidation.

---

[33] Thus, the aggravating circumstances of abuse are covered in Article 181. 5. "The penalties set forth in this article shall be imposed in the upper half if the third or fourth circumstance of those provided for in paragraph 1 of article 180 of this Code is applicable."

[34] See, Article 180 et seq.

[35] See, Article 36 concerning sexual violence, including rape, paragraph 2 of which states: "Consent must be given voluntarily as a manifestation of the free will of the individual considered in the context of the surrounding conditions." Feminism, in general, has interpreted this provision as a slogan to change the notion of consent and its proof for the purpose of establishing sexual offenses: the general rule is that consent to sexual intercourse must be express, conclusive and unequivocal.

[36] See, De Vicente (2018).

[37] Faraldo Cabana and Ribas (2018), p. 291. The reform proposal, in fact, on the contrary, adds a disvalue to the behavior consisting of pharmacologically overriding the victim's will (aggravating circumstance 180. 6th).

[38] The victim, for example, is left unprotected when it is considered undue advantage instead of intimidation (abuse instead of assault) in cases where there is a plurality of attackers and the victim

In fourth place, the distinction between abuse and undue advantage leads to a highly negative consequence regarding sexual assaults against minors, since in such cases the violence or intimidation is usually considered insufficient to establish sexual assault, because, for example, "the victim has not shown real, true, decisive, continued and constant resistance, as required by jurisprudence, which gives rise to the application of sexual abuse."[39]

Finally, the distinction between abuse and assault leads to judge the victim's attitude and personality, which raises problems of "secondary victimization," i.e., damages arising from the judicial system itself in addition to those arising from the commission of the offense.[40]

6 Towards a New Concept of Sexual Assault

6.1 Sexual Assault: Every Non-Consent Sexual Intercourse Seriously Infringes Sexual Freedom

The need for a criminal legislation free of prejudices about the sexual morality of women and aware of the dysfunctions identified, so as to provide effective protection to victims of sexual offenses, has guided a feminist strategy to change the criminal legislation with two workhorses: a new concept of assault and a new concept of consent, as an essential element that allows distinguishing between a contact that is a sexual relationship and an offense.

Therefore, the first demand is to abolish the distinction between two different criminal offenses, abuse and assault, eliminating the term "abuse," considered too benign for the seriousness of the behaviors involved and not very representative of social perceptions regarding offenses against sexual freedom. From a gender

---

is in shock. The facts concerning the famous La Manada case were qualified as constituting abuse and not assault, both in the first instance (Judgment 38/2018, of April 20, issued by the 2nd section of the Provincial Court of Navarra), and on appeal (Judgment 473/2018, of November 30, issued by the Civil and Criminal Chamber of the Supreme Court of Justice of Navarra). On appeal, Judgment 344/2019, dated July 4, 2019, issued by the Second Chamber of the Supreme Court, recognizes sexual assault, overturning the conviction of sexual abuse.

[39] Faraldo Cabana and Ribas (2018), pp. 293–294.

[40] See, Marco Francia (2018), pp. 311–313. The dysfunctions caused by the distinction between violence and intimidation, on the one hand, and undue advantage, on the other hand, makes the criteria adopted in other sexual offenses preferable, as in the case of submission to prostitution conditions and human trafficking, where "this comparison has not only not raised doubts, but has softened the evidentiary problems. In addition, it has also helped to avoid in many cases the secondary victimization of the victim during a criminal proceeding that often deviates the attention completely to the victim, leaving behind the aggressor, thus failing to fulfill the obligation imposed by Articles 19 and 25 of Law 4/2015, of 27 April, on the Statute of the Crime Victim," Faraldo Cabana and Acale Sánchez (2018), p. 28.

perspective, all acts and ways of infringing on sexual freedom should be included under the term "assault."[41]

And the second feminist demand is the definition of the non-consent, an essential element of assault, understood as the absence of *express consent*, through *external, conclusive* and *unequivocal* acts. It could be said that it is a matter of replacing the "no is no" slogan with the "only yes is yes" slogan.[42]

The first step is the deletion of abuse to include those behaviors under the aggravated assault type. Considering the proposed *penalties*, for the behaviors of the current *assault without carnal access* (involving violence or intimidation), *they can be slightly reduced* if compared to the regulation of the current assault[43] (1–4 years in the bill *versus* 1–5 years in the current legislation). Likewise, if we compare the current *regulation on assault with carnal access*, the penalty decreases

---

[41] Accordingly, the reform proposal maintains three of the four criteria that differentiate offenses: it continues to count whether the victim is older or younger than 16 years old (since Chapter II bis is kept, under the same heading "Sexual abuse and assault of minors under sixteen years old"). Moreover, as with the previous regulation, it is relevant whether the behavior that violates sexual freedom involves carnal access or not, the term "rape" being used in common parlance to refer to non-consensual carnal access. Finally, the concurrence or not of aggravating circumstances is also a modulating criterion for these offenses and their penalties.

[42] The Women Judges Association considers the new wording of the consent to be adequate, although its proposal is more vindictive or demanding from a gender perspective in two ways. First, inspired by the bill to reform the Catalan law 5/2008 on the right of women to eradicate male violence, it proposes to add to the basic type of assault (178.1) the requirement that the person who is going to have a sexual relationship must ensure that consent subsists at all times and for each practice: "consent must remain in force throughout the sexual practice and is limited to one or more persons, to certain sexual practices and to certain precautionary measures, both for an unwanted pregnancy and for sexually transmitted infections." This eliminates defensive arguments such as "since she wanted sex, I performed anal sex, even though she didn't want to do it." Second, the AMJE does propose to distinguish between assault and aggravated assault; that is, between a basic type (paragraph 1 of 178) and an aggravated one (paragraph 2 of 178), but the aggravated one would not be defined by the concurrence of violence or intimidation, but by any other circumstances, including those of the traditional abuses, such as undue advantage or deception. This would be the proposed wording: "the penalties provided for in the preceding paragraph shall be imposed in its upper half when the sexual assault is carried out using violence, intimidation or abuse of a situation of superiority or vulnerability of the victim, as well as those that are perpetrated on persons who are deprived of sense or whose mental situation is abused and those that are performed when the victim's will is suppressed for any reason." These are aggravating circumstances and in all of them the perpetrator uses a kind of "malice aforethought" to ensure the result, so there is no justification for punishing them as the basic form. Based on proportionality, in these cases of malice aforethought, it is proposed to apply the penalty in its upper half: imprisonment of 2 years and 6 months to 4 years.

[43] In fact, the bill lowers the penalties in relation to the current regulation of assault: without carnal access, a maximum of 4 years is established, compared to the current 5 years; and with carnal access, a maximum penalty of 10 years is established, compared to the current 12 years. And without carnal access, but with an aggravating circumstance, a maximum of 6 years is established as opposed to the current 10 years, and with access and an aggravating circumstance, a maximum of 12 years is established as opposed to the current 15 years. Even when multiple aggravating factors are involved, the maximum limits are lower (9 years, without carnal access; 13 years in case of carnal access) than those currently established for aggravated assault.

after the reform, becoming equal to the current one for abuse (4–10 years in the bill *versus* 6–12 in the current legislation). However, the deprivation of liberty may *increase* after the reform for some cases of what was considered *abusive* behaviors (1–4 years in the bill *versus* 1–3 years in the current legislation). The increased penalty for sexual assaults without consent in the case of aggravating circumstances is more clearly observed: they are now punishable in the upper half of 1–3 years (without carnal access) and of 4–10 years (with carnal access); they would be punished with a sentence of 2–6 years (without carnal access) and of 7–12 years (with carnal access). On the other hand, the number of years established for assault with violence or intimidation (assault in the traditional sense) is reduced, because, instead of criminal penalties of 5–10 years, they will face penalties of 2–6 years, without carnal access, and instead of 12–15 years, a sentence of 7–12 years would be applicable, in the case of carnal access.

Looking more closely at the proposed wording of the aggravating circumstances, there are two changes that, as has been said, make the regulation more severe for the traditional cases of abuse:[44] first, the suppression of the victim's will by means of natural or chemical substances, currently a behavior that is included in the less aggravated type of abuse (181.2), would become, no longer an assault, but an aggravated assault, or an aggravated rape if there is carnal access.[45] This aggravating circumstance causes some perplexity if it is compared to the seriousness of the behavior it punishes with violent or intimidating behaviors: assaulting or raping with violence or intimidation, methods of commission for which, we insist, no aggravating circumstance is contemplated in the bill, is punished less severely than assaulting or raping a woman deprived of sense or depriving her of sense for such purpose.

Second, and as expected, the fact that the victim is or has been a wife or a woman who is or has been linked by an analogous emotional relationship, even without cohabitation, becomes an aggravating circumstance. We should remember that this aggravating circumstance for offenses of injury, abusive treatment, threats and intimidations committed by men against women in the aforementioned areas, was introduced by Organic Law 1/2004, which sought comprehensive protection against gender violence, and its application entails a presumption *iuris et de iure* regarding the existence of a situation of undue advantage of a patriarchal sign of the male in

[44]In fact, there is an additional change regarding aggravating circumstances that has already materialized in two circumstances included in the recent LO 8/2021, of June 4, on the comprehensive protection of children and teenagers against violence, whose objective is to protect vulnerable people because they are minors, sick, disabled, etc., or because the attack occurs against people linked by kinship or in the context of cohabitation. These circumstances, therefore, are not specifically aimed at protecting the sexual freedom of women, but of other persons in vulnerable situations.

[45]Thus, in cases where the victim is either deprived of her will or the aggressor or aggressors override it, the penalty is considerably increased, because it goes from being a case of abuse punishable by 1–3 years (without carnal access) or 4–10 years (with carnal access), to being an aggravated assault, punishable by 2–6 years (without carnal access) or 7–12 years (with carnal access).

emotional relationships or in the domestic sphere.[46] The aggravating circumstance of patriarchal undue advantage in emotional relationships, also proposed by the Istanbul Convention,[47] poses problems, especially if it is considered to be applied as a no rebuttable *iuris et de iure* presumption. Thus, this aggravating circumstance transgresses the materiality guarantee (it does not punish facts, but the male condition, and can be considered a manifestation of the "criminal law for the enemy" (*Feindstrafrecht*)) and culpability (there is no individual responsibility, but collective responsibility, for injustices previously perpetrated by men or for the usage of a historical advantage by them). The purpose of the penalty, rather than prevention, is retribution without the limit of culpability, since what is punished is a transgenerational responsibility.[48]

In summary, from the guarantism point of view, de-legitimizing any punitive excess, the problem lies in what will be called *assaults, but without violence or intimidation*, whose essence is the lack of consent, that is to say, the traditional abuses.[49] In other words, classifying all sexual offenses under the category of sexual assault is correct because of the dysfunctions inherent in the distinction between abuse and assault. However, a single concept of sexual assault leaves open two debates.

---

[46] In addition, regarding the circumstances that mitigate criminal liability, it should be noted that the reform contemplates a reduced penalty for the so-called "minor cases of assault that do not involve rape" (carnal access or similar conduct). Thus, it states in Article 179.3: The Judge or Court, explaining the reasoning in the sentence, and provided that there are no aggravating circumstances, may impose a prison sentence of a lesser degree or a fine of 18–24 months, considering the minor nature of the act.

[47] See, Article 46: Aggravating circumstances. "The Parties shall adopt the necessary legislative or other measures in order to ensure that the following circumstances... may be taken into consideration as aggravating circumstances in the determination of penalties for the offenses provided for in this Convention." Section (a) The offense was committed against a current or former spouse or domestic partner, in accordance with national law, by a family member, a person living with the victim or a person who has abused his or her authority (Ratification instrument of the Council of Europe Convention on preventing and combating violence against women and domestic violence).

[48] For García Figueroa, feminism has become the most advanced of all the populist movements. The gender vindication, in the first place, is spiritualized and becomes independent of economics and biology. As it became independent of the economy, it brought together women from all economic groups and social classes. By becoming independent of biology (sex is replaced by gender, a social construct), it brings women and men together because what is being criticized is a system of domination, heteropatriarchy, which would dominate not only women, but also men. In this way, feminism represents the people against the caste. The political scene is divided between friends (feminists regardless of their genes) and enemies (male chauvinists regardless of theirs). García Figueroa (2020), pp. 17–18; García Figueroa (2021).

[49] Thus, in the Report of Judges and Women Judges for Democracy (2021), although it is valued that bringing all sexual offenses under the category of assault implies progress in the sexual self-determination of women, it recognizes an increase in penalties for milder behaviors and a risk of stigmatization and problems of reintegration for those accused of sexual offenses. The also reports a lack of proportionality in the equal punishment of an assault with violence or intimidation as without it. Both reports warn that the failure to distinguish between more and less serious means of perpetration constitutes an obstacle to the adequate fulfillment of the criminal prevention function.

A first debate would be the *number of years of imprisonment or severity of penalties that such offenses deserve*. It would be necessary to reflect regarding the legitimacy of the sanctions in comparison with behaviors that damage other legal rights, and it would also be necessary to consider whether the damage to the legal right under the new aggravating circumstances (such as the deprivation of conscience or gender-based violence in the context of intimate partner relationships) is in proportion to the seriousness of the offense.

A second debate that the bill leaves open is whether *it is more serious to act with violence or intimidation than with undue advantage, deceit or taking advantage of or causing any other defect of consent* that does not involve violence or intimidation. In this sense, we find two evaluations of the bill: the one made by Lascuraín, in favor of the current distinction between abuse and assault, since the behavior of those who want to benefit (current abuse) and that of those who want to harm (current assault) deserve different reproach.[50] And, from a perspective in favor of grouping all sexual assaults under the type of aggression, Rosario De Vicente indicates that although we agree that a serious attack against sexual freedom is produced at the moment in which there is no consent, it remains to be resolved whether cases in which violence or intimidation concur deserve an aggravated criminal treatment.[51]

6.2 Consent to Sexual Intercourse As an **Express Will,** *by Means of* **External, Conclusive,** *and* **Unequivocal** *Acts*

Regarding the second feminist workhorse, the definition of consent, *the bill defines the type of assault in two ways: through a detailed* classification of assault acts *(178.2)*, which are specified in those involving violence, intimidation, abuse of a situation of superiority, vulnerability of the victim, or in which the victim is deprived of sense, which involve abuse of the victim's metal situation, or which are carried out in front of a victim whose will is overridden.

But there is a second form of classification (Article 178.1), *generic*, as a closing or exhaustive precept, which would cover any sexual assault for which "consent is not given." The law determines that such absence of consent shall be given in the absence of *express will*, by means of *external*, *conclusive,* and *unequivocal* acts.[52] The law puts into practice the feminist vindication of "only yes is yes." The bill would entail a new concept of sexual freedom based on a new notion of consent, in

[50] "If the reform goes forward, it will constitute the same punishable offense with the same penal framework a sexual assault imposed by means of a knife on the victim's neck as the same sexual intercourse carried out abusing a situation of superiority of the perpetrator over the victim" (Lascuraín 2021, pp. 90–91).

[51] De Vicente (2018), p. 183.

[52] Thus, 178.1 states that there is no consent when "the victim has not freely expressed by external, conclusive and unequivocal acts, in accordance with the circumstances, his or her express will to participate in the act."

that, as pointed out by the Women Judges Association of Spain, it does not require the woman to prove refusal against sexual intercourse, but rather her refusal is presumed and she must prove that there was no indubitable consent. That means, while currently it is presumed that there is consensual sexual intercourse and therefore there is no offense if there is no refusal or resistance, with the bill it is presumed that there is an offense if there is no express, conclusive and unequivocal consent. This wording avoids, according to the Women Judges, gender bias regarding its interpretation and application:

> If the woman didn't say no, there was a presumption that consent had been given. The message communicated was that women are available for sexual intercourse unless proven otherwise, i.e., unless they are shown to be clearly and strictly opposed to sexual intercourse (active resistance). This message is absolutely unacceptable in a modern and democratic society, which protects women's freedom as a fundamental right.[53]

Thus, the wording of assault in Article 178.2 (detailed classification) does not entail any problems from the point of view of guarantees. But, if the criminal conduct occurs under 178.1, that is, when the victim did not express consent in an external, conclusive and unequivocal manner, without reference, therefore, to the acts from which it can be deduced that there could not have been valid consent, there are objectionable aspects from the point of view of the guarantees.

Regarding the *material guarantees*, i.e., those *that must be observed in the precept's wording*, criminal laws must punish facts or acts (materiality), in a detailed manner (taxativity), harmful to a legal right (harmfulness) and imputable to the person on whom the penalty is imposed (culpability). In this regard, it should first be noted that the penal norm of 178.1, with its generic reference to the lack of consent of the victim (178.1), which does not have to materialize in specific circumstances (178.2), violates the guarantee of materiality and taxativity, which requires that the wording of criminal offenses be precise and refer to empirically verifiable facts. The consequence is, on the one hand, that the applicator finds him/herself before a precept without content or blank, which leaves it up to him/her to determine whether there was assault or rape, filling in the circumstances in which he/she supports the conviction that the victim did not consent. And, on the other hand, that the precept offers a definition of consent that only reflects a part of the reality of sexual intercourse: identifying consent with that which is express, supported by external,

[53] Quoting Women Judges Association... On the other hand, the Report of the General Council of the Judiciary and that of JJpD (Judges and Women Judges for Democracy) emphasize that the current definition of sexual offense, based on the absence of consent, is not the problem that causes victimization. They deny the idea that the current consent conception requires proof of refusal or resistance. Secondary victimization (a process in which it appears that the victim is under judgment for her sexual behavior) does not derive from a definition of consent that is demanding on the female victim, but from the procedural rules of the burden of proof. The presumption of innocence requires, in criminal proceedings, that the defense does not have to prove that the defendant did not perpetrate the criminal act, but that it is the prosecution that bears the burden of proof. As long as this burden of proof of the prosecution is maintained, the conditions for secondary victimization will continue, because the trial will be about the victim's behavior in giving such consent and this in order to determine the ambiguous "concurrent circumstances."

conclusive and unequivocal acts hides a part of the reality, namely, that a sexual intercourse can be based on implicit consent. In this way, the law would be able to punish a behavior that is not at all harmful and, consequently, not guilty. In addition, it could be questioned whether this legal form of valid consent to sexual intercourse, external-express, favors or harms sexual freedom. On the one hand, it generates the awareness that the male must make sure that such consent exists. But, on the other hand, it imposes on women a clear understanding before any sexual contact that does not allow them to experiment with their sexuality.

Taking into consideration the procedural *guarantees that must be given regarding the precept's application*, as the precept is drafted, as soon as the victim declares that there was no consent, there is a reversal of the burden of proof, since the only hypothesis that can be debated is the one related to the facts by virtue of which consent was expressed; clarifying this hypothesis will be the defendant's task. At the same time, there is a practically absolute reduction in the standards ruling the certainty requirement of the evidentiary hypothesis,[54] since in situations of doubt (as to whether there was consent) the legal precept of assault, contrary to the principle of the presumption of innocence, obliges to punish.[55] The confrontation between the legal precept of assault based on express and conclusive consent, on the one hand, and the principle of the presumption of innocence, on the other hand, shows that application practices will determine the interpretation of this precept. As it is to be expected that the presumption of innocence will continue to modulate this precept's application, it should be pointed out that the definition of the concept of valid sexual consent has a performative value, typical of symbolic legislation, that is, legislation that is enacted in the knowledge that it will not produce the effects it intends, but other effects (such as raising social awareness about a problem, changing mentalities, or obtaining an electoral advantage), and may even produce contrary and counterproductive effects. In this case, the effect would be to change the patriarchal mentality that the woman is available for sexual intercourse, threatening the possible perpetration of an offense.

In summary, the reform consisting of grouping any non-consensual sexual intercourse under the category of assault, eliminating the overly benign term of abuse, would be justified, insofar as there are reasons to consider an assault in which the absence of victim's consent is established as a serious offense against sexual

---

[54] Gascón Abellán (1999).

[55] On the one hand, if it is a substantive rule that considers the lack of consent as the lack of a manifest and express will, it will result that the rule is unfair, as it includes the punishment of non-injurious behaviors, of sexual behaviors agreed to by the victim, although with a consent that is not manifested, or not express, or not external, or not conclusive, or equivocal. If it is a procedural rule that indicates when the specific factual element of lack of consent must be considered proven, the rule will be contrary to the fundamental right to the presumption of innocence insofar as it considerably reduces the requirement that the elements of the offense must be established with certainty, beyond reasonable doubt. As stated by Tatjana Hörnle, a specialist in the field and advisor to the German reform in this regard, if for a hypothetical observer "it is not clear whether there was consent, if the situation is really ambivalent, it would be unfair to punish the alleged aggressor (*El País*, March 8, 2020)," Lascuraín (2021), p. 94.

freedom, without the need to require violence or intimidation in the strict sense of the term. However, from the perspective of guarantees it can be pointed out, first, that the severity of the penalty deserving the basic sexual assault and under the different aggravating circumstances is not evident, in the sense that it should not be ruled out that the penalty currently provided for abuse is already the penalty for a serious crime. Second, it violates the premises of guarantism to classify as assault any sexual intercourse without external and unequivocal consent, without precise mention of what the perpetrator's behavior may be, since it leads to the reversal of the burden of proof and to the presumption of culpability for ambivalent assumptions.

The updating of sexual offenses, severely burdened by gender bias, must not renounce the punitive prudence to which guarantism invites. The legitimacy of offenses and penalties lies in their suitability to prevent violations of the *most important legal rights* by means of the *most serious offenses*. Nevertheless, penalties should be kept to a minimum. It is not, therefore, an ordinary policy tool[56] to raise awareness against a patriarchal culture, which, by the way, is far from being the only cause of sexual offenses.

7 Summary

The guarantism philosophy considers that the law, far from having *a priori* justification, is a potentially abusive instrument and must therefore be permanently subject to a demand for justification and to a vigilant and critical viewpoint. The *ius puniendi*, as a manifestation of the greatest coercive force, must be the last resort, always conditioned to the social defense of the most important criminal protected goods or rights and in the face of the most unacceptable injuries to them. The minimization of criminal law is possible thanks to several techniques, *guarantees* or principles that should guide its *creation* and *application*. Many of these guarantees, beyond being supported by solid extra-legal reasons, are based on positive law, on constitutional precepts. Consequently, the guarantism represents an optimal model of criminal legal science for the Constitutional State under the rule of law.

[56] As Demetrio Crespo (2020) clearly points out, democratic constitutions, such as the Spanish one, impose a minimum, necessary and proportionate model of criminal law, but the spirit of the current times seems to play against this model. Dogmatics is becoming less and less critical and is placed at the service of the practice of the new criminal trends, where the enlightened, guarantism-based principles are disregarded and we are witnessing a real metamorphosis of criminal law. This metamorphosis is expressed, first, in the "deconstruction" of the "guarantism-based paradigm," as we know it delegitimizes criminal law; second, in its trivialization-expansion; third, in the rise of the retributionist approach; fourthly, in the justification of exceptions to legislative and procedural guarantees, appealing to the confrontation between citizens and enemies of security (enemy criminal law); and, finally, in populism, which is evidenced in a repressive euphoria against different criminal sectors, encouraged by ideologically polarized parties or social groups in competition for votes and power.

Feminist philosophy considers that criminal law must protect against gender-based violence, which refers to the different forms of discrimination that cause physical, psychological and economic damage to women, as well as the fact that this violence is made possible by the situation of discrimination and at the same time helps to perpetuate discrimination. One of the main postulates of current feminism is that gender violence cannot be seen as the sum of individual cases of deviation from social behavior, but as a structural problem involving social, political, economic, etc., concluding that it is not fought like other forms of violence, but rather by transforming and perhaps also *criminalizing patriarchal structures*.

The basic conclusion of this paper is that *criminal* legislative and judicial practices should be analyzed by criminal dogmatics from two equally relevant points of view: the feminist perspective and the guarantism.

Thus, and in relation to the reform of sexual offenses carried out by the *Bill Organic Law on the Comprehensive Guarantee of Sexual Freedom*, it can be concluded that, on the one hand, making sexual assaults previously punished in a milder form more serious requires more than just arguing the gender perspective. The undoubtedly existing heteropatriarchal structures are, however, typical of a reductionist explanation of sexual violence. It is necessary to refine the reasons for the aggravation of penalties, considering first the suitability of such aggravation with a view to the general and special prevention of sexual offenses, and then its legitimacy, focusing on the proportionality between the seriousness of the offenses (not only sexual offenses, but all other offenses with a similar range of penalties) and the harshness of the penalties imposed, according to the principle or guarantee of proportionality.

On the other hand, the advantages of the consent conception as express, unequivocal and conclusive, established by the reform, as the only way to exclude the offense, must be examined, in the first place, from the point of view of its *suitability* for the achievement of the feminist purposes pursued (greater awareness among men when seeking consent and less secondary victimization of women), and also from the point of view of its legitimacy, taking into consideration the possible weakening of the presumption of innocence principle and the burden of proof in the accusation.

References

Acale Sánchez M, Faraldo Cabana P (2018) Introducción. In: Faraldo Cabana P, Acale Sánchez M (Dir) La manada: un antes y un después en la regulación de los delitos sexuales en España. Tirant Lo Blanch, Valencia

Amorós C, De Miguel A (2005) (eds) Teoría feminista. De la Ilustración a la globalización (3 vols). Ediciones Minerva, Madrid

Añón MJ (2008) Una reflexión crítica sobre la reciente legislación española en materia de igualdad entre mujeres y hombres. Sociologia del Diritto XXXV:77–107

Atienza M (2019) Mejor abandonemos el neoconstitucionalismo (con comillas o sin ellas). I. Latina 1-16:486–493

Beauvoir S (2005) El segundo sexo (1949). Cátedra, Madrid

Beccaria C (2008) De los delitos y de las penas (1764). Trad. De Juan A. de las Casas. Alianza Editorial, Madrid
Bodelón E (1998) Cuestionamiento de la eficacia del Derecho penal en relación a la protección de los intereses de las mujeres. In: AAVV Análisis del CP desde la perspectiva de género. Instituto Vasco de la Mujer, Vitoria-Gastéiz
Butler J (2007) El género en disputa. Paidós, Buenos Aires
De Lora P (2019) Lo sexual es político (y jurídico). Alianza, Madrid
De Vicente R (2018) El delito de violación: problemas que plantea su vigente redacción. In: Faraldo Cabana P, Acale Sánchez M (Dir) La manada: un antes y un después en la regulación de los delitos sexuales en España. Tirant Lo Blanch, Valencia
Demetrio Crespo E (2004) Del Derecho penal liberal al "Derecho penal del enemigo.". Revista de Derecho penal y criminología 14:87–115
Demetrio Crespo E (2020) El Derecho penal del Estado de Derecho entre el espíritu de nuestro tiempo y la Constitución. Reus Editorial, Madrid
Faraldo Cabana P, Ribas ER (2018) La sentencia de la Manada y la reforma de los delitos de agresiones y abusos sexuales en España. In: Faraldo Cabana P, Acale Sánchez M (Dir) La manada: un antes y un después en la regulación de los delitos sexuales en España. Tirant Lo Blanch, Valencia
Ferrajoli L (1997) Derecho y razón. Teoría del garantismo penal (1989). Trad de Andrés Ibáñez P, Ruiz Miguel A, Bayón Mohino JC, Terradillos Basoco J, Cantarero Bandrés R, Prólogo de Bobbio N. Trotta, Madrid
Ferrajoli L (2011) Principia Iuris. Teoría del Derecho y de la Democracia (2007), 3 vols. Trad de Andrés P, Bayón JC, Gascón M, Prieto L, Ruiz Miguel A. Trotta, Madrid
García Figueroa A (2020) Populismo y feminismo de Estado. In: Martín T, Velasco JM (eds) Tirant Lo Blanch, Valencia (forthcoming)
García Figueroa A (2021) ¿Unidas podemos? La deriva populista del feminismo. In: Escribano MC (Coord) Estudios sobre mujeres y feminismo. Aspectos jurídicos, políticos, filosóficos e históricos, Ediciones de la Universidad de Castilla La Mancha, Toledo
Gascón Abellán M (1999) Los hechos en el Derecho. Bases argumentales de la prueba. Marcial Pons, Madrid
Jakobs G, Cancio Meliá M (2003) Derecho penal del enemigo. Thomson Civitas, Madrid
Lascuraín JA (2021) Delitos sexuales: no todo vale. Claves de Razón Práctica 277:88–97
MacKinnon CA (1982) Toward feminist jurisprudence. Stanf Law Rev 34:703 ff
MacKinnon CA (2001) Sex equality. Foundation Press, New York
Marco Francia MP (2018) Victimización secundaria en los delitos sexuales. Consentimiento y enjuiciamiento a la víctima. Con especial referencia al caso de "La Manada". In: Faraldo Cabana P, Acale Sánchez M (Dir) La manada: un antes y un después en la regulación de los delitos sexuales en España. Tirant Lo Blanch, Valencia
Montesquieu (2007) Del espíritu de las leyes (1748). Trad. Blázquez M, De Vega P. Tecnos, Madrid
Poggi F (2019) Sobre el concepto de violencia de género y su relevancia para el Derecho. Doxa 42: 285–307
Prieto L (2011) Garantismo y Derecho Penal. Iustel, Madrid
Senese S (2002) La reserva di códice. In: Curi U, Palombarini G (eds) Diritto penale minimo. Donzelli, Roma
Tubert S (ed) (2003) Del sexo al género. Los equívocos de un concepto. Cátedra, Madrid
Turégano I (2011) Derecho y violencia contra las mujeres: la perspectiva feminista. In: Zurilla MA, Domínguez P (eds) Violencia contra las mujeres: un enfoque jurídico. Septem Ediciones, Oviedo
Valcárcel A (2008) Feminismo en un mundo global. Cátedra, Madrid
VVAA (2019) Populismos. Revista Anales de la Cátedra Francisco Suárez 53
Wolstonecraft (1792) A vindication of the rights of woman with strictures on political and moral subjects

Legal Defeasibility: The Limits Between *Ductile Law* and *Arbitrary Law*

Ángeles Ródenas

1 Introduction

The claim that legal rules are defeasible means that, according to our legal practices, it may sometimes be justified for judges to set aside applicable rules in the resolution of disputes and to take other considerations into account in their place.[1] Naturally, this first approach to the concept of defeasibility in no way seeks to avoid all the complexity that the question raises; on the contrary, it only aims to introduce the main problems associated with defeasibility: what do we mean by "an applicable rule"? What does to "set aside" an applicable rule mean? When is it justified to proceed in this way? What kind of considerations should be taken into account in place of the defeated rules?

In this paper, I will try to answer these questions but, before addressing them, it seems pertinent to illustrate the phenomenon of the defeasibility of rules by mentioning some examples from Spanish legal practice.

[1] As a starting point for this theoretical approach to the problem of defeasibility I am going to take the manifestations of defeasibility in our legal practice. Therefore, I will not follow the logical approaches inspired by Alchourrón and Bulygin's conceptual apparatus (Alchourrón and Bulygin 1971; Alchourrón 2010, pp. 77–127, 141–153 and 155–177). In the wake of this kind of logical approach to the problem of legal defeasibility, see *The Logic of Legal Requeriments* (Ferrer and Ratti 2012).

Á. Ródenas (✉)
Faculty of Law, University of Alicante, Alicante, Spain

E. Demetrio Crespo et al. (eds.), *Crisis of the Criminal Law in the Democratic Constitutional State*, Legal Studies in International, European and Comparative Criminal Law 6, https://doi.org/10.1007/978-3-031-13413-5_9

2 Some Examples of Defeasibility from Spanish Legal Practice

Specifically, I am going to provide three examples that will allow us to introduce the phenomenon of the defeasibility of rules.

1. I will start with an example from our criminal legal practice: that the shared consumption of narcotics in a small group of people has been excluded from the criminal definition of drug trafficking by the Supreme Court in its judgments. The Supreme Court in its judgments of February 9, 1994 and May 27, 1994 restricted the punitive scope of the crime of drug trafficking in Article 344 of the former Spanish Criminal Code.[2] Even if consider everything that the grammatical terms of the rule allow, it barely establishes limits on the punishment; both sentences, however, do exclude cases of shared consumption in a small group of people from the criminal definition of drug trafficking (Silva Sánchez 1997, p. 316), adopting a position that is now well-established in our legal doctrine.

   It is interesting to note that in this example the court refuses to subsume in the generic case of the rule the case of the shared consumption in a reduced group, moving away from the literality of the rule. Instead, the court inclines towards a "teleological" interpretation, which leads it to defend the exclusion of the criminal classification for narcotics trafficking, arguing that the legally protected value in the rule—public health—has not been endangered.[3]
2. Moving away again from the literality of the rules involved, the Supreme Court refuses to subsume in the generic case of burglary all those cases in which the irregular entry into a home does not show "a skill or significant effort" that justifies the aggravation of the punishment with respect to the crime of theft.[4] In these cases, the court makes a reduction in the generic case of burglary because it considers that, although an illegal entry into a building has occurred, the seriousness of the associated penalty violates the principle of proportionality (Silva Sánchez 1997, p. 318).

   What I am interested in highlighting from this second example is that, unlike in the previous example, the reduction in the criminal definition of burglary is not

---

[2] Article 368 of the current Criminal Code.

[3] "Starting from the doctrinal distinction between 'apparent realization' and 'effective realization' of the criminal conduct of the norm, the Supreme Court introduces the political-criminal principle of 'exclusive protection of legally protected value'. Thus, the Court refuses to subsume in the generic case of the rule cases in which the conduct of the active subject has not put at risk the value underlying the rule, although this conduct is grammatically perfectly subsumable in the generic case of the norm" (Silva Sánchez 1997, p. 315).

[4] For example, cases of entry through an open window located on the ground floor (STS of April 20, 1999), or "at street level" (STS of January 18, 1999), or "when there is no evidence of a special height concerning the ground floor or of a special way in which the defendant has managed to get onto the windowsill that reveals the special ability or effort inherent to climbing" (STS of March 10, 2000).

because the legally protected value in the rule has not been endangered: the legitimate relationship of control over something has indeed been disturbed, but the severity of the penalty is not justified. What happens in this case is that a new principle comes into play—the principle of proportionality—which motivates the non-application of the rule, due to the excessive penalty established in the rule.

3. But where the defeasibility of the rules takes a more dramatic turn is in those cases in which the courts entirely object to the legislator's decision, declaring a rule to be unconstitutional and, therefore, null and void. For example, the Constitutional Court, in the famous judgment 341/1993, of November 18, annulled Article 21, n° 2 of the LOPSC, better known as "Corcuera Law" or "Law of the kicking down the door". This rule considered "a legitimate cause for entry and registration of a home, because of flagrant delicto, the founded knowledge of the Security Forces that leads them to the certainty that a crime is being committed or has just been committed."[5] The Constitutional Court argues that "the effectiveness in the prosecution of crimes has an unquestionable legitimacy, but it cannot be imposed at the cost of fundamental rights and freedoms." The legal expressions "founded knowledge" and "certainty" "show a breadth and indeterminacy in their wording that is incompatible with the rigor required by Art. 18.2 of the Constitution," which recognizes the inviolability of the home.[6]

3 Legal Defeasibility vs. Authoritative Nature of Law

These three examples offer a preliminary illustration of the phenomenon of the defeasibility of rules and they will prepare the ground to undertake the theoretical analysis of the problem later on. However, before embarking on this analysis, it is worth noting the lack of consideration given to the problem of legal defeasibility by traditional legal theory. Although manifestations of legal defeasibility, such as those illustrated in the previous examples, are not unusual in the courts' application of law, it may seem rather shocking that there has been a clear mismatch between the demand for theoretical analysis from our legal practices and legal theory's response.

The explanation for this mismatch is not a trivial issue. Contemporary legal theory has been largely built on the foundations of the last century's positivist legal science. This model has resisted the integration into its analysis of phenomena that could weaken one of the most characteristic features of modern positive law: the authoritative nature of law. This is true to such an extent that the phenomenon of defeasibility constitutes one of the main problems dealt with by contemporary legal theory (Ródenas 2017, pp. 11–13).

---

[5] The aforementioned rule referred to "crimes regarding toxic drugs, narcotic drugs or psychotropic substances, that the Criminal Code punishes."

[6] "The domicile is inviolable. No entry or registration may be made in it without the consent of the owner or judicial resolution, except in the case of flagrante delicto."

Without any doubt, Joseph Raz is one of the legal philosophers who has dealt with the authoritative nature of modern law in the deepest and most suggestive way. According to Raz, the authoritative nature of law is revealed in its claim that legal norms provide their addressees with protected reasons for action.[7] This means two concurrent things in relation to judges. First, the rules constitute first order reasons for judges to take the required action, that is, to dictate a resolution whose content corresponds to that of the rule. Second, that rules are also exclusionary reasons for judges to disregard the result that would lead to an independent deliberation on the arguments for and against the adoption of that resolution, i.e., a reason that excludes the content of the resolution being based on the judge's assessment of what the best resolution would be (Raz 1990).

However, although judges adopt pre-existing legal rules as protected reasons in most cases, there are also exceptional occasions—such as those illustrated in the examples in the previous section—in which they understand that there are important legal reasons to set aside a rule.[8] We speak of defeasibility precisely when, according to our legal practices, we understand that the rules should not be taken as exclusionary reasons in judicial deliberations.

How can rules, characterized in the terms we have just seen, be defeasible? Apparently, their characterization as protected reasons excludes their defeasibility. This dilemma largely explains why contemporary legal theory has been resisting the rational reconstruction of the phenomenon of defeasibility, either by ignoring it (considering to be a marginal phenomenon, completely unrelated to legal rationality) or by regarding it as a legal power to solve a legal dispute using out of law considerations.[9]

---

[7] Atienza and Ruiz Manero have maintained that this characterization of rules as protected reasons is applicable only to one type of rules: mandatory rules, but not to other types of legal statements such as principles—which constitute mere first-order reasons—or power conferring rules—which would be auxiliary reasons (Atienza and Ruiz Manero 2007).

[8] Thus, according to Silva Sánchez, "there is an increasingly clear tendency in precedents towards overcoming legalistic positivism, which conceives the application of Law as a merely logical operation, as pure subsumption that applies a syllogism. The requirement in art. 5.1 of the Organic Law of Judicial Power, regarding the 'interpretation of legal norms in accordance with the Constitution' may have contributed to some extent to this positivistic tendency. However, it seems to be evident that judges and courts ... are aware of the need to adopt a certain evaluative perspective when they proceed to interpret positive law, in such a way that the process of applying law can be correctly characterized as a process of obtaining law. In the case of our Supreme Court, it seems that this evaluative perspective acquires significant teleological features, in such a way that the interpretation of rules is subject to material political-criminal purposes of criminal law, leading to a guarantee-based application of the law" (Silva Sánchez 1997, p. 314).

[9] According to Raz, it is possible to distinguish between "reasoning to establishing the content of Law" and "reasoning according to Law." In the first case, the interpreter makes a reasoning based solely on the sources of law and, therefore, autonomous. But it is possible that the result of such reasoning is the granting of discretion to judges to depart from what the law establishes if relevant moral reasons are given for it. If this were the case, the second type of reasoning, reasoning according to law, would enter the scene and the judge would have the discretion to deviate from

The consequence of this strategy of denial has had repercussions on our discipline. Nevertheless, if we insist time and time again on the authoritative or directive dimension of law and ignore the tensions that arise within it between its directive and its value dimensions, then our understanding of law will be impoverished. If we seek to understand the problem of defeasibility of rules, we have to stop seeing law exclusively as a set of authoritative rules, and to focus our attention on the judge's and courts' challenges when applying it. Following Dworkin's suggestion, we can only capture the complex nature of law by taking as a starting point the image legal operators have of it when facing hard cases (Dworkin 1995); that is, those cases that are not solved by the mere subsumption of the individual case in the generic case of an authoritative rule (Ródenas 2017, p. 12).

To sum up, if legal philosophers want to elaborate an interesting theory for legal dogmatics, we must incorporate the problem of defeasibility of rules into our agenda. To begin with, we must be able to construct a *general theory of defeasibility*; that is a theory that, beyond the specificities in each branch of law, or the variations in different legal orders, captures common features of defeasibility. But, in turn, we must also be able to subject the matter to severe critical control, asking ourselves whether there is a rational basis for judges' claims that in certain cases they have the legal duty to set aside an applicable rule, and try to define in what type of cases and under what conditions such an attitude would be rational.

4 Three Types of Defeasibility

To deal with the above challenge, I will start with the idea that the phenomenon of defeasibility does not always appear in the same form in law. Specifically, I propose to differentiate between three types of situations in which this phenomenon appears. Each of these types of situations has its own distinctive characteristics, which, in turn, will lead me to differentiate between three types of defeasibility, which I will call, respectively, D1, D2, and D3[10] (Ródenas 2001, pp. 72–82; Ródenas 2012, pp. 33–51).

---

the legal guidelines identified according to the sources' thesis and apply moral reasons (Raz 1994, p. 310).

[10] As will be seen shortly, I am going to characterize D1 as defeasibility at the level of prescriptions contained in the formulation of rules, D2 as defeasibility at the level of the justifications underlying rules, and finally, D3 as radical defeasibility or defeasibility of reason provided by law.

4.1 D1: Defeasibility at the Level of Prescriptions Contained in the Formulation of Rules

Let us start with a fairly simple example. Imagine a rule that—to avoid greater subtle differences—prohibits smoking in workplaces. This rule could have been approved for certain reasons that operate together as its underlying justification. We are usually able to understand the rule that prohibits smoking in workplaces without clarifying what the underlying reasons for it are. According to Frederick Schauer, many normative formulations have semantic autonomy, that is, we can determine their meaning—what they prescribe—without considering their underlying justification (Schauer 1991, pp. 53–62).

Generally speaking, following rules without asking for their underlying reasons is a good strategy, but in some cases, there may be mismatches between what the normative formulation demands and what the underlying justification requires. Returning to the example of no smoking in workplaces, let us accept that we can clearly determine that the underlying justification of this rule is the protection of the right to health of non-smokers. It is easy to imagine cases that are instances of application of the rule, but to which the underlying justification would not be applicable.

1. Let us consider, primarily, the case of a company employee whose job it is to attend the telephone enquiries of the company's clients, outside office hours, when the other employees have left. The prohibition seems to affect him, although there are no non-smokers rights at stake. We could say that the prescription contained in the formulation of the rule exceeds what the underlying justification allows to be forbidden. In fact, the rule was designed for other types of situations. The reasons underlying this rule are not applicable at all in this case.
2. Something similar would happen in the case of a clinical trial carried out in a hospital to show the amount of smoke that a non-smoker who shares a closed space with smokers inhales. Since the hospital is a workplace, the prohibition also seems to be applicable to this case. Also, in this case we could say that the prescription contained in the formulation of the rule exceeds what its underlying justification allows. However, in this second example there is a significant difference to the previous one: clearly the clinical trial endangers the health of the non-smokers who participate in it, but it is estimated that the advantages obtained from the experiment, in terms of its contribution to public health policies, are greater than the disadvantages derived from the harm to the participants' health.

These two examples—the isolated smoker in his office and the clinical trial—help us to illustrate the first type of defeasibility, D1. In these cases, it might seem reasonable for judges to decide not to take the rule that prohibits smoking in workplaces as a basis for their decision, precisely because, if they applied the rule, they would go beyond the balance of reasons underlying this rule. When judges deliberate in this way, they are considering that a rule is defeated at the level of the prescriptions contained in the formulation of rules (D1); judges understand that the result of applying a rule with semantic autonomy is at odds with what is required by the underlying reasons.

To be more precise, defeasibility at the level of prescriptions may be due either to the fact that the main reasons that support the rule are not applicable to the case—as in the example of the employee who smokes alone—or to the fact that, although some of the main reasons for the rule are applicable, there are other available reasons that have not been considered in the balance of reasons that the rule contemplates—as in the clinical trial example. The first type of situations can be considered as cases beyond the scope of the rule; and the second as exceptions to the rule (Raz 1990, p. 82; Ródenas 1998, pp. 113–115; Fernández 2005, pp. 45–48).

If we consider the first two examples that I used in the previous section to illustrate the phenomenon of the defeasibility of rules—the example of shared consumption in reduced groups and that of entry into a home without permission, which shows neither skill nor significant effort—we can establish a parallel with the cases I have just referred to—the isolated smoker in his office and the clinical trial.

1. The first parallelism is between (a) the case of the isolated smoker in his office and (b) the exclusion of the definition of drug trafficking in cases of shared consumption in reduced groups. This parallelism lies in the underlying justification of the two cases. Reasons for the exclusion of the definition of drug trafficking in cases of shared consumption in reduced groups are not very different from those used in the example of the isolated smoker in his office. The main reason underlying the rule—the protection of public health in the first case and the rights of passive smokers in the second—do not apply in either case. In both cases, the prescription contained in the formulation of the rule is defeated because it is beyond the scope of the underlying reasons.
2. The second parallelism is between (c) the example of the clinical trial that I have just used, and (d) the exclusion from the generic case of burglary of cases in which the irregular entry does not show "significant skill or effort." In both cases, even when some of the main reasons for the rule are applicable, other reasons are present that have not been properly considered in the balance of reasons for the rule, i.e., the principle that the penalty should be in proportionate to the offence.

To sum up, in all four cases the prescription contained in the formulation of the rule is defeated due to the decisive weight of a principle that has not been considered in the balance of reasons underlying the rule.

4.2 *Defeasibility at the Level of Underlying Justifications of Rules (D2)*

As we can see in the two previous examples, defeasibility in the D1 sense concerns the prescription contained in the normative formulation by which the rule is expressed, but it is not related with the balance of reasons underlying it. This is the case because we can perceive the excesses of the prescription contained in the formulation of the rule without reopening the balance of the underlying reasons. However, does it make sense to also speak of defeasibility on this second level? Can we talk about defeasibility at the level of reasons underlying rules?

To answer this question, we must consider again the third of the defeasibility examples that I mentioned in the previous section: the Constitutional Court judgment 341/1993, of November 18, annulling the "Law of the kicking down the door" that allowed the police to enter a home without a judicial order by setting extremely imprecise conditions. This rule was not valid because effectiveness in the persecution of the crime had prevailed in its underlying balance of reasons over the right to inviolability of the home. It is this last right and not the effectiveness in the persecution of the crime which constitutes the legal reason that has more constitutional weight, insofar as it is a constitutional right and not a mere policy. In short, given that the fundamental right is protected by the constitution, the balance between reasons underlying the annulled rule was clearly wrong.

Of course, it is not always easy to determine exactly what the balance between reasons which underlie a rule is. However, when it is possible, situations could appear in which the balance of reasons that operates as a justification under a rule is wrong. This possibility allows us also to speak of defeasibility at the level of justifications underlying rules (D2). We speak of defeasibility at this level when, in accordance with another balance between reasons, which is implicit or explicit in other hierarchically or axiologically superior norms in the legal system, and which are applicable to the case, we perceive a mistake in the balance between reasons underlying the rule. In short, it is possible that what is defeated is not the prescription contained in the normative formulation—as in the previous examples—but the commitment (judgment of prevalence) between reasons underlying the rules.

In addition, normative consequences that result from defeasibility at the level of justifications underlying rules are characteristically different from those which result from defeasibility at the level of prescriptions contained in normative formulations. When defeasibility takes place at the level of justifications underlying rules, the rule has failed as a reason for guiding decisions both in this case and in successive cases. The balance between reasons itself, operating as the underlying justification of the rule, is what is considered a mistake, so it is assumed that the rule should not play any role in making future decisions. Therefore, the consequences resulting from defeasibility in the D2 sense are those characteristic of voidness.

4.3 *Radical Defeasibility of Legal Rules (D3)*

Therefore, when we speak of the defeasibility of rules, we may be alluding not only to the defeasibility of prescriptions contained in normative formulations (D1), but also to the defeasibility of justifications underlying such prescriptions (D2). Although the first two meanings of defeasibility—D1 and D2—are those that best reconstruct the way in which defeasibility is understood in our legal practice, there is a third meaning of defeasibility to be explored: radical defeasibility or D3. Radical defeasibility is by no means a reiterative experience in law, but it is a theoretical possibility which cannot be completely ruled out in any real legal system. We speak of defeasibility in this third sense when, according to law, there are reasons for basing the response to a problem of indeterminacy on extralegal standards, that is, standards which have nothing to do with what law establishes.[11]

Radical defeasibility is highly controversial as it implies that law accepts that legal reasons are not the ones that decide the solution to cases. The characteristic claim of the authority of law is radically compromised if the final legal decision is the result of an exercise of strong discretion on the part of law applying organ. For this reason, radical defeasibility is presented by legal theory more as a theoretical possibility than as a real phenomenon. However, since by hypothesis, we cannot exclude the possibility that radical defeasibility can take place in some real legal systems, it is worth reflecting, even briefly, on the analysis of the conditions in which it is possible to speak of radical defeasibility or D3 in law.

One of the authors who has explored defeasibility in this third sense (D3) is Juan Carlos Bayón (Bayón 2000, pp. 87–117). According to Bayón, the presence in law of defeasible norms with this third meaning depends on the concurrence of two variables.

1. The first variable is the existence in law of rules whose order of preference in relation to some of the other norms in the system is not pre-established, according to existing interpretative conventions. If the system does not contain a complete set of all orders of preference between norms, it is necessary that it should contain at least some defeasible rules (Bayón 2000, pp. 107–108).[12]

   Although Bayón is not very explicit about which type of situation he is referring to, I believe I am not misrepresenting him if I point out that what he is considering is a situation of indetermination in the *hierarchy of reasons provided by Law*: a situation in which law lacks an ulterior legal criteria which allows us to resolve a conflict between two or more incompatible legal solutions which are applicable to the same case.[13] This is what would happen if, for example, the result of the balancing of two principles were a draw. If this happened, the legal organ responsible for resolving the case as consequence of the *non liquet* principle, would have to resolve the case by applying a non-legal criteria.
2. The second variable whose concurrence makes it possible to speak of radical defeasibility or D3 is much more difficult to explain. According to Bayón, this variable takes place when law lacks any interpretative convention (applicable to one, several or all norms) which obliges judges to follow conventionally

[11] These legal standards include legal practices that remit to dominant semantic conventions and to interpretative conventions.

[12] Or more precisely, some defeasible rules in the third sense of defeasibility or D3.

[13] Juan Ruiz Manero has worked on a type of conflict that can illustrate this type of situation in Ruiz Manero (2018), pp. 30 ss.

determined criteria to select the relevant features for the normative qualification of a conduct. If such a convention does not exist, rules should be understood as mere rules of thumb, which means that they alone cannot lead to any concrete decision regarding any particular case, since a legal official's choice between open alternatives is always necessary to reach a decision, i.e., a decision whose foundation does not stem from the system (Bayón 2000, pp. 104–105). If this is the case, rules should be understood as rules of thumb, which means that they alone cannot provide any concrete solution concerning any particular case since, to arrive at a solution, a decision by the law applying organ between open alternatives will always be necessary, a decision that cannot be based on the legal system (Bayón 2000, pp. 104–106).

Although Bayón is again not very explicit about which type of situation he is referring to, everything suggests that it could be a type of situation in which reasons provided by law would be ignored. However, the idea that the reasons provided by law could be relegated to the category of mere rules of thumb is surprising: the authoritative nature of law seems to be in total contradiction with the idea of setting aside the reasons provided by law.

Despite its paradoxical nature, we can find an example that illustrates this type of situation without resorting to science fiction. The peculiar Spanish regulation of the "exercise of legal power to grant pardon"[14] can be an example of what we are looking for.[15] This regulation confers almost unlimited discretion on the government to enforce political acts of this kind, since the only limit it imposes is that "reasons of justice, equity or public utility" can be inferred from the "pardon agreement."[16]

Given the wide margin of discretion that the law has conferred on the government in these political acts, their judicial control has been a great problem for the Supreme Court. It is worth mentioning the Supreme Court's famous judgment of November 20, 2013, in which the Court recognized that its power to control the granting of pardon has an external character and is limited to the verification of the concurrence of sufficient factual requirements to support the reasons required by the legislator.

> It is a purely external control. The content of the Pardon Agreement cannot be reviewed. On the contrary, the review must be limited to the verification of whether the agreement has sufficient factual basis to support the reasons required by the legislator, in a process of legal logic. That is, the Supreme Court is only able to reexamine the agreement to verify whether a clear material error, any arbitrariness, or any manifestly logical unreasonableness is present.[17]

[14] Law of June 18, 1870, modified by Law 1/1988, of January 14 in Articles: 2, 3, 10, 11, 15, 20, 22, 23, 24, 26, 28, 29 and 30.

[15] This is how pardon is characterized by the Supreme Court: "pardon is an act with features of atypicality within the framework of the constitutional rule of law... because it involves a certain rejection of the principle of generality of criminal law and of those of independence and exclusivity of the jurisdiction" (ATS of January 18, 2001, Appeal 2940/1997).

[16] Article 11 Pardon Law.

[17] Ground 8.

The Court rules out the possibility that the process of legal logic submitted to review should exceed the external restriction of control of arbitrariness:

> the legal logic in this administrative decision procedure is presented as an external parameter to contain arbitrariness, which is prohibited for all Public Powers in article 9.3 of the Spanish Constitution, as arbitrary decisions are contrary to justice, reason and Law, and obey the exclusive will of the public official. What is prohibited in this constitutional mandate is the lack of support or objective legal basis for an administrative act, and, consequently, the violation of the material order of principles and values of the rule of law. Moreover such a requirement must also be claimed when the granting of pardon is involved, even within the framework of the greater discretion with which it is vested.[18]

Therefore, the regulation of the granting of pardon in our legal system takes away from courts the power to control the coherence between the content of the pardon agreement and the reasons within the law. This limits the review to an external review of arbitrariness, thereby implying that the government is empowered to set aside the reasons that the law itself provides.

In short, either because law allows the setting aside of reasons within it, as happens with the Granting of Pardon, or due to a situation of indeterminacy of the hierarchy of reasons stipulated by law, radical defeasibility, or D3, can appear in law.

To sum up, we can speak of radical defeasibility of rules (D3) in two theoretical hypotheses: (1) when a complete set of all preference relationships between norms in the system does not exist—indeterminacy of the hierarchy of reasons stipulated by law—or (2) when there are no closure rules regarding relevance—law empowers someone to set aside reasons that law itself provides (Ródenas 2001, pp. 72–82).

5 Legal Defeasibility and Discretionality of Legal Operators

Finally, we must deal with one last question: to what extent can we consider *legal* the set of alternative considerations to which operators must resort, when they consider that they should set aside applicable rules?

Clearly our answer must be negative regarding the marginal third kind of defeasibility (D3) that we have just considered. Courts are not obliged to submit themselves to law in cases of radical defeasibility, i.e., (1) when there is an indeterminacy of the hierarchy of reasons stipulated by law and, (2) when law allows the setting aside of reasons within it.

In contrast, defeasibility in D1 and D2 cases does not imply denying that law positively determines judges' decisions. As we have just seen, defeasibility in the D1 sense assumes that judges can set aside a rule when a case is beyond the justified scope of the prescription, as happened with the shared consumption of narcotics in a small group of people, or when the case constitutes an exception to that prescription, as happened with the irregular entry into a home that does not show "a skill or

[18] Ground 8.

significant effort." But judges are not free to formulate as many exceptions or exclusions of the scope of the rules as they wish and when they wish; legal officials must clearly show that, in accordance with the system of principles that gives meaning to the institution, or normative area concerned, the controversial case must be considered either an exception to the prescription or excluded from the scope of the prescription.

Neither do judges have discretion to establish a new balance between first order reasons which underlie rules in cases of D2 defeasibility. Judges can only set aside a rule when they can show the prevalence of other explicit or tacit pre-existing balances in the system among the first order reasons applicable to controversial cases.

In short, only defeasibility in the D3 sense gives judges a genuinely discretional power to make law. However, this sense of defeasibility is an unusual and marginal phenomenon. In D1 and D2 cases—those that best reconstruct the way in which our legal practices understand defeasibility—judges must base themselves on the system of principles that gives coherence to the institution or normative area concerned to legitimately set aside a prima facie applicable rule. Therefore, they must allude to reasons that are closely related to the ideas of normative coherence or congruence.

6 Conclusions

To conclude, I would like to return to a question that I formulated at the beginning of this work: in the opening pages I pointed out that if legal philosophers want to build a general theory of defeasibility which could be useful for legal dogmatics, it has to be able to respond to two challenges. First, it must capture common features of defeasibility beyond both the specificities in each branch of law, or the variations in different legal orders. Second, it must also be able to subject the matter to severe critical control, asking ourselves whether there is a rational basis for judges' claims that in certain cases they have the legal duty to set aside an applicable rule, and try to define in what type of cases and under which conditions such an attitude would be rational.

Throughout the pages of this work, I have tried to provide some elements that allow us to face both challenges. Starting from the observation that legal defeasibility does not always have the same characteristics, I have differentiated between three types of situations in which defeasibility appears. These three types of situation present their own distinctive characteristics, which in turn have led me to differentiate between three different types of defeasibility, which I have called D1, D2, and D3, with different justifying conditions.

Do these differences mean that it makes no sense to speak of defeasibility in a broad sense, beyond its three manifestations? We have seen how, despite the differences between D1, D2, and D3 defeasibility, a common denominator underlies them all: the three types of defeasibility limit the authority of law by expressing rational conditions to set aside applicable prima facie rules; whether the decision is discretionary or arbitrary will depend on whether these conditions exist.

From this lowest common denominator underlying the three types of defeasibility an important reason arises to explain why it makes perfect sense to speak of defeasibility in the broad sense: defeasibility plays a common role in law. The common function of defeasibility, in any of its three manifestations, is to guarantee a sufficient degree of ductility of law[19] for it to pursue the ends and values that we entrust to it. In other words, conditions for defeasibility express the limits of the ductility of law, establishing the point of inflection between ductile law and arbitrary law.

References

Alchourrón C (2010) Fundamentos para una teoría general de los deberes. Marcial Pons, Madrid

Alchourrón C, Bulygin E (1971) Normative systems. Springer, New York

Atienza M, Ruiz Manero J (2007) Las piezas del Derecho. Teoría de los enunciados jurídicos. Ariel, Barcelona

Bayón JC (2000) Derrotabilidad, indeterminación del Derecho y positivismo jurídico. Isonomía 13: 87–117

Dworkin R (1995) Positivismo y Derecho. In: La crisis del derecho y sus alternativas. Consejo General del Poder Judicial, Madrid, pp 73–93

Fernández TR (2005) Del arbitrio y de la arbitrariedad judicial. Iustel, Madrid

Ferrer J, Ratti J (eds) (2012) The logic of legal requirements. Oxford University Press, Oxford, Essays on defeasibility

Raz J (1990) Practical reason and norms. Princeton University Press, New Jersey

Raz J (1994) On the autonomy of legal reasoning. In: Ethics in the public domain. Oxford University Press, Oxford

Ródenas A (1998) Entre la transparencia y la opacidad: análisis del papel de las reglas en el razonamiento judicial Doxa. N. 21, vol 1:99–122

Ródenas A (2001) En la penumbra: indeterminación, derrotabilidad y aplicación judicial de normas, Doxa. Cuadernos de filosofía del Derecho 24:63–83

Ródenas A (2012) Los intersticios del Derecho. Marcial Pons, Madrid

Ródenas A (2017) La investigación en Filosofía del Derecho. Lineamientos metodológicos para la investigación jurídica 3:1–38

Ruiz Manero J (2018) Rule of Law y ponderación. In: Juan Pablo Alonso (coord) Imperio de la ley y *ponderación de principios*. Astrea, Buenos Aires

Schauer F (1991) Playing by the rules: a philosophical examination of rule-based decision-making in law and in life. Clarendon Press, Oxford

Silva Sánchez JM (1997) Nuevas tendencias político-criminales y actividad jurisprudencial del Tribunal Supremo. In: Romeo Casabona CM (ed) Dogmática Penal, Política Criminal y Criminología en evolución. Centro de Estudios Criminológicos-Universidad de La Laguna, La Laguna

Zagrebelsky G (2003) El Derecho dúctil. Ley, derechos, justicia. Trotta, Madrid

[19] The expression "ductility of Law" is inspired by the title of the renowned book in the continental legal culture by Gustavo Zagrebelsky *El Derecho dúctil. Ley, derechos, justicia* (Zagrebelsky 2003).

Punishment and Communication in the Post-Truth Society

Fernando Guanarteme Sánchez Lázaro

1 Communicative Theory and Reality of Punishment: Introduction

One of the most serious criticisms of general-prevention theories of punishment points to their lack of empirical evidence. So much so, that it is accepted among its advocates. Thus, for example, *Roxin* understands, on the one hand, that "the starting point for any justification of criminal law is ... of a preventive nature," distinguishing "between special and general prevention, that is, between the impact on the perpetrator and on the general public," and successively, in relation to the latter, between "the deterrent influence that the criminal justice system exerts on the general public," in the sense of negative general prevention, and in the sense of positive general prevention, between "the strengthening of society's legal awareness" through a "'learning effect', achieved through the public function of the criminal justice system," a "'trust effect', which results when the citizen sees that the law is imposed," and a "'pacifying effect', which is achieved when general legal awareness is calmed down through the sanctioning of the legal infraction and the

This paper has been prepared within the framework of the projects: "Derecho Penal y Comportamiento Humano (Criminal Law and Human Behavior)" (MICINN, RTI2018-097838-B-I00), IP: Eduardo Demetrio Crespo; "Crisis del Derecho penal del Estado de Derecho. Manifestaciones y Tendencias (Crisis of Criminal Law in the Rule of Law. Manifestations and Trends)" SBPLY/17/180501/000223 (IP: Eduardo Demetrio Crespo, Alfonso Jaime García Figueroa and Gema Marcilla Córdoba) "Proyecto Nexo: DER2017-86204-R (Nexus Project: DER2017-86204-R)", IP: Fernando Miró Llinares.

F. G. Sánchez Lázaro (✉)
Faculty of Law, University of La Laguna, Tenerife, Spain
e-mail: fsanche@ull.es

E. Demetrio Crespo et al. (eds.), *Crisis of the Criminal Law in the Democratic Constitutional State*, Legal Studies in International, European and Comparative Criminal Law 6, https://doi.org/10.1007/978-3-031-13413-5_10

conflict with the author is considered resolved" (Roxin 2015, pp. 190, 202).[1] Next, the author adds that, in practice, "little is known about how general prevention works" (Roxin 2015, p. 191),[2] concluding, however, that criminal law cannot be explained, much less justified, without the pursuit of such empirical-social goals (Roxin 2015, p. 190).[3]

This, as a theory, weakens it accordingly: if in practice, in this regard, nothing is known, the justification it offers is reduced to the mere assertion of such, of the pursuit of such empirical-social ends; thus, it reveals its fallacious component, as a theory that obviates the practice toward which—only in theory—it points. This fallacy is successively materialized in problems of legitimacy in its application, in the concrete case, as well as in the absence of answers to the real communicative problems of general prevention.

2 Punishment and Communication

2.1 In General: The Problem of the Channel

In this sense, and in general, it should be noted that the vast majority of judicial decisions do not transcend to the general public. Thus, there are numerous resolutions on issues that are not necessarily minor, which appeal to such reasons of general prevention, but which do not actually reach the general public. Thus, PAA (Provincial Audience Archives) of Madrid 518/2019, of 28 June, resolved "the liquidation of [a] private sentence of freedom ... in relation to the convicted person ... with a date of commencement on 19/3/2019, which expired on 19/11/2020," since the latter had violated the expulsion measure by which it had been replaced. It is particularly pointed out, in the second legal basis, that it is considered "necessary to comply with it 'in order to re-establish confidence in the legal rule infringed' -as the literal wording of the article states- since it has infringed the 'fidelity to the rule' (JAKOBS) that imposed the prohibition to return to the national territory within the indicated period, carrying out the penalty of fulfilling an 'expressive and

---

[1] On the difficulty of these distinctions, in practice Bachmann and Goeck (2013), p. 50.

[2] In relation to the jurisprudence, recently Warner et al. (2019), pp. 26 ff., 40, pointing out: "Interviews with... judges show that some judges admit that 'general deterrence is a fiction' and that they use it, despite doubting its efficacy."

[3] Also see Hassemer (2012), p. 197; Hörnle and von Hirsch (2005), pp. 20 ff. In general, Greco (2010), pp. 18 ff. With further references Goeckenjan (2015), p. 203, pointing out how the counterfactual construction of the hypotheses immunizes them against any falsification and verification. In a different sense Pawlik (2012), p. 50: "In essence, Roxin is content either to appeal expressly to the equally preordained feelings of justice of her readers, or more subtly, to rely on the intuitive plausibility of her assessments." Otherwise, for more detail Demetrio Crespo (2016), pp. 36 ff., 105 ff.

communicative' function (KINDHAUSER) within the framework of general prevention."[4] However, despite such an expressive and communicative claim, the resolution does not mention the rule of conduct first infringed—from which the prohibition to return derives. The result is a decision of a technical nature that omits the normative content it seeks to communicate, thereby restoring the community's confidence. As for the communicative significance, its circulation channel is limited—it seems—to specialized databases.[5]

The aforementioned contradictions, in a second moment, affect the basis of the decision. When the reasons behind the decision—fidelity to the norm, expressive and communicative function in the framework of general prevention—are displaced by the will of the legal operator who is in charge of their appreciation, correlative costs of legal standing ensue. Therefore, the basis for the effective imposition of the penalty is based on the will of the operator who imposes it, rather than the reasons set forth in the law. When in fact, the operator is entitled to apply the law, not his own will (Günther 2005, p. 253).[6] However, the emotional element that—generally—underlies this willingness to appreciate[7] is also reflected in the communication difficulties encountered by resolutions that, in fact, go beyond this: the perennial tendency to shape our beliefs according to what we want to believe (Roxin 2015, p. 190), even in cases where they are clearly contradictory to reality (cfr. McIntyre 2018, pp. 63 et seq.).

Moreover, in the area of suspended sentences, that is, when it comes to deciding on the effectiveness of their fundamental rights costs, it is common to refer to "criminal law as a means of communicative prevention -indeed, one that cannot be understood in terms of a dialogical reasoning- in which the sentence fulfills an expressive function," and where the imposition of the sentence "(something dissimilar to its execution) would convey different messages to each member of the interaction: the defendant, the victim, and the community:

---

[4]On the same terms PAA of Madrid 486/2019, decision of 20 of June, third law basis.

[5]See https://www.google.com/search?client=firefox-b-d&q=Auto+Audiencia+Provincial+Madrid+518%2F2019%2C+de+28+de+junio.

[6]More recently BVerfG 2 BvE 7/11, decision of 2 June 2015, 105 f. Critically, Pawlik (2014), pp. 384 f.: "This literally means: the illegitimacy of everything from Roman law to the Prussian CC of 1851."

[7]Illustrative Warner et al. (2019), pp. 26 ff., 34, concluding, on p. 39, that "General deterrence was the most popular purpose for judges, but the least popular for jurors," pointing out, as well, on p. 41, the "possibility that judges, who impose the pain of punishment on their fellow citizens as part of their daily business in the courts, may feel a need to believe that there is some compensating tangible benefit behind the system of imposing hard treatment on those who commit crimes. The continued judicial exposure to the burdensome consequences of criminal punishment may account for the differences between the judges' views and those of the jurors, who experience only temporary and limited exposure to this harsh aspect of the criminal justice system"; in the latter sense, on cognitive bias, generally McIntyre (2018), pp. 64 ff., 69 ff.

- The convicted person is informed that the crime is a fact for which they are responsible, that it is disapproved and that the rule that has been infringed is restored.
- The victim is conveyed that they have suffered an unjust injury and that they have the right to be compensated for it.
- The community is informed that the norm is a valid and current guideline to regulate social coexistence."[8] Resolutions that generally do not go beyond it, but which provide for "the execution of the same -which constitutes an additional evil- ... in those cases in which ... due to the temporary extension ... its imposition was insufficient to ratify the validity of the rule in the community's opinion."[9]

2.2 Context Problems: The Case of "La Manada"

Compared to the previous resolutions, which are found in channels that do not transcend the general public, the resolutions that do transcend find successive problems in the present communicative context of our society. In this sense, the PAR (Provincial Audience Ruling) of Pamplona 38/2018 of March 20, known as the case of "La Manada ('The Pack')," is paradigmatic. As is known, five citizens were sentenced here to 9 years in prison and 5 years of probation for engaging in vaginal, anal, and oral sex with a woman who did not express her opposition to such acts.[10] Of particular interest is the credibility given by the court to the victim, who adopted "an attitude of submission and passivity," doing "what the defendants told her to do, keeping her eyes closed most of the time." It is particularly expressly stated in the ruling: "we have justified the fact that throughout her statements during the trial, in a clear, forceful manner, and without any drift in the testimony in the oral trial, the plaintiff maintains and we give her *full credibility* that, finding herself in this situation, she noticed how they were unbuttoning the fanny pack that she was wearing crossed, how they were taking off her strapless bra by opening a clip and undoing the sweater she had tied around her waist; from which she experienced the sensation of anguish, which increased when one of the defendants approached the

[8] Recently PAA of Salamanca 231/2019, decision of 30 July, second law basis. In the same terms, and among others, PAA of Salamanca 191/2019, decision 21 of June, second law basis; PAA of Guadalajara 249/2018, decision of 24 September, second law basis; PAA Guipúzcoa 482/2018, decision 13 of July, second law basis; PAA Salamanca 488/2017, decision 29 of December, second law basis; PAA of Valladolid 144/2012, decision of 27 of March, single legal basis, all of them with further references.

[9] PAA of Salamanca 231/2019, decision of 30 July, second law basis.

[10] Sentenced later in SCR 344/2019, decision of 4 of July, as perpetrators of a continuing crime of rape, to 15 years' imprisonment, prohibition of approaching the complainant for 20 years and 8 years' probation, as well as, to one of them, to 2 years' imprisonment as perpetrator of a crime of robbery with intimidation.

plaintiff's jaw for her to perform fellatio on him and in that situation she noticed, how another defendant grabbed her from her hip and pulled down her leggings and thong" (the fourth legal basis). The plaintiff was given *full credibility*, even in view of the concordance of the testimony of the convicted persons with certain photograms, recordings, or statements by the hotel employee, the persistence and consistency of their statements, the results of the tests applied to the victim by the forensic experts,[11] or the contradictions between what the victim initially stated in her complaint of July 7, 2016, and then before the examining magistrate, or finally, in the oral trial,[12] that is: "that they did not force her; she did not try to escape or flee; she did not scream; they did not continually cover her mouth, nor did they throw her in the dirt . . . this version, ultimately, totally contradicts her initial complaint, which was ratified the following day in court."[13] This last element should particularly be assessed in light of the doctrine of our SC, which establishes the persistence of the victim's testimony as a criterion of rationality, that is, "a) the absence of essential modifications in the successive statements made by the victim; b) the concreteness of the statement; c) the absence of contradictions, with the account maintaining the necessary logical connection between the various versions narrated at different times."[14]

The resolution does not refer to reasons of general prevention in the determination of the sentence, basically, it complies with the principles of proportionality and guilt (the seventh legal basis), yet it is of particular interest to communication theories, since it imposes a considerable penalty: 9 years in prison, based on the "full credibility" that is explicitly and implicitly granted to the—last—testimony of the victim. However, it is received in a very different sense by the general public: "yo sí te creo hermana (I do believe you, sister)."

[11] Private vote, second law basis: "shows little impulse control, prioritizes its needs by acting in order to cover them up and without taking into account established social rules," "histrionic and borderline (Cluster B) and dependent and anxious (Cluster C) personality traits," assessments not contested by the forensic experts, who did not evaluate the questionnaire in question, the so-called "Salamanca Questionnaire," also pointing out "the fact that the Self-Control Scale is, among all those evaluated, the one that has conspicuously obtained the lowest score . . . that . . . 'she evidences little control by her superego. She is governed by an alternate and personalized system, giving emphasis to her impulses and needs; she does not let herself be carried away by the rules established by society'", as well as the results of the "Symptom Simulation Inventory," which point out that "the evaluated woman reports atypical symptoms of depression and anxiety which would suggest the magnification of this type of symptomatology."

[12] Private vote, second law basis.

[13] Private vote, second law basis.

[14] SCR 678/2018, decision of 20 of December, fifth law basis, with subsequent references.

2.2.1 Dissonant Messages

After the publication of the PAR of Pamplona, the hashtag "#YoSiTeCreo" ("#iDoBelieveYou") approached 1,200,000 interactions on Twitter,[15] becoming the feminist message of greatest impact in the aforementioned social network, in Spanish.[16] Yet, in a radically different sense to that made explicit by the ruling. Subsequently, the hashtag rebounded on June 22, 2018, when the court agreed to release the defendants on bail,[17] and rose sharply again after the resolution of the appeals by our SC. In this sense, it is also worth noting its qualitative significance.[18] Thus, for example, on June 21, 2019, the current Second Vice-President of the government declared about this last resolution: "millions of women said in the streets I do believe you and they have finally been heard by Justice."[19] The current Minister of Equality attributed the sentence to the feminist movement, declaring: "Sister, I believe you until only yes is yes, until the feet of sexism are stopped."[20] While the current president of the government added for his part: "it was a rape. The Supreme Court's ruling on La Manada confirms this. Only yes is yes. Spain continues to make progress in protecting the rights and freedoms of women and will not stop. Because we believed her, because we believe you. Because we want you to live, free, without fear."[21] Of interest here is, firstly, the relationship of opposition between the message contained in the ruling and that received by a large part of the public: "full credibility"/"I do believe you," despite the coincidence between what was granted by the resolution and what was required of it: to give full credibility to the victim.

---

[15] https://elpais.com/sociedad/2018/10/09/actualidad/1539114993_820161.html; although the existence of different hashtags makes it difficult to assess the overall impact on the networks, being related: #YoSiTeCreo, #LaManada, #yosítecreo, #NoEsAbusoEsViolacion, #hermanayositecreo, #Cuéntalo, #NoesNo, #JusticiaPatriarcal, moreover, illustrative Larrondo et al. (2019), p. 211; Orbegozo et al. (2019), pp. 217 ff.

[16] https://elpais.com/sociedad/2018/10/09/actualidad/1539114993_820161.html. Besides that, about its scope, see https://www.nytimes.com/2018/06/21/world/europe/spain-pamplona-sexualassault.html; https://twitter.com/nytimes/status/989764593403621376?lang=es; https://www.bbc.com/news/world-europe-43915551; https://www.theguardian.com/world/2019/apr/23/wolf-pack-case-spain-feminism-far-right-vox. Recently, also in German doctrine, alluding to the shocking "gang rape that occurred in Pamplona, Spain, in 2016," Hörnle (2019), p. 153.

[17] https://elpais.com/sociedad/2018/10/09/actualidad/1539114993_820161.html.

[18] https://www.trendencias.com/feminismo/hermana-yo-te-creo-asi-reaccionan-las-redes-sociales-al-veredicto-del-juicio-de-la-manada. For the rest, among others https://twitter.com/PabloIglesias/status/1142062455914455042; https://twitter.com/sanchezcastejon/status/1142073628919570432?lang=es; https://twitter.com/irenemontero/status/1142059504982474752; https://twitter.com/hashtag/yos%C3%ADtecreo.

[19] https://www.eldiario.es/politica/Unidas-Podemos-sentencia-Manada-feminismo_0_912359477.html.

[20] https://www.eldiario.es/politica/Unidas-Podemos-sentencia-Manada-feminismo_0_912359477.html.

[21] https://www.infolibre.es/noticias/politica/2019/06/21/garzon_sanchez_errejon_apoyan_decision_condenar_los_miembros_manada_por_delito_violacion_96265_1012.html.

But in a second moment, it is equally important to point out the dissonance between the seriousness of the prison sentence imposed in the first sentence: 9 years in prison, and its scarce communicative transcendence; in any case: neither "strengthening of the legal conscience of society," nor effects of "learning," "trust," and "pacification." In fact, in the opposite sense, the first of the three statements gathered is illustrative: "millions of women said in the street I believe you," the number of interactions of the mentioned hashtag,[22] or the belligerence of the massive demonstrations in the networks: "3 years for a rap, 20 years for a referendum, 60 years for a bar fight, 9 years for a rape, #LaManada also wears a gown,"[23] "Judicial system?, call it an insult . . . I curse this deficient system for this insufficient penance, how sad, justice is on the wane . . . judges are on sale,"[24] "Spanish Justice. La Manada can go out and rape in San Juan."[25]

2.2.2 More Specifically: On Public Discourse in the Post-Truth Era

In a recent publication, Valdés Villanueva pointed out the structural problems that characterize public communication in our time: the decline and displacement of contemporary media, the emergence of social networks, the questioning and discrediting of expert discourse, as well as the perennial particularities of social psychology, which have led to the communicative phenomenon known as post-truth (Valdés Villanueva 2018, pp. 13 et seq.; on the concept of post-truth, McIntyre 2018, pp. 31 seq.) Particularly disturbing is its exclusionary character, its authoritarian component of ideological supremacy, through which it seeks to impose itself as a belief, whether there is evidence for it, against it, or not: "Will I be believed only until I get killed?"[26] In this regard, the doctrine criticized the ideological labeling that accompanied the sentence,[27] recalling how "the judges were insulted, they were . . . [asked] to be disqualified, they demanded things that the sentence grants and protested those that it does not say."[28] The same was true when the highest authorities pointed out the lack of "mental reform" on the part of the members of the court.[29] All of these elements are reflected in the case in question:

[22] https://elpais.com/sociedad/2018/10/09/actualidad/1539114993_820161.html; although the existence of different hashtags makes it difficult to assess the overall impact on the networks, being related: #YoSiTeCreo, #LaManada, #yosítecreo, #NoEsAbusoEsViolacion, #hermanayositecreo, #Cuéntalo, #NoesNo, #JusticiaPatriarcal, moreover, illustrative Larrondo et al. (2019), p. 211; Orbegozo et al. (2019), pp. 217 ff.

[23] https://twitter.com/gabrielrufian/status/989487329738940416.

[24] https://www.instagram.com/p/BiC49I2FOJF/?utm_source=ig_embed.

[25] https://twitter.com/emparmoliner/status/1009837643159531524.

[26] https://www.instagram.com/silvia__alonso/, en https://www.trendencias.com/feminismo/hermana-yo-te-creo-asi-reaccionan-las-redes-sociales-al-veredicto-del-juicio-de-la-manada.

[27] Gil and Nuñez Fernández (2018).

[28] Gil and Nuñez Fernández (2018).

[29] https://cadenaser.com/programa/2018/06/21/hora_25/1529603890_931407.html.

Displacement of Facts and Expert Discourse

First, with respect to the aforementioned judgment, it should be noted how a technical-legal issue of the subsumption of the proven facts in various precepts of the Criminal Code is transformed into a movement to reject a decision that, nevertheless, satisfies what is claimed of it: full credibility for the victim. This element is linked to the more general tendency to lose interest in the truth or in the evidence itself (Valdés Villanueva 2018, pp. 13 et seq.): the word "credibility" is used 40 times in the PAR of Pamplona, 38/2018, of March 20, in two of which it appears after the adjective "full," in the first case making explicit the position of the court in relation to the victim's testimony.

This disinterest in the facts drags the expert discourse: "Fuck you! The rapists, their lawyers, the judges, those of the law... And the rest, please #AlasCalles (#hitTheStreets)."[30] This is despite the "evident tension between the rapid transmission of hashtags and the careful attention that requires a critical evaluation of the comments and causes before supporting them."[31] In this sense, the criticism of the legal qualification, "It is not abuse. It is rape," [32] shared, among others, by our president of government, is equally evident as post-truth when it is reduced to an emotion of rejection, stripped of all technical-legal complexity. Or more recently, when the eventual technical deficiencies of an ambitious bill are attributed to "many frustrated sexists."[33]

It is pointed out that "the prefix <<pos>> is intended to indicate not so much the idea that we have left the truth behind in a temporal sense (as happens in <post-war>>) but in the sense that the truth has been eclipsed: that it is irrelevant."[34] For this reason, legal definitions and semantic rules that distinguish between one crime

[30] https://twitter.com/VeroBoquete/status/989522873864806401. Besides that, Iyengar and Massey (2019), pp. 7656 ff., 7659; van der Bles et al. (2020), p. 7672, with subsequent references.

[31] Larrondo et al. (2019), pp. 218 f., pointing out, however, "Twitter makes it possible to democratize the feminist struggle by extending and normalizing it, hence some authors recommend its consideration as a useful discursive and rhetorical platform." In general, McIntyre (2018), pp. 45 ff.; particularly in relation to the tobacco industry's communication strategy, 49 ff.; on climate change, 54 et seq.; besides that, illustrative https://twitter.com/vox_es/status/1201482571571437569: "VOX rejects the exaggerated and unfounded alarmism about #ClimateChange of the globalist elites that demonizes our fishing, livestock and industrial sectors"; in relation to terrorism Innes (2020), pp. 284 ff.

[32] https://navarra.elespanol.com/articulo/tribunales/actriz-hollywood-manada-redes-sociales/20180427194104185741.html.

[33] https://www.eldiario.es/politica/Iglesias-reservas-tecnicas-machista-frustrado_0_1001950693.html. However, relating the distinction between sexual abuse and sexual assault to "revictimization or secondary victimization," without further justification, see Exposición de Motivos III, Anteproyecto de Ley Orgánica de Garantía Integral de la Libertad Sexual, http://www.igualdad.gob.es/Documents/APLOGarantia%20de%20la%20Libertad%20Sexual.pdf.

[34] McIntyre (2018), p. 34; Innes (2020), pp. 284 ff.; expressly, in general, Errejón (2011), p. 132: "It was not, of course, 'decir the truth' about the crisis and its management. It was a matter of situating the political dispute on more advantageous ground for the challenge to the existing order and its elites."

and another have been left in the shadows.[35] These are, moreover, the specialized linguistic conventions that cannot be ignored by the concrete legal operator, and on which a significant part of the fundamental structural decisions of our Constitution are based: the subjection of the judiciary to the law, the separation of powers, and the realization of the democratic principle, including in the discourse of application.[36]

Opinion As a Parallel Truth

The void left by facts and expert discourse is successively occupied by opinion. In this sense, the statements issued by the President of the Government on April 26, 2018: "She said NO. We believed you and we still believe you," or by the well-known actress and film producer Jessica Chastain: "Five strangers told an intoxicated teenager that they would accompany her to her car. Instead, they took her to another place where they filmed her being gang-raped. How many women are killed each year?",[37] the events of this case, however, generate a new reality, divergent from the one that occurred, with which an emotional bond is additionally established. This is the hashtag: "I do believe you," in front of a world in which, in fact, it has been believed.[38] To which contributes the advanced tendency, individual and collective, to confuse what we believe with what we want, that is: we want to believe (Valdés Villanueva 2018, pp. 21 ff.).

With this, the threat to the truth is made concrete in public discourse (McIntyre 2018, p. 27), by means of an alternative truth that, by placing feelings before facts in its formation, lends itself as an efficient tool for mobilization and power.[39] In addition, the definition of post truth was already included in the Oxford dictionaries when it was nominated for Word of the Year 2016, that is, as an adjective "relative or denoting circumstances in which objective facts are less influential in shaping public opinion than appeals to personal emotion and belief" (https://languages.oup.com/word-of-the-year/2016/).

[35] Illustrative in Gil and Nuñez Fernández (2018). Technical complexity which, moreover, does not significantly affect confidence indices, cfr. van der Bles et al. (2020), pp. 7672 ff., 7679 ff.

[36] Klatt (2005), pp. 345 f., 362, 366; Klatt (2004), pp. 19 ff. In our doctrine, recently also Muñoz Conde (2019), pp. 290 ff.

[37] https://navarra.elespanol.com/articulo/tribunales/actriz-hollywood-manada-redes-sociales/20180427194104185741.html.

[38] In relation to the recent SCJR Madrid 86/2020, decision of 10 of March, also illustrative https://twitter.com/IreneMontero/status/1252913686072766467.

[39] About social networks, understood as "explanatory and generating frameworks of the reality that surrounds us," Orbegozo et al. (2019), p. 213, with further references.

Cognitive Irrationalities

To this is added, equally, our tendency to seek and maintain our psychic self-satisfaction, to avoid self-criticism, because "we feel better thinking that we are intelligent, that we are well informed, that we are capable people, than thinking that we are nothing of the sort."[40] Resistance that is collectively reinforced, when the belief is shared, as in the case discussed here, pointing out a social component of belief so powerful that it leads us to "discard even the evidence of our own senses if we think our beliefs are not in harmony with those around us."[41] There is also an equally biased tendency to confirm, to make a selective discrimination of the evidence that confirms what we are emotionally connected to (McIntyre 2018, p. 66).

In fact, it is pointed out from neuroscience that when affective content influences our reasoning, a different part of the brain is operating, which affects our willingness to accept facts and evidence as a basis for belief.[42] This is an element to keep in mind when evaluating the reaction of the defenders of the communicative theories of punishment to studies that provide them with elements of foundation. Although here, it is interesting to point out how the emotional commitment to the case—of La Manada, as well as in general—conditions even the brain to the possibility of developing a rational dialogue.

Displacement of the Media by Opinion Media and Social Networks

Finally, it is worth noting a 2013 study, which established that 69% of Fox News guests were skeptical about climate change, compared to 17% for the Washington Post, or that 68% of the first network's reports reflected the personal opinions of its guests and presenters, compared to 4% for CNN. It is therefore not surprising that Fox News' audience is less well informed than those who do not resort to any source

[40] McIntyre (2018), pp. 63 ff.; on "source amnesia," the "repetition effect" 69 ff.; Innes (2020), pp. 284 ff.; Iyengar and Massey (2019), pp. 7658 f., regarding the crime/immigration correlation, p. 7659.

[41] McIntyre (2018), p. 66, pointing out, however, the existence of emotional turning points, pp. 167 ff.; in this sense, also Innes (2020), pp. 296 f.: "social media is better at coordinating and channeling people's opinions, than changing them," with further references.

[42] Westen et al. (2006), ff. 1947 ff., concluding: "that motivated reasoning is qualitatively distinct from reasoning when people do not have a strong emotional stake in the conclusions reached," linking motivated reasoning "with activations of the ventromedial prefrontal cortex, anterior cingulate cortex, posterior cingulate cortex, insular cortex, and lateral orbital cortex"; besides, on the " counterproductive effect," that is, when the evidence of falsehood instead of distancing us from the error, clings us to it even more, McIntyre (2018), pp. 72 ff., on the "Dunning-Kruger effect," 74 ff.

of information, nor is it surprising that citizens have lost confidence in the general media.[43]

Along the same lines, a 2016 study established that 2/3 of the US adult population obtain their news through social networks, particularly highlighting the 71% reported on Facebook (McIntyre 2018, pp. 110 and s. 124). This is particularly practical when knowledge of the facts requires the reading of a judgment of the scope of the one discussed here. Given that social networks adjust news to the reader's taste, by means of a practical technification of the confirmation bias,[44] as well as, in general, the lack of a minimum of informative rigor, it is not particularly surprising that in 2016, in this social network, the twenty most important false news were shared more times than the corresponding twenty news, with content that could be qualified as true.[45] And so a new power is taking shape, that of the social networks to the detriment of the fourth, the media,[46] which raises serious doubts about its function of informing and forming public opinion.

In fact, in relation to the aforementioned ruling, the informative dynamics of social networks has revealed three of the four identifying elements of propaganda:

1. Provocation of emotions: "How many women are killed each year?", "Will they believe me only until I get killed?",[47] "He who does not punish evil, orders it to be done."[48] Or more recently, in connection with SCJR of Madrid 86/2020, March 10: "Isa Serra helped stop an eviction of a person with a disability. She acted in defense of Human Rights and of Art. 47 of the Constitution, which protects the right to housing. Neither Isa nor any person in Spain fighting against injustice will be alone. We are more";[49]
2. Designation and denigration of scapegoats: "3 years for a rap 20 years for a referendum 60 years for a bar fight 9 years for a rape #LaManada also wears a

[43] McIntyre (2018), pp. 92 f., 106; more recently, in relation to COVID-19 see https://www.elconfidencial.com/mundo/europa/2020-04-05/coronavirus-covid-trump-pandemia_2532600/: "Only 38 percent of Fox News viewers were concerned about the virus... far below those who watch another channel (68 percent) or read newspapers (72 percent) ... even though half of Fox's audience is over 50. In other words, an audience more prone to suffer from the coronavirus." Besides, illustrative Iyengar and Massey (2019), pp. 7656 ff., 7657: "PolitiFact rates 59% of Fox's assertions as mostly or all false," also pointing out: "the figure for CNN is 27%"; in relation to the Iraq war, see p. 7659.

[44] Iyengar and Massey (2019), p. 7657; Innes (2020), p. 285.

[45] McIntyre (2018), pp. 111 f., 124. In general, Vosoughi et al. (2018), pp. 1146 ff., concluding: "Falsehood diffused significantly farther, faster, deeper, and more broadly than the truth in all categories of information"; Lazer et al. (2018), p. 1095; Iyengar and Massey (2019), pp. 7657 f.; Innes (2020), pp. 288 ff., 293. Besides, illustrative Muñoz-Machado (2020), p. 124.

[46] Orbegozo et al. (2019), pp. 220 f., with further references; on the correlation between the two Innes (2020), pp. 290 f.

[47] https://www.instagram.com/silvia__alonso/, in https://www.trendencias.com/feminismo/hermana-yo-te-creo-asi-reaccionan-las-redes-sociales-al-veredicto-del-juicio-de-la-manada.

[48] https://twitter.com/ChristianG_7/status/989576801499394048.

[49] https://twitter.com/IreneMontero/status/1252913686072766467.

gown,"[50] judicial system?, call it an insult . . . I curse this deficient system for this insufficient penance, how sad, justice is on the wane . . . judges are on sale,"[51] "Spanish Justice. La Manada can go out and rape in San Juan,"[52] "Judicial pack (manada judicial). If only read, the sentence produces nausea (literally), I don't even want to think about what she suffered,"[53] "What can't be is that being killed is the only clear sentence,"[54] "Fucking justice. 9 years is not comparable to a shattered life. Sister I believe you,"[55] "What's up, SPANISH JUSTICE? Just another day of being DISGUSTING, isn't it? Weeell, that's all right. . . That's all there is to it, isn't it? Kisses,"[56] "First raped, then questioned. #JusticiaPatriarcal (#PatriarchalJustice)";[57]

3. Falsification: "I do believe you,"[58] "The Pack (La Manada) is 8: 3 judges and 5 rapists,"[59] "What a fear to walk around #Pamplona at night. Now I know that if I am unlucky enough to run into people like those in #LaManada, either I defend myself at the risk of my life or a group of judges will think that I liked it. #shame #verguenza."[60]

Propaganda that is conceived as a totalitarian strategy of power.[61] The next characteristic note is the search for division among citizens (McIntyre 2018, pp. 127 et seq). However, the high emotional content that the discourse can reach:

---

[50] https://twitter.com/gabrielrufian/status/989487329738940416.

[51] https://www.instagram.com/p/BiC49I2FOJF/?utm_source=ig_embed.

[52] https://twitter.com/emparmoliner/status/1009837643159531524.

[53] https://twitter.com/jordievole/status/989527633418387461.

[54] https://twitter.com/lavecinarubia/status/989494568512081920.

[55] https://www.instagram.com/goicoechea22/, in https://www.trendencias.com/feminismo/hermana-yo-te-creo-asi-reaccionan-las-redes-sociales-al-veredicto-del-juicio-de-la-manada.

[56] https://www.instagram.com/p/BiCdwZ1hWvV/?utm_source=ig_embed.

[57] https://twitter.com/TeresaRodr_/status/990150046447558656; besides, in general, Errejón (2011), p. 127; Orbegozo et al. (2019), p. 241.

[58] McIntyre (2018), pp. 127 f.; more specifically Innes (2020), pp. 292 ff.; particularly also see Antwort der Bundesregierung of 7 of February of 2020, Drucksache 19/16552–19/17073, 1 ff.

[59] https://www.facebook.com/Infobae/posts/la-manada-son-8-3-jueces-y-5-violadoresmiles-de-mujeres-se-movilizaron-el-vierne/10156108320306971/.

[60] https://twitter.com/Lurquizu/status/989639983496683521.

[61] Illustrative *Stanley* in: https://www.wbur.org/hereandnow/2017/02/15/how-propaganda-works-fake-news, on the situation of dialogue, also Larrondo et al. (2019), p. 217, questioning "to what extent feminisms should encourage this path of the striking resource that seeks engagement and viralization, leaving in the background the space for dialogue aimed at deliberation on the strategic evolution of the movement," pointing out as well "the most politicized actors appear to be linked to a greater capacity for dialogue or participation in the digital debate, based on more active attitudes and greater listening among users, as well as between users and political leaders, mostly on the left." Besides that, see Orbegozo et al. (2019), pp. 211 ff., pointing out how "feminists still have many alliances to explore," noting on p. 240, the role of "transformative social movements: Spanish republicanism, users who share the narrative of the so-called 'movements of indignation' that emerged in Spain years ago, communist formations and users, and even interrelated groups and individuals who stand out for defending Catalan independence." What, in his opinion, points to the

"How many women are killed each year?", "Will they believe me only until I get killed?", leaves little room for disagreement with other political phenomena of our time that seek, directly, confrontation: "Spain . . . not only robs us, but also kills us."[62]

3 From Communicative Reality to the Theory of Punishment: Epilogue

The above notes outline a communicative reality different from that conceived by the academy in the development of the theory of punishment. However, on the seriousness of what is stated in Sect. 2.2, the 330,000 deaths attributed to Thabo Mbeki for restricting the use of antiretroviral drugs, associating them with a Western conspiracy, and recommending instead the treatment of HIV with garlic, beetroot and lemonade, are illustrative (see Chigwedere et al. 2008, pp. 410 et seq.). Also, recent attempts at political instrumentalization and destabilization in countries around us,[63] or the "Infodemic," in the context of the COVID-19.[64] Within this framework, the opportunity for individual empowerment strategies is particularly pointed out[65] because of the importance of human behavior in shaping and expanding itself,[66] similar to what has been advanced in the section "Cognitive Irrationalities".

---

fact that "the alliances that are erected have a structural character and a clear vocation to build the antagonism to the liberal rule of law that, in this case, embodies the judicial-social power."

[62] https://cronicaglobal.elespanol.com/en-voz-baja/torra-espana-roba-mata_314726_102.html; otherwise, illustrative Errejón (2011), p. 127, pointing to "the stamp of the 'populism' as a form of constituting the political, through the dichotomization and simplification of society in a conflictive process of interpretation... What is interesting for the perspective of discourse analysis and hegemony is to understand the category of people as... an exercise in identity construction marked by tension toward... a part of the political community... The political meaning of such a nomination will always depend, to a large extent, on an otherness -a 'people' [or caste, subsection added]- in order to raise and reinforce its own contours."

[63] Antwort der Bundesregierung of 7 of February of 2020, Drucksache 19/16552–19/17073, 2; in general, also Innes (2020), pp. 294 ff., 297. Besides cfr. McIntyre (2018), pp. 39 ff., 67 ff.; also https://euvsdisinfo.eu/disinformation-cases/?text=catalonia&date=&offset=0.

[64] Antwort der Bundesregierung of 27 of August 2020, Drucksache 19/21259–19/21891, 1 ff., 6.

[65] Lazer et al. (2018), p. 1095, pointing out also the necessary intervention of social networks, 1095 et seq.; after the latter Muñoz-Machado (2020), pp. 129 ff.

[66] Vosoughi et al. (2018), p. 1150: "false news spreads farther, faster, deeper, and more broadly than the truth because humans, not robots, are more likely to spread it," also pointing out "false rumors inspired replies expressing greater surprise. . ., and greater disgust. . ., whereas the truth inspired replies that expressed greater sadness. . ., anticipation . . ., joy . . ., and trust . . . . The emotions expressed in reply to falsehoods may illuminate additional factors, beyond novelty, that inspire people to share false news."

Generally, it also proposes the development of new and more effective communication strategies by science.[67]

But, particularly, in relation to our discipline, there is a need for a theory that, before establishing subtle theoretical-communicative differences, studies the function of communication that in effect fulfills the sentence, when it is not simply displaced, in a discourse that obviates its meaning in terms of the costs of fundamental law: 9 years in prison. Also the study with property of the latter, which supposes, in effect, the imposition to a citizen of a sentence of 1, 9 or 15 years of privation of freedom, in the light of the rights of benefit that the Article 25.2 of the Spanish Constitution consecrates, when it orients its fulfillment towards the reeducation and social reinsertion.[68] Certainly, the communication problems outlined above go beyond punishment and affect transversal debates such as immigration[69] and, in general, public discourse as the basis of our state model.[70] Hence the urgent need for a multidisciplinary approach.[71] Although, within the theory of punishment, general preventive constructions are particularly suitable, due to their fallacious component, as a response to the challenges presented by this post-truth era.

Institutional Documents

Antwort der Bundesregierung auf die Kleine Anfrage der Abgeordneten Benjamin Strasser, Stephan Thomae, Grigorios Aggelidis, weiterer Abgeordneter und der Fraktion der FDP—Drucksache 19/16552—Desinformationskampagnen—Erkenntnisse und Maßnahmen der Bundesregierung, 19/17073, of 7.2.2020, 1-8.

Antwort der Bundesregierung auf die Kleine Anfrage der Abgeordneten Andrej Hunko, Heike Hänsel, Michel Brandt, weiterer Abgeordneter und der Fraktion

[67] In general, see Iyengar and Massey (2019), p. 7660; on the trust/complexity correlation van der Bles et al. (2020), pp. 7672 ff., 7679 ff.; in relation to public institutions, Antwort der Bundesregierung of 7 of February 2020, Drucksache 19/16552–19/17073, 6 f.

[68] Illustrative BVerfG, 2 BvR 2025/12 decision of 10 October 2012, 3, with further references.

[69] On the National Academy of Sciences' report on the fiscal and economic impact of immigration, cfr. Iyengar and Massey (2019), p. 7659; likewise, see Innes (2020), pp. 291, 294 ff.; Muñoz-Machado (2020), p. 133. In relation to crime figures, also McIntyre (2018), p. 60, n. 38.

[70] Antwort der Bundesregierung de of 7 of February 2020, Drucksache 19/16552–19/17073, 1 ff.; Innes (2020), pp. 294 ff., 297; Illustrative, also: "The logical answer from Europe to the Catalonia referendum would have been: recognize the independence of Catalonia and bomb Madrid," in: https://euvsdisinfo.eu/report/the-logical-answer-from-europe-to-the-catalonia-referendum-would-have-been-recognize-the-independence-of-catalonia-and-bomb-madrid/.

[71] Lazer et al. (2018), p. 1096; in relation to communication technique, also van der Bles et al. (2020), pp. 7672 ff., 7680, concluding "natural scientists, statisticians, and social scientists should work together to evaluate how to best present scientific uncertainty in an open and transparent manner," together with "by a common interest in how to effectively communicate the truth in a so-called posttruth world."

DIE LINKE—Drucksache 19/21259—EU-Maßnahmen zu „strategischer Kommunikation" und „Desinformation" im Zusammenhang mit COVID-19, 19/21891, of 27.8.2020, 1-9.

Online Publications

https://cadenaser.com/programa/2018/06/21/hora_25/1529603890_931407.html. Accessed 16 November 2020.
https://cronicaglobal.elespanol.com/en-voz-baja/torra-espana-roba-mata_314726_102.html. Accessed 16 November 2020.
https://elpais.com/sociedad/2018/10/09/actualidad/1539114993_820161.html. Accessed 16 November 2020.
https://euvsdisinfo.eu/disinformation-cases/?text=catalonia&date=&offset=0. Accessed 16 November 2020.
https://euvsdisinfo.eu/report/the-logical-answer-from-europe-to-the-catalonia-referendum-would-have-been-recognize-the-independence-of-catalonia-and-bomb-madrid/. Accessed 16 November 2020.
https://www.bbc.com/news/world-europe-43915551. Accessed 16 November 2020.
https://www.elconfidencial.com/mundo/europa/2020-04-05/coronavirus-covid-trump-pandemia_2532600/. Accessed 16 November 2020.
https://www.eldiario.es/politica/Unidas-Podemos-sentencia-Manada-feminismo_0_912359477.html. Accessed 16 November 2020.
https://www.eldiario.es/politica/Iglesias-reservas-tecnicas-machista-frustrado_0_1001950693.html. Accessed 16 November 2020.
https://www.facebook.com/Infobae/posts/la-manada-son-8-3-jueces-y-5-violadoresmiles-de-mujeres-se-movilizaron-el-vierne/10156108320306971/. Accessed 16 November 2020.
https://www.google.com/search?client=firefox-bd&q=Auto+Audiencia+Provincial+Madrid+518%2F2019%2C+de+28+de+junio. Accessed 16 November 2020.
http://www.igualdad.gob.es/Documents/APLOGarantia%20de%20la%20Libertad%20Sexual.pdf. Accessed 16 November 2020.
https://www.infolibre.es/noticias/politica/2019/06/21/garzon_sanchez_errejon_apoyan_decision_condenar_los_miembros_manada_por_delito_violacion_96265_1012.html. Accessed 16 November 2020.
https://www.instagram.com/p/BiC49I2FOJF/?utm_source=ig_embed. Accessed 16 November 2020.
https://www.instagram.com/p/BiCdwZ1hWvV/?utm_source=ig_embed. Accessed 16 November 2020.
https://navarra.elespanol.com/articulo/tribunales/actriz-hollywood-manada-redes-sociales/20180427194104185741.html. Accessed 16 November 2020.
https://www.nytimes.com/2018/06/21/world/europe/spain-pamplona-sexualassault.html. Accessed 16 November 2020.

https://www.theguardian.com/world/2019/apr/23/wolf-pack-case-spain-feminism-far-right-vox. Accessed 16 November 2020.
https://www.trendencias.com/feminismo/hermana-yo-te-creo-asi-reaccionan-las-redes-sociales-al-veredicto-del-juicio-de-la-manada. Accessed 16 November 2020.
https://twitter.com/ChristianG_7/status/989576801499394048. Accessed 16 November 2020.
https://twitter.com/emparmoliner/status/1009837643159531524. Accessed 16 November 2020.
https://twitter.com/gabrielrufian/status/989487329738940416. Accessed 16 November 2020.
https://twitter.com/hashtag/yos%C3%ADtecreo. Accessed 16 November 2020.
https://twitter.com/irenemontero/status/1142059504982474752. Accessed 16 November 2020.
https://twitter.com/IreneMontero/status/1252913686072766467. Accessed 16 November 2020.
https://twitter.com/jordievole/status/989527633418387461. Accessed 16 November 2020.
https://twitter.com/lavecinarubia/status/989494568512081920. Accessed 16 November 2020.
https://twitter.com/Lurquizu/status/989639983496683521. Accessed 16 November 2020.
https://twitter.com/nytimes/status/989764593403621376?lang=es. Accessed 16 November 2020.
https://twitter.com/PabloIglesias/status/1142062455914455042. Accessed 16 November 2020.
https://twitter.com/sanchezcastejon/status/1142073628919570432?lang=es. Accessed 16 November 2020.
https://twitter.com/TeresaRodr_/status/990150046447558656. Accessed 16 November 2020.
https://twitter.com/VeroBoquete/status/989522873864806401. Accessed 16 November 2020.
https://twitter.com/vox_es/status/1201482571571437569. Accessed 16 November 2020.

References

Bachmann M, Goeck F (2013) Ein Blick in den Abgrund? – Strafrecht auf dem Prüfstand von Verfassung und Kriminologie. In: Brunhöber B et al (eds) Strafrecht und Verfassung. Nomos, Baden-Baden, pp 37–56

Chigwedere P, Seage G, Gruskin S, Lee T, Essex M (2008) Estimating the lost benefits of antiretroviral drug use in South Africa. J Acquir Immune Defic Syndr 49:410–415

Demetrio Crespo E (2016) Prevención general e individualización judicial de la pena (General prevention and judicial individualization of punishment), 2ª edition. B de F., Buenos Aires

Errejón I (2011) El 15-M como discurso contrahegemónico. ENCRUCIJADAS (The 15-M as a counterhegemonic discourse. CROSSROADS). Revista Crítica de Ciencias Sociales 2:120–145

Gil A, Nuñez Fernández J (2018) La Manada y la jauría (La Manada and the wolfpack). https://elpais.com/elpais/2018/04/30/opinion/1525083152_968336.html. Accessed 16 Nov 2020
Goeckenjan I (2015) Überprüfung von Straftatbeständen anhand des Verhältnismäβigkeitsgrundsatzes: überfällige Inventur oder Irrweg? In: Jestaedt M et al (eds) Verhältnismäβigkeit – Zur Tragfähigkeit eines verfassungsrechtlichen Schlüsselkonzepts. Mohr Siebeck, Tübingen, pp 184–209
Greco L (2010) Conveniencia y respeto: sobre lo hipotético y lo categórico en la fundamentación del Derecho penal (Convenience and respect: on the hypothetical and the categorical in the foundation of the criminal law). Dret Revista para el análisis del Derecho 4:1–36
Günther K (2005) Schuld und kommunikative Freiheit. Studien zur personalen Zurechnung strafbaren Unrechts im demokratischen Rechtsstaat. Vittorio Klostermann, Frankfurt am Main
Hassemer W (2012) El principio de proporcionalidad como límites de las intervenciones jurídico-penales (The principle of proportionality as limits of legal-criminal interventions). In: Robles R et al (eds) Límites al Derecho penal. Principios operativos en la fundamentación del castigo (Limits to criminal law. Operational principles in the foundation of the punishment). Atelier, Barcelona, pp 193–200
Hörnle T (2019) #MeToo ¿Implicancias para el derecho penal? (#MeToo: Implications for criminal law?). In Writing: Derecho Penal 9:144–167
Hörnle T, von Hirsch A (2005) Positive Generalprävention und Tadel. In: von Hirsch A (ed) Fairness, Verbrechen und Strafe. Strafrechtstheoretische Abhandlungen. Berliner Wiss. Verl., Berlin, pp 19–39
Innes M (2020) Techniques of disinformation: constructing and communicating 'soft facts' after terrorism. Br J Soc 71:284–299
Iyengar S, Massey D (2019) Scientific communication in a post-truth society. PNAS 116:7656–7661
Klatt M (2004) Theorie der Wortlautgrenze. Semantische Normativität in der juristischen Argumentation. Nomos, Baden-Baden
Klatt M (2005) Die Wortlautgrenze. In: Lerch K (ed) Die Sprache des Rechts II: Recht verhandeln. Argumentieren, Begründen und Entscheiden im Diskurs des Recht. De Gruyter, Berlín, pp 343–360
Larrondo A, Morales J, Orbegozo J (2019) El hashtivismo feminista en España: grado de politización del movimiento en la conversación digital en torno a #YoSiTeCreo, #HermanaYoSíTeCreo, #Cuéntalo y #NoEstásSola (Feminist hashtivism in Spain: degree of politicization of the movement in the digital conversation around #YoSiTeCreo, #HermanaYoSíTeCreo, #Cuéntalo and #NoEstásSola). Commun Soc 32(4):207–221
Lazer D, Baum M, Benkler Y, Berinsky A, Greenhill K, Menczer F, Metzger M, Nyham B, Pennycook G, Rothschild D, Schudson M, Sloman S, Sunstein C, Thorson E, Watts D, Zittrain J (2018) The science of fake news. Science 359(6380):1094–1097
McIntyre L (2018) Posverdad (Post-truth). Cátedra, Madrid
Muñoz Conde F (2019) La vinculación del juez a la ley la reforma de los delitos contra la libertad sexual. Algunas reflexiones sobre el caso 'La Manada' (The linking of the judge to the law reforming crimes against sexual freedom. Some reflections on the 'La Manada' case). Revista penal 43:290–299
Muñoz-Machado J (2020) Noticias falsas. Confianza y configuración de la opinión pública en los tiempos de internet (Fake news. Trust and shaping of public opinion in the times of the Internet). El Cronista del Estado social y democrático de Derecho 86–87:122–137
Orbegozo J, Morales J, Larrondo A (2019) Feminismos indignados ante la justicia: la conversación digital en el caso de 'La Manada' (Feminists outraged at justice: the digital conversation in the case of 'La Manada'). Revista Científica de Información y Comunicación 16:211–247
Pawlik M (2012) Das Unrecht des Bürgers. Mohr Siebeck, Tübingen
Pawlik M (2014) Vom Nutzen der Philosophie für die Allgemeine Verbrechenslehre. Goltdammer's Archiv für Strafrecht 161-7:369–389

Roxin C (2015) Prävention, Tadel und Verantwortung – Zur neuesten Strafzweckdiskussion. Goltdammer's Archiv für Strafrecht 162-4:185–202

Valdés Villanueva LM (2018) Presentación (Presentation). In: McIntyre. Posverdad (Post-truth). Cátedra, Madrid, pp 13–25

Van der Bles A, van der Linden S, Freeman A, Spiegelhalter D (2020) The effects of communicating uncertainty on public trust in facts and numbers. PNAS 117:7672–7683

Vosoughi S, Roy D, Aral S (2018) The spread of true and false news online. Science 359:1146–1151

Warner K, Davis J, Spiranovic C, Cockburn H, Freiberg A (2019) Why sentence? Comparing the views of jurors, judges and the legislature on the purposes of sentencing in Victoria, Australia. Criminol Crim Just 19(I):26–44

Westen D, Blagov P, Harenski K, Kilts C, Hamann S (2006) Neural bases of motivated reasoning: an fMRI study of emotional constraints on partisan political judgment in the 2004 U.-S. Presidential Election. J Cogn Neurosci 18(11):1947–1958

Presumption of Innocence and Pre-Trial Detention in the Light of Directive (EU) 2016/343

Ágata M. Sanz Hermida

1 Introduction

Can judicial decisions concerning the adoption and/or extension of pre-trial detention affect the presumption of innocence recognized in Art. 48.1 of the Charter of Fundamental Rights of the EU—hereinafter the CFREU—and developed, in some of its aspects, in Directive (EU) 2016/343 of the European Parliament and of the Council of 9 March 2016, *on the strengthening of certain aspects of the presumption of innocence and of the right to be present at the trial in criminal proceedings*? And if so, what specific aspects of the presumption of innocence could be achieved? When a Court rules on the adoption of a measure that restricts the right to liberty, such as pre-trial detention or its maintenance, how can the Judge or the Court safeguard the balance between the consideration of the concurrence of the requirements for its adoption and/or modification, including the existence of "reasonable grounds" of the perpetration of the crime by the suspect with the need that the decision does not imply their consideration "as guilty" of the crime? Are the requirements to which decisions on this type of preventive measures compatible with respect for the presumption of innocence regulated in European legislation, in Directive (EU) 2016/343?

This paper has been developed within the framework of the Research Project, Criminal Law Crisis of the Rule of Law: Manifestations and Trends, co-financed by the Castilla-La Mancha Regional Government and FEDER Funds (SBPLY/17/180501/000223). This article pays tribute to Prof. Vicente Gimeno Sendra, with all my gratitude, admiration and affection. The Spanish version of this article was published at ASENCIO MELLADO, J.M. (dir) (2020). Derecho probatorio y otros estudios procesales: Vicente Gimeno Sendra. *Liber amicorum* Castillo de Luna: Madrid. págs. 1841–1860.

Á. M. Sanz Hermida (✉)
Faculty of Legal and Social Sciences, University of Castilla-La Mancha, Toledo, Spain
e-mail: Agata.Sanz@uclm.es

E. Demetrio Crespo et al. (eds.), *Crisis of the Criminal Law in the Democratic Constitutional State*, Legal Studies in International, European and Comparative Criminal Law 6, https://doi.org/10.1007/978-3-031-13413-5_11

The CJEU has had the opportunity to rule on some of these questions in various decisions, either directly or indirectly, providing relevant criteria on the relationship between the presumption of innocence and pre-trial detention in the light of EU law that marks certain differences with the doctrine upheld by the ECtHR, as will be developed in the following sections, although these are limited to the interpretation of this principle in a strictly community setting.

2 Legal Framework of the European Union

2.1 General Definition: The Presumption of Innocence According to the CFREU

Art. 48.1 of the CFREU provides that *States must ensure that everyone who has been charged shall be presumed innocent until proved guilty according to law.* Its content, as stated in the *Praesidium's Explanations*, is in line with paragraphs 2 and 3 of the ECHR[1] and its meaning and scope is the same as the right guaranteed by the ECHR (Art. 52.3 of the CFREU). Hence the provisions of Art. 6 of the ECHR, which, under the heading "right to a fair trial," provides in paragraph 2 that "everyone charged with a criminal offense shall be presumed innocent until proven guilty according to law,"[2] must be considered. According to the framework of the ECHR, the ECtHR has defined the presumption of innocence as a fundamental right which, in addition to being provided under Art. 6.2 of the ECHR, is included among the rights that make up the fair trial in Art. 6.1 of the ECHR.[3]

[1] In the abovementioned *Explanations by the Praesidium* of the European Convention to the CFREU (2007/C 303/02), the full content of Art. 48 which, in its paragraph 2, refers to "the rights to defense," is taken into consideration. Hence, it can be said that Art. 48 contains what could be called "the basic legal position of the suspect or defendant in criminal proceedings" and that, therefore, the correspondence of Art. 48 with paragraphs 2 and 3 of Art. 6 of the ECHR, which lists, in a more extensive manner, the fundamental rights covered by the aforementioned statute, particularly: (a) to be informed of the charge; (b) to have adequate time and facilities for the preparation of the defense; (c) to defend oneself in person or through legal assistance; (d) to examine, or have examined, the witnesses for and against oneself; and (e) to have the free assistance of an interpreter if one does not understand or speak the language used in the hearing, aspects which have been the subject of more detailed study, among others, in Aguilera Morales (2004), pp. 1543–1571; López Escudero (2008), pp. 759–776; Sanz Hermida (2019), pp. 1459–1505.

[2] The recognition of the presumption of innocence is referred to in other important international human rights instruments such as Art. 11.1 of the Universal Declaration of Human Rights of 1948; Art. 14.2 of the International Covenant on Civil and Political Rights of 16 December 1966; Art. 8.1 of the American Convention on Human Rights (Pact of San José), November 22, 1969; Art. 66 of the Rome Statute of the International Criminal Court, July 17, 1998; Art. 40.2b.i) of the UN Convention on the Rights of the Child, November 20, 1989, to name a few of the most important.

[3] In fact, the ECtHR has defined the right to the presumption of innocence in Art. 6.2 of the ECHR, together with the rights of the defense that Art. 6.3 of the ECHR lists in a non-exhaustive manner, as particular manifestations of the general principle set out in Art. 6.1. (ECtHR Ruling (ECtHRR) of

Indeed, in accordance with the ECtHR, respect for the presumption of innocence requires, among other things: (1) that the members of the Court, in carrying out their duties, do not start from the preconceived idea that the accused has committed the offense charged; (2) the burden of proof is placed on the prosecution and (3) doubt benefits the accused *(in dubio pro reo)*.[4] However, the ECtHR has also extended the presumption of innocence to other rights, such as it is for the prosecution to inform the accused of the charge that will be made against him or her, so that he or she may prepare and present his or her defense accordingly, and to adduce evidence sufficient to convict him or her;[5] the right to remain silent and not to confess guilt or the reasonable period of provisional detention.[6] This shows the huge link between these guarantees, with the consequent effect of making it difficult to make a clear distinction between them, especially when they have to be put into context in specific situations and not from a merely abstract perspective.[7]

For its part, for the CJEU, which essentially follows the doctrine of the ECtHR, the presumption of innocence is a fundamental right that confers rights on individuals which the community judge guarantees to uphold.[8] The proper scope of application of this principle refers, in the first place, to criminal proceedings as a whole.[9] Therefore, this guarantee must be observed at all stages of the criminal proceeding and at all instances, including prejudicial statements and provisional detention,[10] although it is at the time of the gathering of evidence that it is most

27 February 1980, Deweer v. Belgium Case, no. 6903/75, paragraph. 56, ECLI:CE:ECHR:1980:0227JUD000690375).

[4]ECtHRR of 12 December 1986, Cases Barberá, Messegué and Jabardo v. Spain, number 10590/83, paragraph. 77, ECLI:CE:ECHR:1988:1206JUD001059083.

[5]ECtHRR of 12 December 1986, Cases Barberá, Messegué and Jabardo v. Spain, number 10590/83, paragraph. 77, ECLI:CE:ECHR:1988:1206JUD001059083.

[6]Thus, some authors critically underscore the ups and downs of the ECtHR, which, on the one hand, in many cases extends the requirements of the presumption of innocence beyond the evidentiary process, and, on the other hand, despite the autonomous nature of Art. 6.2, which is separate from the right to a fair trial, the Court has not managed to construct a "perfectly outlined" concept of the presumption. Allué Burza (2005), pp. 384–385.

[7]The ECtHR points out that criminal proceedings generally involve "a complex interaction of different aspects of the procedure, so that it is often artificial to try to categorize a case from which perspective and in relation to which of the rights set out in Article 6 it is necessary to examine it" [ECtHRR, 13 September 2016, Ibrahim and Others v. United Kingdom, (Cases 50541/08, 50571/08, 50573/08 and 40351/09), par. 274, ECLI:CE:ECHR:2016:0913JUD005054108].

[8]Cf. *inter alia* SPI (Fourth Chamber) of 4 October 2006 (Case T-193/04), par. 221, ECLI:EU:T:2006:292; JCFI (Third Chamber) of 8 July 2008, Yves Franchet and Daniel Byk v. Commission of the European Communities, (Case T-48/05), par. 209, ECLI:EU:T:2008:257.

[9]ECtHRR of 25 March 1983, Case Minelli v. Switzerland, No. 8660/79, ECLI:CE:ECHR:1983:0325JUD000866079.

[10]In our legal system, some authors had already been expressing their opinion on precisely this aspect. Specifically, Gimeno Sendra points out that the presumption of innocence must unfold its effects in the investigative phase, "preventing acts that limit fundamental rights in general, and provisional detention in particular, from being adopted without the prior existence of well-founded reasons for participation in the punishable act of the accused and after a motivated resolution in

widely projected, as has been defined in the jurisprudence of the ECtHR. In addition to these elements, Advocate General Juliane Kokott has added the need to establish guilt (*nulla poena sine culpa*) as a necessary prerequisite for the presumption of innocence, which she understands to be implicit in both Art. 48.1 of the CFREU and Art. 6.2 of the ECHR, and which constitute the procedural expression of this guarantee.[11]

However, it is also a guarantee that must be respected in other disciplinary proceedings, as the CJEU has had occasion to point out that the principle of the presumption of innocence, as it results from Art. 48 of the CFREU, applies to the procedures relating to infringements of the competition rules applicable to undertakings that may result in the imposition of fines or periodic penalty payments, given the nature of the infringements in question and the nature and degree of severity of the penalties.[12]

From these considerations, it can be said that, at the present time, in Europe,[13] the presumption of innocence has been broadly defined as a "*rule of judgement*" in relation to evidence,[14] since a person can only be convicted if the commission of the criminal act and their guilt are proven in accordance with the guarantees in force, and

---

which all the requirements of the principle of proportionality are met." Nevertheless, he emphasizes that the doctrine of the Spanish Constitutional Court in relation to this guarantee has been extremely sparing in claiming its validity in the investigative phase and has been fundamentally redirected to the evidentiary stage. Cf. Gimeno Sendra (2015), pp. 203–204; Gimeno Sendra (2017), pp. 479–480.

[11] Opinion of Advocate General Juliane Kokott of 17 April 2013, Schindler Holding Ltd and Others v. European Commission, (Case C 501/11 P), par. 115, ECLI:EU:C:2013:248.

[12] Cf. *inter alia*, CJEU (Sixth Chamber) of 8 July 1999, Hüls AG v. Commission of the European Communities, (Case C-199/92 P), aps 149-150, ECLI:EU:C:1999:358; CJEU (Sixth Chamber) of 8 July 1999, Montecatini SpA v. Commission of the European Communities, (Case C-3235/92), aps. 175–176, ECLI:EU:C:1999:362; STG (Sixth Chamber) of 12 April 2013, International Confederation of Societies of Authors and Composers (CISAC) v. European Commission, (Case T-442/08), par. 93, ECLI:EU:T:2013:188.

[13] The Inter-American Court of Human Rights has also established a broad concept of the presumption of innocence, which includes both the prohibition of prejudices regarding the guilt of the accused; its link to the scope of the evidence in the terms summarized above; the treatment of the investigated person as not guilty by both the judicial authorities and the rest of the public authorities, including its application to the scope of preventive detention, aspects that are analyzed in depth by Llobet Rodríguez (2018), pp. 493 and following. And this broad conception is also maintained in General Comment n. 32 of the United Nations Human Rights Committee, which states that "According to article 14, paragraph 2 everyone charged with a criminal offence shall have the right to be presumed innocent until proven guilty according to law. The presumption of innocence, which is fundamental to the protection of human rights, imposes on the prosecution the burden of proving the charge, guarantees that no guilt can be presumed until the charge has been proved beyond reasonable doubt, ensures that the accused has the benefit of doubt, and requires that persons accused of a criminal act must be treated in accordance with this principle. It is a duty for all public authorities to refrain from prejudging the outcome of a trial, e.g., by abstaining from making public statements affirming the guilt of the accused" and, among other things, adds that "the length of pre-trial detention should never be taken as an indication of guilt and its degree."

[14] Ovejero Puente (2017), pp. 431–455.

the doubt must be interpreted in a favorable light for the defendant. In fact, the presumption of innocence reaches its greatest expression at the evidentiary stage, since its validity requires the need to prove that a subject has committed the unlawful act attributed to them. This burden is on the prosecution and must be carried out through the presentation of evidence, fundamentally at the trial, obtained without violating fundamental rights and practiced with respect for the right to defense and a fair trial, under the court's immediacy. Also, the *in dubio pro reo principle* (doubts should benefit the accused) is a specific expression of the presumption of innocence.

However, it has also been defined as a "*rule of treatment*" that indicates how the subject of the proceedings should be treated,[15] which requires, among other things, that no representative of the state should declare that a person is guilty of a crime before his guilt has been established by a Court,[16] and that this presumption may be violated by statements or decisions that reflect the feeling that the person is guilty, that encourage the public to believe in their guilt or that prejudice the evaluation of the facts by the competent Court.[17] To assess these circumstances, it is necessary to verify whether, by their action, the grounds of their decisions or the language used in their reasoning, the national authorities and courts which are called upon to give a decision following a judgment in criminal proceedings cast doubts on the innocence of the applicant thereby infringing the principle of the presumption of innocence.[18] However, the assessment of whether a statement by an agent of the state violates this presumption must be made in the context of the circumstances in which it occurred. This right may be infringed if, by its reasoning, a judgment reflects the opinion that a person is guilty of an offense after the criminal proceedings have been closed by his acquittal.[19] A distinction should be made between statements that reflect the feeling that a person is guilty and those that merely describe a state of suspicion.[20]

---

[15] Aguilera Morales (2004), p. 1556. Other authors prefer to refer to the procedural or extra-procedural dimension of the guarantee, including, Arangüena Fanego (2019), pp. 5–40.

[16] ECtHRR of February 10, 1995, Allenet de Ribemont v. France, n. 15175/89, paras. 35–36, ECLI: CE:ECHR:1995:0210JUD001517589; ECtHRR, 28 October 2004, Case YB et al. v. Turkey, (n. 48173/99 and 48319/99), para. 43, ECLI:CE:ECHR:2004:1028JUD004817399.

[17] ECtHRR of 21 September 2006, Pandy v. Belgium, 13583/02, par. 43 ECLI:CE:ECHR:2011: 0524JUD005346607. This doctrine is followed by the CJEU, *inter alia*, in JCFI (Third Chamber) of 8 July 2008, Yves Franchet and Daniel Byk v. Commission of the European Communities, (Case T-48/05), par. 210, ECLI:EU:T:2008:257.

[18] Opinion of Advocate General Yves Bot of 20 March 2014, Kalliopi Nikolaou v. Court of Auditors of the European Union, (Case C 220/13 P), par. 51, ECLI:EU:C:2014:176.

[19] ECtHRR (First Chamber) of 10 July 2014, Kalliopi Nikolaou v. Court of Auditors of the European Union, (Case C-220/13 P), par. 35, ECLI:EU:C:2014:2057 and the ECtHR's caselaw cited therein.

[20] Cf, *inter alia*, ECtHRR of 28 November 2002, Marziano v. Italy, No 45313/99, par. 31, ECLI: CE:ECHR:2002:1128JUD004531399.

It is a fundamental guarantee that applies to the passive subject of the process—investigated, accused, defendant[21]—both natural and legal persons,[22] and that benefits any accused regardless of their recidivism and the seriousness of the crime, until they are condemned by a firm sentence.[23]

Hence, the presumption of innocence has been considered "the key principle of any criminal system,"[24] a "fundamental value of the European criminal system,"[25] "one of the most multifaceted guarantees surrounding the activity of the parties involved" and one of the most frequently invoked by the accused parties to whom it attributes an advantageous position—a "sort of protective armor"—with criminal prosecution being its field of application, without precluding its expansive force from being projected beyond it, such as into punitive law or the extra-procedural sphere.[26]

2.2 *Content and Scope of the Presumption of Innocence in Directive (EU) 2016/343*

2.2.1 Scope of Application: The Limited Scope of Legal Protection

Article 48.1 CFREU has been partially developed in Directive (EU) 2016/343 of the European Parliament and of the Council, of March 9, 2016, which *reinforces certain aspects of the presumption of innocence and the right to be present at the trial in criminal proceedings*. This Directive is a consequence of the roadmap set out in the *Roadmap to strengthen the rights of suspects and accused persons in criminal*

---

[21] Although international normative texts usually refer to the "accused," as is done in the ECHR, this expression, according to the ECtHR, has an "autonomous" meaning in the context of the Convention and should not be delimited based on its meaning in domestic law. The legislation of the defendant state is certainly relevant, but it is merely a starting point for this purpose. The eminent place that the right to a fair trial occupies in a democratic society advocates a "material" rather than "formal" conception of the term "accusation" in Article 6. This requires the Court to set aside appearances and analyze the reality of the proceedings in question to determine whether there really is an "accusation" in the terms of Article 6. Cf., *inter alia*, ECtHRR, 27 February 1980, Deweer v. Belgium, n. 6903/75, especially paras. 42 and 44, ECLI:CE:ECHR:1980:0227JUD000690375.

[22] In this sense, the HCR of 16 March 2016 states that legal entities have the same rights as natural persons "notwithstanding the necessary modulations," particularly affirming, as far as this commentary is concerned, the importance of the presumption of innocence which, also in these cases, places the burden of proof on the accuser, which in the context of the current regulations on the criminal liability of legal persons, means that it is necessary to prove that there has been a serious breach of supervisory duties by the legal person (HCR 966/2016, March 16, rapporteur H.E. Mr. Manuel Marchena, ECLI:ES:TS:2016:966).

[23] López Escudero (2008), p. 762.

[24] Nieva Fenoll (2016), p. 4.

[25] As expressed by Musacchio (2009), pp. 1–10.

[26] As pointed out by Ramos Méndez (2016), pp. 392 et seq.

proceedings [Council Resolution, November 30, 2009 (2009/C 295/01)] and which, in 2010, was extended to the presumption of innocence by the so-called Stockholm Programme ["An open and secure Europe serving and protecting citizens" (2010/C 115/01)].[27] Article 1 emphasizes that its purpose is to establish common minimum rules concerning certain aspects of the presumption of innocence in criminal proceedings to strengthen the Member States' confidence in each other's criminal justice systems and thus to facilitate the mutual recognition of decisions in criminal matters.[28] The name of the Directive and the framework established in Art. 1 mark *ab initio* their vocation clearly limited to "certain aspects" of the guarantees mentioned.

Based on this premise, Article 2 of the Directive establishes the scope of application for the interpretation of which it is also necessary to consider, as is already usual in European normative technique, the *intentio legislatoris* specified in the recitals, which specify, sometimes in a markedly restrictive manner, the interpretation of the stipulations of the various articles that make up the Directive, with consequences, as will be made clear, not always positive for the development and

[27] The above-mentioned *Roadmap* contains a proposal of six indicative measures to strengthen and give effect to procedural rights of suspects and defendants in criminal proceedings at EU level. These measures, which are not a *numerus clausus* and their order is not binding either, range from the right *to translation and interpretation* (measure A), information on rights and Information about the charges (measure B), *to legal advice and legal aid* (measure C), *to communication with relatives, employers and consular authorities* (measure D), special safeguards for suspected or accused persons who are vulnerable (measure E) or *the green paper on pre-trial detention* (measure F). These provisions have resulted, to date, in a number of European directives that refer to different rights of the *suspect or defendant* in criminal proceedings, such as the right to translation and interpretation [Directive (EU) 2010/64 of the European Parliament and of the Council of October 20, 2010 *on the right to interpretation and translation in criminal proceedings*]; information [Directive (EU) 2010/64 of the European Parliament and of the Council of October 20, 2010 *on the right to interpretation and translation in criminal proceedings*]; to legal assistance [Directive (EU) 2013/48 of the European Parliament and of the Council of October 22, 2013, *on the right of access to a lawyer in criminal proceedings and in European arrest warrant proceedings, and on the right to have a third party informed upon deprivation of liberty and to communicate with third persons and with consular authorities while deprived of liberty*]; *the rights of minors suspected or accused of a crime* [Directive (EU) 2016/800 of the European Parliament and of the Council of May 11, 2016, *on procedural safeguards for children who are suspects or accused persons in criminal proceedings*] or the right to legal aid [Directive (EU) 2016/1919 of the European Parliament and of the Council of October 29, 2016, *on legal aid for suspects and accused persons in criminal proceedings and for requested persons in European arrest warrant proceedings*]. On the origins of the Directive, its processing, and the criticisms it received during that process, cf. Cras and Erbežnik (2016), pp. 25–36.

[28] This is based on Art. 82.2 TFEU, which states that, "To the extent necessary to facilitate mutual recognition of judgments and judicial decisions and police and judicial cooperation in criminal matters having a cross-border dimension, the European Parliament and the Council may, by means of directives adopted in accordance with the ordinary legislative procedure, establish minimum rules. Such rules shall take into account the differences between the legal traditions and systems of the Member States." To that end, paragraph (b) of that Article provides that such rules shall relate, inter alia, to the rights of individuals in criminal procedure.

respect of basic procedural guarantees. In this context, the Directive defines its application:

(a) From an objective point of view to the criminal proceedings, as interpreted by the CJEU, without detriment to the caselaw of the ECtHR. This excludes its application to other procedures; particularly, the European Legislature refers to "civil proceedings or to administrative proceedings, including where the latter can lead to sanctions, such as proceedings relating to competition, trade, financial services, road traffic, tax or tax surcharges, and investigations by administrative authorities in relation to such proceedings" (Recital 11). The inclusion of this list is justified by the dual nature that this type of conduct may have in domestic legal systems, either as administrative or criminal offenses, with the former, despite their punitive nature, being expressly excluded from the scope of application.

   However, it is applicable at all stages of the criminal proceedings until the decision on the final determination of whether the suspect or accused person has committed the criminal offense has become definitive (Recital 12).
(b) From a subjective point of view, the Directive is addressed to natural persons suspected or accused in criminal proceedings, expressly excluding legal persons.[29] The basis of this exclusion is found again in the diversity of regulations in the Member States and of caselaw, both at domestic and Union level, as well as the existence of different degrees and needs for the protection of certain aspects of this guarantee to some and other subjects, so the European Legislature renounces to standardize its regulation through this Directive, so for the time being its application to legal persons must be protected by the national law and caselaw, whose evolution may determine in the future the need for an intervention of the Union (cf. Recitals 13–15).

2.2.2 Guarantees to Protect the Presumption of Innocence

As a way to contribute to its full effectiveness, seeking the harmonization of a basic content in the Member States, Directive (EU) 2016/343 indicates various measures to be adopted by the states, among which those aimed at avoiding the perception of the situation of the suspect or defendant as "guilty" on the occasion of information or images that are disseminated about that subject (presumption of innocence as a rule of treatment); aspects relating to the burden of proof and the rights not to declare and

[29]This aspect was criticized, along with others that will be referred to later, as opening the door to possible reversals of the burden of proof, limiting its application to the criminal process, or, to highlight some of the most important objections, not establishing a rigid rule of inadmissibility of evidence obtained through the violation of fundamental rights. On these aspects, see more extensively, Villamarín López (2017), pp. 6–7; Cras and Erbežnik (2016), p. 28. For some, it Is truly a missed opportunity, Lamberigts (2016), pp. 36–42.

not to plead guilty, rights which, notwithstanding their link to the presumption of innocence, constitute manifestations of the rights of defense.[30]

Presumption of Innocence as a Rule of Treatment

The measures that can be brought together in this section are intended to avoid the consideration of a suspect or accused person as "guilty" in criminal proceedings due to the way in which the case is reported or, where appropriate, the image of the subject. In other words, the aim is to avoid the generation of "prejudices" about the guilt of a subject based on elements external to the process itself, which have a great influence on contemporary society, marked by image and information.[31]

The measures envisaged are aimed at the public authorities, which are called upon to play an active role in order, on the one hand, to provide adequate information on the criminal proceedings, avoiding reflecting or conveying opinions that the suspect or accused is guilty (until a firm sentence has been pronounced),[32] as provided under Art. 4, both based on public statements and of judicial decisions other than those of conviction,[33] without affecting, as is obvious, procedural acts aimed at proving guilt and preliminary decisions of a procedural nature taken by the competent authorities—judicial or otherwise—that are based on evidence or proof of the charge.

Like the "neutral" transmission of information about the suspect or accused, the dissemination of images or the manner of presenting the suspect or accused in public should be carried out in such a way as to avoid the identification of the subject with their guilt. This can affect both the use of physical means of coercion (avoiding

[30] In fact, the broad framework of the Directive has been the subject of criticism since its adoption, for departing from the roadmap designed by the Council in 2009 referred to above, and for considering that its articles rather set out general principles of law, rather than providing a legal framework for the protection of the rights of the suspect or defendant. Arangüena Fanego (2019), p. 20.

[31] In this regard, the Human Rights Committee, in General Comment No. 32, notes that "It is a duty for all public authorities to refrain from prejudging the outcome of a trial, e.g., by abstaining from making public statements affirming the guilt of the accused. Defendants should normally not be shackled or kept in cages during trials or otherwise presented to the court in a manner indicating that they may be dangerous criminals. The media should avoid news coverage undermining the presumption of innocence."

[32] Cf. JCFI (Third Chamber), of 8 July 2008, Yves Franchet and Daniel Byk v. Commission of the European Communities, (Case T-48/05), par. 210, ECLI:EU:T:2008:257 citing ECHR, of 21 September 2006, case Pandy v. Belgium, 13583/02, par. 41–42, ECLI:CE:ECHR:2011:0524JUD005346607.

[33] Thus, with respect to the latter, safeguarding the principle particularly requires that in carrying out their duties the members of a court do not start from the preconceived idea that the accused has committed the act of which he is accused. The presumption of innocence is undermined by statements or decisions that reflect the feeling that the person is guilty, that incite the public to believe in his guilt, or that prejudge the judge's assessment of the facts (JCFI (Third Chamber) of 8 July 2008, Yves Franchet and Daniel Byk v. Commission of the European Communities, (Case T-48/05), nr. 210, ECLI:EU:T:2008:257).

handcuffs, shackles, etc.)—unless there are circumstances that justify it (e.g., security reasons) and with respect to the principle of proportionality—and their clothing (avoiding the use of prisoner's clothing) or other external elements that, from the point of view of the image, could lead to the identification of the subject as guilty (Art. 5).

Presumption of Innocence as a Rule of Judgement

The presumption of innocence imposes on the prosecution the burden of proving the charge, guarantees that no guilt can be presumed until the charge has been proved beyond reasonable doubt, ensures that any doubt should benefit the suspect or accused person.

These aspects are referred to in Art. 6 of the Directive which, in its first paragraph, states that states must ensure that the burden of proof lies with the prosecution. In this regard, it is rightly stated that the presumption of innocence would be violated if the burden of proof were shifted from the prosecution to the defense (Recital 22). However, some nuances are introduced here by pointing out, in the recital, that all of this is "without detriment to the possible powers of the court to propose evidence of its own motion, or to the independence of the court in assessing the guilt of the suspect or accused, **or to the use of *de facto* or *de jure* presumptions regarding the criminal responsibility of the suspect or accused**" (emphasis added).

However, in the criminal sphere, the admission of evidentiary presumptions is controversial, and this has been the subject of a major doctrinal debate,[34] to which the ECtHR and the CJEU have also paid attention. The evidentiary difficulties encountered by the justice system with respect to certain types of crimes must be resolved using evidence, whether direct or indirect, without this leading to a reversal of the burden of proof, as is discussed in the case of the use of certain presumptions, such as, for example, the criminalization of unjust enrichment in some Ibero-American legal systems or, in the European context, the French model.[35]

In the EU, we can find different jurisprudential pronouncements in which the validity of the presumptions has been admitted, although generally referred to the sanctioning scope for collusive practices. Thus, the SCJEU upholds the validity of a presumption of "decisive influence" in competition law, stating that it does not constitute in any way a violation of the presumption of innocence, enshrined in Article 48 of the Charter and Article 6.2 of the ECHR, having particular regard to its

[34] Gimeno Sendra (2017), p. 481; Fernández López (2015), pp. 431–466. On the specific debate that arose during the processing of the Directive, see González Monje (2016), pp. 15–16.

[35] On these aspects, see, among others, Fernández López (2015), *passim*; Pérez Cebadera (2013), p. 374.

nature as an "*iuris tantum* presumption."[36] In addition, some authors[37] point out that the ECtHR has also considered the existence of these presumptions of guilt to be compatible with Art. 6.2 of the ECHR, provided that two conditions are met: (1) the presumption is not automatically applied, so that the subject is not deprived of the effective exercise of the right to a defense to introduce elements of contradiction; and (2) that, to determine guilt, the assessment of the presumption is made in conjunction with the rest of the evidence presented.[38]

Precisely, Advocate General G. Pitruzzella, in his Opinion in case C-653/19 (PPU) after stressing the highly articulate nature of the text of Recital 22, which contrasts with the more concise wording of Article 6 of Directive 2016/343, which does not contain any reference to the abovementioned presumptions, points out that with this provision the Union legislature seems to have admitted the possibility of using de facto or de jure presumptions regarding the criminal liability of a suspect or accused without those presumptions infringing the principle of the presumption of innocence, provided that they are "confined within reasonable limits, taking into account the importance of what is at stake and maintaining the rights of the defence, and the means employed should be reasonably proportionate to the legitimate aim pursued. Such presumptions should be rebuttable and, in any event, should be used only where the rights of the defence are respected." [39]

In addition, as has been pointed out, Article 7 regulates the rights to remain silent and the right not to incriminate oneself, which are manifestations of the right to defense, notwithstanding the relationship they may have with the presumption of innocence and to which the Directive refers.[40] Thus, based on the need for states to recognize both rights, various measures are regulated to ensure, on the one hand, that they are known and, on the other, that their exercise can have an impact on the process.[41]

---

[36] CJEU (First Chamber) of 19 June 2014, FLS Plast A/S v European Commission, (Case C 243/12 P), par. 27, ECLI:EU:C:2014:2006 and caselaw cited.

[37] López Escudero (2008), pp. 761–762.

[38] ECtHRR of October 7, 1988, Salabiaku v. France, No. 10519/83, aps. 28–30, ECLI:CE:ECHR:1988:1007JUD001051983; ECHR, 25 September 1992, Pham Hoang v. France, No. 13191/87, aps. 32–35; ECLI:CE:ECHR:1992:0925JUD00131918730.

[39] Opinion of Advocate General Pitruzzella, delivered on 19 November 2019, Criminal proceedings against DK, (Case C 653/19 PPU), par. 30. ECLI:EU:C:2019:983.

[40] Arangüena Fanego points out that in the Directive these rights are defined as "absolute, so that their exercise is not subject to any condition and no negative consequences can be drawn from such exercise," thus clearly departing from the questionable doctrine of the ECtHR in these aspects. Aguilera Morales (2004). Other authors, however, qualify this alleged absolute value, taking into consideration the last sentence of Recital 28: "This should be without prejudice to national rules concerning the assessment of evidence by courts or judges, provided that the rights of the defence are respected." Cras and Erbežnik (2016), p. 32; or, among other aspects, the literal wording of the provisions of Art. 7.3, which refers to the "the use of legal powers of compulsion" which can be interpreted in very different ways by the Member States. Lamberigts (2016), p. 36.

[41] The rights to remain silent and not to incriminate oneself are analyzed in this section because of their important link to evidentiary aspects. However, for some authors, the regulation of these rights must be analyzed from the perspective of the presumption of innocence as a rule of treatment. Villamarín López (2017), p. 14.

1. On the first aspect, the need to ensure that the suspect or accused has effective knowledge of such information is sanctioned, so that under the provisions of Arts. 3 and 4 of Directive 2012/13/EU this information must be provided along with the other rights the suspect holds.
2. On the impact of this information on the process, particularly in relation to evidence, the following measures are established:

   (a) The exercise of the right not to incriminate oneself does not prevent the authorities from gathering evidence that can be legally obtained through the legitimate exercise of coercive powers and that has an existence independent of the will of the suspects or accused. This allows national domestic rules to regulate the collection of genetic samples that may be useful for the purposes of criminal prosecution (to obtain DNA from saliva, blood, urine samples, etc.).
   (b) In addition, the impossibility of considering the effective exercise of these rights—that is, keeping silent or not testifying against oneself—by themselves as evidence of having committed the crime, or as an element against the suspect or accused, is sanctioned.
   (c) In any case, it is reminded that states may allow their judicial authorities to take into consideration the cooperative behavior of suspects or defendants.

Of particular importance in relation to these aspects is the provision in Recital 45, which emphasizes, in summary, the inadmissibility of evidence in violation of human *rights*, since it would affect the right to defense and the fairness of the proceedings, in application of the doctrine of the ECtHR, as well as, among others, the provisions of Art. 3 ECHR and the United Nations Convention against Torture and Other Cruel, Inhuman or Degrading Treatment or Punishment.

As a closing rule, Art. 7.6 provides that the above provisions shall not "preclude Member States from deciding that, with regard to minor offences, the conduct of the proceedings, or certain stages thereof, may take place in writing or without questioning of the suspect or accused person by the competent authorities in relation to the offence concerned, provided that this complies with the right to a fair trial," a stipulation that seems to be intended for minor road traffic offenses (Recital 30) or others that might have a similar consideration.

3 Presumption of Innocence and Pre-Trial Detention According to the Court of Justice

Once the aspects covered by the Directive in relation to the presumption of innocence have been summarized, it becomes necessary to determine which of them, and to what extent, apply to decisions relating to provisional detention. Since the adoption of the Directive on the presumption of innocence, the CJEU has ruled on up to four occasions on the application of the presumption of innocence to provisional detention, [42] with a markedly restrictive line of jurisprudence, based on the limited protection that the Directive confers on the presumption of innocence referring only to "certain aspects." In the light of the minimal degree of harmonization pursued therein, the Court of Justice points out that the Directive on the presumption of innocence cannot be interpreted as being "cannot be interpreted as being a complete and exhaustive instrument intended to lay down all the conditions for the adoption of decisions on pre-trial detention,"[43] so it is necessary to specify which aspects it tries to harmonize and what would be its content and scope.

As regards the regulatory framework, as noted above, Art. 4 of the Directive provides that "Member States shall take the necessary measures to ensure that, for as long as a suspect or an accused person has not been proved guilty according to law, public statements made by public authorities, and judicial decisions, other than those on guilt, do not refer to that person as being guilty. **This shall be without prejudice** to acts of the prosecution which aim to prove the guilt of the suspect or accused person, **and to preliminary decisions of a procedural nature, which are taken by judicial or other competent authorities, and which are based on suspicion or incriminating evidence**" (emphasis added). This provision should be complemented by what is set out in Recital 16 of the Directive, which adds that "before taking a preliminary decision of a procedural nature the competent authority might first have to verify that there are sufficient elements of incriminating evidence against the suspect or accused person to justify the decision concerned, and the decision could contain reference to those elements."

Based on these provisions it can be stated, as pointed out by Advocate General Michal Bobek in the conclusions of the first case of Emil Milev[44] that, although preventive detention is not the subject of any specific European Union legislation, "judicial decisions on pretrial detention are covered by the protection of the presumption of innocence, as guaranteed by Directive 2016/343" and this happens since in certain cases "judicial decisions on pretrial detention may, in specific cases, entail an infringement of the fundamental right to the presumption of innocence, as set out in Article 48(1) of the Charter. The meaning and scope of that provision are the same as those of Article 6(2) of the ECHR, as is clear from Article 52(3) of the Charter and the Explanations relating to the Charter."

In effect, although the Advocate General in the aforementioned conclusions does not obviate the fact that the interpretation of Article 48 of the CFREU must be made

[42] ECtHRR (Fourth Chamber) of 27 October 2016, Criminal proceedings against Emil Milev, (Case C-439/16 PPU), ECLI:EU:C:2016:818; ECtHRR (First Chamber) of 19 September 2018, Criminal proceedings against Emil Milev, (Case C-310/18 PPU), ECLI: EU:C:2018:73; CJEUR (First Chamber) of 12 February 2019, Criminal proceedings against RH, (Case C-8/19 PPU), ECLI: EU:C:2019:110; CJEUR (First Chamber) of 28 November 2019, Criminal proceedings against DK, (Case C-653/19 PPU), ECLI:EU:C:2019:10.

[43] ECtHRR (First Chamber) of 19 September 2018, Criminal proceedings against Emil Milev, (Case C-310/18 PPU), par. 47, ECLI:EU:C:2018:732.

[44] Opinion of Advocate General Michal Bobek of 11 October 2016, Criminal proceedings against Emil Milev, (Case C-439/16 PPU), aps. 61 et seq., ECLI:EU:C:2016:760.

in accordance with the provisions of the ECHR and the caselaw of the ECtHR, he does establish certain interpretative nuances that can be specified as follows (paragraphs 72 et seq.):

1. In general, the requirements for the adoption of a resolution mandating pre-trial detention—particularly those relating to the existence of "reasonable grounds"—have been included by the ECtHR in Art. 5 of the ECHR, which regulates the right to liberty.[45] In this regard, according to the Advocate General, Art. 5 can be considered *lex specialis* in relation to the presumption of innocence.
2. However, according to the Advocate General, although Art. 52.3 of the Charter means that the meaning and scope of the rights guaranteed by the Charter are the same for corresponding rights as those laid down by the ECHR, this does not mean that "specific standards developed in the caselaw of the European Court of Human Rights in connection with a certain fundamental right cannot constitute, in EU law, elements which are part of the content protected by other fundamental right."
3. Hence, when interpreting Directive (EU) 2016/343 in relation to certain aspects of the presumption of innocence, the protection of Union law may be more extensive than that arising from the ECHR.
4. In this framework, the presumption of innocence "entails, in practice, not being authorized to take any repressive measures, with regard to a person who is accused of having committed an offense, before proving at least that there are reasonable grounds for suspecting that that person is the perpetrator." Deprivation of liberty constitutes a serious exception to the principles of individual liberty and the presumption of innocence, so that, in the specific context of pre-trial detention, the requirement that there be "reasonable grounds" is linked to the guarantee of the presumption of innocence, an interpretation that is also supported by a sector of the doctrine.[46]
5. And he concludes that for the purposes of Article 3 and the guarantees provided by Articles 4 and 10 of Directive (EU) 2016/343, the continued detention of a person without any judicial consideration of "reasonable grounds" is, (in my view), likely to infringe the principle of the "presumption of innocence."

The Court of Justice agrees that Directive 2016/343, and Articles 3 and 4, paragraph 1 "do not preclude the adoption of preliminary decisions of a procedural nature – such as a decision taken by a judicial authority that pre-trial detention – should continue, which are based on suspicion or on incriminating evidence, provided that such decisions do not refer to the person in custody as being guilty." Moreover, on the conditions under which decisions of pre-trial detention may be adopted, particularly those relating to the degree of certainty which it must have concerning the perpetrator of the offense, the rules governing examination of various

[45] Aspects also highlighted in the Opinion of Advocate General G. Pitruzzella, delivered on 19 November 2019, (Case C 653/19 PPU), aps. 40 et seq., ECLI:EU:C:2019:983.

[46] Gimeno Sendra (2017), pp. 479–480.

forms of evidence, and the extent of the statement of reasons that it is required to provide in response to arguments made before it, such questions are not governed by that directive but rather fall solely within the remit of national law.[47]

Despite the forcefulness of this declaration, the Court of Justice does consider some aspects of "reasonable grounds" in the Order of the CJEU of 12 February 2019, which it puts into context in the framework of Article 5 paragraph 1, letter c) of the ECHR, in Arts. 4 and 6 of the Directive and in what is established in Recital 16. Thus, after recall the need to preserve the presumption of innocence in public statements, it reminds that the declaration does not affect preliminary decisions of a procedural nature, taken by judicial or other competent authorities and based on evidence or proof of charges. It concludes that Article 4 of Directive 2016/343, read together with Recital 16 thereof, "must be interpreted as meaning that the conditions relating to the presumption of innocence require that, where the competent court examines the existence of reasonable grounds for believing that the suspect or accused person has committed the offence alleged, in order to adjudicate on the legality of a pre-trial detention decision, that court must weigh the elements of inculpatory and exculpatory evidence presented to it and it must give grounds for its decision, not only indicating the evidence relied on, but also ruling on the objections of the defence counsel of the person concerned."[48]

It cannot be concluded from the above considerations, however, that the requirements relating to the burden of proof in Art. 6 of the Directive apply to the preliminary decisions, since "reference to establishing 'guilt' in Article 6(1) and (2) of Directive 2016/343 must therefore be construed as meaning that the aim of that provision is to govern the allocation of the burden of proof only in the adoption of judicial decisions on guilt," which is not the case in decisions relating to pre-trial detention, a statement which is also supported by Recitals 16 and 22 of the Directive.[49]

In conclusion, it can be stated that the EU Legislature intended, on the one hand, to establish the notion that decisions concerning pre-trial detention do not in themselves constitute a violation of the presumption of innocence, even if they mention the existence of evidence. On the other hand, and notwithstanding the above, the obligation of the courts to base such decisions on sufficient information to justify them has been explicitly provided for. Hence, Advocate General Michal Bobek states that the guarantees relating to the presumption of innocence can be invoked "in the case of both 'positive' action by the court (for example a decision containing statements of guilt) and a 'negative' omission, in the form of the complete

[47] ECtHR (First Chamber) of 19 September 2018, Criminal proceedings against Emil Milev, (Case C-310/18 PPU), par. 48, ECLI:EU:C:2018:732.

[48] CJEUR (First Chamber), of 12 February 2019, Criminal proceedings against RH, (Case C-8/19 PPU), aps. 49, ECLI:EU:C:2019:110.

[49] CJEUR (First Chamber) of 28 November 2019, Criminal proceedings against DK, (Case C-653/19 PPU), aps. 33 and 34, ECLI:EU:C:2019:1024.

absence of judicial consideration of suspicion forming the basis for a pretrial detention measure during the litigation stage of criminal proceedings."[50]

Thus, in adopting these decisions, the courts must consider the existence of the evidence on which the decision is based and must rule on both the evidence on which it is based and the objections of the defense of the person concerned. However, the opportunity has been missed to harmonize the conditions under which preventive detention decisions can be taken, those relating to the degree of certainty that the court must have about the author of the offense, the evaluation of the various pieces of evidence and the scope of the motivation that must be provided, which remain exclusively in the hands of the national legislator, thus demonstrating, once again, the limited scope of protection afforded by the Directive, including pre-trial detention.

References

Aguilera Morales ME (2004) Presunción de inocencia y derechos de la defensa. In: Conde A, Mayol G (coords) Comentarios a la Constitución Europea. Tirant lo Blanch, Valencia, pp 1543–1571

Allué Burza A (2005) Una presunción de inocencia extensa y poco intensa. In: Roca G, Santolaya P (coords) La Europa de los Derechos. El Convenio Europeo de Derechos Humanos. Centro de Estudios Políticos y Constitucionales, Madrid, pp 367–387

Arangüena Fanego C (2019) Las Directivas europeas de armonización de garantías procesales de investigados y acusados. Su implementación en el Derecho español. Revista de Estudios Europeos (I):5–40

Cras S, Erbežnik A (2016) The directive on the presumption of innocence and the right to be present at trial. Genesis and description of the new EU-measure. Eucrim (1):25–36

Fernández López M (2015) Consideraciones procesales sobre el delito de enriquecimiento ilícito. In: Demetrio Crespo E, González-Cuéllar Serrano N (dirs) Halcones y palomas: Corrupción y delincuencia económica. Castillo de Luna, Madrid, pp 431–466

Gimeno Sendra V (2015) El derecho a la presunción de inocencia. In: González-Cuéllar Serrano N, Demetrio Crespo E (Dirs), Sanz Hermida AM (coord) Legalidad y defensa. Garantías constitucionales del Derecho y la Justicia penal. Castillo de Luna, Madrid, pp 201–218

Gimeno Sendra V (2017) Los derechos a la presunción de inocencia y de defensa. In: Sendra G, Del Moral T, Allard M, Martínez D. Los derechos fundamentales y su protección jurisdiccional. Edisofer, Madrid, pp 479–505

González Monje A (2016) La presunción de inocencia en la Unión Europea: Directiva 2016/343 del Parlamento Europeo y del consejo de 9 de marzo de 2016 por la que se refuerzan en el proceso penal determinados aspectos de la presunción de inocencia y el derecho a estar presente en el juicio. Revista General de Derecho Europeo (39):1–28

Lamberigts S (2016) The directive on the presumption of innocence. A missed opportunity for legal persons. Eucrim (1):36–42

Llobet Rodríguez J (2018) La Corte Interamericana de derechos humanos y las garantías penales. Editorial Jurídica Continental, San José de Costa Rica

[50] Opinion of Advocate General Michal Bobek of 11 October 2016, Criminal proceedings against Emil Milev, (Case C-439/16 PPU), par. 82, ECLI:EU:C:2016:760.

López Escudero M (2008) Artículo 48. Presunción de inocencia y derechos de la defensa. In: Mangas Martín A (dir) Carta de los derechos fundamentales de la Unión Europea. Comentario artículo por artículo. BBVA Foundation, pp 759–776.

Musacchio V (2009) La presunción de inocencia como un valor del sistema penal europeo. Revista General de Derecho Penal (11):1–10

Nieva Fenoll J (2016) La razón de ser de la presunción de inocencia. InDret. Revista para el análisis del Derecho (1):1–23

Ovejero Puente AM (2017) Protección del derecho a la presunción de inocencia. Teoría y Realidad Constitucional, UNED (40):431–455

Pérez Cebadera MA (2013) La prueba del origen ilícito de los bienes y el decomiso ampliado. In: González-Cuéllar N (Dir), Ortiz Pradillo JC, Sanz Hermida AM (coords) Problemas actuales de la Justicia Penal. Colex, Madrid, pp 365–382

Ramos Méndez F (2016) El sistema procesal español. Atelier, Barcelona

Sanz Hermida ÁM (2019) Título IV. Justicia. Artículo 48. In: López Castillo A (dir) La Carta de Derechos Fundamentales de la Unión Europea. Diez años de jurisprudencia. Tirant lo Blanch, Valencia, pp 1459–1505

Villamarín López ML (2017) La Directiva Europea 2016/343, de 9 de marzo, sobre presunción de inocencia y el derecho a estar presente en el juicio. InDret. Revista para el análisis del Derecho (3):1–39

Part III
Expansion and Trivialization of Criminal Law in the Democratic Constitutional State

Criminal Law Protection of Competition: An Instance of Punitive Excess?

Demelsa Benito Sánchez

Abstract This chapter aims to study the legal value (*Rechtsgut*) of free market competition as a possible legal value worthy of protection under criminal law. In this regard, two key issues arise: the concept of competition in itself and adherence to two fundamental principles of criminal law (the principles of exclusive protection of legal values and minimal intervention). Thus, to avoid arguing in the abstract, a concrete political-criminal issue is discussed: the crime of corruption involving private individuals as a crime against market competition. This paper concludes that legislators have partially disregarded the minimal intervention principle in this area.

1 Introduction

This paper aims to study market competition as a possible legal value worthy of protection under criminal law.[1] It particularly seeks to provide an answer to the question as to whether criminal law intervention to protect this legal asset is justified in terms of two fundamental principles of criminal law, namely the principles of exclusive protection of legal values and minimal intervention. Protecting the proper functioning of the market under criminal law is certainly nothing new. The Criminal Code has a long tradition of crimes such as bid rigging in public tenders and

[1] This chapter is a result of the following research projects. (A) "Crisis del Derecho Penal del Estado de Derecho: Manifestaciones y tendencias" (SBPLY/17/18501/000223) granted by Junta de Comunidades de Castilla—La Mancha, and co-funded by the European Regional Development Fund, principal investigators: E. Demetrio Crespo, A. J. García Figueroa y G. M. Marcilla Córdoba (University of Castilla-La Mancha). (B). "Hacia un modelo de justicia social: alternativas político-político criminales" (RTI2018-095155-A-C22), granted by the Ministry of Science, Innovation and Universities of the Government of Spain, principal investigator: D. Benito Sánchez (University of Deusto).

D. Benito Sánchez (✉)
Faculty of Law, University of Deusto, Bilbao, Spain
e-mail: demelsa.benito@deusto.es

E. Demetrio Crespo et al. (eds.), *Crisis of the Criminal Law in the Democratic Constitutional State*, Legal Studies in International, European and Comparative Criminal Law 6, https://doi.org/10.1007/978-3-031-13413-5_12

auctions, the removal of raw materials or basic commodities from the market, and price fixing. However, in recent years we have seen demands from supranational authorities to intensify criminal justice response to behaviours that may harm market competition. The European Union, for example, is calling for criminal law intervention to deal with so-called private corruption[2] and behaviours leading to market abuse.[3] The Organisation for Economic Co-operation and Development, for its part, requires states to criminally punish corruption in international business transactions,[4] while recommending the criminalisation of cartels.[5]

In view of these supranational requirements, Spanish legislators have gradually added new criminal definitions to criminal legislation such as corruption in business (Articles 286a and 286b of the Criminal Code, hereinafter CC), and have also broadened the scope of what is punishable in existing offences such as price fixing (CC Article 284), all of which are criminal definitions aimed at protecting market competition.

Criminal law protection of free competition does, however, present some problems. The first concerns the indeterminate nature of the notion of competition in itself, which undoubtedly makes it difficult to attach material content to the legal value to be protected. The second concerns observance of two crucial principles of criminal law in democratic states and states governed by the rule of law, essentially the offense principle and the principle of minimal intervention. In this respect, it should be remembered that a state's *ius puniendi* intervention should be allowed only when it seeks to protect an interest that is indispensable to life in society against the most severe attacks on it, and where action preceding criminal law—by definition less harmful to individual rights than criminal law—is unable to provide effective protection. In short, criminal law in this area faces two classic questions: what is to be protected, and how is it to be protected?

To answer the question posed earlier in the introduction, this paper will first seek to explore the concept of market competition, and then analyse whether criminal law intervention to protect market competition is legitimate based on the aforementioned principles. Thus, to avoid arguing in the abstract, a concrete political-criminal issue will be discussed; that of incorporating the crime of corruption involving private individuals into the Criminal Code (CC Article 286a), which punishes behaviours that are already sanctioned in other branches of the legal system. Only by observing

---

[2] See Council Framework Decision 2003/568/JHA, 22 July 2003, on combating corruption in the private sector Official Journal of the European Union L 192, 31 July 2003.

[3] See Directive 2014/57/EU of the European Parliament and Council, 16 April 2014, on criminal sanctions applicable to market abuse (Market Abuse Directive) Official Journal of the European Union L 173, 12 June 2014.

[4] See OECD: Convention on Combating Bribery of Foreign Public Officials in International Business Transactions, 17 December 1997. Spanish instrument of ratification: Official State Bulletin (hereinafter, BOE) No. 46, 22 February 2002.

[5] See the document draw up by the OECD Secretariat entitled On Co-operation and Enforcement. Criminalisation of cartels and bid rigging conspiracies: a focus on custodial sentences, 9 June 2020, and related documents available from this link (last accessed 25.4.2021).

the offense principle and minimal intervention (subsidiarity and fragmentarity) would recourse to criminal law in this area be legitimate. The contrary would be a sign of punitive excess that would be difficult to justify in a democratic state governed by the rule of law.

2 Competition As a Legal Value Worthy of Criminal Law Protection

2.1 *On the Concept of Competition*

If there is one criticism to be made of contemporary criminal law, and especially of economic criminal law, it is the dematerialisation of collective legal values (Mendoza Buergo 2001, p. 69), which are usually the objects of protection in this branch of criminal law. That is why this section seeks to shed light on the concept of market competition—a legal value of an obviously collective nature.

At present, the concept of competition is in no way peaceful in any field, not even in economic science, where the term comes from (Stucke 2012, pp. 28–29). The problem is even greater in the field of economic criminal law, where concepts such as free competition, loyal competition, honest competition, fair competition, etc. are often used interchangeably without specifying exactly what is meant by them. Providing a precise definition of the term is an ambitious task, so here we attempt to take an approach that will subsequently enable us to address the issue raised in the introduction concerning the crime of corruption involving private individuals.

According to the dictionary, the word "competition" is associated with terms such as contest, dispute or rivalry. More specifically, for the case at hand, it is defined as "the situation of companies vying in a market offering or demanding the same product or service".[6] The dictionary does not, however, specify what the purpose of such rivalry is. In essence, the aim is to increase a company's sales of products and services to the detriment of rival companies to make higher profits (Signes de Mesa et al. 2013, p. 29). Such rivalry or competition between firms, despite the negative connotations of these terms, has beneficial effects for society as a whole. Economic theory has shown that competition between firms is a means of efficiently allocating the resources available to a society, leads to the lowest possible prices of goods and services in the market, and stimulates innovation and improvement of goods and services (Signes de Mesa et al. 2013, p. 55). In other words, economic theory justifies maintaining a perfect competition system in the pursuit of so-called allocative efficiency, productive efficiency and dynamic efficiency.

Allocative efficiency focuses on the effects of competition on consumers. Under perfect competition conditions, resources are allocated across different goods and

[6] Royal Spanish Academy Dictionary, entry "competition". Available from https://dle.rae.es/competencia (last accessed 25.4.2021).

services in such a way that no better level of allocation is possible. Consumer surplus, i.e. the consumer's net gain when buying a product, is the largest. Goods and services are allocated according to the price consumers are willing to pay—a price that ultimately will not exceed the marginal production cost. Productive efficiency centres on the effects on producers and distributors. In a perfect competition system, goods and services are produced at the lowest possible cost. This is because the way companies sell more cheaply than their competitors is by cutting production costs. Finally, dynamic efficiency refers to the effect of competition on stimulating innovation to produce new and improved products to offer consumers as part of the ongoing battle between competing companies. Competition must therefore have the effect of stimulating research and technological development (Whish and Bailey 2015, pp. 5–6).

Advocates of each of the three trends, or a combination of them, can be found in the doctrine. Some consider that overall welfare should be enhanced through a combination of allocative and productive efficiency. Others believe that essentially consumer welfare should be promoted, which will undoubtedly lead to stimulation in consumption, and therefore in production. There are also those committed to promoting dynamic efficiency.[7] The first and second positions are in fact very similar, and the third appears to be wholly related in that innovation by companies leads to improved products for consumers (Whish and Bailey 2015, pp. 4–5). In short, it seems clear that a perfect competition system, which pursues these efficiencies, must be oriented towards maximising social welfare (Motta 2004, pp. 17–22). Therefore, the intervention of law in this field, either by regulating it or by sanctioning certain behaviours, will only be justified if such a goal is to be achieved (Paredes Castañón 2019, *et passim*, especially, p. 137).

However, it should be remembered that markets cannot always maintain efficient order in the above sense, as there are market failures and behaviours by the agents themselves that distort its functioning. In fact, experts agree that perfect competition does not appear to be an achievable goal (Stucke 2012, p. 35), barring exceptional situations, and so the proclamation by the legal system of business freedom does not necessarily imply an objective situation of free competition (Calvo Caravaca 2009, p. 58). Indeed, from an economic perspective, a model of effective or functional competition is chosen, that is, the real competition possible in a specific market considering the economic and legal context. From this point of view, a model consisting of competitive and monopolistic elements is chosen, where other market structures beyond perfect competition would be present, such as monopoly and oligopoly. In this respect, the existence of certain processes of economic concentration would be advocated, with limits, to ensure technological progress and the efficiency level deriving from optimal company size (ibid.).

From a legal perspective, the aim is to ensure both the subjective and objective dimensions of competition, i.e. competition as a subjective right (business freedom) and objective competition or competition as an institution, since one cannot exist

[7] See for further references, Artaza Varela (2017), pp. 348–349.

without the other (Fikentscher 1984, pp. 474–477). As a subjective right, competition is seen as equal opportunities for economic agents (Calvo Caravaca 2009, p. 58), which implies freedom of access to the market, as well as freedom to pursue the activity and to cease it (Solernou Sanz 2018, p. 69). Competition as an institution transcends the purely subjective, and refers to the existence of a series of appropriate social, legal and economic conditions for economic freedoms to be exercised and developed effectively (ibid., p. 75). Protecting competition as an institution will not only be in the interest of competitors, but also of consumers and society as a whole insofar as it serves to maintain the economic order, and thus ceases to be solely a private affair but takes on indisputable public significance, for what must be preserved is a competitive market to the benefit of all (Abanto Vásquez 2010, p. 162), in the aforementioned sense of maximising social welfare.

Ultimately, protecting competition by means of the law is justified insofar as it is aimed at maintaining competitive markets that have beneficial effects for society as a whole. The law, in its various branches, must safeguard these competitive markets by penalising practices restricting them, and thereby undermine social welfare. *Criminal* law, for its part, is entitled to intervene solely where the offense principle and the principle of minimal intervention are observed, as explained in the following section.

2.2 *On Free Competition As a Legal Value Worthy of Criminal Law Protection*

Evolution of the model of state towards a social state in the second half of the twentieth century had major consequences on the content of criminal law as it had to incorporate the protection of collective legal values. Indeed, even in nineteenth century criminal codes there were crimes protecting legal values that transcended purely individual values such as, for example, crimes against public administration or crimes against public faith. Nevertheless, when it is said that one of the major challenges facing criminal law today revolves around specifying the content of collective legal values, we think of objects of protection different from those in nineteenth century criminal codes (Berdugo Gómez de la Torre 2012, p. 205); objects of protection now associated with the social state. The environment and economic order have traditionally been mentioned as paradigmatic examples (Mendoza Buergo 2001, p. 70). Within economic order, which is the object of protection under economic criminal law (Bajo and Bacigalupo 2010, p. 11), there is market competition, a legal value that transcends the purely individual. The previous section focused on the study of the concept; this section aims to examine its suitability to be deemed a legal values worthy of *criminal* law protection.

As Paredes Castañón (2003), p. 100 has shown, particularly for the field of economic criminal law, identifying a criminal-legal value involves analysis of two previous issues. The first refers to the reality in which economic criminal law operates. The second relates to the values and behavioural patterns it should foster and, hence, what should be punished. On the first point, the economic reality at the time, that is, a social market economy, must be considered in this case. In effect, Article 38 of the Spanish Constitution advocates this model, as does Article 3.3 of the Treaty on European Union, guaranteeing that public authorities will not intervene in the economy other than to prevent and eventually punish behaviours that jeopardise this economic model. In other words, the role of the state is to ensure that the social market economy model functions properly; but this model can never be changed (Zabala López-Gómez 2011, pp. 21–22), all the more so as this is also the model that has been championed since the economic constitution of the European Union (Gordillo Pérez 2018, pp. 266–274). Areas can be identified in this model where objects worthy of legal protection (albeit not necessarily criminal) can be found, i.e. individual or collective needs, which must be fulfilled to the greatest extent possible (Paredes Castañón 2003, p. 103). These needs may relate, for example, to the production and allocation of goods and services, whose assurance requires that other needs be acknowledged, such as the right to private property, business freedom and free competition (ibid., p. 104). Having determined these needs, the human behaviours that will contribute, in causal terms, to bringing about and maintaining the required state of affairs must be specified, for which scientific knowledge is an essential resource (ibid., pp. 105–106). The empirical basis effectively becomes an indispensable methodological presupposition to analyse the harmfulness of behaviours that can be punished under criminal law (Berdugo Gómez de la Torre 2012, p. 209; Demetrio Crespo 2020, p. 19; Soto Navarro 2003, p. 81, among others). For instance, in the field under consideration, economic science will determine which human behaviours help to create or maintain free competition, and which restrict or eliminate it, and the law must rely on such data.

The fact that empirical science passes this information on to us does not mean that we are automatically presented with legal values worthy of criminal law protection. On this point, Paredes Castañón (2003), p. 107 notes that, to draw such a conclusion, we must examine whether legal protection of the object is desirable from an ethical-social perspective; and then, from the perspective of instrumental rationality, we must study whether, rather than coercive regulation, other means of state intervention in the economy are possible (ibid., pp. 111–112). Moreover, even if it were concluded that coercive regulation is required, this does not imply that *criminal* law should be applied. This is because not every legal value is a *criminal*-legal value. As noted by Mir Puig (2006b), p. 129, the concept of legal value is broader than that of criminal-legal value. Indeed, free competition is a clear example of this. As a legal value, it is protected by other branches of the legal system, such as private law or administrative law, such that criminal law can only intervene to protect it where the principles of exclusive protection of legal values and minimal intervention are observed.

The first of these principles states that criminal law can only be applied to protect "vital values that are indispensable for the coexistence of people in the community" (Jescheck and Weigend 1996, p. 7), that is, fundamental interests geared towards the individual, enabling their participation in a given social system (Berdugo Gómez de la Torre et al. 2010, p. 71). In this sense, criminal law cannot punish behaviours that do not cause social harm. However, relying solely on this criterion "entails the danger of totalitarian roots, of attending to the needs of the social whole while neglecting the individual" (Silva Sánchez 1992, p. 269). Hence, beyond purely sociological approaches which understand that criminalised behaviours must affect social functions and structures, from a value point of view, it is argued that for a legal value to be protected by criminal law, it must have a foundation in the constitutional order of values (Berdugo Gómez de la Torre et al. 2010, pp. 71–77). This does not imply that the catalogue of legal values is redirected to a specific article of the constitution; what is relevant is that the legal values are associated with the constitutional framework (Berdugo Gómez de la Torre et al. 2015, p. 90; Quintero Olivares, 2020, p. 51). This reference to the constitution is, nonetheless, a negative criterion (Martínez-Buján Pérez 2016, p. 310) as not all interests with constitutional projection should be protected by criminal law, and certainly not interests without a constitutional reference. At all events, it is understood that the constitution must be open. In addition, it can and should be interpreted according to the social reality at the time (Berdugo Gómez de la Torre 2012, pp. 208–209).[8] That reference is not being made to the constitution as a mere instrument for organising the state, rather as the supreme legal standard in the legal system, with direct normative value, and founded on fundamental rights (Berdugo Gómez de la Torre et al. 2010, p. 8).

The legal value under consideration here, namely market competition, is of unquestionable importance in today's society. As seen in the previous section, competition constitutes a means of efficiently allocating the resources available to a society, results in the lowest possible prices for goods and services, and encourages technological innovation and improvements, all contributing to social welfare. And, as mentioned above, eliminating or reducing competition leads to a decline in the standard of social welfare. Moreover, market competition currently enjoys clear constitutional support, particularly in the so-called economic constitution, understood as "the [constitutional] norms aimed at providing the fundamental legal framework for the structure and functioning of economic activity".[9] Article 38 of the Spanish Constitution is the cornerstone of constitutional economic law (Bajo and Bacigalupo 2010, p. 16), insofar as it acknowledges the right to business freedom within the social market economy framework, the only limits being those arising from the demands of the economy in general and planning. Although the guarantee of free competition is not expressly mentioned, it is understood to be inherent to the right to business freedom in Article 38, within citizens' duties and rights (De la Mata Barraco et al. 2018, p. 368; Gordillo Pérez and Rodríguez Ortiz 2019; p. 48; Martínez-Buján Pérez 2016, p. 189).

These references can also be found in the European economic constitution, which is essential as it sets out the guidelines for the Member States' economic model. The

[8] In fact, the Constitutional Court decided early on in favour of an open and flexible concept of an "economic constitution".

[9] See Constitutional Court ruling 1/1982, 28 January 1982, the primary legal basis.

European economic constitution considers competition to be inherent to the single market, and Articles 101 and 102 of the Treaty on the Functioning of the European Union are responsible for its protection, prohibiting practices that restrict or distort it.[10] Competition, despite being a collective legal value, ultimately refers to the individual person concerned, to the free development of their personality, which, together with the person's dignity and their inherent inviolable rights, constitute the foundation of political order and social peace, as stated in Article 10 of the Spanish Constitution. This is worth highlighting because it has been pointed out that in constitutional systems such as Spain's, legal values, albeit collective, must ultimately refer to the individual.[11] In this sense, as noted above, competition is intimately related to the free development of personality. In fact, business freedom (the subjective dimension of competition) is considered a further manifestation of the free development of personality (Solernou Sanz 2018, p. 68).

Together with the offense principle, the second principle that must be observed is the minimal intervention principle, which functions as a limiting principle of the state's *ius puniendi*. Particularly in the field of economic criminal law, examination of this principle merits detailed analysis as this sector of criminal law is made up of criminal offences that punish behaviours which, for the most part, are already sanctioned by other branches of the legal system, such as private law or administrative law.[12] The following section addresses this issue, taking the crime of corruption involving private individuals as an example. It should be particularly noted that this principle refers to two elements: the subsidiary and fragmentary nature of criminal law.

3 An Example of Criminal Law Protection of Competition: The Crime of Corruption Involving Private Individuals

As mentioned in the introduction, the issue of competition as a legal value worthy of criminal law protection will be addressed in the study of a criminal definition that has been included in the Criminal Code relatively recently: corruption involving private individuals. This criminal definition was added to criminal legislation under

[10] Reference to the economic constitution of the European Union is essential on this point because a large part of the criminal law protection of competition in the Criminal Code derives precisely from European mandates. See, among others, Doval Pais (2020), *et passim*, particularly pp. 117–120; Gómez-Jara Díez (2017), pp. 29–48; Zabala López-Gómez (2011), pp. 23–32.

[11] See in this respect, among others, Bustos Ramírez (1987), pp. 196–197; Mir Puig (2006a), p. 91; Roxin (2006), p. 56; Santana Vega (2000), pp. 94–95; Silva Sánchez (1992), p. 272; Silva (2006), pp. 270–271; Soto Navarro (2003), pp. 231–232.

[12] The need to observe the minimal intervention principle in criminal law protection of competition was already raised in the 1980s in connection with proposals to amend the Criminal Code. See Berdugo Gómez de la Torre (1985), *et passim*, particularly p. 405.

Constitutional Law 5/2010[13] to transpose the aforementioned Council Framework Decision 2003/568/JHA on combating corruption in the private sector. Article 286a was thus introduced in a new section entitled "Corruption involving private individuals" in Chapter XI, Title XIII, Book II of the Criminal Code. The precept was changed in the amendment implemented by Organic Law 1/2015[14] to incorporate technical improvements, as noted in the preamble of the law. The title of the section was also changed to "Offences of Corruption in Business", as the offence of corruption in international business transactions was included. Article 286a now reads as follows:

> 1. The director, administrator, employee or collaborator of a commercial enterprise or company who, personally or by intermediary, receives, requests or accepts an unjustified benefit or advantage of any nature, or offers or promises to obtain one, for themselves or for a third party, as compensation for unduly favouring another in the procurement or sale of goods, or in the hiring of services or in business relations, shall be punished by imprisonment from six months to four years, specific disqualification from engaging in industry or commerce for a period of one to six years and a fine amounting to three times the value of the benefit or advantage.
>
> 2. The same penalties shall apply to any person who, personally or by intermediary, promises, offers or grants to the directors, administrators, employees or collaborators of a commercial enterprise or company, an unjustified benefit or advantage of any nature whatsoever, for them or for third parties, as compensation for unduly favouring them or a third party over others in the procurement or sale of goods, hiring of services or in business relations.
>
> 3. Judges and courts, in view of the amount of benefit or value of the advantage, and the importance of the offender's functions, may impose the lesser penalty and reduce the fine at their discretion.[15]

The legal value that this criminal definition aims to protect was the subject of a broad doctrinal discussion before it was even included in criminal legislation, when some supranational bodies were already calling for its punishment. This paper will not enter into the details of the discussion for reasons of space, but start from the clearly predominant perspective which, following the German model, links this offence to market competition, especially after amendment of the precept in 2015 (when the term "failing to comply with their obligations" was withdrawn from the definition of the offence), although various formulas are used to refer to legal values, such as loyal, honest and fair competition, etc.[16] Thus, it is stated that payment of a

[13] Organic Law 5/2010, 22 June, amending Organic Law 10/1995, 23 November, of the Criminal Code, BOE No. 152, 23 June 2010.

[14] Organic Law 1/2015, 30 March, amending Organic Law 10/1995, 23 November, of the Criminal Code, BOE No. 77, 31 March 2015.

[15] The precept continues with a fourth paragraph criminalising so-called corruption in sport. This is not the object of analysis in this paper because the legal value protected, despite its emplacement, is not market competition. See in this respect Sánchez Bernal (2018), *et passim*.

[16] See, among others, Bustos Rubio (2019), p. 238; Cerina and Bravo Vesga (2009), pp. 379–447; Galán Muñoz and Núñez Castaño (2018), p. 182; Gil Nobajas (2015), pp. 574–580; Gili Pascual (2007), pp. 8–13; Gómez-Jara Díez (2012), pp. 420–421; Herrero Giménez (2017), p. 206;

bribe by a company employee to the employee of another company to benefit their company with respect to third party competitors in the procurement or sale of goods, or hiring of services, unduly places them in a privileged competitive position, which may lead to the expulsion of competitors from the market or restrict entry of new competitors. This circumstance may result in a loss in the efficiencies referred to in the economic theory explained above Sect. 2.1, and a consequent loss in social welfare. An example would be where restrictions on competition generate monopolistic situations that lead to the limitation of production (Calvo Caravaca 2009, p. 60).

As stated in the previous section, market competition is a value of unquestionable social importance and is also reflected in both the national and European Union's economic constitution. However, this does not simply empower criminal law to exercise a protective function with respect to this legal value as the minimal intervention principle must always be observed, which is precisely what is called into question in relation to this crime (Estrada i Cuadras 2020, p. 495). The subsidiary (*ultima ratio*) and fragmentary nature of criminal law appear to have been overlooked by legislators in some respects, as explained below.

Outside criminal law, there are two regulatory bodies that protect market competition, namely the Unfair Competition Act (hereinafter, UCA)[17] and the Defence of Competition Act (DCA).[18] The question that must now be asked is whether the bribery practices punished under Article 286a of criminal legislation can already be sufficiently resolved before resorting to criminal law. Article 4.1 of the Unfair Competition Act contains a standard clause stating the following:

> All behaviour which is objectively contrary to the requirements of good faith is deemed unfair.
>
> In relations with consumers and users, the conduct of an entrepreneur or professional contrary to professional diligence, understood as the level of competence and special care to be expected from an entrepreneur in accordance with honest market practices, which significantly distorts or is likely to significantly distort the economic behaviour of the average consumer or average member of the practices' target group, shall be deemed contrary to the requirements of good faith where the business practices are targeted at a particular group of consumers.

Indeed, the offer of a bribe must be understood as contrary to the requirements of objective good faith. This being so, "any natural or legal person participating in the market, whose economic interests are directly harmed or threatened by unfair practices" (UCA Article 33) is entitled to bring a series of actions, including, for example, "action seeking compensation for damages caused by the unfair practices" (UCA Article 32.5). The limited active legitimation provided for in the Act seems to

---

Mendoza Calderón (2017), pp. 28–29; Navarro Frías and Melero Bosch (2011), *et passim*; Otero González (2013), *et passim*; Sánchez Bernal (2017), pp. 270–277. The French model, by contrast, places emphasis on the protection of the employee's duties of loyalty towards their employer.

[17] Act 3/1991, 10 January 1991, on Unfair Competition, BOE No. 10, 11 January 1991.

[18] Act 15/2007, 3 July, on the Defence of Competition, BOE No. 159, 4 July 2007.

be inadequate as a deterrent against such practices, which, besides the individual economic harm that might be compensated, may result in a decline in the welfare of society as a whole.

Furthermore, behaviours relating to the payment of bribes to gain market share could also be sanctioned under the DCA. This law particularly punishes two types of behaviour: collusive behaviour and abuse of a dominant position (DCA Articles 1 and 2, respectively, in line with TFEU Articles 101 and 102). We shall begin with the second scenario. In Spanish law, as in European Union law, a dominant position is not in itself unlawful conduct; abuse of it is, insofar as it is understood that competitors and consumers are harmed (Laguna de Paz 2019, p. 35). In essence, abuse of a dominant position is deemed to occur when the company so positioned imposes conditions on customers or users above the competitive level, or when it creates obstacles to expansion or the entry of new competitors into the market (Signes de Mesa et al. 2013, p. 213). Of course, one might think that a company in a dominant position does not need to pay bribes "when procuring or selling goods, or hiring services or in business relations" (CC Article 286a), precisely because of its position, so conduct involving bribery does not seem to be punishable as abuse of a dominant position. Nonetheless, this scenario cannot be ruled out either, one merely needs to recall the Tabacalera case.[19]

The payment of a bribe, however, may be the mechanism to carry out a collusive behaviour. Article 1 of the aforementioned Act states:

> All agreements, decisions, collective recommendations or concerted or consciously parallel practices that aim at, lead to or are liable to lead to the prevention, restriction or distortion in all or part of the national market are prohibited.

The corrupt pact between the bribe giver and bribe taker can effectively be understood as the "agreement" referred to in the law,[20] and will fall within the scope of the law where it leads to or is liable to lead to the prevention, restriction or distortion of competition. This administrative infringement is deemed to have been committed even where the agreement has not been implemented or put into practice; the fact that the agreement *may* have negative effects on free competition is sufficient. Moreover, the conduct referred to in DCA Article 1 is also prohibited, although the parties involved were unaware of the harmful effects on the market,

[19] In the case in question, the then Court of Defence of Competition ruled on "the carrying out of practices of abuse of a dominant position by sale at a loss and distortion of free competition by unfair acts, *consisting of giving gifts to retailers* who buy their products, thereby infringing the regulations in force on tobacco monopolies in Spain" (italics added). The Court found that there had been abuse of a dominant position, but did not consider that giving gifts constituted "sufficient disruption of the market", and therefore did not consider that the DCA should be enforced in this respect. See Court of Defence of Competition Resolution, 16 February 1999 (Case 375/96, Canary Islands Tobacco).

[20] The term "agreement" has in fact been broadly interpreted, allowing, for example, written or oral, formal or informal pacts and "gentlemen's agreements" (Signes de Mesa et al. 2013, p. 110).

or had no intention of restricting competition.[21] In any event, DCA Article 5 provides for limitation in terms of the effect on the legal asset, such that the law will not be applied to "behaviours which, given their insignificant nature, are not capable of significantly affecting competition. The criteria for defining conduct of minor significance will be determined by regulation, taking into account, among other things, market share".[22]

Taking all this into consideration, the question that must now be asked is what the extra harmfulness in CC Article 286a is in relation to the DCA. It is certainly not easy to find. In fact, the crime of corruption involving private individuals does not seem to require any additional elements in relation to the administrative infringement, which calls into question the minimal intervention principle that should govern criminal law. CC Article 286a could even sanction behaviours that fall outside the DCA, as is the case, for example, of conduct of little or minor significance. Administrative law has chosen to leave out such behaviours, whereas the Criminal Code has not. It should be noted that the attenuated type of offence in the third paragraph of CC Article 286a bears no relation, at least directly, to the reduced effect on legal assets in market competition. It provides for the reduction of the penalty—which is facultative, not mandatory as in DCA Article 5—in two cases: the amount of benefit or value of advantage, and the importance of the offender's functions in the organisation (extensively on this subject, Sánchez Bernal 2017, pp. 426–429).

Furthermore, it should be noted that, according to the current wording of classic bribery offences, Article 286a does not require actual payment of the bribe to be made for the offence to be consummated, the mere offer or request being sufficient; a situation where risk to the legal value is truly remote. Precisely due to the fact that such risk to market competition is so remote, this advancing of the protection barrier must be questioned, given that behaviours permitted by administrative legislation could be sanctioned because of their scarce or lack of impact on the market. The precept must therefore be interpreted in a restrictive manner on this point (Bolea Bardón 2013, pp. 17–19).[23]

In short, the wording of CC Article 286a allows for the punishment of behaviours that are not sanctioned by competition law, contravening the minimal intervention principle, which should govern criminal action in democratic states, subject to the

[21] In this respect, see, for example, the National Competition Commission Resolution, 20 March 2013, file S/0359/11, ATASA, pp. 34–35.

[22] Article 1 of the Regulations on the Defence of Competition (Royal Decree 261/2008, 22 February, approving Regulations on the Defence of Competition, BOE No. 50, 27 February 2008) sets out the market shares to be considered when assessing whether the conduct is of minor significance. Moreover, Article 2 precludes the application of this *de minimis* rule in cases where behaviours among competitors aim at: (a) fixing the product sales prices for third parties; (b) limiting production or sales; (c) sharing markets or customers, including fraudulent bids, or restricting imports or exports.

[23] Gili Pascual (2007), p. 13 also expressed the same opinion regarding the bill to include this crime in the Criminal Code.

rule of law. Particularly, the fact that behaviour is criminalised which may not be punishable under administrative law is undoubtedly a breach of the fragmentary nature that criminal law must possess, whereby criminal law must intervene only in the case of the most serious forms of attack on the legal asset in question. Article 286a should therefore introduce a precept limiting *ius puniendi* intervention to behaviours which significantly affect market competition, as is the case with other economic crimes.[24]

Nevertheless, further analysis needs to be carried out to ensure that the criminal law response in this area observes the *ultima ratio* principle. To this end, it must be ascertained whether the sanctions provided for in the DCA are effective, for if they are, criminal law intervention would not be justified. DCA Article 63 provides for possible fines to be imposed by competition authorities. Fines can be imposed on companies (literally stating the precept, economic agents, firms, associations, unions or groups) and, in the case of a legal person, the fine can also be imposed on the natural person representing the legal person or director.

The heaviest fine envisaged for companies can amount to "up to 10% of the offending company's total turnover in the financial year immediately preceding the year in which the fine is imposed" (DCA Article 63.1.c). This doctrine reveals the limited deterrent nature of fines imposed by the National Commission for Markets and Competition when enforcing to the aforementioned provision (Costas Comesaña 2017, *et passim*), especially after the Supreme Court (Section 3) ruling of 29 January 2015 declared the calculation method adopted by the then National Commission for Competition to be unlawful in an official statement issued on 6 February 2009.[25] The empirical evidence has certainly revealed the inadequacy of such sanctions. The study carried out by García-Verdugo Sales (2016), analysing the fines imposed by the National Commission for Markets and Competition between 2011 and 2015, categorically concludes that they "have proved to be insufficiently dissuasive, and should therefore tend towards heavier penalties that are closer to the optimal deterrent fine" (p. 35). It is indeed striking that in more than 90% of the cases studied, the fine failed to reach even 40% of the value of the optimal deterrent sanction, which considers the illicit benefits and annual probability of infringement detection.

On natural persons, DCA Article 63.2 states the following:

> In addition to the sanction provided for in the previous section, where the offender is a legal person, a fine of up to 60,000 Euros may be imposed on each of their legal representatives or on the persons forming the managerial bodies involved in the agreement or decision. Those persons who, forming part of corporate administrative bodies, have not attended the meetings or voted against or dissented shall be excluded from the sanction.

---

[24] For example, CC Article 284.1.2, 284.1.3, 285.

[25] Official statement issued on 6 February 2009 from the National Competition Commission, on the quantification of penalties arising from infringements of Articles 1, 2 and 3 of Act 15/2007, 3 July, on the Defence of Competition and Articles 81 and 82 of the European Community Treaty, BOE No. 36, 11 February 2009.

This section of the Act, however, has traditionally been seldom applied. In fact, the aforementioned Supreme Court ruling of 29 January 2015 drew attention to the limited use made by the National Competition Commission of the power to impose fines on natural persons for infringement of the DCA. Since then, the National Commission for Markets and Competition has imposed some fines on these natural persons, but the modest amounts and fact that the company may ultimately pay the fine means that they have limited deterrent effect (Costas Comesaña 2017, p. 63; Díez Estella 2016, pp. 12–13).[26]

It is claimed that where action preceding criminal law proves to be ineffective at protecting market competition because their sanctions fail to act as a deterrent, criminal law intervention could then be legitimised (subsidiarity or *ultima ratio* principle). Nevertheless, it cannot simply be concluded that criminal penalties will be more effective than administrative sanctions. For example, it is unlikely that the criminal fine will surpass the administrative fine on account of the way fines are calculated in criminal law (Baucells Lladós 2013, p. 195; Corcoy Bidasolo 2014, p. 172; Faraldo Cabana 2013, p. 91). Thus, the fine imposed on the natural person, according to Article 286a, is calculated in proportion to the bribe, not to the benefit gained, which may have limited deterrent effect because it is easy to imagine that the bribe is lower than the benefit gained. The fine imposed on the legal person for this offence (under Article 288) can be calculated using the day-fine system (which would lead to a maximum fine of nine million Euros) or proportionally, in this case, to the benefit gained or sought, which could act as a greater deterrent. However, the resource to exorbitant fines may lead to fall into the *deterrence trap* (Coffee Jr 1981, pp. 389–393), that is, that situation in which the legal person cannot afford the fine, so finally it does not have any deterrence effect since the legal person knows that it will not pay it.

However, it is also true that in the criminal field, the penalty par excellence for natural persons is the prison sentence, which in the case of Article 286a must be between 6 months and 4 years. In this respect, it has been noted that imposing a prison sentence as a non-transferable sentence, unlike a fine (Gutiérrez Rodríguez and Ortiz de Urbina Gimeno 2017, p. 111), could be more dissuasive in this area than fines imposed on natural persons under the DCA, but other variables should be considered: the effective enforcement of the prison sentence (over and above the formal provision for this penalty under the precept in question), the probability of it

[26] In any event, and despite being unable to elaborate here for reasons of space, in order to assess the effectiveness of competition law sanctions, private enforcement of competition law must now also be considered, which has been strengthened in the Spanish case by transposing the so-called "Damages Directive" (Directive 2014/104/EU of the European Parliament and Council, 26 November 2014, on certain rules governing actions for damages under national law for infringements of the competition law provisions of the Member States and of the European Union, Official Journal of the European Union L349/1, 5 December 2014), by Royal Decree Act 9/2017, 26 May, which transposes European Union directives in the financial, business and health fields, and in relation to the movement of workers (BOE. No. 126, 27 May 2017). See Díez Estella (2019), *et passim*.

being imposed and speed in enforcing the sentence (ibid., pp. 112–113). Finally, the fact that the penalty must observe other principles such as proportionality and re-socialisation should not be overlooked.

4 Criminal Law Protection of Competition As an Example of Punitive Excess and Symbolic Criminal Law

Based on what has been said thus far, the question arises as to why legislators have incorporated Article 286a into the Criminal Code, which could punish behaviours that are not punishable under competition law. As stated above, the inclusion of this precept in criminal legislation is based on supranational legislation, specifically Framework Decision 2003/568/JHA.[27] The problem that currently exists with the transposition or implementation of criminal measures emanating from the supranational sphere is that they are undertaken without the corresponding preliminary political-criminal debate (especially on corruption involving private individuals, Corcoy Bidasolo 2014, p. 178; Gili Pascual 2007, p. 10, Martínez-Buján Pérez 2016, p. 381; Sánchez Bernal 2020, p. 531). This fact leads to the inclusion of excessively vague, at times technically deficient, criminal definitions that make them extremely difficult to enforce, which can turn them into purely symbolic criminal law (particularly for corruption involving private individuals) (Corcoy Bidasolo 2014, p. 192; Sánchez Bernal 2020, p. 531; in general, for economic crimes, Terradillos Basoco 2020, p. 37).

Indeed, one of the problems facing criminal law today is symbolic criminal law: criminal definitions that are added to criminal legislation to satisfy the demands of certain sectors or lobbies, but which have no practical application. The expression symbolic criminal law has essentially been used to refer to those criminal policies which do not so much seek to reduce crime as to allay social fears regarding crime (Díez Ripollés 2005, pp. 23 ff.). It is true that crimes under economic criminal law are not the kind of crimes that typically instil fear in society; nevertheless, one can also speak of their symbolic nature in that many of them are included in criminal legislation to satisfy certain demands. These demands made by supranational bodies, fall into oblivion once included in the Criminal Code. Such is the case of the crime under study here, which has rarely been rarely enforced in 10 years of existence. The same applies to the provision contained in Article 286a of the Criminal Code under section "Crimes of corruption in business", also aimed at protecting market competition, albeit in its transnational dimension, in CC Article 286b.[28]

[27] The 1999 Council of Europe Criminal Law Convention on Corruption and 2003 United Nations Convention against Corruption, both ratified by Spain, also call for criminal punishment.

[28] In 20 years, only one ruling is reported regarding this issue, the National High Court (Audiencia Nacional) ruling of 23 February 2017. The peculiarities of this legal value merit further analysis, which could not be conducted here for reasons of space. See, recently, in this respect, Berdugo Gómez de la Torre (2020), *et passim*.

Such lack of enforcement contrasts with the range of criminal definitions, which, as has been pointed out in the case of corruption involving private individuals, could give rise to a myriad of behaviours, even punishing those causing slight harm to the legal value, inasmuch as they have not been expressly excluded from the precept's scope of application and no limit has been imposed in this respect.

In any event, what has been said so far is no obstacle to understanding that behaviours which seriously affect market competition should be criminally punished. As Terradillos Basoco (2008), p. 24 pointed out, "*ultima ratio* does not equate to *nulla ratio*". In other words, what has been criticised up to this point is the incorrect use of criminal law to protect the legal value in the crime under study, which does not mean that criminal law intervention to punish behaviours affecting the market should be rejected. It can and must do so. It can do so provided that, as has been shown, competition is a legal value that is indispensable to life in society, and it must do so when this is significantly attacked, and previous proceedings have proved insufficient. Failure to do so would indeed suggest that criminal law is somehow protective of so-called white-collar criminals, those who engage in economic crime. In other words, state *ius puniendi* intervention in economic matters is necessary so that it ceases to focus solely on the most disadvantaged strata of society (Berdugo Gómez de la Torre 2012, p. 211), as Sutherland noted in the early twentieth century.

5 Conclusions

In recent years, legislators have broadened the scope of criminal law intervention in relation to protecting market competition by incorporating new criminal definitions such as corruption involving private individuals or in international business transactions, and by extending those existing, such as the offence of price fixing. This has led this study to consider the legitimacy or otherwise of punitive expansion in this area. The following conclusions have been drawn in this respect:

1. Criminal protection of market competition presents two essential issues. First, the indeterminate nature of the concept of competition in itself makes it difficult to endow the legal value with any material content. Second, observance of the principles legitimising criminal law in democratic states governed by the rule of law. In this respect, it must be remembered that resorting to criminal law is only justified as a means of protecting interests that are indispensable to life in society (offense principle), and against the most severe attacks on them, insofar as an effective response cannot be provided by action preceding criminal law (minimal intervention principle).
2. The definition of market competition must be based on studies provided by economic theory, which states that competition is essential for the maximisation of social welfare. This is so because competition generates a series of efficiencies

(allocative, productive and dynamic) that precisely result in the maximisation of social welfare.
3. Market competition can be deemed a legal value worthy of criminal protection. There is no doubt that it is an indispensable legal value in today's society insofar as it is essential to maintain the constitutionally proclaimed economic order (social market economy). Where it cannot be protected by other branches of law (subsidiary nature of criminal law) and where it is gravely affected (fragmentary nature of criminal law), state *ius puniendi* is entitled to intervene.
4. The specific example discussed, corruption involving private individuals, presents certain legitimacy issues. Legislators have included this criminal definition in Criminal Code to cater for the demands of certain supranational bodies, particularly the European Union, but have done so without considering, or at least apparently, existing competition law (administrative law). The crime under consideration does not appear to observe the fragmentary nature of criminal law in that the criminal definition allows for certain behaviours to be penalised that are exempt from punishment under competition law due to their negligible harmfulness to the market. On the principle of subsidiarity, the experts consider the existing administrative sanctions for behaviours that restrict competition to be ineffective because of their limited deterrent effect, and thus call for criminal law intervention in this area on the grounds that criminal law is more dissuasive. It should be noted in this regard that this may be the case for a prison sentence (which must always observe the limits deriving from the principles of proportionality and re-socialisation), but not for a fine, either for natural persons or legal persons, as it may be even lighter in criminal law.
5. The crime of corruption involving private individuals is an instance of punitive excess typical of modern times. Of course, behaviours that gravely affect the market can and must be punished under criminal law where previous proceedings prove to be insufficient. Not to do so would be an indication of how discriminatory criminal law can be by failing to punish the behaviour of powerful people, the main players of economic crime, but to do so the principles of subsidiarity and fragmentarity must be observed, which are essential for designing rational criminal policy.

References

Abanto Vásquez MA (2010) Delitos contra el mercado, viejas prácticas, nuevas figuras: delitos contra la libre y leal competencia. In: Serrano-Piedecasas Fernández JR, Demetrio Crespo E (dirs) Cuestiones actuales de derecho penal empresarial. Colex, Madrid, pp 139–176

Artaza Varela O (2017) La colusión como forma de agresión a intereses dignos de protección por el Derecho Penal. Primera aproximación. Revista de Derecho XXX(2):339–366

Bajo M, Bacigalupo S (2010) Derecho penal económico, 2nd edn. Editorial universitaria Ramón Areces, Madrid

Baucells Lladós J (2013) Las penas previstas para la persona jurídica en la reforma penal de 2010. Un análisis crítico. Estudios Penales y Criminológicos XXXIII:175–218

Berdugo Gómez de la Torre I (1985) La tutela de la competencia en la propuesta de anteproyecto de nuevo código penal. In: Santos B (ed) La reforma penal: delitos socio-económicos. Servicio de publicaciones de la Facultad de Derecho, Madrid, pp 393–421
Berdugo Gómez de la Torre I (2012) Viejo y nuevo Derecho penal. Principios y desafíos del Derecho penal de hoy. Iustel, Madrid
Berdugo Gómez de la Torre I (2020) El soborno internacional: normas, obstáculos y propuestas. In: Demetrio Crespo E, (ed), De la Cuerda Martín M, García de la Torre García F (coords) Derecho penal económico y teoría del delito. Tirant lo Blanch, Valencia, pp 569–602
Berdugo Gómez de la Torre I et al (2010) Curso de Derecho penal. Parte General. Ediciones Experiencia, Madrid
Berdugo Gómez de la Torre I, Pérez Cepeda AI, Zúñiga Rodríguez L (2015) Lecciones y materiales para el estudio del Derecho penal. Iustel, Madrid
Bolea Bardón C (2013) El delito de corrupción privada. Bien jurídico, estructura típica e intervinientes. InDret. Revista para el análisis del Derecho 2:1–29. http://diposit.ub.edu/dspace/bitstream/2445/53524/1/624079.pdf. Last accessed 25 Apr 2021
Bustos Ramírez J (1987) Los bienes jurídicos colectivos. In: Bustos Ramírez J (dir) Control Social y sistema penal. PPU, Barcelona
Bustos Rubio M (2019) Los delitos de corrupción en los negocios. In: Gómez Pavón P, Bustos Rubio M, Herradón P (eds) Delitos económicos. Wolters Kluwer, Madrid, pp 235–256
Calvo Caravaca AL (2009) Derecho antitrust europeo. Tomo 1. Parte general. La competencia. Colex, Madrid
Cerina G, Bravo Vesga C (2009) La corrupción en el sector privado. Apuntes de derecho comparado e internacional. In: Romero Guzmán J, Rodríguez García N, Olivares Tramón JM (eds) Bueno gobierno y corrupción: algunas perspectivas. Pontificia Universidad Católica de Chile, Santiago de Chile, pp 379–447
Coffee JC Jr (1981) "No Soul to Damn: No Body to Kick": an unscandalized inquiry into the problem of corporate punishment. Mich Law Rev 79:386–459
Corcoy Bidasolo M (2014) Algunas cuestiones político-criminales sobre la corrupción privada. Límites y eficacia de los *compliance*. In: Mir Puig S, Corcoy Bidasolo M, Gómez Martín V (dirs), Hortal Ibarra JC, Valiente Ivañez V (coords) Responsabilidad de la empresa y compliance: programas de prevención, detección y reacción penal. BdF, Buenos Aires, pp 161–194
Costas Comesaña J (2017) La imposición de multas por conductas anticompetitivas en España. In: Martín-Laborda R (coord) La lucha contra las restricciones de la competencia. Sanciones y remedios en el ordenamiento español. Colex, Madrid, pp 11–78
De la Mata Barraco N, Dopico Gómez-Aller J, Lascuraín Sánchez JA, Nieto Martín A (2018) Derecho penal económico y de la empresa. Dykinson, Madrid
Demetrio Crespo E (2020) Derecho penal económico y teoría del delito: otra vuelta de tuerca. In: Demetrio Crespo E (ed), De la Cuerda Martín M, García de la Torre García F (coord) Derecho penal económico y teoría del delito. Tirant lo Blanch, Valencia, pp 17–45.
Díez Estella F (2016) La persecución internacional de los cárteles empresariales: entre laclemencia para los delatores y la criminalización de los directivos. Revista de fiscalidad internacional y negocios transnacionales, 31–27
Díez Estella F (2019) La aplicación privada del Derecho de la competencia: acciones de daños y pronunciamientos judiciales. Cuadernos de Derecho Transnacional 11(1):267–305. https://e-revistas.uc3m.es/index.php/CDT/article/view/4620. Last accessed 25 Apr 2021
Díez Ripollés JL (2005) El nuevo modelo penal de la seguridad ciudadana. Anuario de Filosofía del Derecho 22:13–52. https://www.boe.es/publicaciones/anuarios_derecho/abrir_pdf.php?id=ANU-F-2005-10001300052. Last accessed 5 Dec 2020
Doval Pais A (2020) La confusa armonización de los delitos de manipulación de mercado (art. 284 CP) by L.O. 1/2012. Estudios penales y criminológicos XL:113–178. http://rua.ua.es/dspace/handle/10045/106247. Last accessed 25 Apr 2021

Estrada i Cuadras A (2020) Protección de la propiedad, intelectual e industrial, del mercado y de los consumidores. In: Silva Sánchez JM (dir), Robles Planas R (coord) Lecciones de Derecho penal económico y de la empresa. Atelier, Barcelona, pp 495–570

Faraldo Cabana P (2013) ¿Es la multa una pena apropiada para las personas jurídicas? In: De la Cuesta Arzmendi JL, Pérez Machío AI, Ugartemendia Eceizabarrena JI (dir) Armonización penal en Europa. Instituto Vasco de Administración Pública, pp 77–113

Fikentscher W (1984) Las tres funciones del control de la economía (Derecho antimonopolio). Revista de Derecho Mercantil 172–173:475–477

Galán Muñoz A, Núñez Castaño E (2018) Manual de Derecho penal económico y de la empresa, 2nd edn. Tirant lo Blanch, Valencia

García-Verdugo Sales J (2016) Valoración económica de las sanciones a la competencia. Document AE-01/16(0428).2. CNMC. https://www.cnmc.es/sites/default/files/editor_contenidos/CNMC/DocumentosReferencia/Documento%20AE-01_16(0428).2.pdf. Last accessed 25 Apr 2021

Gil Nobajas MS (2015) El delito de corrupción en los negocios (art. 286 bis): análisis de la responsabilidad penal del titular de la empresa, el administrador de hecho y la persona jurídica en un modelo puro de competencia. Estudios penales y criminológicos XXV:567–624. https://revistas.usc.es/index.php/epc/article/view/2604. Last accessed 25 Apr 2021

Gili Pascual A (2007) Bases para la delimitación del ámbito típico en el delito de corrupción privada. Contribución al análisis del art. 286 bis del Código Penal según el Proyecto de reforma de 2007. Revista Electrónica de Ciencia Penal y Criminología 09(13):1–35. http://criminet.ugr.es/recpc/09/recpc09-13.pdf. Last accessed 25 Apr 2021

Gómez-Jara Díez C (2012) El delito de corrupción entre particulares (art. 286 bis). In: Silva Sánchez JM (dir), Pastor Muñoz N (coord) El nuevo Código Penal. Comentarios a la reforma. La Ley, Madrid

Gómez-Jara Díez C (2017) El delito de manipulación de mercado (arts. 284.2 y 284.3 CP). Tirant lo Blanch, Valencia

Gordillo Pérez L (2018) Constitución económica, ordoliberalismo y Unión Europea. De un derecho económico nacional a uno europeo. Revista de Derecho UNED 23:248–293. http://revistas.uned.es/index.php/RDUNED/article/view/24017. Last accessed 25 Apr 2021

Gordillo Pérez LI, Rodríguez Ortiz FR (2019) Constitución económica y gobernanza económica de la Unión Europea. Thomson Reuters, Aranzadi

Gutiérrez Rodríguez M, Ortiz de Urbina Gimeno, I (2017) Conductas restrictivas de la competencia y Derecho penal. In: Martín-Laborda R (coord). La lucha contra las restricciones de la competencia. Sanciones y remedios en el ordenamiento español. Colex, Madrid, pp 79–121

Herrero Giménez R (2017) El tipo de injusto en el delito de corrupción entre particulares. Doctoral thesis, Universidad Complutense de Madrid. https://eprints.ucm.es/48108/1/T40042.pdf. Last accessed 25 Apr 2021

Jescheck HH, Weigend T (1996) Lehrbuch des Strafrechts. Allgemeiner Teil, 5th edn. Duncker & Humblot, Berlin

Laguna de Paz JJ (2019) Ámbito de aplicación del Derecho de la competencia. Revista de Administración Pública 208:17–49. http://www.cepc.gob.es/publicaciones/revistas/revistaselectronicas?IDR=1&IDN=1410&IDA=38613. Last accessed 25 Apr 2021

Martínez-Buján Pérez C (2016) Derecho penal económico y de la empresa. Parte general, 5th edn. Tirant lo Blanch, Valencia

Mendoza Buergo B (2001) El Derecho penal en la sociedad del riesgo. Civitas, Madrid

Mendoza Calderón S (2017) La corrupción en el sector farmacéutico: análisis de su incidencia en el ámbito europeo y su trascendencia en el derecho penal español. Revista General de Derecho Penal 27:1–45

Mir Puig S (2006a) Bien jurídico y bien jurídico penal como límites del ius puniendi. In: Mir Puig S (dir) Estado, pena y delito. BdF, Montevideo, Buenos Aires

Mir Puig S (2006b) Derecho penal. Parte general, 7th edn. Reppertor, Barcelona

Motta M (2004) Competition policy. Theory and practice. Cambridge University Press, New York

Navarro Frías I, Melero Bosch LV (2011) Corrupción entre particulares y tutela del mercado. InDret. Revista para el análisis del Derecho 4:1–40. https://indret.com/corrupcion-entre-particulares-y-tutela-del-mercado/. Last accessed 25 Apr 2021

Otero González P (2013) Corrupción entre particulares (Delito de). Eunomia. Revista en Cultura de la Legalidad 3:174–183.

Paredes Castañón JM (2003) Los delitos de peligro como técnica de incriminación en el Derecho penal económico: bases político-criminales. Revista de Derecho penal y Criminología 11:95–164. http://revistas.uned.es/index.php/RDPC/article/view/24840. Last accessed 25 Apr 2021

Paredes Castañón JM (2019) El mercado como objeto de regulación y protección jurídica: el caso de las restricciones verticales a la competencia. Revista de Derecho penal y Criminología 22:107–158. http://revistas.uned.es/index.php/RDPC/article/view/26441. Last accessed 25 Apr 2021

Quintero Olivares G (2020) Estado actual de la teoría del delito y Derecho penal económico. In: Demetrio Crespo E (ed), De la Cuerda Martín M, García de la Torre García F (coord) Derecho penal económico y teoría del delito. Tirant lo Blanch, Valencia, pp 50–63

Roxin C (2006) Derecho penal. Parte general (trans: Luzón Peña DM, Díaz y García Conlledo M, de Vicente Remesal J). Civitas, Madrid

Sánchez Bernal J (2017) El delito de corrupción entre particulares. Especial referencia a la corrupción en el deporte. [Unpublished doctoral thesis]. Universidad de Salamanca

Sánchez Bernal J (2018) El delito de corrupción deportiva tras la reforma de 2015. Tirant lo Blanch, Valencia

Sánchez Bernal J (2020) Algunos *highlights* sobre el delito de corrupción privada en España. Entre la necesidad y la exasperación legislativa. In: Bustos Rubio M, Abadías Selma A (dir) Una década de reformas penales. Análisis de diez años de cambios en el Código Penal (2010–2020). Bosch Editor, Barcelona, pp 515–533

Santana Vega DM (2000) La protección penal de los bienes jurídicos colectivos. Dykinson, Madrid

Signes de Mesa JI, Fernández Torres I, Fuentes Naharro M (2013) Derecho de la competencia. Thomson Reuters, Civitas Cizur

Silva Sánchez JM (1992) Aproximación al Derecho penal contemporáneo. Bosch Editor, Barcelona

Silva Sánchez JM (2006) La expansión del Derecho penal. Edisofer, Madrid

Solernou Sanz S (2018) La ordenación jurídica del mercado de transportes de mercancías por carretera. Thomson Reuters, Aranzadi

Soto Navarro S (2003) La protección penal de los bienes colectivos en la sociedad moderna. Granada, Comares

Stucke M (2012) What is competition? In: Zimmer D (ed) The goals of competition law. Edward Elgar, Cheltenham, pp 27–52

Terradillos Basoco J (2008) Concepto y método del Derecho penal económico. In: Serrano-Piedecasas JR, Demetrio Crespo E (dir) Cuestiones actuales de Derecho penal económico. Colex, Madrid, pp 11–35

Terradillos Basoco J (2020) Aporofobia y plutofilia. La deriva jánica de la política criminal contemporánea. Bosch Editor, Barcelona

Whish R, Bailey D (2015) Competition law, 8th edn. Oxford University Press, Oxford

Zabala López-Gómez C (2011) Introducción: la autonomía de los delitos bursátiles. La Ley 18560(2011):1–82

The Impact of Soft Law on the Expansion of Criminal Law

Mónica de la Cuerda Martín

Abstract The basic elements on which this contribution is based are: on the one hand, the recognition of the basic characteristics of soft law instruments and the appreciation of their denaturalization. On the other hand, the analysis of the expansive phenomenon of criminal law and its link with globalization and the risk society. Their joint analysis will allow me to determine the effective incidence of the soft law in the expansion of criminal law, in the light of what has happened in the case of self-laundering of capital which, together with the criminalization of the conducts of using and possessing (Art. 301 CC), and tax fraud being considered a prior offense (Art. 305 CC), generates important breaches in one of the most basic and elementary principles of Criminal Law of the Rule of Law, the *non bis in idem* principle.

1 Introduction

Could the non-regulatory legal instruments (soft law) have an impact on the expansion-modernization of (economic) criminal law? This question is the backbone of my contribution. With it, I intend to offer some insight not only into the complexity of these instruments, but also into the expansive phenomenon itself. This will be done through one of the most illustrative and controversial examples, particularly the introduction of self-laundering in our legal system. For this analysis, I will start from the following premises:

I. Duality of Legal Instruments in the International Legal Order Without prejudice to their different manifestations, we dispose at this level of instruments of hard

---

Professional mailing address; Universidad de Castilla-La Mancha, Facultad de Ciencias Jurídicas y Sociales de Toledo, Cobertizo de San Pedro Mártir, 45071, Toledo (España).

M. de la Cuerda Martín (✉)
Faculty of Legal and Social Sciences, University of Castilla–La Mancha, Toledo, Spain
e-mail: Monica.CuerdaMartin@uclm.es

E. Demetrio Crespo et al. (eds.), *Crisis of the Criminal Law in the Democratic Constitutional State*, Legal Studies in International, European and Comparative Criminal Law 6, https://doi.org/10.1007/978-3-031-13413-5_13

law and soft law that have, respectively, the ability to direct or influence national legal systems, and whose characteristics will be defined by exclusion.

The denaturalization of the specific features of hard law and soft law instruments and their conversion into tacitly binding instruments through the recognition of a pseudo-sanctioning system, lead us to enter into the study of a dichotomy that, as far as I can see, has not yet been addressed, and which could eventually be identified with the necessary differentiation between *dogmatic soft law (should be) and real-practical soft law (is).*

II. The Expansive Tendency of Our Legislation Although its origin must be placed in the promulgation of the Criminal Code (hereinafter, CC) of 1995, we must bear in mind that, with the passage of time, this expansive tendency has done nothing but consolidate due, among other reasons, to the increasing globalization and the so-called risk society. This leads us to consider a difficult balance between the need to protect legal assets (existing and new) and the dangers it poses to the protection of the most essential guarantees of the criminal law of Constitutional State.

All this is particularly relevant in the field of economic criminal law, where its continuous expansion, the international demand for reforms and the relevant role played by the Financial Action Task Force (hereinafter, FATF) make it a paradigmatic example of the problems addressed here.

III. The Impact of Soft Law on the Expansion of Criminal Law Thanks to a joint vision of the above premises, it is possible to advance that, in fact, the FATF Recommendations (soft law) have the capacity to direct, and not only to influence the feeling of national legal systems, to the point that, by virtue of its content, criminal law expands with the inclusion of new criminal offenses, such as self-laundering which, moreover, can lead to breaches of essential principles such as *non bis in idem*.

2 Soft Law: Concept and Scope

2.1 General Approach to Soft Law

The term soft law was coined by Lord Macnair and, despite its various interpretations,[1] it can currently be understood as a lax, soft or flexible law characterized by being identified as a set of instruments emanating from international bodies or

[1]Initially, the term soft law was used "to describe normative statements formulated as abstract principles that became operative through their judicial application." See, in this sense, Mazuellos Bellido (2004), p. 2: Alarcón García (2010), p. 274.

Barberis has also enunciated, in my opinion with great accuracy, the different meanings that this term can have. In this sense, Barberis (1994), pp. 282–283.

organizations endowed with authority and which, lacking binding effectiveness and a sanctioning system, can take different forms, such as recommendations, principles, advice, declarations, or regulatory guidelines.[2]

The main objective of this type of instrument is identified with the search for international consensus,[3] the voluntary adoption of these regulations being, in Mostacci's opinion, synonymous with integration into the international community.[4] This denotes, according to Feler Alan, the incipient intention of directing efforts towards the achievement of certain objectives through common expectations of conduct.[5]

This being the case, I understand that we can configure soft law as a "*final*" instrument aimed at establishing general guidelines for action to guarantee the achievement of a specific objective, but which, at the same time, is sufficiently "*open*" to leave it in the hands of the states the power to carry it out in the manner that best suits their constitutional parameters and the requirements and basic principles of a respectful and protective Constitutional State. Consequently, when states accept the content of these instruments, they would only be committing themselves to take the necessary measures to achieve a common overall objective (for example, the fight against money laundering in a given area), but the authorities would keep the sovereignty to decide how and when establish the general tips of the soft law.

However, it should be noted that at the international level we also have hard law tools, understood as "those instruments or general practices of a mandatory nature whose non-compliance may be demanded by the institutional means of conflict resolution and lead to the international responsibility of the State."[6]

By virtue of this, and without prejudice to later nuances, it is possible to appreciate the existence of a phenomenological binomial derived from the contraposition between hard law and soft law, with these two concepts being antagonistic points whose own characteristics shall be defined by exclusion[7] and having in common only the institutional order from which they emanate. In any case, this does not mean understanding that they are non-interrelated watertight compartments, since the international legal system describes a series of legal techniques[8] designed to convert those instruments that are born as soft law into hard law, so that the latter can be incorporated with full effects into national legal systems. However, this

---

[2] Garrido Gómez (2017), p. 4.

[3] Notwithstanding the above and considering not only their exceptional nature but also the fact that they are characterized by being atypical acts and instruments, we must emphasize that they are also present in Spanish public law through different forms and categories, such as circulars, instructions or service letters (Sarmiento 2006, p. 231).

[4] Mostacci (2008), p. 90.

[5] Feler (2015), p. 292.

[6] Del Toro Huerta (2006), p. 528.

[7] On the conceptual differences between hard law and soft law: Sánchez Cáceres (2019), p. 468.

[8] It deals specifically with: (1) Incorporation in hard law; (2) Incorporation by reference or resubmission; 3) Incorporation by endorsement of the legislator. For more information on the content of these techniques: Sarmiento (2006), p. 249.

conversion faces a temporal problem, in other words, it "arrives late," since in general the conversion of soft law into hard law takes place after the introduction into national legal systems of the content of the soft law. This is due, as will be seen below, to the denaturalization of the characteristics of the latter, thus turning them into legal instruments with a tactical binding nature.

2.2 Elements of Soft Law

In the words of Garrido Gómez, soft law can be described as "new governance arrangements"[9] which, while having a normative legal nature,[10] do not have enforceability, uniformity, justiciability, sanctions and/or authorities that require them.[11] It is important to appreciate that the main characteristics of this typology of instruments are derived from the above-mentioned conceptualization.

First, *they are instruments that are not legally binding*, Mostacci, Ramajoli, del Toro Huerta and Mazuelos Bellido[12] reflect the practically unanimous opinion of the doctrine that they are not binding on the states, which is why they normally take the legal form of a recommendation. However, for Mazuelos Bellido this binding force can be questioned.[13] This, in my opinion, is a nuance of great transcendence and, to understand it, it is necessary to bear in mind the rest of the characteristics of this institution, since this questioning is a consequence, precisely, of its denaturalization.

However, the fact that soft law is not binding does not prevent us from understanding that it is *endowed with authority*. This authority derives precisely from the fact that it has been drafted by internationally relevant bodies or organizations. For this reason, soft law would acquire the authority of the institution that dictates it.

[9]On the relationship between soft law and governance: Laporta San Miguel (2014), pp. 51–56 and 60.

[10]There is an intense debate about the understanding, or not, of soft law as a source of international law, the answer to which depends to some extent on the interpretation given to Art. 38 of the ICJ Statute. Thus, while for Alarcón García soft law under a strict interpretation cannot be considered a source of international law (Alarcón García (2010), p. 528), for Escudero Alday, through a moderate interpretation, it can be considered as such as long as it is introduced into the legal system through a hard law rule (Escudero Alday (2012), p. 109 et seq.). The third option would be a *flexible interpretation* by virtue of which soft law can be considered a source of international law, insofar as it is a consequence of the will of the states with respect to a specific global problem.

[11]Garrido Gómez (2017), p. 56.

In similar terms Escudero Alday also expresses himself, for whom soft law is "a formula of normative production that is placed next to the traditional forms of legal regulation and that at this initial moment can be characterized through the following notes: it responds to the scheme of advice or recommendation, proposes and does not impose the performance of behaviors" (Escudero Alday (2012), p. 128).

[12]In this sense, see, Mostacci (2008), p. 2-3; Romajoli (2017), p. 150; Del Toro Huerta (2006), p. 519; Sperti (2012), p. 108.

[13]Mazuellos Bellido (2004), p. 2.

More specifically, soft law can come both from the European Union's own bodies[14] and from international organizations aimed, in general terms, at ordering our life in society (FATF, OECD, WHO, IMF, etc.). Particularly, the main drawbacks arise when soft law is issued by such organizations which, without prejudice to the important role they play, in my opinion, the instruments issued by them (such is the case of the FATF) would give them a greater capacity to affect national legal systems in a greater measure than they would dogmatically be entitled to do.

The third characteristic of soft law is identified with the *(formal) absence of a sanctioning system and of authorities that require it*. Indeed, if we analyze the wording of these instruments, we cannot find a sanctioning system established in them *strictu sensu*, hence, it is formally said to be lacking in the same at face value. With all, if we place ourselves in a more practical, more real context, we will be able to appreciate that, in reality, they do have such a sanctioning system, inasmuch as failure by the states to comply with the content established therein entails the imposition of "honorary" sanctions based on international discredit and public condemnation.[15] Sanctions which, by the way, can be even more harmful than economic sanctions. This is what authors such as Alarcón, Caamaño Anido or Calderón Carrero[16] have described as soft coercion and would come to be identified with the very channels of sanction of soft law when the traditional formulas are not applicable.[17] An additional problem derived from this type of non-quantifiable sanctions is the possible *violation* of essential principles such as, for example, the principle of proportionality. The indirect consequences of international marking as a non-compliant country are difficult to quantify and could entail, among other things, a slowdown or partial suppression in the arrival or establishment of capital.

---

[14] Under Article 249 of the Treaty on European Union, the European Parliament, the Council and the Commission have the power to issue non-binding recommendations and opinions, i.e., soft law.

[15] Ibánez is of this opinion when he says: "these are norms that lack one of the elements of the concept of legal norm, that is, the legal effect or consequence, which is also usually called 'sanction'; what happens if the proposition that determines what must be done in a specific situation, what the norm orders, is not fulfilled. These 'soft, green or flexible' norms, come to recover for the legal field the basic characteristic of social norms, endowed with a tacit sanction that only entails to a greater or lesser extent a discredit or loss of public consideration" (Ibánez García (2018), p. 3).

[16] More specifically, Caamaño Anido and Calderón Carrero, after recognizing the existence of modifications to national legal systems in the light of soft law provisions, understand that, in those cases in which states do not carry them out, "they may suffer certain types of countermeasures by the organizations and institutions that have dictated them, such as, for example, inclusion in a 'black list', economic sanctions, obstruction of operations with the defaulting country by a block of countries that establish legislation to that effect, or simply the suspension of payments of an international credit" (Caamaño Anido (2002), pp. 245–288).

[17] Alarcón García (2010), p. 277.

2.3 *Dogmatic Soft Law (Should Be) vs. Real-Practical Soft Law (Is): An Analysis of the Interdependence of the Basic Characteristics of Soft Law Instruments*

Of all the aforementioned characteristics, perhaps the most relevant for the purposes of establishing the differentiation between a dogmatic soft law and a real soft law is the third one, that is, the absence of a formal system of sanctions, insofar as it would be identified as the unification of the two previous features and, at the same time, it is the one that allows for a better understanding.

Honorary sanctions would be a tactical recognition of the binding nature of soft law, and it would be possible to appreciate the existence of a pseudo-sanctioning system derived from the need for recommendations, advice or principles to be respected by all states, thus becoming binding due to the authority of the institution that issues them. Consequently, and although authority and binding nature are not synonymous, they become directly proportional: the greater the relevance or international authority of the organization issuing the soft law instrument, the greater the binding nature. With this in mind, it is possible to differentiate between:

- *Dogmatic soft law (should be).* This would take the form of the definition of these instruments: They are endowed with authority, but this does not imply either a binding nature or the existence of an economic and/or honorary sanctioning system.
- *Real-practical soft law (is).* it implies the denaturalization of the characteristics of these instruments, thus showing a tactical binding nature and a *pseudo-sanctioning* system of an honorific nature. In reality, this *practical* soft law would differ from hard law in that the latter is born with a real binding will and the former acquires it later.

At present, unfortunately, we would be moving towards the acceptance of a *real-practical soft law* that would place us outside the margin of what this type of instrument should be. This "*step*" would appear to be a consequence of the increasing interdependence between states and those who dictate it.

In my opinion, it is not appropriate to give soft law an implicit binding nature based on the reinterpretation of its own and configuring characteristics (should be), since this would be recognizing its capacity to direct and not only influence the meaning of our domestic legal system and, beyond the fact that the techniques for converting soft law into hard law are being ignored, this would endanger in a quite serious way the validity of some of the most basic and essential principles of a state governed by the Rule of Law, which must be understood, in the words of Bacigalupo, as "a directive principle that requires a concretization of its details in each situation" and which is characterized, continues the aforementioned author "–at least– by guaranteeing the security of all citizens, through a linking of the updating of the State to known legal norms and principles of justice in such a way that it is in any case understandable."[18]

2.4 FATF Recommendations: An Example of the Denaturalization of Soft Law

The FATF's main objective is to set standards and promote the effective implementation of legal, regulatory and operational measures to combat money laundering, the financing of terrorism and the financing of the proliferation of weapons of mass destruction, and other threats to the integrity of the international financial system,[19] and to this end it issues its well-known 40 Recommendations, which exert an important and undeniable influence on the legislation of its member states, becoming a success of international compliance.[20]

With this in mind, the question arises: *are the FATF recommendations a soft law instrument?* The answer is yes and, moreover, they are identified as a clear example of the denaturalization of these legal instruments, placing them in the realm of practical soft law. More specifically:

I. They Take the Legal Form of a Recommendation But Are Mandatory To recommend means "to give advice" and not to force or bind with respect to a given issue. In the case of FATF recommendations, we can observe how recommendatory language is interspersed with language of a binding nature, such as "countries should"[21] (recommendation) or "countries must"[22] (imposition).

II. Absence of a Sanctioning System and of Authorities That Require Them In its literal wording no sanctioning system has been established which would suggest that it is intended, at least dogmatically, not to be binding. However, the issuance of verification or evaluation reports, based on predefined and objective parameters, on the level of compliance and the quality of the measures adopted by the states in the fight against money laundering would suggest the opposite.

The FATF thus has a system of indirect sanctions by means of which, according to authors such as Blanco Cordero, has achieved a strategy of publicly pointing out those countries that do not comply with the recommendations, that is, compliance

---

[18] Bacigalupo (2005), p. 103.

[19] Information extracted from the following web link (in Spanish): https://www.uiaf.gov.co/asuntos_internacionales/organizaciones_internacionales/grupo_accion_financiera_7114 (Retrieved 14.04.2021).

[20] Blanco Cordero (2012), p. 173.

[21] "Introduction to the FATF Recommendations: The FATF Recommendations set an international standard that countries should implement through measures adapted to their particular circumstances."

[22] Recommendation B. 3. Money laundering crime "Countries should criminalize [. . .]"

with the recommendations has been achieved primarily for reputational reasons.[23] For this reason, it could be said that the sanction imposed by the FATF will consist of the issuance of a negative report.[24]

The appreciation of this sanction implies understanding that the recommendations must cease to be considered as such to be understood as mandatory (tacit binding effect), this being a consequence of the authority held by the organization in question. Hence, it can be concluded that the FATF Recommendations are identified as a hard law instrument masked in the legal form of soft law, i.e., they are *real-practical soft law*.

3 The Expansion of Criminal Law

3.1 The Expansive Phenomenon: Particularly the Case of Economic Criminal Law

Criminal expansion consists, broadly speaking, in the increase of the punitive intervention of the state and is characterized, according to Demetrio Crespo, "by three main features: administrativization,[25] regionalization/globalization and the progressive deconstruction of the liberal paradigm."[26] Thus, both criminal law in general, and economic criminal law in particular, have been placed under the umbrella of the so-called "modern criminal Law."[27]

---

[23] Blanco Cordero (2012), p. 173.

[24] In the latest FATF report evaluating Spain, the FATF gave it a score of 10 out of 11, which places it "as one of the countries with the safest money laundering prevention systems"

(https://www.mineco.gob.es/stfls/mineco/prensa/ficheros/noticias/2018/191204_np_2gafi.pdf) (Last consulted 07.11.2020).

[25] With respect to this feature, a parallel dilemma could be posed, which I will only indicate, and which would involve answering the following question: *are all the conducts typified in the Criminal Code really worthy of reproach?* In my opinion, no. It is necessary to recognize the existence of a transfer between the administrative (sanctioning) and criminal systems, which has only blurred the limits of the controversial boundary between the administrative illicit and the criminal infraction.

In this regard: Terradillos Basoco (2006), p. 70; Sotomayor Acosta (2008), p. 152; Navarro Cardoso 2020, p. 268 et seq.

[26] Demetrio Crespo (2020), p. 38.

[27] This would be a consequence of the fact that, "for reasons other than prevention or retribution, it strives to cover all corners of antisocial behavior" (Bajo Fernández (2013), p. 407). In similar terms, Díez Ripollés takes the position that "the modernization of criminal law is a consequence of the accommodation of the new post-industrial societies to the social rule of law model," and where, in his opinion, "the increases in criminal intervention derive from the emergence of new social realities and conflicts that highlight the existence of relevant collective interests whose criminal protection is justified" (Díez Ripolles (2005), p. 01:7). On the case of economic criminal law: Gracia Martín (2003), p. 65.

In this regard, it is regrettable that our 1995 CC decided to embark on this path. This path has been progressively consolidated due to the multiple and successive reforms, which in the case of economic criminal law have mainly been the result of international requirements,[28] which have led to the introduction of such controversial figures as the extension of money laundering to the conduct of using and possessing and the punishment of self-laundering.

This has caused the current economic criminal law, as Bajo Fernández argues, to participate in "the particularities to enter into the criticizable condition of expansive criminal law and symbolic criminal law, and its legitimacy and justification will therefore depend on how it manages to avoid the negative characteristics of both categories."[29] expressions that according to the aforementioned author define the dangerous situation to which the criminal law of parliamentary democracy has arrived.[30]

However, without prejudice to the fact that the expansive phenomenon is a fact that we can and should criticize, it is no less true, according to Corcoy Bidasolo, that it is a phenomenon that we can hardly avoid,[31] insofar as criminal law has gone beyond its traditional role of individual risk prevention to become an instrument for the management of social problems that,[32] in a globalized world such as the one we live in, require a joint and uniform response.

In this sense, it would be possible to delimit the expansive phenomenon of the so-called *minimum criminal law*, responsible for reducing criminal law to the minimum necessary is needed "to avoid informal social violence, such as possible spontaneous punitive reactions by aggrieved citizens."[33] In contrast to this axiological model, Demetrio Crespo recognizes that "there is currently a phenomenon of expansion of the scope of what is punishable in clear contradiction with the pretension of reducing criminal law to a hard core corresponding in essence to the so-called 'classic criminal Law' and which would be aimed at protecting new legal assets characteristic of post-industrial society." Thus—for this author—"the axiological postulates of the minimum criminal law model seem to impose themselves, then, on the demands of criminal intervention coming from a society characterized as a modern risk society."[34]

---

[28] This is made clear by Bajo Fernandez, when he says "many economic crimes have arisen due to international pressure from technocratic officials ignorant of the principles of criminal law. The point is that these same officials who are tutors of international norms, when they take up the tasks of government in their own countries, invoke the norms that they themselves developed in international organizations to force their annexation to domestic law. Thus, crimes as debatable in their conception or scope as money laundering have been incorporated into Spanish criminal law" (Bajo Fernández (2013), pp. 409–410).

[29] *Ibíd.*, p. 409.

[30] *Ibíd.*, p. 407

[31] Felip and Saborit (2010), p. 64.

[32] Felip and Saborit (2010), p. 64.

[33] Demetrio Crespo (2020), p. 34.

[34] Demetrio Crespo (2020), p. 36.

I agree with Demetrio Crespo,[35] in that it is not possible to understand minimum criminal law in the terms of classical criminal law,[36] but we must recognize that, as a consequence of globalization, new risks have arisen that require protection and that force us to modernize and adapt our criminal law. Today we should opt for a minimum criminal law that responds to the need to protect all the interests that are currently at risk and which are inevitably not the same as they were, for example, 50 years ago. The problem lies in the tendency to criminalize, and expand criminal law, not only beyond what is necessary, but also in the fact that this expansion is not carried out in accordance with the correct use of adequate legal-regulatory instruments (see FATF Recommendations).

Consequently, following Corcoy Bidasolo, there would be no choice but to ask ourselves "what criminal Law we want -should be- and above all, what guaranteeing and 'average' criminal Law we can achieve -is-."[37]

Precisely, the crime of money laundering has been described, according to Abel Souto, as a clear expansionist example that forgetting the principle of subsidiarity breaks with a "guaranteeing criminal Law," but also transforms the overflowing type of money laundering into a genuine representative of the criminal law of the enemy.[38] More specifically, the main modifications introduced in this criminal type are: on the one hand, the extension of the typical conducts of possessing and using. [39] And on the other hand, the punishment of self-laundering, thus arising the main problems when the joint application of both occurs, that is, in those cases of self-laundering in which the typical conduct of possession or use is pursued, which are precisely the cases in which there is a breach of essential principles, as we will see in later moments.

Be that as it may, we are in a position to recognize that all this punitive intensification of which economic criminal law is the object places us in a plane of enormous complexity in the application of criminal types[40] and, consequently, we

---

[35] In the same sense: Jímenez Díaz (2014), p. 08:3.

[36] According to Díez Ripollés "classic criminal law would remain anchored in the protection of the catalog of traditional legal goods and where the usual and rigorous criteria of imputation and guarantees for the alleged offender would continue to govern" (Díez Ripolles (2005), p. 01:7).

[37] Corcoy-Bidasolo (2012), pp. 46–47.

[38] The reason for this would lie, according to this author, in the fact that "it punishes with disproportionate and unjustifiable penalties, behaviors far removed from the endangerment of the legal right and derogating or reducing the guarantees of the accused, transmutes it, within the framework of a logic of emergency or securitarian discourse, incompatible with the demands of a democratic *ius puniendi*, in one of the most clamorous examples of the sociotechnological foundation of a criminal Law converted into a political instrument with a breakdown of constitutional values and principles, into a tool to investigate and prosecute anomalous patrimonial situations" (Abel Souto (2016), p. 124).

[39] On the content of both types of conduct: Ibid., p. 127 et seq.

[40] More specifically, according to Quintero Olivares, this complexity of application is due to the large number of exceptions or variations, which, in his opinion, and due to an amalgam of complex causes, gives rise to the assertion that it is disfigured (Quintero Olivares (2020), p. 50).

are forced to rework the traditional theory of crime[41] to adapt it not only to the emerging typical conducts, but also to those traditional ones that have been the object of reformulation/modernization.[42]

Notwithstading, this does not mean opting for the creation of a new criminal law,[43] but only the adaptation of the existing one to the needs arising from the evolution of economic criminal law. To this effect, three options could be considered: (1) Create a new general part within the Spanish CC, different from the existing one, in which these necessary reformulations would be established; (2) Given that the problems in the field of economic criminal law are due to the attempt to apply doctrinal and jurisprudential interpretations typical of traditional criminal law, the solution would involve a criminal legal awareness that certain traditional institutions or consolidated doctrines cannot be applied as they are known, but must be adapted; (3) Opting for a model like the Italian model of specific complementary legislation in which all the economic criminal law and the administrative laws that complete it are collected, remembering that most of them are blank criminal types.

Of these options, first, I would rule out the second one, since I consider it to be a utopia that would be against discretion and would constrain the judiciary to solve certain problems in the field of economic criminal law through specific doctrines and interpretations.

Between the first and the third, I would favor the latter. I would thus opt for the enactment of a special law that breaks down the subsystems into which criminal law is composed and provides legal certainty in this complex area, which in turn would mean recognizing that the current structures of the theory of crime are not sufficient to deal with its intense problems. However, the solution is not so simple and the justification must not be so brief, since in parallel a series of problems would be generated that are difficult to solve, and which for obvious reasons I cannot address here but simply state.

---

[41] See, in this regard, Gracia Martín (2003), pp. 86–88; Martinez - Buján Pérez (2014), p. 62.

[42] Martínez - Buján, among other authors, is of this opinion when he states: "one of the most important issues that have arisen as a result of this phenomenon of expansion is the fact that a situation of tension has arisen, when trying to project on the new socioeconomic crimes general principles and dogmatic structures that were developed for the exegesis of traditional crimes, when the criminal law had not yet begun its modern phase of expansion to the protection of new legal goods" (Martinez - Buján Pérez (2014), p. 62).

[43] Quintero Olivares takes the opposite view when he understands that, as a result of the problems and specialties posed by economic criminal law, it has been preferred to "renounce the traditional theory of crime and admit that we are dealing with 'another criminal law', such as, for example, military criminal law. Thus we would have a criminal subsystem, in which there would be a special 'General Part' for economic crimes, at the center of which would be a reformulated theory of crime, in which all the particularities of economic crimes would be inserted, including general problems that are especially important for economic crime, such as, for example, the criminal liability of legal entities" (Quintero Olivares (2020), p. 51).

3.2 *The Criminal Expansion of Globalization and Its Relationship with the Society of Risk*

Allusion has already been made to globalization[44] as one of the main causes of criminal expansion and to the close relationship between it and the so-called society of risk that is based on "the observation of a set of social realities that could perhaps be summarized in three main blocks: (1) The generalization in modern society of new risks, affecting large groups and that could be described as artificial [. . .]; (2) There are growing difficulties in attributing responsibility for such risks to certain individuals or groups of people [. . .]; (3) Risk-generating activities are intertwined with one another, so that risk control is not only beyond one's control, but it is also unclear in whose hands it lies [. . .]; (4) Risk-generating activities are intertwined with one another, so that risk control is not only beyond control, but it is also unclear in whose hands it lies [. . .]"[45]

In other words, supranational economic integration, the evolution of markets, cybercrime and transnational organized crime[46] are concrete social risks of globalization, without which there would have been less need to criminalize new offenses or reform pre-existing ones. Moreover, given the characteristics of this type of crime, in general terms, a coordinated and joint fight by a plurality of states is required, hence the need to resort to supranational legal instruments that have the capacity to direct (hard law) or influence (soft law) the feeling and the unanimous response of the different countries to a specific global problem.

For this reason, authors such as Silva Sanchez understand that the fundamental objective of the criminal law of globalization is to provide a uniform or, at least, harmonious response to transnational crime that avoids the creation of "*legal-criminal paradises,*" since the existence of such "*paradises*" is particularly dysfunctional when it comes to combating a type of crime in which the place and time of the intervention of the main leaders of the organizations can be perfectly available.[47]

I believe that at this point it is of interest to bring up the statement by Demetrio Crespo when he says: "The debate about the suitability of criminal Law to protect collective legal goods has been taken to its ultimate consequences in the framework of the political-criminal and dogmatic discussion about the expansion of criminal Law in the 'society of risk' as a consequence of the transformation of socio-economic structures in post-industrial society, which has led to a very important punitive inflation." [48] This, from my perspective, could not be more accurate. The

[44] On the concept of globalization: Romeo Maldana (2012), pp. 314–314.

[45] Díez Ripolles (2005), pp. 01:3–01:4.

In similar terms: Schünemann (1996), pp. 30–31; Jímenez Díaz (2014), p. 08:2; May (2012), pp. 304,306.

[46] More specifically, the relationship between transnational organized crime and the phenomenon of globalization is highlighted by authors such as: Terradillos Basoco (2006), pp. 91 et seq. Donini (2003), p. 96.

[47] Silva Sánchez (1999), p. 72.

[48] Demetrio Crespo (2020), p. 37.

evolution of the social and economic structures inherent in the transformation of post-industrial society towards worldwide globalization has led to the emergence of collective legal assets (see the socio-economic order in the case of money laundering) which have inevitably led to an increase in the number of criminal offenses. However, as noted above, this criminal inflation does not necessarily have to be on the margins of minimum criminal law, understood in the sense of punishing the minimum necessary for the proper protection of legal assets, whether traditional or modern (socio-economic order, for example).

But *is any expansion of criminal law an evil in itself against which we must fight because it implies the violation of essential guarantees?* Demetrio Crespo reminds us that "the modernization of criminal Law is necessary and, moreover, unstoppable. There has been a transformation of criminality that undoubtedly entails a change in the legal approaches that must deal with it"[49] and, indeed, I am of the same opinion. We cannot say that every criminal expansion is "harmful," since sometimes it may be justified insofar as it is necessary to protect new interests at risk that were unimaginable years ago. For this reason, and briefly, it is necessary to differentiate between the different types of expansion:

I. Extensive Expansion vs. Intensive Expansion while the former consists of the introduction of criminal types derived from the need to protect new legal assets characteristic of the current society of risk. In this sense, in the opinion of Demetrio Crespo, this type of expansion would refer to "that which seeks a certain democratization of criminal prosecution in the face of economic determinism."[50] *Intensive expansion* is characterized, among other aspects, by enhancing the profile of the perpetrator as opposed to the seriousness of a specific act, a severe increase in penalties or a hardening of the penitentiary execution, its most acute manifestation being the *criminal law of the enemy,*[51] in short, it would be the one that supposes an intensification of punitivism.

In similar terms, Jimenez Díaz takes a similar position, for whom "Current criminal law is a law in expansion as a response to the society of risk, so that what comes to be described as expansion of criminal law is basically linked to its use to defend modern society from the new dangers of the current post-industrial era" (Jímenez Díaz (2014), p. 08:3).

[49] Demetrio Crespo (2020), p. 69.

[50] Demetrio Crespo (2014), p. 5.

[51] Felip and Saborit (2010), p. 65.

For Demetrio Crespo, "The criminal law of the enemy is that which seeks to strip certain subjects of the category of citizens, who must be treated as mere 'sources of danger', who must be neutralized at any cost" and "is a consequence, among other factors, of the symbolic use of criminal Law and of the crisis of the Social State itself" and can thus "be identified without too much difficulty with a regressive current, which lacks constitutional legitimacy" (Demetrio Crespo (2020) pp. 15,17,38).

However, as the aforementioned author argues, "the expansion/modernization of criminal Law and the criminal Law of the enemy, must in principle be adequately differentiated because while the former focuses mainly on the field of economic criminal law, the latter mainly affects organized crime and terrorism." However – continues Demetrio Crespo – "neither are phenomena to be treated

II. Unreasonable or Unjustified Expansion vs. Justified Expansion the first is that which implies, or may imply, the breakdown of the guarantees of a state governed by the rule of law. On the other hand, the second would be identified with the one developed within the margins of the guiding principles of our legal system.

Well, considering that expansion-modernization is a phenomenon that is difficult to avoid and to a certain extent necessary, since it would be the result of the adaptation of criminal legislation to the protection of the new existing risks, it should be noted that, in principle, not all expansion has the capacity to undermine the criminal law of a state governed by the rule of law, but we must focus our attention on intensive expansion and, fundamentally, on that which can be qualified as unreasonable or unjustified.

However, this generates a further problem identified with the absence of objective criteria that allow us to qualify, in one way or another, the expansive phenomena. Therefore, the only possible characterization is based on general subjective criteria such as, for example, the assessment of criminal policy motives or respect for the general principles of law, in which the principle of proportionality plays an important role.[52] It goes without saying that we are all aware of the difficulty of these subjective evaluations, thus placing us in a plane of total uncertainty where our opinions will take center stage.

4 The FATF and Its Recommendations: An Example of the Impact of Soft Law on the Expansion of Criminal Law

The FATF Recommendations, as I have already stated, are an instrument of *practical soft law*, so that we are in a position to affirm that they have ceased to have a mere capacity to influence the sentiment of the national legal systems and have come to direct their content. It should also be borne in mind that in the field of economic criminal law, practically all the reforms introduced in recent years, which characterize it as one of the most peculiar manifestations of the expansionary phenomenon, have come from international bodies. This is without prejudice to recognizing the important role played in this field by the hard law instruments identified with the legally binding Community directives or regulations issued by the European Parliament and the Council.

in isolation because both share certain trends of contemporary criminal policy, in particular, the search for effectiveness and security" (Demetrio Crespo (2020), p. 68).

[52] Hassemer reminds us that "in the system of a Law of intervention, and above all criminal Law is such, the guarantees of the Rule of Law have normally played the role of conditioning the intrusions and their intensity to certain presuppositions, minimizing them and controlling them. In this context, the central principle is the proportionality of interventions, which must therefore be necessary and appropriate to achieve their objective, as well as reasonable in each case" (Hassemer (1998), p. 39).

This being the case, one might ask: *are the consequences of criminal expansion, and therefore the possible breach of guarantees, just as relevant when it occurs through the use of hard law instruments as when it is the result of the adoption of soft law?* The answer to this question is to recognize that, in the first case, states are directly obliged to transpose and introduce into their legal systems the provisions emanating from a hard law mechanism. On the other hand, in the case of soft law (in its dogmatic version), states have a dual power: on the one hand, to decide on the relevance of their introduction. And on the other hand, to determine the terms in which the content of the instrument in question is to be adopted, thus guaranteeing respect for the most basic and elementary principles of a criminal law of the Rule of Law.

Therefore, considering that any breach of guarantees, regardless of where it comes from, is unacceptable, in my opinion, the "severity" of the aforementioned violation is not the same in both cases, since in the case of soft law instruments, the states would be renouncing their own powers, that is, they are rejecting their power to decide for the mere purpose of avoiding the honorific sanction that non-compliance entails.

Precisely, this is what happened in the case of the introduction of self-laundering in our legal system through the reform carried out in 2010, thus obeying the need to respect the content of the sixth consideration of the interpretative note of the 3rd FATF recommendation, and in which the following circumstances would be highlighted to specify the effective impact of soft law in the expansion of criminal law:

I. Waiver of Their Own Powers If we look closely at the content of this recommendation, we can see that the legislator of the time did not assess the need to introduce this figure in our legal system, nor did they make a special justification for it, but simply transcribed the content of the recommendation in question in Art. 301 CC.

II. Breach of Guarantees The introduction of self-laundering combined with the criminalization of the conduct of possessing and using leads to breaches of the *non bis in idem* principle.

The specific situation in which such a violation would be occurring, according to a restrictive interpretation developed by the caselaw of the SC, would be as follows: Based on the understanding that the tax offense can and should be considered as an offense prior to money laundering,[53] the question is to determine the relationship between the two offenses, especially in those cases where the active subject is the same. Thus, leaving aside the possibility of accepting a continuous crime, the solution would be redirected to the concursal level, having to choose between a concurrence of rules or a concurrence of crimes, and in this delimitation a

[53] On this aspect, see among others, the following works: Martínez-Arrieta Márquez del Prado (2014); Demetrio Crespo (2016), pp. 1–19; Blanco Cordero (2011), pp. 01:1–01:46); Almagro Martín (2016), pp. 173–212.

determining role is played by the fact of understanding that the purpose of concealment or concealment of the laundered assets is essential for the purposes of the concretion of the crime of money laundering.[54]

In the case of self-laundering, it could be asked whether there is a purpose of concealment or concealment of the laundered assets when the person committing the predicate offense uses the funds for ordinary consumer expenses and, if so, whether there are one or two typical conducts. In my opinion, in these cases there is only one typical conduct and the punishment for both would lead us to a violation of the *non bis in idem* principle, since, based on the theory of co-opted acts, if convicted for the crime of tax fraud and for money laundering, there would be a violation of the mentioned principle since the laundering conduct is considered as the exhaustion of the tax crime. This being so, there would be a unity of act and only one final offense would be committed, and it would not be possible to consider the laundering as completed since the purpose of concealment or disguise, which is an essential element of it, is not present. In this sense, we find SCR 265/2015, of April 29, 2015, according to which, the mere possession or use of illicit funds (such as the defrauded quota) in ordinary consumer expenses does not constitute self-laundering, since these are not acts whose purpose is to integrate funds into the economic-financial system with the appearance of legality, and in the case of being punished for both offenses (fraud and laundering) two simultaneous offenses would be punished, it seems obvious that the type of tax evasion already contemplates, covers and punishes the devaluation caused by the fact that the active subject, instead of declaring and paying into the state's coffers the money that should be paid in accordance with tax regulations, uses it for other purposes.

III. The Conversion of Soft Law Into Hard Law "Arrives Late" When addressing the characteristics of this type of instruments, I mentioned that, in general terms, such conversion was carried out after the inclusion of the content of the soft law in the national legal systems. Well, in the case of self-laundering precisely this happens, Directive (EU) 2018/1673 of the European Parliament and of the Council of 23 October 2018, on combating money laundering by means of criminal law, establishes in its recital 11 the need for such criminalization. However, Spain, to comply with the FATF Recommendations, did so in 2010, and this was only due to the need to avoid the existence of international sanctions as a non-compliant country, i.e., honorary sanctions.

[54] Among others: SCR 1080/2010, of October 10 (JDE 2010/264941); SCR 690/2015, of October 27 (JDE 2015/216244).

5 Final Assessment

I. Dogmatic Soft Law (Should Be) vs. Real-Practical Soft Law (Is) This dichotomy is the main consequence of the denaturalization that this legal institution has undergone.

The relevance and necessity of these instruments for the sake of reaching an international consensus is undeniable, but this cannot justify a blurring of their own elements. At least in the case of the FATF, these instruments no longer have a mere capacity to influence but now boast a capacity to direct and, under a label that does not correspond to them (soft law), real hard law instruments are masked.

II. Necessary Expansion of Criminal Law Certainly, criminal expansion is necessary insofar as there are new interests, derived from globalization and the society of risk, in need of special protection. However, this is not the means to violate the most elementary principles of a criminal law proper to the Constitutional State.

For this reason, we cannot say that expansion is "harmful" per se, just as I do not even believe that it is considered an evil in itself. But, on the other hand, neither can we determine that the expansion is always and, in any case, "valid" and in accordance with our legal system and with the demands derived from the society in which we are inserted. I believe that, above all, we must ensure that criminal expansion does not lead to the denaturalization of criminal types and their distancing from the purposes for which they were originally intended, as happens in the case of money laundering.

We must therefore opt for a criminal expansion as much in line as possible with a minimum criminal law understood, as has been said, in the sense of punishing the essential conducts to protect all legal assets (old and new). The search for points of balance between all the conflicting interests is the goal to which we must aspire, since otherwise we would be encouraging a malicious punitive populism that would lead us directly to a criminal expansion governed by parameters that are far removed from necessity and reasonableness.

III. The Impact of Soft Law on the Regulation of Self-Money Laundering As mentioned above, soft law gives states the power to decide on the relevance of criminalization and where appropriate, on its terms, conditions, and limits.

In this regard, we must consider that: (1) Spain introduced self-laundering without being formally obliged to do so; (2) It waived the power to adapt it to our Criminal Code; (3) The conversion of soft law into hard law has been delayed in time.

In any case, and beyond the legal qualification of the recommendations as soft law, I consider that what is really relevant is the waiver of the state's powers of reflection and adaptation. Frankly, if we had made an effort to analyze and justify this figure, we would undoubtedly have appreciated the incongruities it enters into, avoiding, or at least reducing, its capacity to affect the essential principles of criminal law of the Rule of Law.

Moreover, if we were not really willing to carry out the aforementioned analyses and reflections, we would only have had to wait for this figure to appear in an international directive (hard law). In this case, even if the contravention of principles were still maintained, at least the classification would have been made in accordance with mandatory rules, both formally and materially speaking.

Finally, and in answer to the question posed in the first lines of this contribution, I must say that soft law instruments do indeed influence the expansion of criminal law.

References

Abel Souto M (2016) La expansión penal del blanqueo de capitales. Centro Mexicano de estudios en lo penal y trbutario A.C. México

Alarcón García G (2010) El soft law y nuestro sistema de fuentes. En Arrieta Martínes de Pisón J. C (Dir.) Tratado sobre la ley general tributaria. Homenaje a Álvaro Rodríguez Bereijo. Tomo I. Cizur Menor-Aranzadi, Navarra, pp 271–298

Almagro Martín C (2016) Reflexiones sobre el delito fiscal como antecedente al blanqueo de capitales. En Almagro Martín C (Dir.) Estudios sobre el control del fraude fiscal y prevención del blanqueo de capitales. Aranzadi, Navarra, pp 173–212.

Bacigalupo E (2005) Derecho penal y el Estado de Derecho. Editorial jurídica de Chile, Santiago de Chile

Bajo Fernández M (2013) "Los delitos económicos como manifestación caracteristica de la expansión del Derecho Penal". En Álvarez García F J (Dir.) Libro Homenaje al Profesor Luis Rodríguez Ramos. Tirant lo Blanch, Valencia, pp 407–416

Barberis JA (1994) Formación del Derecho Internacional. Ábaco, Buenos Aires

Blanco Cordero I (2011) El delito fiscal como actividad delictiva previa al blanqueo de capitales. Revista electrónica de ciencia penal y criminología (13-01):01:1-01-46

Blanco Cordero I (2012) El delito de blanqueo de capitales. 3ª Ed. Thomson Reuters Aranzadi, Navarra

Caamaño Anido MA (2002) Globalización económica y poder tributario: ¿Hacia un nuevo Derecho tributario? Revista española de derecho financiero 114:245–288

Corcoy-Bidasolo M (2012) Expansión del derecho penal y garantías constitucionales. Revista de Derechos fundamentales 8:45–76

Del Toro Huerta M I (2006) El fenómeno del soft law y las nuevas perspectivas del Derecho Internacional. Anuario Mejicano de Derecho Internacional (VI):513–549

Demetrio Crespo, E. (2014) El significado político del Derecho penal económico. En Demetrio Crespo, E & Maroto Calatayud, M (Dirs.) Crisis financiera y derecho penal económico. BdeF, Montevideo – Buenos Aires, pp 3–22

Demetrio Crespo E (2016) Sobre el fraude fiscal como actividad delictiva antecedente al blanqueo de capitales. Revista General de Derecho penal 26:1–19

Demetrio Crespo E (2020) El Derecho penal del Estado de Derecho entre el espíritu de nuestro tiempo y la constitución. Reus, Madrid

Díez Ripolles J L (2005) De la sociedad del riesgo a la seguridad ciudadana: Un debate desenfocado. Revista electrónica de Ciencia Penal y Criminología (07-01): 01:1-01:37

Donini M (2003) ¿Una nueva edad media penal? Lo viejo y lo nuevo en la expansión del Derecho penal económico. Nuevo foro penal 63:92–119

Escudero Alday R (2012) El concepto de soft law. En Moreso JJ (Dir.) Contribuciones a la Filosofía del Derecho. Marcial Pons, Madrid pp 127–148

Feler A (2015) Soft Law como herramienta de adecuación del derecho internacional a las nuevas coyunturas. Lecciones y Ensayos 95:281–303

Felip I Saborit D (2010) Observaciones a la expansión 10 años después. Robles Planas R (Dir.) La crisis del Derecho penal contemporáneo. Atelier, Barcelona.
Garrido Gómez MI (2017) El soft law como fuente del Derecho extranacional. Dykinson, Madrid
Gracia Martín L (2003) Prolegómenos para la lucha por la modernización y la expansión del Derecho penal de resistencia. Tirant lo Blanch, Valencia
Hassemer W (1998) Perspectivas del Derecho penal del futuro. Revista penal 1:37–41
Ibánez García I (2018) Notas sobre el soft law. Actualizdad Administrativa 8
Jímenez Díaz MJ (2014) Sociedad del reisgo e intervención penal. Revista electrónica de Ciencia penal y criminología (16-08):08:1 - 08:25.
Laporta San Miguel FJ (2014) Gobernanza y soft law: Nuevos perfiles jurídicos de la sociedad internacional. En Ruiz Miguel A (Dir.) Entre Estado y Cosmopolis; Derecho y justicia en el mundo global Trotta, Madrid, pp 41–81
Martinez - Buján Pérez C (2014) La expansiíon, la reducción y la legitimidad del Derecho penal económico. Revista penal Mexico 5:61–75
Martínez-Arrieta Márquez del Prado I (2014) El autoblanqueo. El delito fiscal como delito antecedente al blanqueo de capitales.Tirant lo Blanch, Valencia
May S (2012) Nuevos riesgos, seguridad y prevención: sobre la transformación del estado moderno y sus formas de actuación jurídica. En Pérez Alonso E, Arana García P, Mercado Pachecho, Serrano Moreno J (Dirs.) Derecho, globalización, riesgo y medio ambiente. Tirant lo Blanch, Valencia, pp 303–322
Mazuellos Bellido Á (2004) Soft law: ¿mucho ruido y pocas nueces? Revistsa electrónica de estudios internacionales (VIII):1–40
Mostacci E (2008) La soft law nel sistema delle fondi: un studio comparato. Cedam, Padova
Navarro Cardoso F (2020) A vueltas con la vieja delimitación entre el iícito administrativo e ilícito penal, a propósito de algunos nuevos problemas. Demetrio Crespo E (Dir.) Derecho penal económico y teoría del delito. Tirant lo Blanch. Valencia, pp 263–292.
Quintero Olivares G (2020) Estado actual de la teoría del delito y Derecho penal económico. En Demetrio Crespo E (Dir.) Derecho penal económico y teoría del delito. Tirant lo Blanch, Valencia, pp 49–69
Romajoli M (2017) Soft law e ordinamento amministrativo. Rivista trimestrale. Diritto amministrativo 1:147–162
Romeo Maldana S (2012) Un nuevo modelo de Derecho penal transnacional: El derecho penal de la Unión Europea tras el Tratado de Lisboa. Estudios penales y criminológicos (XXXII):313–386.
Sánchez Cáceres LF (2019) El sistema de hard law y sofr law en relación con la defensa de los derechos fundamentales, la igualdad y la no discriminación. CEFD: Cuadernos Electrónicos de Filosofía del Derecho 39:467–488
Sarmiento D (2006) La autoridad del Derecho y la naturaleza del soft law. Cuadernos de Drecho público 28:221–226
Schünemann B (1996) Consideraciones críticas sobre la situación espiritual de la ciencia jurídico-penal alemana. Universidad Externado de Colombia, Colombia
Silva Sánchez JM (1999) La expansión del Derecho penal. Aspectos de política criminal en la sociedades postindustriales. Civitas, Madrid.
Sotomayor Acosta JO (2008) ¿El derecho penal garantista en retirada? Revista penal 21:148–164
Sperti A (2012) Una soft law constituzionale? Politica del diritto 1:107–140
Terradillos Basoco JM (2006) Globalización, administrativización y expansión del Derecho penal. Nuevo foro penal 70:86–115

Enlaces Web

https://www.mineco.gob.es/stfls/mineco/prensa/ficheros/noticias/2018/191204_np_2gafi.pdf
https://www.uiaf.gov.co/asuntos_internacionales/organizaciones_internacionales/grupo_accion_financiera_7114

Contentious Politics and Penal Expansion in Spain: A Decade of Criminalization of Protest

Manuel Maroto Calatayud

Abstract In this chapter we address some notable processes of criminalization of protest in the last decade in Spain, trying to highlight that, although there has been a punitive expansion in this area, it has not been continuous or free of contradictions and it has met both internal and external resistances. The complex dynamics of penal expansion in relation to the repression of protest in Spain will be illustrated through the analysis of four different sociolegal processes: the prosecution of the organizers of the demonstration which triggered the Indignados Movement (2011–2020); the ruling of the Constitutional Court declaring the criminalization of flag desecration in accordance with Constitution (2013–2020); the ruling of the Constitutional Court declaring the Law for the Protection of Citizen Security in accordance with the Constitution (2015–2020), and the denial of the early release from prison to convicted Catalan pro-independence politicians (2017–2020). The chapter concludes with some considerations on the prominence given in the specialized literature to police institutions and the control of demonstrations, rather than to the role of the judiciary and limitations of free speech.

1 Introduction

In April 2021, the Spanish Congress repealed the crime of "coercion to strike," until then provided for in Article 315.3 of the Penal Code. In the preamble to the law that removed this article from the Code,[1] one could read the following description of the use to which this offence had been put over the last decade:

[1] See the preamble of *Ley Orgánica 5/2021, de 22 de abril, de derogación del artículo 315 apartado 3 del Código Penal.*

M. Maroto Calatayud (✉)
Faculty of Law, Complutense University of Madrid, Madrid, Spain
e-mail: manumaro@ucm.es

E. Demetrio Crespo et al. (eds.), *Crisis of the Criminal Law in the Democratic Constitutional State*, Legal Studies in International, European and Comparative Criminal Law 6, https://doi.org/10.1007/978-3-031-13413-5_14

> With the crisis as an opportunity, since the Popular Party came to power in December 2011, a constant and systematic process of dismantling freedoms began, especially those related to the public expression of disagreement with the government's economic policies. [. . .] The labor reform, which practically excluded workers' collective bargaining and which devalued or directly eliminated many other of their rights, did not seem sufficient, and therefore all the measures that externalised the conflict were reinforced, with direct attacks, using the legislation in force, such as Organic Law 4/2015, of 30 March, on the protection of citizen security, and article 315. 3 of the Penal Code, in the short term, and working, in the medium term, to deploy a framework of laws that suffocate the capacity of reaction, protest or resistance of citizens and trade union organisations, towards the government's policies.

That the *Boletín Oficial del Estado* contained an explicit depiction of the strategy of repression of protest set in motion by the *Partido Popular* caused unease among jurists, including many politically progressive. The preamble and the law itself seem certainly remarkable, not so much because of that political explicitness (which is otherwise very common in the legal and sociological literature on repression of protest), as because the last decade has clearly been dominated by legal reforms oriented towards "penal expansion," and examples of "penal retraction" are very rare.

In this chapter we will address some notable processes of criminalization of protest in the last decade, trying to highlight that, although there has been a clear punitive expansion in this area, the way in which this expansion has taken place has not been continuous or free of contradictions and, even if ultimately successful, it has met both internal and external resistances.

2 Repression of Protest in Spain: Political Contingency or Post-Authoritarian Inherency?

The last decade of Spanish "contentious politics"[2] can be read from a dialectical logic ("the state reacts to a political thread") that is common in approaches to the study of the repression of protest (Russell 2020). The 2008 financial crisis and its political and economic consequences soon leads to intense social unrest; increased anti-austerity mobilization in the streets is followed by police, judicial and political repression from the state. After some time, the combination of "mobilization fatigue"[3] and new opportunities to access to positions of institutional power eventually give rise to new electoral actors, and the political focus substantially shifts from the activities of social movements to the party system dynamics.[4] These new initiatives trigger some political innovations, within a restricted framework of institutional reform. While social mobilization stays relatively low, an authoritarian response sponsored by different actors gains new strength at the political, police,

[2] See Tarrow (2013).

[3] See Toivonen (2017).

[4] See Orriols and Cordero (2016).

legislative and judicial level: a reactionary partnership of state and non-state groups which remained mostly on the defensive during period of strong social mobilization, increasingly takes the initiative.

At the time this chapter is written, Spain seems to be in such a peculiar political moment. The national government is participated, for the first time since the third decade of the twentieth century, by members on the left of social democracy; but, at the same time, the far-right is enjoying a cultural and political relevance unseen in the last four decades. In 2021, 10 years after the peak of mobilization of the anti-austerity protest cycle, we have witnessed the consolidation and strengthening, both legal and factual, of some of the instruments and practices of repression of political dissent common during the last decade (particularly, of the administrative legislation on public order, which has become with the COVID-19 crisis central legal and police device of social control). But, at the same time, we have also seen how, as we already mentioned, Article 315.3 of the Penal Code, that was used for years to criminalize trade union actions during strikes, was repealed.

Although a general trend towards penal expansion seems clear, specially at a time when instruments traditionally used against specific groups are now being massively employed to manage the entire population due to the pandemic, it is also true that the different actors and processes involved in this process of expansion sometimes demonstrate divergent directions.

The last decade of penalization of dissent in Spain may seem too complex to be conceived just as a political regression to the latent authoritarian dynamics of Francoism.[5] Different processes of criminalization can be identified, seen as diverse and discontinuous, evolved in different and rhythms and stages, and involving different actors which sometimes hold conflicting and contradictory interests. The end of the decade can be explained as the closing of a cycle that underpins neoliberal domination and exposes the authoritarian legacy inherited by Spanish democracy. It can also be argued that the outcome of these years might be, however, more contingent to political practices and processes than that.

3 Processes of Criminalization of Protest: Four Examples

I want to illustrate the complex dynamics of penal expansion in relation to the repression of protest in the last decade in Spain using four specific examples of processes of criminalization. The four are social and legal processes that have developed over several years and have more recently reached a resolution.

i. *The prosecution of the organizers of the demonstration of May 15, 2011 which triggered the Indignados Movement (2011-2020)*

[5] For an account from the perspective of the literature on postfascism, see Bernat and Whyte (2020).

ii. *The ruling of the Constitutional Court declaring the criminalization of flag desecration in accordance with the Constitution (2013-2020)*
iii. *The ruling of the Constitutional Court declaring the Law for the Protection of Citizen Security in accordance with the Constitution (2015–2020)*
iv. *The denial of early release from prison to convicted Catalan pro-independence politicians (2017–2020)*

It is reasonable to say that, when each of these four processes began, what their outcome would finally be seemed to be a relatively uncertain question to most analysts. Analyzing the factors that lead different institutions to opt for one solution instead of another is an interesting way to approach the issue.

3.1 The Prosecution of the Organizers of the Demonstration of May 15, 2011 Which Triggered the Indignados Movement (2011–2019)

What would later become known as the *Indignados* or *15M movement* started on May 15, 2011 with a series of demonstrations called in fifty different Spanish cities and towns by a platform called *Democracia Real Ya*, under the slogan "We are not puppets in the hands of politicians and bankers." In Madrid (Comisión Legal Sol 2015), the demonstration gathered 20,000 people and resulted in antiriot police charging protesters and arresting nineteen people in the early morning of the 16th for public disorders and damage to property. They were between 18 and 26 years old. Several of them reported having been ill-treated by the police during their detention, as explained in a statement released a week later. The same morning of May 16, a dozen people decided to camp at the *Puerta del Sol* in protest for those previous arrests. The forced eviction of protesters from this camp by the police provoked a chain reaction: the next day thousands of people returned to the square, in a phenomenon that was reproduced with the same force in the squares of many cities and towns in the country.[6]

This was the beginning of a cycle of social mobilization, inspired by the Arab Spring, which would remain active at least until 2014. The number of annual demonstrations registered rose from 21,297 in 2011 to 44,233 in 2012. The number of administrative sanctions (fines) imposed for failure to comply with the requirement of prior notification of demonstrations to the authorities increased from 376 in 2011 to 1,722 in 2012. The repression of the cycle of protests against austerity peaks between 2011 and 2013. Arrests and charges for misdemeanors against public order increased by 300% from 2008 to 2012 (from 638 to 1934); for "offences" against public order they grew by 20% (from 20,329 to 24,841). After a new *Law on the Protection of Public Security* (LOPSC) was passed in 2015, 4,311 sanctions were

[6] See Camps Calvet and Di Nella (2020).

imposed for "disobedience" (Art. 36.6 LOPSC) that year, and one year later, in 2016, 12,094, three times more. The growth in sanctions for "disrespect and disregard" to authority (37.4 LOPSC) is even more pronounced: from 3,130 in 2015 to 19,497 in 2016 (i.e., 622% more).[7] These are all figures that only indirectly reflect another phenomenon: the increase in the disproportionate use of police force. Direct police intervention indeed became a privileged mechanism of protest containment, often subject to very little oversight beyond public scrutiny. In October 2020, the European Court of Human Rights condemned Spain for failing to effectively investigate cases of police assaults on demonstrators during protests in 2012.[8]

Several things seem noteworthy about the criminal prosecution of the nineteen people who were arrested in the early hours of May 16, 2011 and charged and convicted years later.[9]

One of them is the extraordinary delay in the proceedings, which lasted for no less than eight years. No formal accusation was made until 2014 regarding events that had occurred in 2011. There was not a conviction until 2019. During these years, many things had happened, including a far-reaching reform of the Criminal Code and the adoption of the already mentioned new *Law for the Protection of Citizen Security,* both enacted in 2015. Both legislative reforms were perceived as a reaction of authoritarian tones to the anti-austerity social mobilization triggered by the events of May 2011. Both reforms reconfigured in a significant way the Spanish legislation on "public disorders." When the court handed down the conviction of the nineteen persons that were arrested that night, it did so in accordance with the Criminal Code in force in 2011, but in the mid of the different repressive culture of 2019.

Another critical aspect is that, after so many years, the process ended with a negotiated sentence which reduced to fines the original proposal of the prosecution: imprisonment of up to 6 years. The sanctions were also reduced by the application of the mitigating circumstance of undue delay of the criminal process. The very long proceedings ended in an ambivalent manner: relatively lenient sentences, but a recognition of responsibility of the organizers, and without the trial itself having any significant social or political impact.

A third issue to be stressed is that the trial of the nineteen May 15th detainees seems representative of some of the features that characterized the judicial response to police repression of political dissent during the anti-austerity cycle. Specifically, it is a quintessential instantiation of its ambivalent and sometimes contradictory role. I have remarked elsewhere how, although the number of arrests and charges for crimes against public order increased considerably from 2011 to 2012, the number of judicial convictions for these crimes remained stable.[10] Some of the most

---

[7] According to the official data of the Ministry of Interior. See Ministerio de Interior, Portal Estadístico de Criminalidad. Available at https://estadisticasdecriminalidad.ses.mir.es/publico/portalestadistico/.

[8] See Laguna Guzman v. Spain, Application No. 41462/17, 6 October 2020.

[9] See Red Jurídica (2019).

[10] See Maroto Calatayud (2016).

significant protests of the anti-austerity cycle received the support of judges. The *Audiencia Nacional,* for example, quickly dismissed the charges against the organizers of a massive demonstration that surrounded the Spanish Parliament (*Rodea El Congreso*, September 25, 2012) declaring that the event was protected by the constitutional freedom of assembly and explicitly (and surprisingly) recognizing that it was a legitimate response to the "agreed upon decadence of the political class."[11] The trial against the nineteen detainees, highly symbolic in 2011 but progressively deprived of political importance, was an uneasy case for the courts to handle. The outcome of the proceedings could be interpreted as a case of judicial leniency, given the relatively mild penalties that were finally imposed. But an also be read as the opposite, a particular harsh treatment that entailed eight years living under the fear of being imprisoned for having participated in a demonstration. It can also be simply considered as the result of a certain institutional disorientation on what to do exactly with these protesters.

Another aspect of this process deserves, I think, further research. It seems that, regarding the role of courts during the anti-austerity cycle in Spain, we could distinguish a first "safeguard phase" in which the judiciary considerably contained the repressive anti-protest impulse promoted by the Ministry of Interior. In fact, this generated enough unrest among the minister and the whole conservative party for them to initiate significant administrative and criminal law reforms to facilitate the direct policing of protests by the executive, resorting to administrative fines, without depending on the sometimes uncooperative criminal courts. However, that phase did not last long, and an "anti-safeguards" agenda very soon developed and was put into practice also within the judiciary, although not specifically against the anti-austerity protesters of the *Indignados* movement.

3.2 The Ruling of the Constitutional Court Declaring the Criminalization of Flag Desecration in Accordance with the Constitution (2013–2020)

Soon after his appointment in December 2011, the Minister of Interior Jorge Fernández Díaz declared his intention to criminalize activities such as passive civil disobedience during demonstrations.[12] From 2014 onwards, a different and peculiar phenomenon begins. Not demonstrators on the streets, but social networks users

[11] See the decision of the Audiencia Nacional dated October 4, 2012. Available at: https://e00-elmundo.uecdn.es/documentos/2012/10/05/autopedraz.pdf. In another example of delayed "recriminalisation," in 2021, 8 years after the demonstration of September 29, 2012, the prosecution is demanding sentences ranging from three years and eight months in prison to seven years and four months. The court has not investigated the ill-treatment that the detainees reported having suffered at the hands of police officers. See Ter García (2021).

[12] See Dopico (2012).

began to be prosecuted for messages posted mainly on Twitter. Song lyrics, political statements, jokes on victims of terrorism or the holocaust, abstract calls to revolution and political violence, black humor, or anti-religious statements were suddenly the matter of criminal proceedings. Some of the now prosecuted were plainly labelled as anarchists or terrorists (that is how the so-called *Operación Araña* was framed by the police: as a prospection for supporters of terrorism in social networks) but many were musicians (Cesar Strawberry, Valtonyc, Pablo Hasel), politicians (Guillermo Zapata), comedians, actors or TV hosts (Facu Diaz, Guillermo Toledo, Dani Mateo), even puppeteers (Caso Titiriteros). Others were just anonymous Twitter users (Casandra Vera) that only achieved public relevance after being prosecuted and charged. Their main common denominator was a taste for provocative or subversive messages, and often being leftists. The prosecutions were based on some of the most problematic sections of the Spanish Criminal Code, due to their potential impact on freedom of expression: glorification of terrorism, humiliation of the victims of terrorism, hate crimes. Many of these categories of offences had been scarcely enforced before, some had not produced any caselaw at all and were somehow considered to be relics of other times, such as the offence against religious feelings. Between 2014 and 2016, 76 people were arrested for their comments on Twitter, accused of glorifying terrorism and humiliating victims.[13] Many were dismissed without even going to trial, but there were also a significant number of convictions. This trend, which was then truly striking, contrasts with the relative judicial restraint in the prosecution of public disorders.

I think there are several possible interpretations of this. It could be said, for instance that the 2011 *Indignados* were "non suitable enemies." Young middle-class people recently politized, with frustrated aspirations and demands not detached from the dominant political discourse (housing, jobs, democracy, anticorruption, citizenship), they were not the usual suspects. The *15M movement* also constituted an elusive and not easily framed political identity, and the movement was relatively successful in resisting being labelled as anarchists or subversive anti-system activists. By contrast, the prosecuted social media users were somehow easier targets. They were presented as attached to morally reprehensible messages that could be linked to violence or terrorism. These "crimes" were easy to detect in prospective operations, literally through simple twitter searches. Another relevant factor is that during these years the police and judicial knowledge on how social networks operated was still rather poor,[14] and these prospective raids might be seen as a form of "acting out" against a new and dangerous technology of unknown political potential. It seems that these prosecutions served therefore to achieve some expressive and symbolical ends (engaging in a cultural counteroffensive against "left radicalism," promoted by certain moral entrepreneurs, under the auspices of the Ministry of Interior), and at the same time to domesticate social networks.

---

[13] See Cadena Ser (2017).

[14] See Maroto Calatayud and Segura Vázquez (2018).

This judicially backed offensive of the executive branch against freedom of expression by means of the criminal law has continued throughout the following years, until today. It has done so in a sinuous, conflicting manner. In February 2020, for instance, the Constitutional Court overturned one of the most notorious convictions, namely that of musician Cesar Strawberry, on the grounds that freedom of expression had been violated.[15] However, on December 15, 2020, the same Constitutional Court in a new ruling has accepted as constitutional the criminalization of flag deprecation, despite the obvious contradiction with the doctrine of the European Court of Human Rights.[16] Striking as it is, the future of this particular process of criminalization is difficult to predict.

3.3 The Ruling of the Constitutional Court Declaring the Law for the Protection of Citizen Security to be in Accordance with the Constitution (2015–2020)

When it came to government in 2011, the conservative *Partido Popular* was already under strong social scrutiny for several corruption scandals under judicial investigation since 2009. The party elite was very concerned about the hostile political and social climate sparked in 2011. After the initial unsatisfactory attempt to criminalize protest in the courts, the Ministry of Interior launched several initiatives to address political criticism and contentious politics. One of them, as we have already mentioned, was the expansion of police administrative powers to identify, sanction and arrest. The legal basis for these police functions was then the 1992 *Ley Orgánica de Protección de la Seguridad Ciudadana* as well as a multitude of local ordinances that had proliferated since the beginning of the century and gave city councils the power to sanction incivilities.[17] The discretionary power that both instruments (LOPSC and local ordinances) placed in the hands of police forces was already remarkable. However, the Council of Ministers decided on November 29, 2013 to reform the LOPSC to significantly expand police powers.

A draft of the bill was leaked to the press a few days later, a movement that some interpreted as a "trial balloon" to test public opinion, acclimate it to regressive reforms, and to present as concessions some of the final changes in the law, foreseen beforehand (Legal Sol 2015). The new LOPSC contains a broad catalog of infractions linked to public order. In many cases, the definitions of the infractions directly described the repertoire of social movements during those years: entering company headquarters without authorization, calling for demonstrations without authorization, removing fences or other delimiting elements placed by the police, etc. Other prohibitions were classic infractions of public order defined in vague terms:

[15] See ruling of the Constitutional Court 35/2020, February 25.

[16] See Judgment 190/2020 of 15 December 2020. Appeal for amparo 1691-2018.

[17] See Maroto Calatayud (2013).

breaching the peace, generating public disorder. Other provisions were even more generic infractions that constituted general habilitations to sanction: resistance and disobedience to authority (Article 36.6 LOPSC) and of lack of respect and consideration to authority (Article 37.4 LOSPC). The fines provided for in the new law ranges between 300 and 600,000 euros, sometimes becoming notably harsher than penal fines.

Despite the fact that the draft law generated an impressive mobilization against it and was strongly criticized even from important consultative bodies of the state, which partially questioned its constitutionality,[18] the law was approved on March 26, 2015 with the vote of the Partido Popular. On the same day and with the same parliamentary majority, the party passed a reform of the Criminal Code with notable regressive measures, including new crimes against public order, or the reintroduction of life imprisonment in the Criminal Code (a penalty that had been abolished in the Spanish legal system since 1928) and, remarkably, the transformation of the category of misdemeanors in administrative infractions. Together with a series of minor legislative measures against corruption approved a few months later, this was how the government pretended to confront the crisis: severe measures of order and authority in the street, on the one hand, and timid reforms against corruption, on the other.

The repeal of the 2015 reform soon became one of the political mottos of the opposition parties. After the municipal elections of May 2015, some city councils that became governed by the left (such as Barcelona or Madrid) refused to apply the LOPSC. Some cities also launched initiatives to reform the functioning of local police forces, such as revising the local ordinance on coexistence in Barcelona,[19] or reducing the municipal anti-riot unit in Madrid. These initiatives, along with other attempts at community-oriented police reform, generated, particularly in Madrid, strong police hostility toward the city government, and ultimately failed.

A subsequent political shift at the national level did not bring about a repeal of the 2015 reform, either. Here I would like to point out an aspect that I believe is relevant to understand the dynamics of this decade of repression of protest in the Spanish case: the regressive reforms put in place to suppress protest have proved insistently difficult to reverse, even after major changes in political majorities. In May 2018, a ruling of the *Audiencia Nacional* established that the Partido Popular had been illegally financed, in a systematic way, for several decades.[20] This ruling led the parliament to appoint a new president of the government in June: the social-democrat Pedro Sánchez (PSOE). In September 2019, a coalition of PSOE and Podemos won the general elections. Although the repeal of the so-called "Gag

[18] See, for example, the report by the Consejo General del Poder Judicial, "Informe al Anteproyecto de Ley Orgánica de Protección de la Seguridad Ciudadana," 7 de enero de 2014; also the report on the proposal by the Consejo General de la Abogacía, "Observaciones que presenta el consejo general de la abogacía al proyecto de ley orgánica de protección de la seguridad ciudadana," October 17, 2014.

[19] Fernandez Bessa, 2018.

[20] See Judgement of the Audiencia Nacional 20/2018, May 17, 2018.

Law" (LOPSC) had been one of the usual electoral commitments in the electoral programs of both parties since 2015, the repeal has not yet taken place. The new government of the PSOE preferred to wait for the Constitutional Court to rule on the revision of constitutionality that the parliamentary opposition had requested regarding the law in 2015.

The new government not only failed to repeal the LOPSC but made extensive use of it during the COVID-19 crisis. The LOPSC indeed served as the (precarious) legal basis to justify police controls during the first months of the confinement. During the first weeks of "hard confinement," the police imposed massive sanctions for non-compliance with the rules of the state of alert declared in March 2020 (i.e., leaving home during unauthorized hours, or for unauthorized purposes). All these sanctions were issued in a creative application of the provision against disobedience of the LOPSC. First a factual police practice, this interpretation was then formally supported by the Minister of Interior, who issued internal instructions regarding sanctions for disobedience.[21] While in 2018 this infraction implied seriously disregarding the direct orders of a police officer, in 2020 it was enough to generically disregard the provisions of the law, not necessarily a direct order. A new expansion of police power was thus set in motion. In a few weeks, the police issued more tickets for disobedience than in the previous four years combined (Lopez Riba 2020).

On November 19, 2020, the Constitutional Court finally ruled on the LOPSC.[22] The Constitutional Court declared the law constitutional, except for a provision concerning the prohibition of using images of police officers without prior authorization, which was declared contrary to the constitutional prohibition of prior censorship. The position of the Constitutional Court was in 2020 more conservative and regressive than the stance adopted by other state agencies in 2015. This seems in line with the overall deterioration of the institutional protection of freedom of expression that has been developing since 2013, and as is exemplified in the ruling on the criminalization of flag desecration.

It might be said that it is only after years (2013–2020) of erosion of the freedom of expression in the "legal field" that this kind of decision by the Constitutional Court was possible. In other words, the sustained devaluation of freedom of expression through the criminal repression of subversive or offensive messages on online social networks has been a necessary step to make "imaginable" a declaration of constitutionality of a criminal conviction for messages about burning a flag in contemporary Spain. As recently as in 2018, the *Audiencia Nacional*, for instance, hesitantly acquitted a person who promoted on Facebook a call to booing the king of Spain

---

[21] See Ministry of Interior "Comunicación del Ministro del Interior a los Delegados del Gobierno sobre incoación de procedimientos sancionadores por presunta infracción del art. 36.6 de la ley orgánica 4/2015, de 30 de marzo, de protección de la seguridad ciudadana, y criterios para las propuestas de sanción," April 14, 2020.

[22] See Ruling 172/2020 of 19 November 2020. Appeal of unconstitutionality 2896-2015.

during a football match, considering it to be protected by freedom of criticism.[23] The regressive trend seems clear but however not continuous or completely lineal.

3.4 *The Denial of Early Release from Prison to Convicted Catalan Pro-Independence Politicians (2017–2020)*

The police operation and subsequent judicial prosecution against the Catalan independence referendum of October 1, 2017 takes place in a legal and cultural context of protest that is already different from 2011. We will not go into detail here about the differences between the social control of anti-austerity protests and the Catalan independence demonstrations, but we can point out some discontinuities. First, in 2017 the legal context was different: the strongly symbolic reforms of the Criminal Code and the LOSC had already been passed. Moreover, the offensive from a sector of the judiciary against freedom of expression had already been consolidated. The confrontation with Catalan secessionism also appealed to core ideas of traditional Spanish conservative discourse, i.e., the need to "defend the unity of Spain." Catalan separatism, in short, constituted a defined political identity, more easily criminalized than the diffuse political subject of precarious young people that made up the 15M movement.

The year 2017 was also a year of several judicial proceedings on government corruption. In July 2017, the conservative Mariano Rajoy was the first president of the Spanish democracy to testify as a witness in the trial of a notorious corruption scandal, the so-called *Gürtel scandal.*[24] In February 2017, Iñaki Urdangarin, the current king's brother-in-law, had been convicted of maintaining a corrupt scheme.[25] The repression of Catalan independence was an unbeatable opportunity to retake control of the media agenda and to reaffirm certain institutions and dynamics (the traditional political parties, the monarchy) in a conflict with a distinctive enemy: separatism.

Some of the criminalization attempts that failed in relation to the *15M movement* were successful against the pro-independence process. At the time, the Ministry of Interior failed in its goal of labeling demonstrations such as *Rodea el Congreso* on September 25, 2012 as "coup attempts" or "crimes against state institutions."[26] However, the leading organizers of the Catalan process were convicted through

---

[23] See Judgement 035/2017 of the Juzgados Centrales de lo Penal, December 21, 2017, and Judgement N° 14/18 of the Audiencia Nacional. Sala de lo Penal, May 4, 2018. The accused was first convicted of an offence of insulting the king, and then acquitted by the higher body. Similar complaints had been outright rejected in 2009 by the Audiencia Nacional. See Resolution of the Juzgado Central de Instrucción n. 1, July 15, 2009.

[24] See note 21.

[25] See Ruling No. 277/2018 Supreme Court. Criminal Chamber, 8 June 2018.

[26] See "La delegada del Gobierno en Madrid compara el 25S con 'un golpe de Estado'", eldiario.es, September 25, 2012.

old, almost forgotten, categories of offences in the criminal code: *rebellion* and *sedition* were added to the list of crimes creatively "rediscovered" since 2011 to persecute political dissidence. The conviction for sedition, issued in October 2019,[27] was not surprising. It came from the same *Tribunal Supremo* that two years earlier had overturned the previous acquittal by the *Audiencia Nacional* of the protesters in the Parliament of Catalonia in June 2011.[28]

It might be said that the ruling was not clearly predetermined either: during the 2019 trial there was a certain public consensus in the academic legal community against the possibility of applying those crimes of rebellion and sedition, and the sense that the outcome of the process would inevitably be reviewed by the European Court of Human Rights marked the procedural development of the trial. However, the reactionary judicial impulse that was set in motion in 2013 reached a new landmark with the judgement on the Catalan *procés*.

Although its supporters present the Supreme Court ruling as a sort of relatively lenient decision, a supposedly moderate decision which had not convicted for rebellion but "only for sedition" and "misuse of public funds," the penalties imposed were unprecedented, both attending the nature of the political activities criminalized and the severity of the prison sentences (of up to 9 to 13 years in prison). Even after formalizing the convictions, the judiciary could have opted, now that the Catalan pro-independence movement can be considered demobilized, to adopt certain measures, such as placing the prisoners in open or semi open prison regimes or allowing them to work and take care of their relatives outside prison, measures that are provided for in the Spanish prison legislation. However, in 2020, the *Tribunal Supremo*, against the previous decision of the *Juez de Vigilancia Penitenciaria*, revoked these measures for Catalan prisoners. The different resolutions, which should address rather technical aspects of individualized prison treatment, contain on the contrary broad remarks aimed at depoliticizing the nature of the conviction. In what can be understood as the pursue of symbolic and expressive goals (accommodating the existence of political prisoners in a democracy), the rulings insistently stress the absolute separation between political processes and criminalization processes.[29] That notion of separation is in itself hardly compatible with a constitutional culture aimed at maximizing the exercise of fundamental rights, and expresses, in short, a commitment to a concept of democracy that is strongly limited by penal means.

[27] See Ruling No. 459/2019. Supreme Court Criminal Chamber, 14 October 2019.

[28] See Judgment of the Audiencia Nacional No. 31/2014 of 7 July, and Judgment of the Supreme Court No. 161/2015 of 17 March.

[29] See Supreme Court, Special Cause 20907/2017, ejecutorias 1.2019 to 9-2019. Available at: https://www.poderjudicial.es/cgpj/es/Poder-Judicial/Tribunal-Supremo/Noticias-Judiciales/El-Tribunal-Supremo-revoca-el-tercer-grado-a-los-nueve-presos-de-la-causa-del-Proces-por-considerarlo-prematuro. For the most complete account of the open prison regime, see Rodriguez Yagüe (2021).

4 Conclusions

Analyses of the repression of protest in Spain in the last decade have focused on police control of demonstrations. Less emphasis has been placed on judicial proceedings against political dissent. Part of the emphasis on policing and demonstrations has to do with specific methodological traditions.[30] This has often left out of the analysis, for example, the patent process of criminalization of political speech in social networks, since criminal prosecutions have been aimed at individual actors who might not even be particularly politicized or organized. This shifts the focus away from social movements, which is the usual object of analysis. The penalization of freedom of expression in social networks might constitute, however, one of the fundamental transformations of the decade in Spain.

Another reason the judicial processes of criminalization of dissent may have received less attention than police-based processes of penalization is because of their more ambiguous nature. In the past decade, different phases, sectors, and responses can be distinguished at different levels of the judiciary. Public disorders associated with the cycle of protests against austerity were treated with relative restraint in criminal justice courts, particularly at the beginning of the protest cycle. The resort to administrative law and fines through police was clearly a preferential option for the executive bodies of the state. From 2013 onwards, the judicial penalization of dissent seems to become more selectively authoritarian, through the criminalization of social media. From 2017, a phase of selective incapacitation by means of the criminal law of leaders of the Catalan independence movement seems to develop, combined with the prosecution of hundreds, if not thousands, of other people in different judicial proceedings.[31]

This option for "selective authoritarianism" in the Spanish developments supports the idea of a predominance of symbolic and productive functions in the processes of criminalization of protest, derived from the sociology of punishment.[32] The erosion during the past decade of the institutional protection of freedom of expression in Spain can be considered, in this sense, as a fundamentally productive task: there are, at the present time, no strong social movements to contain, and yet 2020 has been a year of consolidation of regressive steps in regard to freedom of speech and protest. What I suggest here is that a judicial-political reaction within the state, which in 2013 was fundamentally short-sighted and defensive, has managed to become in 2020 a considerable motor for the promotion of a limited

---

[30] See Gonzalez Sanchez (2019), p. 3.

[31] See "Òmnium denuncia una segunda ola de juicios políticos contra independentistas," www.elnacional.cat, March 5, 2021. According to Òmnium, a pro-independence organisation whose own leader, Jordi Cuixart, has been in prison since 2017, 3,301 people have been "repressed" and 115 legal cases have been opened for "political reasons" since 2017.

[32] See Gonzalez Sanchez (2019).

notion of democracy.[33] This limited democracy seems particularly functional for the neoliberal capitalist project.[34] The criminalization of activities which are still today socially considered as harmless, such as the burning of the national flag, recently consecrated by the Constitutional Court, can be interpreted as a proactive agenda of symbolic production that advances towards the legal alienation of a significant part of the population. An alienation that operates, first, through the generation of shock and stupefaction[35] which later might turn into acceptance and resignation.

With these notes on the Spanish case, I also wanted to highlight the importance of addressing the legal sociology of the processes of criminalization of protest in legal and criminological research. It seems particularly important to address the changes, conflicts, and internal contradictions existent within judicial institutions and other actors in the legal field. It seems similarly relevant to further research to keep track of how certain political activities that were treated as harmless or tolerable are transformed into potentially criminalized conduct, especially when such processes occur in short periods of time.

References

Bernat I, Whyte D (2020) Postfascism in Spain: the struggle for Catalonia. Crit Sociol 46(4–5)

Cadena Ser (2017) Ingresa en prisión Alfredo Remírez, el primer tuitero detenido en la Operación Araña. Cadena Ser, November 4, 2017. Available at: https://cadenaser.com/emisora/2017/11/04/ser_vitoria/1509784511_561655.html

Camps Calvet C, Di Nella D (2020) Contrahegemonías antirrepresivas. Un estudio de caso de la protesta en Barcelona (2011-2015), Politica y Sociedad 57(1). Available at: https://revistas.ucm.es/index.php/POSO/article/view/60271

Comisión Legal Sol (2015) La ciudadanía como enemiga: balance tras cuatro años de represión de la protesta, en Bondia, David (dir.) Daza, Felip & Sánchez, Ana (coords). Defender a quien defiende. Leyes Mordaza y criminalización de la protesta en el estado español, Icaria. Available at: http://defenderaquiendefiende.org/wp-content/uploads/2019/08/defender-a-quien-defiende_Libro.pdf

Dopico J (2012) "Ciudadano terrorista," El País, April 14, 2012. Available at https://elpais.com/sociedad/2012/04/12/vidayartes/1334259638_936971.html

Fishman RM (2019) Democratic practice: origins of the Iberian divide in political inclusion. Oxford University Press

García T (2021) La Fiscalía pide penas de hasta 7 años y 4 meses de cárcel para 21 personas por el Rodea el Congreso de 2012, elsaltodiario, February 21, 2021

Gonzalez Sanchez I (2019) Symbolic violence and the penalization of the protest, Revista Internacional de Sociologia, v. 77(4). Available at http://revintsociologia.revistas.csic.es/index.php/revintsociologia/article/view/1040

[33] See an important contribution to the understanding of the exclusionary characteristics of Spanish democracy, in comparison with Portuguese democracy, in Fishman (2019). I would like to thank José Ángel Brandariz for sharing the reference with me.

[34] See González Sanchez and Maroto Calatayud (2018); Maroto Calatayud et al. (2020).

[35] See Comisión Legal Sol (2015), p. 126.

González Sanchez I, Maroto Calatayud M (2018) The penalization of protest under neoliberalism: managing resistance through punishment. Crime Law Soc Change 70(4)

Lopez Riba JM (2020) La gestión policial de la crisis sanitaria, CTXT, April 1, 2020. Available at https://ctxt.es/es/20200401/Politica/31731/Jose-Maria-Lopez-Riba-policia-coronavirus-confinamiento-estado-alarma.htm

Maroto Calatayud M (2013) Seguridad ciudadana y civismo como instrumentos de burorrepresión de la protesta, en Oliver Olmo, P. Burorrepresion: sanción administrativa y control social, Bomarzo, Albacete

Maroto Calatayud M (2016) Punitive decriminalisation? The repression of political dissent through administrative law and nuisance ordinances in Spain. In: Persak N (ed) Regulation and social control of incivilities. Routledge

Maroto Calatayud M, Segura Vázquez A (2018) Mobilisation and surveillance on social media. The ambivalent case of the anti-austerity protests in Spain (2011–2014). In: Melgaço L, Monaghan J (eds) Protests in the information age: social movements, digital practices and surveillance. Routledge

Maroto Calatayud M, González-Sánchez I, Brandariz JA (2020) Editors' Introduction: Policing the Protest Cycle of the 2010s. Soc Just 46-2/3. Available at: http://www.socialjusticejournal.org/wp-content/uploads/2020/07/156_01_Introduction1.pdf

Orriols L, Cordero G (2016) The breakdown of the Spanish two-party system: the upsurge of Podemos and Ciudadanos in the 2015 general election. South Eur Soc Polit 21(4):469–492

Red Jurídica (2019) Las acusadas del Juicio del 15-M alcanzan un acuerdo de conformidad con Fiscalía, February 2, 2019. Available at: https://red-juridica.com/juicio-15m/

Rodriguez Yagüe C (2021) La pena de prisión en medio abierto. Un recorrido por el régimen abierto, las salidas tratamentales y el principio de flexibilidad, Reus, Madrid

Russell Z (2020) Resistance and movement in neoliberal society: a literature review on the criminalisation of dissent. Spark Stirling Int J Postgrad Res (6). https://spark.stir.ac.uk/wp-content/uploads/2020/10/Russell-Criminalisation-article.pdf

Tarrow S (2013) Contentious politics. The Wiley-Blackwell encyclopedia of social and political movements, 14 January 2013

Toivonen A (2017). When all hope is lost: mobilization fatigue and the aftermath of demobilization. In: Academy of Management Proceedings (2017(1)). Academy of Management, Briarcliff Manor, NY 10510, p 16852

Ceilings for the Criminal Liability of Internet Service Providers

Jesús Iván Mora González

Abstract Article 270.2 of the Spanish Penal Code makes internet service providers responsible when their behaviour can be regarded as active and non-neutral facilitation of copyright infringements. This approach has resulted in an uncertain mechanism that encourages uncritical collaboration with copyright holders neglecting the social value of creativity in transformative uses of the work. This article suggests the analysis of authorship as a distinctive sign with the aim of reducing this normative uncertainty by a restrictive interpretation of exclusive rights, eliminating derivative uses for any notice and take-down procedure. At the same time, it is required the recognition of a counter-notification mechanism to protect fair use and transformative uses as key elements to protect social creativity.

1 Safe Harbour and Neutrality on the Internet

The concept of neutrality on the Internet has become a fundamental postulate to delimit internet service providers' liability and their duties of collaboration with intellectual property holders. These duties of collaboration have a marked international scope, whose most relevant regulatory representatives are the *Digital Millennium Copyright Act* (1998) of the United States and Directive 2000/31/EC of the Parliament and the Council of 8 June 2000 on certain legal aspects of internet society services, in particular electronic commerce, in the internal market. Through an indeterminate concept such as the *safe harbour,* internet service providers are treated as neutral actors and therefore not subject to any liability, as long as they do not infringe their duties of collaboration with the intellectual property rights holder. This approach, at the same time, has not been free of problems when seeking an international consensus for the fight against counterfeiting and piracy, the most

J. I. M. González (✉)
Faculty of Social Science of Melilla, University of Granada, Granada, Spain
e-mail: jesusivanmora@ugr.es

E. Demetrio Crespo et al. (eds.), *Crisis of the Criminal Law in the Democratic Constitutional State*, Legal Studies in International, European and Comparative Criminal Law 6, https://doi.org/10.1007/978-3-031-13413-5_15

significant failure being the European Parliament's rejection of the *Anti-Counterfeiting Trade Agreement (ACTA)* on July 4, 2012.

Thus, despite the fact internet service providers play a key role in an international context such as the Internet, there is no consensus on what kind of liability and under what circumstances the service provider should be liable. This is particularly relevant when the holder performs surveillance functions in the identification of possible infringements by *a notice and take down process requesting* the collaboration of the online service provider to withdraw the infringing use from the network under the need for an efficient process.

In this context, several judgments of the European Court of Justice (ECJ) deserve to be mentioned in the delimitation of the scope of the *safe harbour* linked to the concept of neutral actor as a space where the intermediary service provider would not be subject to liability. First, the *Google AdWords* case where the ECJ in its ruling of March 23, 2010 understood that the fact that Google set forms of remuneration for the service of marketing keywords associated to distinctive signs and the hosting of advertising links referring to those keywords was not sufficient to consider that Google had effective knowledge or control over the data entered into its system by advertisers. Thus, the *safe harbour* exemption provided for in the E-Commerce Directive was maintained on the understanding that such activity was neutral in nature. At the same time, the Court held that such neutrality would be applied as long as the AdWords service was exclusively technical, automatic and passive. In other words, it recognised that if the intermediary acted as an aggregator of information from third parties, collaborated or actively intervened in the appearance and presentation on screen, on its own online site, of data, information or services that were harmful to the rights of third parties, it could incur liability, depending on the circumstances, without being able to invoke in its defence the system of exemption from liability.

This linkage of the concept of neutrality to the technical, automatic and passive treatment is confirmed in L'Oreal v eBay. The relevant events occurred in 2007, when L'Oreal SA (L'Oreal) sent a letter of notification to eBay International AG (eBay) expressing its concern about the continuous transactions that were taking place on the eBay platform regarding the non-consensual use of its trademark in several countries of the European Union, filing a lawsuit against eBay before the *High Court of Justice of England and Wales* making it responsible for the sale of L'Oreal products marketed on the website, www.ebay.co.uk. Although L'Oreal and eBay agreed that two of the 17 products were counterfeit, L'Oreal claimed that the rest also infringed the trademark rights since they were not intended for sale as they were mere testers or parallel imports and were destined for North America. The *High Court of England and Wales* held that although it was possible for eBay to implement new control measures in the supply and distribution of goods on its platform, this did not imply the generation of a duty of general surveillance. In view of this situation, the *High Court of England and Wales* decided to refer several questions to the ECJ for a preliminary ruling, one of which concerned cases where an intermediary service provider would play an active and non-neutral role and would be excluded from the *safe harbour*. The ECJ responded to this question by linking the active role of the intermediary to the concept of neutral position, which would only extend to a purely technical and automatic processing of the data, while arguing that the optimisation of the presentation of offers for sale or the promotion of the same would imply the loss of such condition.

Finally, and derived from both Judgments of the ECJ, it is worth highlighting in the Spanish context the Judgment of the Provincial Court of Madrid of January 14, 2014. The plaintiffs in this case were Gestevisión Telecinco S.A. and Telecinco Cinema S.A.U. and the defendant was Youtube LL.C. The controversy is focused on the dissemination and use on YOUTUBE of broadcasts and audiovisual recordings over which Telecinco held copyright, requesting compensation for damages caused by the understanding that YOUTUBE was carrying out an activity of a content provider, and therefore responsible for the acts of reproduction and disposal of the work without the consent of the owner. The Provincial Court rejected such claim, understanding that YOUTUBE acted as an intermediary and that it was not its duty to supervise in order to sustain an effective knowledge of the infringements that could occur.

In this regard, the Provincial Court stressed that the work of cataloguing "featured videos" was not sufficient to avoid applying the exemption from liability provided for in the Spanish Act 34/2002, since the conditions under which it is carried out imply a high degree of predetermination on the part of the system's users, which allows the attribution of a proactive role based on such tasks to be questioned, and because, in any case, the scope of such action would be restricted to a very limited number of contents. This would mean that, given that YOUTUBE is under no obligation to supervise ex-ante the content hosted on its servers, the copyright holder would have to cooperate by informing them "individually and specifically" of the infringing content.

These relevant cases show that intellectual property owners have stopped focusing their efforts on the identification of "primary" infringers to focus their monitoring activity on internet service providers (ISP) based on secondary liability. In this way, and regardless of the "label" used, intellectual property enforcement is partially shifted to these actors through a notice and take down process to remove the infringing material. Therefore, the intermediaries are granted the ability to enforce intellectual property rights as a way of collaboration with intellectual property holders under the threat of losing their status as neutral actors and being subject to civil, administrative, or criminal sanctions (which the Spanish case would have as a specific reference in Article 270.2 of the Criminal Code).

This generates a situation of uncertainty that has two major negative effects. The first one derives from ISP secondary liability and their rejection to be subject to a sanction and therefore, their desire to maintain their condition of neutral actor regardless of whether this implies to reach to lawful uses (*over-deterrence*). The second, and derived from the first, is the effect this has on competitiveness and creativity without the due process guarantees.[1]

This problem is generated by the balancing of interests between the need for an efficient process required by the intellectual property holders through ISP and the need for the due process guarantees to protect the interests of competitors in promoting social creativity, and ultimately, in protecting freedom of expression. In this sense, the Internet allows us to give greater value to the dialogical capacity of citizens by playing a role that goes beyond the passive condition of consumer of works, and that positions him in the *produser* paradigm,[2] which requires a clear and concise protection of fair uses to protect its creative activity from previous works.[3]

On the other hand, *copyright* holders who find their capacity for supervision on primary infringers limited, and therefore need other private actors to control any derivative use and enforce their property rights in an efficient way avoiding the litigation costs at Court. This efficient way is found currently in the notice and takedown process, although it raises some important problems with the due process guarantees.[4]

Finally, and as the main actor, internet service providers, whose normative motivation for collaboration is based on the loss of their status as a neutral actor granted by the so-called *safe harbour*, that is, the duty to collaborate with the intellectual property owner through the implementation of a sanctioning privatisation.[5] This model is based on the need for speed that e-commerce requires, but it generates multiple incentives to remove creative material, and few incentives

[1] *Carpou (*2016*) p. 567 "(. . .) In the nondigital world, when an individual receives a cease-and -desist letter for a non-digital work (a painting, for example) alleging that the work infringes someone's copyright, the individual is able to contest the letter while her work remains undisturbed. In the digital world, by contrast, takedown requests result in the removal of content as a first step, with any dispute over the fact of infringement occurring later. This creates the potential for chilling effects on free speech in the digital world only, with the notice-and-takedown mechanism serving as a form of pre-emptive censorship". Blevins (*2013*), pp. 1833–1835 "(. . .) it creates incentives for internet platforms to become co-enforcers of third- party copyright holders (. . .) uncertainty expands the breadth of secondary liability, making it more likely that a platform will face damage or penalties (. . .)".*

[2] Grinnell (2009), pp. 577–578; Rosenblatt (2019), pp. 377 ff.

[3] Wong (2009), p. 1075; Heyman (2008), p. 455 "(. . .) What the fair use doctrine should be concerned with, then, is not what an author does when she creates-whether the second author changes the first author's expression in some ascertainable or substantial way-but rather whether the reader perceives an interpretive distance between one copy and another (in other words, a lack of similitude)".

[4] Thornburg (2001), p. 171 "(. . .) A rational ISP, then, will always choose to takedown when it receives a notices of alleged infringement. The safe harbour provisions turn the ISP into the copyright owner's enforcer and the copyright owner will not need to file a legal proceeding or even directly confront the alleged online infringer (. . .)".

[5] Urban and Quilter (2006), p. 687 "(. . . .) OSPs have significant financial disincentive to attempt to distinguish between spurious and valid copyright claims. Doing a more detailed and costly check on notices would often simply result in an assessment of risk of secondary liability in a grey situation, exactly what OSP's hoped to avoid through legal safe harbour (. . .)".

to carry out a prior investigation to assess the existence of such infringement and a possible fair use of the work of reference.[6]

At this point, the questions to be answered would be diverse. This article, however, does not aim to answer every one of them, but mainly seeks to legitimise a restrictive interpretation of Article 270.2 of the Spanish Criminal Code (due to its express provision) so that the criminal sanction does not become an instrument generating incentives for uncritical collaboration with the copyright holder by ISP.

To this end, this article raises the need for a multidisciplinary approach, treating authorship as a historical concept and highlighting the shortcomings of the economic analysis of romantic authorship. From this historical vision, a change of model called "distinctive authorship" is proposed, based on a semiotic analysis of distinctive signs, which aims (among others) to give greater normative value to the citizen's dialogic capacity in the process of meaning creation from previous works protected by copyright, highlighting the abuses to which the romantic model of authorship tends. Once the distinctive model of authorship has been delimited, the next point would consist of using this model to delimit the scope of Article 270.2 of the Criminal Code, reducing its application by means of a restrictive reading that establishes the cases where online ISP may refuse to collaborate with the copyright holder without losing the condition of neutral actor.

2 Economic Analysis of Copyright and Romantic Authorship

The romantic construction of authorship takes as a relevant reference the abolition in 1695 of the *Licensing Act of* 1662 in England and the disappearance of a monopolistic privilege granted to the Stationers' Company in London with a mostly censorial purpose. This implied the need to find a new justification in the granting of a copyright, which was found in the displacement of the author as the responsible subject (eventually criminal) for a subject deserving an economic retribution through a copyright on the work. In 1710, the Statute of Anne was passed by the British Parliament, becoming the best normative representative of this paradigm change. This economic retribution was first linked to the justification of the fruits of Locke's work, and was gradually refined through the exaltation of the direct relationship between the author-god and his predicate, the work.[7]

The recognition of the work protected by copyright as an immaterial good obtained an outstanding formalisation at the end of the 18th century in Fichte's

[6]Blevins (2013), p. 1875 "(. . . .) the practical effect of shifting enforcement costs to platforms will be overbroad removal of content as platforms owner operating under uncertain secondary liability standards would have incentives to remove any material that copyright owners have identified o may identify as an infringement (. . .)". See as well, Yen (2000), pp. 45 ff.

[7]Woodmansee (1984), pp. 425 ff Rose (1992), p. 475.

Proof of the Unlawfulness of Reprinting: a Rationale and a Parable (1793). Fichte distinguished between the physical object, the ideas and the form in which the ideas are presented, justifying the right of copy in the individuality of the original work. In this way the differentiation between idea and expression of the idea was formalised, where the expression of the idea would be the object on which the copyright would be delimited. William Wordsworth, in his *Preface to Lyrical Ballads* (1798), contributed significantly to the intersection between romantic aesthetics and copyright by highlighting concepts such as *vivid sensation* or *spontaneous overflow of powerful feelings* which were intimately connected with the author and his creativity. This consolidation of romantic aesthetics and legal discourse would be highlighted again by William Wordsworth in *Poems (*1815), allowing to consolidate the author as a creator of original works. This romantic view of authorship reaches our days in the positive regulation of intellectual property where the differentiation between idea and expression of the idea plays a fundamental role through the substantial copy as a cornerstone in the scope of copyright.[8]

And on this historical view, classical economic analysis holds that copyright is a regulatory system that protects monopolistic markets to correct market failures in the production of public goods. In this way, the romantic model is presented as a natural concept that comes to recognise the individuality of a creator-god and the protection of freedom of expression through the differentiation between the idea and the expression of the idea. This model is projected at the same time on a utilitarian legitimisation of a right of exclusive use where the weighting between monopolistic prices and marginal costs would allow the maximisation in the production of works through the correction of asymmetric market failures caused by the non-rival character of public goods and a deficient exercise of price discrimination on consumers.[9]

In other words, since ideas can be reproduced by infinite expressions, access to the idea should not imply a cost for every potential author. All expressions protected by an exclusive use right could and should be created independently and differently, where originality would be intimately connected with the concept of novelty. The necessary difference between original expressions (substantial similarity) would translate into an exclusive use right generating a monopolistic market due to the broad conceptualisation of derivative use and the high level of transformation required among the works protected in the market.

This concept, at the same time, can be easily transferred to the concept of neutrality and to the way in which the notifications from the *copyright* holders reach the intermediary service providers, where the substantial similarity marks an ambiguous hermeneutic criterion translated into the generation of incentives to collaborate uncritically. However, could copyright cease to be defined as a necessary monopolistic market through its dissociation from substantial copying?

[8]Lemley (1997), pp. 873–880; Aide (1990), pp. 191 ff.

[9]Lunney (1996), pp. 656 ff; Landes and Posner (1989), pp. 353 ff.

Copyright is linked to monopolistic markets to correct asymmetric market failures arising from the non-exclusive and non-rivalrous nature of public goods. Without a legal rule restricting the freedom of copying in the market, the level of production of works would be reduced due to the impossibility of efficient price discrimination on consumers due to their refusal to disclose the intensity of their preferences. If this economic approach to social creativity is analysed through the lens of the romantic model of authorship, the expression of the idea should be protected by a temporary exclusive right while the idea should remain in the public domain. Consequently, copyrighted works should be treated as a non-substitute *output* allowing free access to the "world of ideas" while promoting creativity through an exclusive right linked to a deified creation model of the original works.[10]

The insufficient incentives to create new works corrected by an exclusive right to promote creativity, however, should not be the main point of discussion, but the scope of exclusive rights based on an authoritarian creativity through the romantic model of authorship. This model has the capacity to reduce the access to creative sources in the process of creation of meaning through the substantial similarity or the complete internalisation of the social value. And both become fundamental criteria in the notice and takedown process used by copyright holders that delimit, at the same time, the scope of secondary liability on ISP.[11]

The replacement of authoritarian creativity, however, does not imply that any weighting approach between incentives and access must be invalidated, but merely that the external guidance for delimiting this weighting must be kept away from any remuneration criteria linked to the romantic exaltation of authorship. It only generates punitive models that in the context of ISP make uncritical collaboration prevail instead of the weighting of interests in the network.

At this point, an alternative definition of authorship could be useful to distance oneself from romantic aesthetics, without delegitimising the need for a copyright to promote social creativity, that is, a more ponderous model through a stricter delimitation of the situations where the online service provider is obliged to collaborate with the copyright holder in the identification and elimination of infringing uses.

3 Distinctive Authorship and Criminal Enforcement

According to a dialogical vision of culture, citizens have the capacity to participate in the processes of meaning creation. This would be an intertextual flow never completed that would limit the possibilities of communicative interaction between

[10] Yoo (2004), pp. 281 ff; Lemley (1997), pp. 1084 ff.

[11] Pessach (2003), pp. 104 ff; Ku (2002), pp. 324 ff; Heller (1998), pp. 688–690; Rotstein (1992), pp. 804–815.

human beings.[12] This dialogical capacity, however, can be restricted by exclusive rights that delimits the type of competitive behaviour that is prohibited, allowing its owners to manage the social impact of the protected works in the attention of the audiences.[13]

This restriction in the dialogical capacity of the individual that the *copyright* exercises does not imply the delegitimisation of this normative institution, but would require a formulation in dialogical terms, that is, what kind of legal interest has the capacity to justify a dialogical restriction in the participation of the processes of creation of meaning of every work? From the wide variety of possibilities that semiotic analysis offers us, I consider that Pierce's sign theory is an interesting approach to the reformulation of the concept of authorship. According to this approach, every distinctive sign should be analysed as a holistic structure composed of three main parts: the representamen, the object, and the interpretant. The mediation process between the representamen and the object of the distinctive sign would produce interpretants in the qualitative characteristics of the goods traded in the market that should be protected through the trademark holder responsibility.[14]

If this economic and semiotic approach of the distinctive sign is translated into terms of authorship, the key points would be the following:

a. Authorship should be defined as responsibility for the selection of any expression or work from a set of alternatives available in the market.
b. Authorship should be divided into three main elements: the author's name (representamen), the work (object) and the author's responsibility for the work (interpretant).
c. Social creativity should be explained in terms of trademark competition through two main functions: the classificatory function and the attributive function.
d. The purpose of the classification function of authorship would be to explain how works are distinguished in the marketplace through a differential variable composed of the author's name and the work. Transformative uses should be considered a necessary right of access to copyrighted works to promote social creativity, and thus, to protect freedom of expression in a democratic culture.
e. The attributive function of authorship would aim to explain how social creativity is promoted, which would require four fundamental variables: subjective, qualitative, disciplinary and retributive. The romantic paradigm of authorship based on original expressions should be replaced by the dialogical capacity of citizens in the production of reasonable substitutes that promote the competition of authors in the market.

[12] Coombe (1991), p. 1859 "(..) Individuality and consciousness are embedded in and realized through language and share cultural symbols (. . .) subjectivity, then, is fundamentally dialogic: what is most characteristic of our humanity is that we are dialogical or controversial beings in whom language is a reality".

[13] Heyman (2004), pp. 1448–1452; Lange (1992), pp. 152–160.

[14] Beebe (2005), pp. 704–710.

f. The purpose of the subjective variable within the attributive function would be to recognise property rights as a means through which the person obtains social recognition and at the same time to highlight the intersubjective symbolic relations that allow us to visualise authorship as a complex variable that provides meaning to communicative relations through the responsibility for the speech.[15]
g. The qualitative variable within the attributive function should aim to efficiently satisfy the needs of the consumer through the production of goods (works) in the market. The consumer's search cost savings would be the result of a system of exclusive use rights that rewards and encourages distinctive creativity and where authorship would provide useful information to consumers in the selection of competitive products (works).
h. The disciplinary variable should aim to promote the value of author´s responsibility for the qualitative characteristics of the product (work), allowing consumers to identify the products they want to buy or reject, promoting consumer search cost savings.
i. The retributive variable within the attributive function would be linked to the work substitutive level in the promotion of competition between authors. The substitutive capacity of the creative resources of the work should be considered as a hermeneutic instrument in the delimitation of the right of expressive access that citizens have in the participation of the process of creation of meaning of culture.

Thus, citizens should have an exclusive right to produce perfect substitutes regardless of the tangible medium where the work can be distributed. This exclusive right, therefore, would be the fundamental axis to delimit the legally protected interest to be enforce by criminal law and, at the same time, to delimit the scope of ISP collaboration duties. This is particularly relevant because Article 270 of the Spanish Criminal Code is characterised by its broad scope through actions such as reproduction, plagiarism, distribution, public communication, or any other form of economic exploitation. This implies an open model that reflects a substantial identity between criminal and civil protection contained in the Spanish Act 1/1996, especially in Article 17 and following. In addition to the conducts of reproduction, distribution and public communication, there are those of transformation, which take on special relevance to give meaning to other forms of economic exploitation and, at the same time, convert the substantiality of the copy into a fundamental axis to delimit the ISP secondary liability.

In this ambiguous context, the distinctive model of authorship has the capacity to provide a restrictive vision of the criminal enforcement of copyright that allows delimiting the concept of neutrality with greater clarity, and therefore, avoiding that criminal law becomes an instrument generating incentives of uncritical collaboration, but on the contrary, in one of weighting all the interests that exist in the internet with the purpose of protecting and promoting the dialogical citizen capacity.

[15] Hughes (1998), pp. 81–95; Radin (1982), pp. 34–50.

In this way, the distinctive model of authorship would provide following hermeneutic criteria to delimit the cases in which ISP would be subject to a criminal sanction:

A. The criminal enforcement of *copyright* would have as its purpose the promotion of expressive diversity, where citizens would be recognised the capacity to compete through exclusive rights in the production of perfect substitutes without consideration of the tangible medium where the work may be distributed. Considering this right as a legally protected interest, it would have the capacity to delimit the scope of safe harbour identifying cases where ISP did not have to collaborate with intellectual property holders.
B. Interpretative approaches that take as a reference the substantial similarity to delimit the scope of copyright infringements (such as the fragmented literal similarity test, levels of abstraction test, total concept and feel test), have the quality of reducing the substitution capacity of the public goods and increasing the cost of audience attention. Substantial similarity, therefore, should not be considered as a hermeneutic criterion to justify the criminal enforcement of copyright, since this would imply analysing not only the substantial similarity between two works, but between every expression that has been able to influence the author, an activity that far exceeds the capacity of any online service provider.[16]

   The distinctive model of authorship, by contrast, would require recognition of the social value of transformative uses, and thus of the creative resources that are necessary to compete efficiently online through the production of reasonable substitutes. Thus, the criminal enforcement of *copyright* should not be legitimised when it aims at restricting transformative uses and increasing the scope of derivative uses. Consequently, it should not be a criterion that creates an obligation for the online service provider to collaborate with the copyright holder.
C. The concept of public domain should not be defined metaphorically as objects that can only be used after some time (as general rule, the author's life plus 70 years). The alternative would be to define public domain with a markedly fluid character. The public domain would be defined an essential creative resource for the dialogic capacity of every citizen in the production of reasonable substitutes potentially adequate to impact the attention of the audience.

---

[16] See for those tests, Carter (2013), p. 678 "(. . . .) fragmented literal similarity is based on literal elements scattered throughout an infringing work. Though the criteria for deciding fragmented literal similarity vary, the generally weigh the element's qualitative and quantitative value to the copyrighted works (. . .)". Khong (2007), p. 722 "(. . . .) a copyrighted work is to be abstracted into different levels of abstraction, the non-protection elements filtered out and what remains are to be compared with the alleged infringing work (. . .)". Brashears "Total concept and feel or dissection: Approaches to the misappropriation test of substantial similarity" (1993), pp. 918–920.

4 Criminal Liability of Intermediary Service Providers: The Need for Restrictive Interpretation

The amendment of Article 270.2 Penal Code by the Spanish Act 1/2015 comes to delimit the ISP criminal responsibility through the active and non-neutral facilitation of works protected by copyright. Although this section does not cover the different types of providers of intermediary services, it tries to copy, with an unclear technique, the harmonisation process undertaken by Directive 2000/31/EC on certain legal aspects of information society services (transposed by Spanish Act 34/2002 on information society services and electronic commerce).

From a joint reading of the criminal and civil regulations, a first interpretative restriction is linked to the knowledge requirement of the existence of an infringement. It means that there is not a duty of general supervision to maintain the condition of neutral actor. In addition, Article 16 of Spanish Act 34/2002 should be highlighted, due to its importance in the interpretation of the criminal norm when establishing the requirements that must be met for the service provider to have knowledge. This article establishes the intermediary liability linked to effective knowledge, and once he has obtained it, he acts with due diligence to remove the offending content. This knowledge is deemed to be proven when a competent body has declared it unlawful or when it derives from voluntary agreements and other means of effective knowledge that may be established, which refers to the supervisory activity that the *copyright* holders carry out and the notifications that they may make to the intermediary and its legal effects.

This interpretation is confirmed by some recent caselaw of the Spanish Supreme Court. It is worth highlighting judgments of February 10, 2011, February 26, 2013, March 17, 2013 and January 7, 2014, where the Supreme Court holds that for the existence of an effective knowledge is not essential that a sentence or an injunction has been issued by the Court regarding a copyright infringement, but that such knowledge can be given by other means, particularly by a reliable and reasoned notification of the affected party or even when it is evident. In this sense, it could be interpreted as an obligation to act uncritically when faced with the notification of a *copyright* infringement by its owner, encouraging the abuse of this figure as neither formal requirements for notification of a possible infringement nor the existence of a counter-notification are foreseen. At the same time, this interpretation would fit perfectly in the light of the aforementioned caselaw, since knowledge would not require a judicial decision, but merely a reliable and well-founded notification, or simply when it is evident by itself.

These issues only show a lack of clarity regarding the scope of criminal liability of internet service providers, which would allow to develop a comparative analysis to find a regulatory model that protect the due process guarantees. It is believed that the best example for this debate can be found in the requirements given by section 512 of the *Digital Millennium Copyright Act* 1998, where there is a regulated procedure of notification and counter-notification to ensure (at least formally) certain basic guarantees of due process without imposing an excessive supervisory burden on intermediaries. If both regulatory instruments are compared, the main feature derived from Article 270.2 Penal Code and from the European and Spanish regulations on the electronic market is the lack of a counter-notification procedure that would allow the alleged infringer to defend himself before the online service provider and the lack of some formal notification requirements as a mechanism to activate a duty of collaboration with the copyright holder to maintain the safe harbour status and therefore not be subject to a criminal penalty.

Everything seems to indicate that not losing this condition would require a collaborative activity with the *copyright* holders in a diligent way and especially with celerity. However, these appeals to an efficient model in the identification and punishment of *copyright* infringements should always be weighed against the demand for minimum requirements for the exercise of a private sanctioning power. Unlike a criminal procedure, where there are a series of guarantees, the intermediary supervisory activity can take on the form of private censorship with low levels of visibility, since it is not coordinated or reviewed, and it is never known how the dialogical and creative capacity of the citizenry has been deformed.[17]

And this can be explained through an economic analysis. If it is costly to distinguish a licit use from an illicit one on a work protected by copyright, the intermediary will probably abandon all efforts and develop a policy of self-censorship by blocking that content which may carry a threat of sanction for the loss of its status as a neutral actor. At the same time, in the Internet, the benefit derived from a marginal consumer can easily be absorbed by the imposition of a sanction, i.e. it is much cheaper to remove a parody of a *copyright* work (which the owner understands negatively affects his reputation) or to block a website without granting a prior right of defence than to carry out an exhaustive study of fair use with the risk of subsequently losing the status of neutral actor and being subject to a sanction (possibly criminal) because it is considered an active and non-neutral facilitation of the work.[18]

If to this cost-benefit assessment by ISP is added a situation of legal uncertainty (such as that present in Article 270.2 of the Spanish Penal Code), the solution seems to be directed in only one direction: the uncritical collaboration of the intermediary

---

[17] Thornburg (2001), pp. 151–160.

[18] Kreimer (2006), p. 31 "(. . .) efforts to generate proxy censorship by targeting intermediaries are less likely to be challenged in court than censorship efforts directed at speakers or listeners, and are therefore more likely to be consciously manipulated to suppress protected speech. Given the divergence between their interest and those of the speakers, intermediaries are unlikely to expend much time or energy contesting dubious demands that can be satisfied by sacrificing a marginal user of their services. Unlike a speaker, who has an interest in all of the profits to be earned from a determination that speech is protected, the intermediary's interest is limited to the profits from speech conveyed over its own network, and a regulator intent on suppressing a particular type of communication can take advantage of that fact (. . .)".

as a way of ensuring the neutral condition derived from not being able to capture the full value of the use on the work.[19]

And it is here where the distinctive model of authorship could play an important role in a restrictive reading of Article 270.2 of the Spanish Penal Code, advocating the delimitation of a concrete and clear space of non-collaboration on the part of the online service provider, maintaining the condition of neutral actor and therefore, not subject to a criminal sanction. To do so, it is necessary to abandon the postulates of the romantic concept of authorship. Substantial similarity as a paradigm to delimit the copyright infringements derived from the romantic model of authorship based on substantial copying normally aims at reducing the substitutive capacity of public goods and increasing the cost of attention of the audience in the market. Beyond this restrictive effect on creativity, the main problem that such approach brings with it is the inability in many cases or the excessive cost that the service provider would incur in delimiting what is fair use or infringement using such criterion (especially in transformative uses through expansive conducts that take as a basis "any other mode of economic exploitation") when it must be weighed against the efficiency of the response and the non-loss of the safe harbour to avoid the imposition of a sanction.

From a cost-benefit perspective, the service provider does not have the capacity to delimit what is substantial similarity and whether it constitutes a licit or illicit activity, which generates an important incentive to reduce its costs by means of an uncritical collaboration with the *copyright holder,* understanding that there is indeed an infringement as claimed by the *copyright* holder.

The distinctive model of authorship would, however, require the identification of creative resources that are necessary to compete efficiently in the marketplace through the production of reasonable substitutes. Thus, when the notification by the *copyright* holder is intended to protect derivative uses, such notification should not generate any obligation to act on the part of the online service provider and therefore an attitude of non-cooperation with the *copyright* holder would entail the loss of the status of neutral actor and its eventual submission to a criminal penalty. And this does not mean that the *copyright* holder is unprotected, but rather that an informal process of identification and removal of creative content by ISP is not the appropriate scenario, but rather a judicial process with the due process guarantees despite the fact this may slow down the sanctioning process. Thus, any private notification (generating an obligation to collaborate) should require a justified information by the *copyright* holder indicating that the infringement does not affect uses derived from the works protected by *copyright.*

---

[19]Kreimer (2006), p. 40 "(. . .) there is an important class of regulation targeted at intermediaries where the claim that commercial forces will moderate censorship is almost wholly illusory. In the case of threatened criminal punishments, side payments will almost always be insufficient to induce intermediaries to avoid censorship. A speaker who is willing herself to risk imprisonment is not often in a position to 'cash out' that willingness and pay it to the intermediary. Moreover, the risk preferences of an intermediary regarding criminal conviction are likely to differ substantially from those of a committed first-party speaker. The threat of criminal conviction is not something that can be insured against by plausibly available policies (. . .)".

At the same time, the distinctive model of authorship is a faithful reflection of the dialogical capacity of citizens in the use of creative resources that would require at least an efficient system of counter-notification that values the fair use of the work and its non-elimination as a manifestation of the weighting of interests that *copyright* is called upon to protect. This minimum guarantee of counter-notification would prevent the criminal law from becoming a sanctioning instrument to motivate the service provider in an uncritical collaboration with the postulates of the romantic model of authorship, to become an instrument to protect the fair use of creative resources, being the obligation of the *copyright* holder to prove such unlawful use not through informal sanctioning channels but through a judicial process with due guarantees when the alleged infringer makes a well-founded statement through a counter-notification.

Considering both postulates, the existence of minimum requirements in the private notification are fundamental to delimit the scope of Article 270.2 of the Spanish Penal Code by identifying space where ISP would not be liable, maintaining the condition of neutral actors. Thus, a restrictive interpretation would imply requiring at least the following key points:

4.1 Capacity of the Internet Service Provider

The online service provider should have a right to make a declaration of capacity to examine such content. In this sense, Article 270.2 of the Criminal Code does not make any classification of service providers, as regulated in the E-Commerce Directive in Articles 12, 13 and 14 respectively. This implies, from the outset, a deficient technique in the wording of the norm since an obligation on a service provider regarding mere transmission is not the same as an obligation to host data. This is especially relevant in a chain of transmission and dissemination of content.[20] This regulatory criterion, therefore, would make it possible to recognise the safe harbour when it is beyond the service provider´s capacity to directly control the infringing content and it is justified through a declaration of capacity to examine such content. If the copyright holder disagrees with that declaration of capacity, the alternative should be a judicial process with the due process guarantees.

[20] Longke (2019), pp. 153–154 "(. . .) the paper holds that the standard for determining the existence of the ISP's criminal liability is (. . .) service provider's direct control over illegal and criminal information" "(. . .) 1. ISP has control over illegal and criminal information and decides whether certain illegal on criminal information can be transmitted through certain channels and with certain scope (. . . .) the service provider is not responsible for safety management regarding illegal and criminal information beyond its influence and control (. . .). 2. The ISP's control over illegal and criminal information is direct: 2.a. If an ISP has the capability to control over illegal and criminal information and such control is not direct but needs help on intermediation of other ISP's, the former ISP's management obligation in terms of criminal liability shall be denied. 2.b. In the chain of information transmission and dissemination, the ISP is only responsible for the illegal information of the first link and level under its direct control (. . .)".

4.2 Counter-Notification As a User Right

If there is a positive answer from ISPs regarding their ability to examine the infringing content, they will proceed to notify the person allegedly responsible for the copyright infringement. In that notification should be clearly identified the possibility of counter-notification to defend not only a fair use of the work but also the possibility to demand the copyright holder based on the abuse of their rights.

If there is a counter-notification by the alleged infringer, and such counter-notification is based on a legitimate use of the work that can be identified by the online service provider, he or she will contact the *copyright* holder again to inform that the work will not be removed, and that his or her interests should be redirected through a judicial process. This type of behaviour by ISP should be part of the safe harbour, and in consequence, the refusal to cooperate in the removal of content will not in any case lead to the loss of the status of neutral actor subject to a sanction.[21]

Therefore, according to this model, in notice and take down processes implemented by copyright holders, the criminal law cannot appear as a sanctioning instrument that encourages automatic and uncritical collaboration in favour of copyright holders by ISP, but rather a normative instrument to promote the development of a considered and weighting examination of the interests not only of the copyright holders, but also the copyright users with the due process guarantees.[22]

This implies a restrictive reading of Article 270.2 of the Spanish Penal Code with the aim of not linking the lack of an automatic response or the infringing of duty to collaborate uncritically with the copyright holder with the loss of the neutral condition and the possibility to be subject to a criminal sanction. Conversely, the criminal liability of ISP will require a passive behaviour after the counter-notification if from this counter-notification there is an acceptance of the copyright infringement, there is no justified fair use of the work, or the response of the alleged infringer is non-existent after a prudent period granted by the ISP.[23]

---

[21] Carpou (2016), p. 585.

[22] On the deficiencies of the NTD counter-notice in the USA, see Urban et al. (2017), p. 44 "(. . .) As rightsholders press for faster takedown from the major services, some DMCA Auto OSPs now respond to most takedown requests in minutes. Action on counter notices, on the other hand, is still measured in days or weeks. Service providers must restore content based on a valid counter notice no later than fourteen days after receipt, but also, no sooner than ten days—the period in which the rightsholder must decide whether or not to sue OSPs expressed concern about this statutorily mandated delay, pointing out the potentially dangerous effects on expression or competition. As one OSP described it, ten to fourteen days represents an eternity on the Internet for small businesses, for community sites where content has a short lifespan, or for political speech (. . .)".

[23] On the abuse of notice and take down processes, suggesting a new normative criteria in the USA which is called "Anti-Slapp Relief" "(. . .) 1. The plaintiff lacks a legitimate economic motivation to preserve an established market for the licensing of its copyrighted works; 2. The defendants use of the work at issue advances the expression of basic facts or community matters of public concern (. . .)".

5 Conclusions

The Court of Justice of the European Union has played a fundamental role in delimiting the scope of liability of internet service providers, but at the same time, it has provided a broad criterion that clashes with the requirements of legal certainty demanded by the criminal law. Article 270.2 of the Spanish Penal Code requires for such liability the existence of an active and non-neutral facilitation of works protected by *copyright, which* has resulted in an uncertain mechanism generating incentives for uncritical collaboration with *copyright* holders without adequately considering social creativity through the transformative use of the work, and therefore, ignoring the dialogical capacity of every citizen beyond the passive role of consumer.

The alternative suggested by this article is based on a historical analysis of authorship. It highlights how the romantic construction was developed and the abusive effects that it produces in the economic analysis of *copyright* through substantial copying as a paradigm delimiting the scope of exclusive rights, and how this is transmitted to the concept of neutrality over internet service providers. These abusive effects, however, do not imply that *copyright* should be delegitimised, but rather that an alternative vision is needed in the concept of authorship. This article proposes the analysis of authorship as a distinctive sign to emphasise the value of the dialogic capacity of every citizen through the transformative use and the social function that internet service providers are called to fulfil as a channel of creativity and freedom of expression and, therefore, requiring a restrictive interpretation to justify a criminal sanction for internet service providers.

Thus, substantial copying is rejected as an interpretative criterion derived from the romantic model of authorship, suggesting a restrictive view on the scope of copyright. This approach suggests the elimination of derivative uses as a paradigm for the notice and take down procedure. At the same time, this vision appeals to the need to implement a counter-notification mechanism that allows the alleged infringer to effectively defend his interests before the intermediary, without losing the condition of neutral actor, that is, a mechanism for weighing interests that respects the basic guarantees derived from the due process, despite the fact this implies less efficiency in the identification and elimination of infringements of works protected by *copyright.*

References

Aide C (1990) More comprehensive soul: romantic conception of authorship and the copyright doctrine of moral rights. Toronto Faculty Law Rev 8:185–209

Beebe B (2005) The semiotic analysis of trademarks. UCLA Law Rev 51:621–704

Blevins J (2013) Uncertainty as enforcement mechanism: the new expansion of secondary copyright liability to internet platforms. Cardozo Law Rev 34:1821–1888

Brashears-Macatee S (1993) Total concept and feel or dissection: approaches to the misappropriation test of substantial similarity. Chicago-Kent Law Rev 68:913–937
Carpou Z (2016) Robots, pirates and the rise of the automated takedown regime: using the DMCA to fight piracy and protect end-users. Colum J Law Arts 39:551–589
Carter M (2013) Applying the fragmented literal similarity test to musical work and sound recording infringement: correcting the Bridgeport Music, Inc. v Dimension Films Legacy. Minn J Law Sci Technol 14:669
Coombe R (1991) Objects of property and subjects of politics: intellectual property law and democratic dialogue. Tex Law Rev 69:1853–1880
Grinnell C (2009) From consumer to prosumer to produser: who keeps shifting my paradigm? We do! Public Cult 21:577–598
Heller M (1998) The tragedy of the anti-commons: property in the transition from Marx to markets. Harv Law Rev 111:620–688
Heyman L (2004) The birth of the authornym: authorship, pseudonymity and trademark law. Notre Dame Law Rev 80:1378–1448
Heyman L (2008) Everything is transformative: fair use and reader-response. Columbia J Law Arts 31:445–466
Hughes J (1998) The personality interest of artists and inventors in intellectual property. Cardozo Arts Entertain 16:81–182
Khong D (2007) Copyright doctrines, abstractions and court error. Rev Law Econ 3:715–743
Kreimer S (2006) Censorship by proxy: the First Amendment, Internet Intermediaries and the problem of the weakest link. Univ Pennsylvania Law Rev 155:11–101
Ku R (2002) The creative destruction of copyright: napster and the new economics of digital technology. Univ Chicago Law Rev 69:263–324
Landes W, Posner R (1989) An economic analysis of copyright. J Legal Stud 18:325–353
Lange D (1992) At play in the fields of the word: copyright and the construction of authorship in the post-literature millenium. Law Contemp Probl 55:139–151
Lemley M (1997) Romantic authorship and the rhetoric of property. Texas Law Rev 75:873–906
Longke T (2019) On an internet service provider's content management obligation and criminal liability. J Eastern-Eur Crim Law 1:145–158
Lunney G (1996) Re-examining copyright's incentives-access paradigm. Vand Law Rev 49:483–656
Pessach G (2003) Copyright law as a silencing restriction on non-infringing materials: unveiling the scope of copyright's diversity externalities. 76. South Calif Law Rev 76:1067–1104
Radin M (1982) Property and personhood. Stanley Law Rev 34:957–1016
Rose M (1992) The Author in Court: Pope v Curl 1741. Cardozo Arts Entertain Law J 10:475–493
Rosenblatt E (2019) Fair use as resistance. UC Davis Legal Stud Res 9:377–400
Rotstein R (1992) Beyond metaphor: copyright infringement and the fiction of the work. Chicago Kent Law Rev 68:725–804
Thornburg E (2001) Going private: technology, due process and internet dispute resolution. U.C Davis Law Rev 34:151–220
Urban J, Quilter L (2006) Efficient process or chilling effects? Takedown notices under Section 512 DMCA. Santa Clara Comput High Technol Law J 22:621–693
Urban J, Karaganis J, Schofield B (2017) Notice and Takedown in Everyday Practice. UC Berkeley Public Law Research Paper, N° 2755628,1-182
Wong M (2009) Transformative user-generated content in copyright law: infringing derivative works or fair use. Vanderbilt J Entertain Technol Law 11:1075
Woodmansee M (1984) The genius and the copyright: economic and legal conditions of the emergence of the author. Eighteen Cent Stud 17:425–448
Yen A (2000) Internet service provider liability for subscriber copyright infringement, enterprise liability and the first amendment. Georgetown Law J 88:1–56
Yoo C (2004) Copyright and product differentiation. N Y Univ Law Rev 79:212–281

Part IV
Paradigm of Danger and Security in the Criminal Law in the Democratic Constitutional State

Why Do They Call It 'Dangerousness' When They Mean 'Risk Assessment'? Using Risk Assessment in the Spanish Criminal Justice System

María Pilar Marco Francia

Abstract We are currently living through tempestuous times where the new currents in Spanish Criminal law seem to be leading us towards a progressive abandonment of the guarantee-based paradigm and a definite approximation towards the paradigm of dangerousness. The issues of criminal dangerousness and its treatment are highly topical, and the assessment of risk seems a difficult issue to resolve insofar as there may be a conflict of rights in the always disheartening struggle between freedom and security. The question for debate is whether it would be advisable to introduce to our legal systems in Spain actuarial techniques, which could contribute to making better predictions as to the degree of dangerousness of dangerous individuals.

1 Dangerousness and Dangerous People

With the introduction in 2015 in Spain of the life sentence (in Spanish law, the literal translation would be 'the reviewable permanent prison sentence'), the post-prison security measure of supervised release (as an extended sentence), as well as other matters already present in Spanish law, such as: assessing dangerousness when determining the granting of prison leave or the imposition of determining the dangerousness of an individual when imposing penal precautionary measures, and specifically when establishing penal protection measures for the victims of gender-based violence, matters relating to the contextual and media bias (Díez Ripollés 2015) towards the legislative/regulatory treatment of certain issues that are motivating political-criminal decisions and which are at the very least hurried, it seems necessary to introduce an actuarial element to support decision-making.

Thanks to the Faculty of Legal and Social Sciences of Toledo (UCLM) for its financial support.

M. P. Marco Francia (✉)
Faculty of Law, Complutense University of Madrid, Madrid, Spain
e-mail: pilar.marco@ucm.es

E. Demetrio Crespo et al. (eds.), *Crisis of the Criminal Law in the Democratic Constitutional State*, Legal Studies in International, European and Comparative Criminal Law 6, https://doi.org/10.1007/978-3-031-13413-5_16

The legislative changes appear to lead us to a shift in the dangerousness paradigm, towards an offender-based criminal law incorporated into postulates of the enemy criminal law. However, we need to understand that perhaps we are facing a new border, something 'new' to limit and define, which is ongoing, in the same way that modern neuroscientific techniques are raising new and passionate challenges for criminal law, just as González-Tapia (2018) propounds, when we refer to enemy criminal law, it could well be 'one more piece of a political-criminal model in progress, of a general trend towards the reconstruction of the criminal law of dangerousness in current criminal law. It would be an exceptional offender-based model (due to its greater repressive intensity) within a criminal law that, globally and progressively, incorporates criminal dangerousness from the very heart of the unjust and which is increasingly deployed in the punitive reaction, which is increasingly becoming multidimensional, with a progressive elimination of the boundaries between genuine punishments and security measures. This Law would be inserted as a complement to the criminal Law of liability, resulting in a mixed or individualised model whose dogmatic shape is yet to be determined'.

As we have already said, in Spanish criminal law, the determination of an individual's criminal dangerousness, considered as a judgement of the probable risk of reoffending, will be very important when deciding between the precautionary measures of provisional release and pre-trial detention or agreeing on a precautionary measure prohibiting approach and communication, or on issues as whether or not to impose a security measure of supervised release, to grant the benefit of the suspension of the execution of the custodial sentence, to grant prison leave or when deciding whether to grant parole.

Unfortunately, when we have to take decisions, legal practitioners increasingly frequently apply a more professionally cautious law. The point is we are afraid of incurring false negatives, and of making an assumption of non-dangerousness in case the subject violates it (for example, when not requesting a precautionary measure prohibiting approach). For this reason, actuarial aid, with properly calibrated risk-prediction instruments, could help to avoid future victimisations and contribute to reducing the institutional cost of the subjects, avoiding unnecessary measures of pre-trial detention and therefore maximising the available resources in caring for individuals who do require it (Pérez Ramírez et al. 2009).

We must not forget that risk prevention techniques in matters of interpersonal violence still do not have a satisfactory level of prediction, for several reasons (Daffern 2010), such as not considering the basic rates of assault, which are low and therefore more difficult to predict, thus producing more false positives than negatives. We are speaking in eminently probabilistic terms, so the possibility of error exists, although there is training in risk predictor instruments (Storey et al. 2012, p. 299).

It is worth emphasising that the question of criminal dangerousness was already mentioned in the Bible, with the first Christians being dangerous subjects and the question of dangerousness was already brought to light by the Italian positivists, who defined the dangerous condition as that of a person who combines criminal capacity and social inclusion (Garófalo 1912).

Dangerousness is very difficult to conceptualise. On occasion, carried along by the mainstream notion of dangerousness and risk control, we tend to categorise as dangerous terrorists, sex offenders and, recently, the perpetrators of gender-based violence, who appear to epitomise the dangerous offender in the public imagination.[1]

The natural progression seems to be to move from an apparently ineffective concept, to that of 'risk of violence' which seems to be more conceptually limited[2] and which doctrine defends as more appropriate (Andrés Pueyo and Echeburúa et al. 2010, p. 1).

A classic definition of criminal dangerousness would be that of Romeo Casabona (1986, Urruela Mora 2009, p. 5), who defines it as the likelihood of reoffending in the future. The judgment criteria for assessment are natural, meaning that morality is not involved, and it is carried out in two stages: the diagnosis of dangerousness and the prognosis of criminality, that is, how this dangerousness is related to a criminal future, which is where considerations of genetic vulnerability come in.

We are facing a moral and social dilemma (Walker 1996). While we want to prevent dangerous people from causing harm to others, we must also adapt the legal safeguards and restrict their lives as little as possible, especially when we are talking about probabilistic judgments that can lead to false negatives.

2 Assessing Dangerousness: Clinical Judgement and Structured Judgement

Although it is more usual to use clinical judgement, structured and actuarial clinical judgement approaches are gradually being adopted. It seems that actuarial instruments offer the greatest preventative validity (Monahan 2010, p. 17).

2.1 Clinical Judgement

Starting with clinical judgements or unstructured future violence risk judgements, it must be pointed out that these are based on the subjective judgement of professionals who carry out predictive judgements, usually psychiatrists, psychologists and social workers, who base their prognoses on their experience and theoretical orientation. Clinical judgement combines risk factors holistically and intuitively to produce an opinion on an individual's future risk of committing criminal offences. In clinical

---

[1] As Wacquant (2010, p. 63) points out 'the paedophile has become the vile incarnation of any threat to the integrity of the family and is feared to the same extent that the family is subjected to the hardships caused by the informalisation of employment. In short, it is "the other", the enemy to beat and whom we depersonalise in order objectify'.

[2] For a critical analysis of the concept of dangerousness, see Andrés-Pueyo (2013).

judgement, the allegedly dangerous subject undergoes an interview of a predominantly clinical nature by an expert who, in addition to examining the court records, previous convictions and other reports in court records, and after forming a clinical opinion, produces a prognosis about the individual's future criminal behaviour and whether the individual is likely to reoffend or not (Seto 2008, p. 145). This method is the most widely used throughout Europe, and is used almost exclusively (Padfield 2010, p. 7). It is the most common however, as it does not follow fixed rules, it is eminently discretional and so the inter-judge reliability is low (Andrés Pueyo and Echeburúa 2010). The assessment is generally negative, since it incurs many false positives (it is understood that the offenders are going to commit a violent action, but they do not), and there is even doubt as to whether its use is ethical, given that more precise assessment methods are available (Levenson and Morin 2006). Furthermore, it must be assumed that the experts who carry out clinical judgements are affected by personal bias which may spill over into their assessments (Monahan 2006).[3]

In the oldest scientific literature, the assessment of clinical judgment is defended in preference to statistical methods, despite the numerous false positives that both generate (Cohen et al. 1978). The advances in statistical and actuarial methods, which have been recognised in numerous scientific studies, must make us see that both are complementary and necessary. There will always be a clinical judgement, there will always be someone who assesses and pours out all their knowledge when the test is taken and similarly, the results of the programmes will also be interpreted by human beings.

In Spain, medical-legal expertise on the dangerous condition should be attributed to forensic doctors, as they are medical professionals with a comprehensive knowledge of psychiatry (specialised de facto, although the content of their public sector examination includes an extensive set of psychiatry topics) and which could be extended to forensic psychologists dependent on Spanish medical-legal institutions. According to Villanueva and Valenzuela (2005, p. 1089), as the term 'dangerous' is so ambiguous and predicting human behaviour so difficult, the attribution of 'dangerousness' to a subject is usually determined by means of typological classification, assigning it to the subjects with traits that occur more frequently in dangerous individuals, as opposed to those with the traits of 'normal' people. The assessments will refer to: the harmfulness of the act (regarding the harm caused by the act and where aggressiveness and emotional indifference will be assessed) and 'unintimidation', considered to be the subject's lack of restraint, and where egocentricity and emotional lability will be assessed. The subject's social (non-)adaptation will also be assessed, and the (always approximate) typology of the dangerous subject will be the result of both assessments.

[3] Monahan points to two studies carried out on the validity of the predictions of clinical judgment. In one of them it was found that only 39% of the defendants who had a medium-high risk of reoffending committed crimes in the following two years, while 26% of those classified as low risk committed a crime. With respect to the other study to which Monahan alludes, of the patients with a predicted high risk of recidivism, one in two committed an offence, and one in three of those classified as low risk or no risk of recidivism committed a violent criminal offence.

The procedure of forensic assessment is based on a medical-psychological examination whereby a psychiatric exploration is carried out, which assesses, by means of an interview; the biographical clues relevant to the psychological analysis (anamnesis), a psychopathological examination of the subject, their family history, the possible consumption of toxics and their attitude to rules will also be studied.

Psychometric surveys can also be carried out through test batteries to explore the traits that interest us, such as intelligence, personality, impulsivity, aggressiveness or anxiety. In addition, it would be advisable to contrast the information acquired with the family, social and personal circumstances of the subject being assessed, but this is not usually possible, since the specialist's report is basically based on the interview with the patient and on complementary information that can be found in the court records or which comes from other administrations (Gisbert Calabuig 2005).[4]

Clinical judgement consists of the assessment by a professional of pre-existing data and of that obtained by the clinical subject who is going to act as judge, while in actuarial assessment human bias is eliminated and replaced by the statistics selected (Janus and Prentky 2003, p. 1453). The use of statistical or actuarial risk assessment tools could provide greater clarity and therefore improve the assessment of the future risk of an offender.

2.2 *Structured Clinical Judgement*

It would appear that the best way to obtain correct predictions is by combining psychological and behavioural variables, or also actuarial variables, rather than using clinical judgment as the sole method (Rodríguez et al. 2002).

In structured clinical judgement we have the relevant expert or clinical specialist, who in turn is in possession of the court records, but who uses a guide to the risk factors to be assessed, both structured and unstructured; that is, whether they have been empirically verified or are the result of the expert's 'clinical eye'. For Andrés-Pueyo and Echeburúa (2010, p 408), this is the best technique to prevent crime because it avoids bias or forgetfulness on the part of the assessor, and they consider that the assessor cannot be dispensed with and that these tools indeed help the assessor to decide.

As we have already stated, these methods are used as a guide to support clinical professionals, but they do not establish how to measure or evaluate the variables; that is at the discretion of the professional. The main structured clinical methods are:

[4]For Padfield (2010, p. 7), it is imperative to clarify who is an expert in the assessment of dangerousness and if a psychiatrist is more qualified than anyone else to predict dangerousness, in principle because the very concept of dangerousness is basically a political and flexible label. In addition, the experts must be independent, and the affected people must have the right of access to independent reports and experts. Third, since the subject is eminently subjective, the assessments must be carried out with caution, and the judges or other institutions that use these reports must be warned of the weaknesses inherent in any future prediction made by an expert.

PCL-R, PCL-SV, HCR-20, SVR-20, MnSOST, HCR-20, SRA y MMPI-2 (Tiffon Nonis 2009; Marco Francia 2016).

2.3 General Considerations on Actuarial Models

If we understand from Steadman (Dresdner and Gutiérrez 2010) dangerousness as a 'probabilistic estimate that something will occur', it seems appropriate that to assess it, a probabilistic estimate should be carried out and will be achieved by performing a probability calculation. When we talk about an actuarial model we are referring to 'a method that uses statistics and probability calculation in the study of questions pertaining to social welfare. In Psychology, actuarial methods have been used to make predictions in fields such as the appearance or development of behavioural disorders and school failure, amongst others' (Moreno Rosset 2005, p. 186), in addition to dangerousness, that is the area which concerns us.

Most states in the USA use these actuarial risk assessment instruments for sex offenders at some point during their monitoring (Storey et al. 2012, p. 4). However, the statistical instruments have to be considered together with a clinical judgement and the static and dynamic elements must be assessed in an integrated manner (Ansbro 2010).

These models make decisions based on algorithms used after research findings. Therefore, the risk is calculated mathematically by including only variables that have been considered in the model. The most used actuarial models are the VRAG, the SORAG, RRASOR, STATIC-99 and ICT (Tiffon Nonis 2009).

Risk assessment tools such as the STATIC-99, RRASOR and the Minnesota Sex Offender Screening Tool-Revised are mainly based on so-called static (or unalterable) risk factors and, although they undoubtedly have limitations, we can affirm that they are more trustworthy than mere clinical judgement. Therefore, we could consider it unethical to remain anchored to clinical judgement when it has been empirically proven that statistical methods are more accurate. On the accuracy and to predicting recidivism in sexual crimes, clinical judgement has a prediction of $r = 0.40$, while statistical methods have $r = 0.60$. Other variables that assessors can consider, as well as strong predictors of recidivism in sexual violence, are: previous sexual crimes, failure of previous treatment and whether we are facing an offender with a psychopathic personality. As for dynamic elements[5] that may modify the level of risk, we can mention, amongst others: having access to the victims, lacking social support or having negative social influences, sexual concerns, tolerant attitudes towards sexual assault and/or poor self-management strategies, as well as a lack of cooperation with different types of monitoring. However, other variables which at an

[5]The latest research indicates that risk assessments would be greatly improved if we advanced our understanding of the evidence surrounding dynamic factors (Ansbro 2010, p. 266; Padfield 2010, p. 9).

intuitive level we may think do relate to possible reoffending, such as: the number and age of the victims, substance abuse and the non-assumption of having committed a crime, amongst others, have not been scientifically established. Levenson and Morin (2006) consider that when assessing and subsequently recommending civil commitment, experts' clinical judgment may be tainted by those fears and beliefs, as well as demographic factors (race, social class, etc.) that may make them recommend internment when it has not been scientifically proven that these variables make it more likely for the dangerous criminals to reoffend. In this regard, Ansbro (2010) conducted research with a small risk assessment group where the information provided by the actuarial programs was inconsistent with the clinical judgment. The results of the study revealed that the experts were more inlined to use their own criteria, contradicting the actuarial information that indicated low risk, than when it was high, thus confirming the precautionary principle. Furthermore, there was found to be a reluctance to accept a reduction of the risk for sex offenders even when there was evidence for it, and the opposite occurred with non-sex offenders, to whom the risk was reduced with weak evidence and against the actuarial criteria.

Actuarial systems are widely used in medicine regarding life expectancy for certain diseases such as cancer, and also in life insurance. However, we have to consider that such predictions are carried out with a massive amount of data and, as we know with statistics, the larger the sample size, the greater the precision in future predictions. Nevertheless, as far as crime is concerned, appropriate predictions could be made for less serious crime, of which there are many cases, but not for serious or very serious crime, of which fortunately there are few cases, and so the chances of false positives are very high. According to Harcourt (2007, p. 185), it has to be said that the fact that a certain life insurance premium is awarded will not affect someone's chances of dying, while ruling that leave or parole will not be granted or that a post-prison measure will be applied in response to the dangerousness will change the way that person behaves and how they are seen by society, and so it will affect the likelihood of that person reoffending. In addition to what Harcourt (2007) refers to as the 'ratchet effect', which is none other than defining a certain profile of people as dangerous via statistical methods, as an indirect result, surveillance of such people will increase and therefore, more cases will be detected and so we will see a self-fulfilling prophecy.

3 The Case of Spain

3.1 Criminal Dangerousness in Spain

The Spanish Royal Academy (of the language) understands dangerousness as that which has the 'quality of dangerous' and 'dangerous'. In its first meaning, it means 'that which has a risk and can cause damage' and its second meaning refers to a person, 'that may cause harm or commit criminal acts'. For Villanueva and Valenzuela (2005, p. 1085) a dangerous condition would constitute 'behaviour which there is a strong chance will result in damage to legally-protected goods, or as behaviour that is socially condemned'. Of course, if these dangerous conditions do not result in criminal dangerousness; that is, if a crime is not committed, they would constitute social dangerousness and therefore be beyond legal reproach, but not beyond social reproach.

In Spain, there is no definition of legal dangerousness, nor is there one of a dangerous subject. However, we can find direct and indirect references to dangerousness and criminal dangerousness in the regulation of pre-trial detention, in the Criminal Code, as well as in prison legislation:

(1) The regulation of pre-trial detention

In the day-to-day course of judicial life, we find ourselves in situations of having to decide between the precautionary measures of provisional release or pre-trial detention.[6] The existence of appropriate actuarial instruments could help the judge when deciding, beyond their 'clinical eye' or personal intuition regarding reoffending or any other of the cases of application of the precautionary measure of pre-trial detention.

(2) The Spanish Criminal Code

   (a) In Article 6 of the Criminal Code, Section 1, which bases the imposition of security measures on the dangerousness of the subject, provided that said dangerousness manifests itself in the commission of a crime (post-offence security measures); and Section 2 which limits its duration to the penalty abstractly applicable to the crime committed and to the time necessary to prevent the offender from being dangerous.
   (b) Articles 36.1 and 92 of the Criminal Code where the review of the reviewable permanent prison (life) sentence is authorised in accordance with the progression to the third degree in prison (open prison) and also article 36.4 referring to certain very seriously ill inmates with incurable diseases and of

[6]Pre-trial detention is regulated by Articles 502 and 503 of the Criminal Procedure Act (henceforth CPA), as a deprivation of the fundamental right to liberty (Article 17 of the Constitution), meaning that it is exceptional and will only be imposed when there are no other less burdensome measures applicable to the case, and the repercussions for the life of the individual that the measure will produce must always be considered; that is, in accordance with the principles of exceptionality (since the *favor libertatis* or *in dubio pro libertatis* governs), that of proportionality, to which we have already alluded, and the principle of judiciality; it must be imposed by the judge or magistrate examining or judging; and the principle of provisionality, by which said prison must be reviewed as the circumstances that justified its imposition change (STC 128/1995 of 26th July).

The judge must weigh up whether to establish pre-trial detention between the *favor libertatis* and the possible danger of escape, destruction of evidence or of acting against the victim/witness. Furthermore, the second paragraph alludes to the possibility of the accused reoffending, always concurrently with the first and second requirements, together with the seriousness of the crime already committed and those that they could commit, concluding that the requirement of two years in prison is not even necessary, as long as it can be inferred from the court records that they are a habitual criminal or that they collaborate with others in an organised way to commit crimes.

septuagenarians, assessing their low dangerousness, the main reasons being humanitarian and human dignity.

(c) Article 83 of the Criminal Code regulates the condition of the suspension of the execution of the term of imprisonment (similar to probation) on the fulfilment of certain prohibitions and duties. Sections 3 and 4 establish the obligation of the law enforcement agencies and the services for the management of penalties and alternative measures of penitentiary institutions to notify the Judge or Enforcement Court and the Prosecution Service if there is a violation or non-compliance with them (or other circumstances) because it will be relevant to assess the prisoner's dangerousness and the likelihood of their reoffending in the future.

(d) Reference is also made to the dangerousness of the subject in the regulation of parole, specifically in Article 90.5 of the Criminal Code, where the judge responsible for the enforcement of sentences is empowered to revoke the suspension of the execution of the rest of the sentence and parole granted when there has been a severe modification of the situation that allowed the suspension of the execution, which no longer permits the prognosis of lack of danger on which the decision was based.

(e) In the case of seriously ill inmates with proven incurable conditions, or septuagenarians (or those who reach that age during their sentence), Article 91 of the Criminal Code empowers the penitentiary institutions to raise their parole with the judge responsible for the sentence, even when they have not completed the necessary part of the sentence established in Article 90 of the Criminal Code. In the ruling, the judge responsible for the enforcement of sentences will have to assess, together with the subject's personal circumstances, the likelihood of their committing a crime and the subject's low dangerousness. In the case of Section 3, in cases of obvious danger to the life of the inmate due to illness or age and considering the subject's lack of dangerousness, it establishes the granting of parole, with no other procedures except for a report from the prison on the final prognosis to be able to assess it. Clearly, we are dealing with humanitarian assumptions that try to preserve the dignity of the inmate.

(f) In Article 92.3 *in fine* of the Criminal Code, which deals with the revocation of the benefit of the suspension of the enforcement of the term of imprisonment, when there has been a change in circumstances that make it impossible to maintain the prognosis of lack of dangerousness which motivated the granting of the benefit in the first place.

(g) Article 97 b) enables the judge or sentencing court to order the cessation of the security measure imposed if the criminal dangerousness of the subject disappears.

(h) In the regulation of probation in Article 192.1 of the Criminal Code when it is empowered to not impose supervised freedom after the custodial sentence in the case of a less serious crime committed by a primary offender of scarce dangerousness. It is established in the same way by the Criminal Code in Article 579.3 for crimes of terrorism.

If we look at the regulation of the post-criminal and post-prison supervised release security measure in our country, it seems that the dangerous subjects *ab initio* in the 2010 regulation were sex offenders (Article 192.1 CP) and terrorists (Article 579 bis 2). Subsequently, as the cases of application were increased in 2015, the concept of dangerous imputable subjects would be extended to those convicted of crimes against life (Articles 138 and subsequent Criminal Code), injuries with victims of Article 173.2 Criminal Code (Article 156 *ter* Criminal Code) and habitual domestic abuse (Article 173.2 Criminal Code *in fine*).

(1) Prison regulations

Without claiming to be exhaustive, the prison regulations refer to dangerousness with regard to the closed regime, the most severe (Article 10 of the General Prisons Act (LOGP) 1/1979, of September 26, 74, 91 Royal Ordinance 190/1996, of February 9, Prison Regulations (PR), the regime for prisoners on remand (Article 96.3 RP), the assessment for carrying out prison transfers (Article 38 PR), the intensity of internal security measures (Article 65 PR); Article 102.3 of the PR with reference to Article 10 of the General Prisons Act (LOGP) indicates the factors that need to be weighed up to examine extreme dangerousness or manifest and serious maladjustment to the general rules of orderly coexistence that makes them deserving of the first degree. In this article, we can distinguish defining notes on the concept of prison dangerousness that can be categorised as follow: (1) Criminological factors of the offender's personality in relation to their criminal record sheet: (a) The nature of the crimes committed throughout their criminal history, which denotes an aggressive, violent and antisocial personality. (2) Criminal typology: (a) Commission of acts that threaten the life or physical integrity of persons, sexual freedom or property, committed in particularly violent ways, (b) Belonging to criminal organisations or armed gangs, as long as they do not demonstrate, in both cases, unequivocal signs of having escaped the internal discipline of said organisations or gangs. (3) Eminently penitentiary issues as regards their effect on the security of the prison, such as: (a) Active participation in riots, protest strikes, physical attacks, threats, or coercion. (b) Commission of disciplinary offences classified as very serious or serious, repeatedly and sustained over time. (c) Introduction or possession of firearms in prison, as well as the possession of toxic drugs, narcotic drugs and psychotropic substances in significant amounts, giving reason to believe they are intended for trafficking.

Having said that, can we and should we limit our 'dangerous' setting to this type of criminal? We have a series of preconceived ideas about what is and is not dangerous, and as we mentioned before, this will depend on our subjective vision of what we consider dangerous or not and the social alarm that is unleashed and magnified by the media regarding certain crimes that occur in our communities. Armaza Armaza (2013) considers influential factors for highlighting the issue of dangerousness: the existence of global communication media, the existence of new forms of response to crimes and the fact that there is great interest in the effective protection of the most important legal assets, closely related to the development of the global communication media.

When assessing dangerousness, we have to predict whether a delinquent is going to commit another crime, using as the indicative criterion the previous commission of a crime, considering that a fundamental problem with prediction is that two possible errors can always be made: either someone who is mistakenly thought not to be dangerous is released or someone who has been wrongly diagnosed as dangerous remains in prison and, as we have pointed out, when the recidivism rate is low, it is statistically more difficult to predict human behaviour and so the risk of making mistakes increases (Van Zyl Smit and Spencer 2010, p. 332).

3.2 The Risk Assessment of Dangerousness

Risk assessment can refer to two tracks on the same trail in the victim/delinquent pairing. On the one hand, there is the risk of victimisation; that is, the probability of experiencing the crime, and on the other, the risk of a violent aggressor reoffending.

On the assessment of the risk of the offender reoffending, we will refer to the assessment of risk and the methods we have to predict the potential risk of recidivism. On risk assessment in Spanish law, we must consider what is established by the Criminal Procedure Law in its Articles 456 to 485, and what is established regarding imputability in Article 20 of the Criminal Code.

The role of experts in brain damage or cognitive disorders, specialists in neuroscience,[7] neuropsychologists or psychiatrists, is to provide the courts with information pertaining to their expertise in brain damage and its consequences, not only cognitive, but also social, and in emotional and behavioural issues of both the accused and the victim (Naharro et al. 2010, p. 44).

As far as the predictive methods that have been used or are in use are concerned, they are basically clinical judgment (structured or unstructured) and actuarial methods. The future is by definition an unknown quantity and although scientific methods can give us a reasonably clear idea of matters in the near future (for example, regarding the weather), foreseeing what a person is going to do in the future is difficult. Since not even you yourself know how you will react in five minutes, it is even more difficult for a person to foresee that another person will commit a violent act in the future, even when there has been a previous act of violence.

---

[7] By neurosciences, we refer to the disciplines that study 'the development, structure, function, pharmacology and pathology of the nervous system', see Mora and Sanguinetti (2004, p. 173).

3.3 *The Gradual Introduction of Actuarial Methods in Spain*

Although there are some scales that have been adapted to the characteristics of the Spanish sex offender population, such as: HCR-20, VRAG, PCL-R, SARA (Andrés Pueyo and Echeburúa 2010; Jiménez Gómez et al. 2014),[8] EPV, SVR-20 and SAVRY (Andrés Pueyo and Echeburúa 2010; Marco Francia 2016), we will briefly examine below the scales that are used in Spain, referring the reader to works that deal in detail with the adapted instruments that we have just mentioned.

In Spain, we have been making and adapting actuarial tools as a scientific alternative to clinical judgement for more than a decade. Arbach-Lucioni and Andrés-Pueyo (2016), in a study of Spanish professionals—psychologists ($n = 35$, 87.5%) and other professionals in the mental health area ($n = 5$, 12.5%)—who had worked in Spain for at least the 12 months prior to receiving the survey, indicated as a result of their research that professionals in the legal and health systems use these tools regularly, in varying ways, the most frequent use being when the person to be assessed is a male suffering from a personality disorder and/or substance use disorder. According to the study, the psychopathy scales (PCL-R and PCL: SV) and the HCR-20 were the most used tools, the LSI-R[9] being the instrument that seemed the most useful in risk management and monitoring.

3.3.1 Risk Assessments on Gender-Based Violence

Given the serious concern about the criminal and social phenomenon of gender-based violence in Spain, we will analyse the different instruments regarding gender-based violence which have been adapted or developed in our country.

[8] This instrument (SARA), owned by the British Columbia Institute on Family Violence, is used to predict the risk of violent manifestation of domestic abusers with respect to their partner or ex-partner. Its second version has been adapted in Spain by the Group for Advanced Studies in Violence of the University of Barcelona and analyses criteria of psychosocial adjustment, history of aggressions and living together as a couple. The contexts of application are both civil proceedings for custody, as well as criminal charges and assessment of the risk of violence or recidivism (Andrés Pueyo and Echeburúa 2010, p. 407). The Spanish adaptation is used in other Spanish-speaking countries as Chile (Gallardo and Concha-Salgado 2017).

[9] The Level of Service Inventory—Revised (LSI-R) is a quantitative tool, designed to be used on subjects aged 16 and over. It has 54 items and examines different characteristics of offenders and relevant situations in which they can be found to determine both the level of supervision and decisions regarding treatment, in the correctional or penitentiary environment. On its use in Spain, see Graña et al. (2014).

Severe Intimate Partner Violence Risk Prediction Scale (Revised) VRS-R

The VRS-R is also used in the context of intimate partners, but applied to the sphere of violence and designed by ECHEBURÚA and collaborators for the Spanish situation, specifically in the law enforcement area (it is used by the Basque Country Police force to determine the assessment of risk in the preparation of reports of gender-based violence), as well as in the judicial and forensic fields. However, according to its creators, it has not been tested outside the Basque Country and it has not been studied on intimate partner violence in general, only with respect to police reported violence. Furthermore, its validity has not been contrasted with other instruments such as the SARA (Echeburúa et al. 2010, p. 1059).

This tool was established to provide mental health professionals, lawyers and the law enforcement agencies the means to identify the protection measures that were required according to the needs of the victims. The scale shows good levels of consistency (Arbach-Lucioni 2015).

Protocol for Assessing the Risk of Intimate Partner Violence

This instrument was developed for the Spanish National Police and the Military Police (Guardia Civil). Regarding the Military Police and according to technical standard no. 1/2008 of July, which regulates the procedure of the Military Police units on this matter, the first risk assessment is carried out if the instructor of the report understands that the facts reported require a protection measure to be adopted. For this purpose, the standardised assessment form is used on the Police's computer system and the woman is subsequently informed of the result and the measures that can be applied. The score can be low, medium, high, or extreme.

Protocol for Assessing the Risk of Intimate Partner Violence Against Women (RVD-BCN)

This protocol was created by the Barcelona Circuit Against Gendered Violence.[10] It is aimed at professionals with experience in intimate partner violence so that they can use a validated and rigorous risk assessment guide which can predict the risk of serious violence against women by their partner or ex-partner in the period between 3 to 6 months after the risk assessment date (Andrés Pueyo and Echeburúa 2010; Arbach-Lucioni 2015, p. 284).

[10] See BCNROC. Repositori Obert de Coneixement de l'Ajuntament de Barcelona: RVD-BCN: protocol de valoració del risc de violència contra la dona per part de la seva parella o exparella). It has been made freely available to the public under the Creative Commons licence.

3.3.2 Instruments Used in Prison Systems

Assessment Scale for Violent Behaviour and Risk of Recidivism (SPVB-RR)

This instrument was created in Spain by Jiménez Gómez et al. (2014) to assess prisoners who are considered violent, following a study supported by the University of Salamanca and the National Autonomous University of Mexico. This scale has two adaptations, one Spanish and the other Mexican, and consists of 27 items, which are administered through a guided interview conducted by professionals who have experience both with the inmates and with the scale. It is applied in a prison context and, in addition to the interview, previous reports and files from the centre are also used, regarding three variables: recidivism, violence and psychopathy.

Table of Risk Variables (TRV)

The risk variables that are studied in the TRV are very similar to those that the Technical Team must assess, in addition to others, to decide whether or not to grant leave.[11]

Drawn up by CLEMENTE and collaborators for a prison context, it claims to be able to predict the risk of breach regarding the inmates' furloughs and scale 10 variables (Jiménez Gómez et al. 2014).

The variables were collected after a study by the Complutense University of Madrid (Daunis Rodríguez 2016, p. 240), in collaboration with the former Directorate General of Penitentiary Institutions, regarding breaches occurring among of large samples of inmates. Variables were applied to 1581 subjects in three groups depending on whether they had returned from prison leave (group C), did not rejoin (group B), or were not granted furlough (group A). After applying various statistics, an instrument was developed based on the variables that most decisively influenced the breach cases.

Administrative Instruction 3/2008[12] establishes the assessments of the variables that will not score 0, or will be assigned a 1, 2 or 3 (not all variables mark 3 points); they will be added up and it will be understood that the greater the result, the greater

[11] Article 156.1 of the Prison Regulations, R.D. 190/96, of February 9th, states that: 'The mandatory report of the Technical Team will be unfavourable when, due to the particular criminal trajectory, the anomalous personality of the inmate or the existence of unfavourable qualitative variables, breach of sentence, the commission of new crimes or a negative impact of the release on the prisoner from the perspective of their preparation for life in freedom or their individualised treatment programme are likely'.

[12] Available at: instruccion_3_2008.pdf (acaip.info) [last consultation date 17-9-22]. Previously established in Administrative Instruction 22/96, of December 16th, available at: INSTRUCCIÓN 22-96 permisos.doc (acaip.info) and Administrative Instruction 1/12, of April 2nd, available at: Instruccion_penitenciario_1_2012.pdf (igualdad.gob.es) [date of last consultation 17-9-22]. The latter Administrative Instruction has introduced two new special circumstances, the existence of administrative or judicial removal orders and the commission of crimes of gender-based violence.

the risk of breach. In those related to the person we can mention the following (Daunis Rodríguez 2016):

1. Immigration (if the person is a Spanish national, has a Spanish spouse or has had a work permit in Spain for more than 5 years, the score will be 0).
2. Drug addiction will score 0 (if the individual is not a user or remains abstinent for 5 years, having been released (even partially released) for at least a year, 1 (where there is sporadic drug use and unconsolidated rehabilitation attempts) or 2 (if there is a history of dependency without attempts at rehabilitation or repeated unsuccessful attempts).

On those related to criminal activity: 3. Criminal professionalism (isolated crimes will not score), 4. Recidivism (a first crime will not score, previous crimes will be assigned one point).

On the variables related to prison behaviour, we can distinguish between:

5. Breaches (if there are previous breaches in custody (3), no custody (1) and no breaches (0)).
6. Article 10 LOGP (or first degree in prison, if classed as such (1) or if the inmate has committed 4 very serious offences in 2 years (1)).
7. Lack of prison furloughs (score 0 if the inmate has benefitted from them in the last two years and 1 if they have not benefitted from them).

On the variables related to furloughs:

8. Cohabitation failure.
9. Distance between the place where furlough is taken and the place of execution of the sentence (1point if the place where the inmate will go on furlough is located at a distance greater than 400 km from the prison).
10. Internal pressures from other inmates in the unit.

Following the TRV and to complete the information to assess whether or not furlough is granted by the Technical Team, another prediction instrument is used, the Table of Concurrence of Special Circumstances (called M-CCP[13]), that is, if there are particular circumstances that may influence a possible misuse of the leave/furlough: The result of the TRV, if the risk is equal to or greater than 65 points, the type of crime for which the individual was convicted, especially if it was a crime against people, against sexual freedom, or gender-based violence, and if the person belongs to an armed gang or to an international criminal organisation.

In the cases of foreign convicts (non-EU and without legal residence) who also have an administrative or judicial removal order, as well as those who have committed serious crimes (punished with a prison sentence of more than five years), such specific circumstances and granting of permission will be assessed, the agreement must be specially justified and motivated so that the concurrence of such circumstances will not affect the risk of misuse or breach.

[13]This table consists of factors indicative of the risk of breach which could not be statistically validated. Cruz Márquez and Moya Guillem (2017, p. 6).

RisCanvi Protocol

The Autonomous Community of Catalonia, who has powers in prison matters along with the Basque Country in Spain, has used the RisCanvi risk assessment and management protocol for the entire Catalan prison population. This protocol emerged at the end of 2007 after the recommendations of the MENA Commission (Legal Ruling/2363/200, DOGC No. 4937, of 24th July 2007), which demanded the establishment of a technical protocol for risk assessment that could be applied in police forces, prison and judicial administrations. In its limited version (screening), the RISCANVI-S includes inmates' data, age, gender, marital status, procedural and prison situation, prison lifestyle, type of crime and relationship with the victim. Subsequently, 10 items appear, of which 7 are static, and therefore cannot be modified by the inmate (Rivera Beiras 2015): (1) the age of the first violent incident or the beginning of the violent behaviour; (2) the existence of violence prior to the main crime; (3) the subject's previous prison behaviour (serious or very serious offences); (4) escape, breaches or non-compliance with sentence; (5) problems with drugs or alcohol; (6) previous mental health problems; (7) self-harm attempts or behaviour; (8) absence of family and social network; (9) work-related problems and (10) a lack of future plans. In the event that the subject is found to be high risk according to the screening, the Riscanvi complet (Riscanvi-C) will be applied, which consists of the examination of criminal and prison factors, personal or psychosocial factors, and clinical and personality factors, distributed in 43 items and which result in a low, medium or high-risk classification. Good predictive results have been obtained for intra-institutional violent offences (Arbach-Lucioni 2015).

In research carried out by Férez Mangas and Andrés Pueyo (2016), of the ten risk factors that make up the RisCanvi-S assessment protocol, 'prison behavioural problems', 'escape, breaches or previous violations' and 'lack of family support' were established as powerful predictive factors of the risk of breach of furlough (OR = 1,92).

4 Conclusions

As has been emphasised in this analysis, risk assessment instruments currently used only incidentally in Spain, although their use has been increasing in recent years.

Even though there is no danger of decreeing a civil commitment or indefinite detention, as they do not exist in our legal system, actuarial techniques, with due precautions, can be useful guides regarding the application of issues as varied as precautionary measures, the security measure of supervised release, as well as those related to prison furloughs and the granting of parole.

The risk assessments for gender-based violence used by the National Police and the Military Police are very generalised and, depending on the assessed risk, relevant protection methods are recommended to the victim. Before carrying out further studies, it would be very interesting to determine how the National Police or Military

Police operator codifies the impressions of the interview with the female victim of violence, in addition to the objective data resulting from the report, or documentation from records, such as police or criminal records. It would be equally interesting to see how this result is reflected in the assessment of the aggressor's risk and, therefore, in the number and types of protection measures to adopt. Similarly, it would be necessary to study the correlation between the risk perceived by the computer program and whether there was afterwards any kind of breach or incident which confirmed that risk and equally, to try to determine through qualitative means to what extent the granting of the precautionary measures of a restraining order or pre-trial detention are based on the recommendations of the program.

In the same way, more critical research is needed on the actuarial instruments in Penitentiary Institutions, to enable us to know more about the strengths and weaknesses of these instruments, eschewing automatisms which violate the fundamental rights of people who have to be reintegrated into society. We should bear in mind that many of the matters that actuarial instruments assess, such as reoffending, are already considered by the legal operator performing the assessment, and other static offender issues, impossible to modify, must imply the involvement of public administrations for their removal, in accordance with Article 9.2 of the Constitution, and not pose an obstacle to the offender's re-education and social reintegration.

The practical applications which are already underway, together with those carried out by various university research teams regarding the application of instruments such as those mentioned above, encourage us to foresee a positive future for the use of statistical instruments as an auxiliary means that contributes to the decision of the Judge, court or administrative body, which may reach a conviction using, in addition to the actuarial instrument, the knowledge of technicians and experts. Our current scientific knowledge of human beings and their important individual differences, as well as the low incidence of violent issues at statistical levels, makes it more difficult for predictions to be successfully adjusted. Therefore, we must never forget that we are talking about probabilities, not certainties. These probabilities can be exceeded and the *ratio decidendi* of an actuarial instrument cannot entail the making of decisions limiting a person's fundamental rights, without other compelling arguments to support it especially, as indicated by Rivera Beiras (2015) if it creates a severe violation of those fundamental rights.

References

Andrés-Pueyo A (2013) La peligrosidad criminal: Análisis crítico de un concepto polisémico. In: Demetrio E, Maroto M (eds) Neurociencias y Derecho Penal. Edisofer S.L., Madrid, pp 483–503

Andrés-Pueyo A, Echeburúa E (2010) Valoración del riesgo de violencia: instrumentos disponibles e indicaciones de aplicación. Psicothema 22(3):403–409

Ansbro M (2010) The nuts and bolts of risk assessment: when the clinical and actuarial conflict. Howard J Crim Just 49(3):252–268. https://doi.org/10.1111/j.1468-2311.2010.00614.x

Arbach-Lucioni K (2015) La práctica de la evaluación del riesgo de violencia en España. Revista de la Facultad de Medicina 63(3)

Arbach-Lucioni K, Andrés-Pueyo A (2016) Violence risk assessment practices in Spain. In: Singh JP, Bjørkly S, Fazel S (eds) International perspectives on violence risk assessment. Oxford University Press, Oxford, pp 280–295

Armaza Armaza EJ (2013) El tratamiento penal del delincuente peligroso. Editorial Comares S.L., Granada

Cohen M, Groth A, Siegel R (1978) The clinical prediction of dangerousness. Crime Delinq 24:28–39. https://doi.org/10.1177/001112877802400103

Cruz Márquez B, Moya Guillem C (2017) Concesión de permisos de salida al agresor de género. Revista Electrónica de Ciencia Penal y Criminología:1–40

Daffern M (2010) Risk assessment for aggressive behavior in personality disorder. In: Tennant A, Howells K (eds) Using time, not doing time. Practitioner perspectives on personality disorder and risk. Wiley-Blackwell, Chichester, pp 15–32

Daunis Rodríguez A (2016) Criterios para la valoración de la peligrosidad y el riesgo en el ámbito penitenciario. Cuadernos de Política Criminal:239–280

Díez Ripollés JL (2015) Delitos y Penas en España. Los libros de la catarata, Madrid

Dresdner R, Gutiérrez O (2010) Los trastornos de comportamiento y cambios permanentes en la personalidad. In: Jarne A, Aliaga Á (eds) Manual de neuropsicología forense. Herder, Barcelona, pp 117–158

Echeburúa E, Amor PJ, Loinaz I, Corral P (2010) Escala de predicción del riesgo de violencia grave contra la parejarevisada (EPV-R). Psicothema 22(4):1054–1060

Férez Mangas D, Andrés Pueyo A (2016) Predicción y prevención del quebrantamiento de los permisos penitenciarios. Revista Española de Investigación Criminológica:1–28

Gallardo R, Concha-Salgado A (2017) Propiedades psicométricas del Manual para la Valoración del Riesgo de Violencia contra la Pareja (SARA) en agresores chilenos. Terapia Psicológica 35 (2)

Garófalo R (1912) La Criminología. Estudio sobre la naturaleza del crimen y teoría de la personalidad. Daniel Jorro Editor, Madrid

Gisbert Calabuig JA (2005) Medicina Legal y toxicología. Masson, S.A., Barcelona

González-Tapia MI (2018) Derecho penal de la peligrosidad y neuropredicción: hacia un "Derecho penal individualizado". In: Suárez JM, Barquín J, Benítez I, Jiménez MJ, Sáinz JE (eds) Estudios Jurídico Penales y Criminológicos. En homenaje al Dr. Dr. H. C. Mult. Lorenzo Morillas Cueva. Editorial Dykinson S.L., Madrid, pp 327–351

Graña JL, Andreu JM, Silva T, Pozuelo F, Ruiz A (2014) Evaluación de las propiedades psicométricas del LSI-R en una muestra penitenciaria. Psicopatología Clínica, Legal y Forense 14(2014):7–23

Harcourt B (2007) Against prediction, profiling, policing and punishing in actuarial age. University of Chicago Press, Chicago

Janus E, Prentky R (2003) Forensic use of actuarial risk assessment with sexual offenders: accuracy, admissibility and accountability. Am Crim Law Rev 40(4):1443–1499

Jiménez Gómez F, Sánchez Crespo G, Merino Barragán V, Ampudia Rueda A (2014) Evaluación de la peligrosidad en la población penitenciaria. Ratio Legis Ediciones, Salamanca

Levenson J, Morin J (2006) Factors predicting selection of sexually violent predators for civil commitment. Int J Offender Ther Comp Criminol 50(6):609–629. https://doi.org/10.1177/0306624X06287644

Marco Francia MP (2016) La peligrosidad criminal y las técnicas de prevención de riesgos: especial referencia a la delincuencia sexual peligrosa. Anuario de Derecho penal y ciencias penales:277–320

Monahan J (2006) A jurisprudence of risk assessment: forecasting harm among prisoners, predators, and patients. Virginia Law Rev 92(3):391–435

Monahan J (2010) Structured risk assessment of violence. In: Simon RI (ed) Textbook of violence assessment and management. American Psychiatric Publishing Inc., London

Mora F, Sanguinetti AM (2004) Diccionario de neurociencia. Alianza Editorial, Madrid
Moreno Rosset C (2005) Evaluación psicológica. Concepto, proceso y aplicación en las áreas del desarrollo y de la inteligencia. Editorial Sanz y Torres S.L., Madrid
Naharro ML, Soler J, Falcone D (2010) El rol del neuropsicólogo forense en los tribunales. In: Jarne IA, Aliaga Á (eds) Manual de neuropsicología forense. De la clínica a los tribunales. Herder, Barcelona, pp 13–45
Padfield N (2010) The sentencing, management and treatment of the 'dangerous' offenders. In: Final report. European Committee on crime problems, Council for Penological Co-operation. Council of Europe, Strasbourg
Pérez Ramírez M, Redondo Illescas S, Martínez García M, García Forero C, Andrés Pueyo A (2009) Assessing risk of recidivism in sex offenders. Psychol Spain 13(1):55–61
Rivera Beiras I (2015) Actuarialismo penitenciario. Su recepción en España. Revista Crítica Penal y Poder:102–144
Rodríguez A, López JM, Andrés Pueyo A (2002) Personalidad y comportamiento penitenciario. Psicothema 14(supl):90–100
Romeo Casabona CM (1986) Peligrosidad y Derecho Penal preventivo. Bosch, Barcelona
Seto M (2008) Pedophilia and sexual offending against children: theory, assessment, and intervention. American Psychological Association, Washington
Storey JE, Watt K, Jackson K, Hart S (2012) Utilization and Implications of the Static-99 in practice. Sex Abuse J Res Treat 24:289–302. https://doi.org/10.1177/1079063211423943
Tiffon Nonis BN (2009) Manual de actuación profesional en Psicopatología clínica, criminal y forense. Librería Bosch, Barcelona
Urruela Mora A (2009) Las medidas de seguridad y reinserción social en la actualidad. Editorial Comares, Granada
Van Zyl Smit D, Spencer J (2010) The European dimension to the release of sentenced Prisoners. In: Padfield N (ed) Release from prison. European policy and practice. Willan, Abingdon, pp 9–48
Villanueva Cañadas E, Valenzuela Garach A (2005) La prognosis criminal. In: J. A. Gisbert Calabuig, Medicina legal y toxicología. (Sexta edición. Reimpresión ed.), Masson, S.A., Barcelona, pp 1085–1093
Wacquant L (2010) Castigar a los pobres. El gobierno neoliberal de la inseguridad social. Gedisa editorial, Barcelona
Walker N (1996) Dangerous people. Blackstone Press Limited, London

Criminal Law of Security: Serious Crime and Visibility

Laura Zúñiga Rodríguez

Abstract The current criminal law of security expressed in punitive populism has a bias towards the criminal prosecution of street and violent crimes, while the crimes of power and business run with greater tolerance of society and legal operators, because they are carried out in standardized contexts. To support this thesis, we analyze what society understands by serious (dangerous) crime, the visibility of crime and crime statistics, principally. This analysis leads us to the consideration that the perception of social harm, the fear of being a victim of crime, social tolerance of certain behaviors, the media that construct stereotypes, and the visibility shown in statistics, all combined, give rise to a social construction of the material content of serious crime in a selective manner, oriented toward crimes against persons, leaving socioeconomic crimes out of focus.

1 Introduction

The hypothesis I try to illustrate in this article is the following: The punitive populism and the criminal law of security that is predominant in the current political-criminal scenario are fundamentally oriented towards the prevention of street crime, of the violent type, forgetting that at the current period of social development there are other forms of criminality, non-violent and non-street, which are carried out in normalized contexts of business and power, which have not received sufficient social attention and, consequently, there is a weak criminal prosecution in this area.

To support this proposition, I will analyze two conceptual tools that are closely linked: serious crime and visibility. Both of them allow us to unravel the expansion bias of criminal law, perhaps not so much in the always hyper-punitive (frequently symbolic) criminal legislation, but above all in the criminal prosecution itself, that is,

L. Zúñiga Rodríguez (✉)
Faculty of Law, University of Salamanca, Salamanca, Spain
e-mail: lzr@usal.es

E. Demetrio Crespo et al. (eds.), *Crisis of the Criminal Law in the Democratic Constitutional State*, Legal Studies in International, European and Comparative Criminal Law 6, https://doi.org/10.1007/978-3-031-13413-5_17

in the prosecution and conviction of crime, for which criminal statistics should be a good barometer.

What is intended to be emphasized is that the punitive populism in vogue, in practice, does not affect all social sectors in the same way, because there is a clear emphasis on certain forms of crime, those committed by the marginal sectors; while the crimes perpetrated by the economic and political power elites, although they are affected by primary criminalization (criminal classification), are not—or, at least not to the same extent – in secondary criminalization (criminal prosecution), nor in tertiary criminalization (serving prison sentences).

There are, of course, different factors that determine this criminological reality: tolerance (or intolerance) of certain behaviors, the social perception of the crime type and/or the type of offender, the media's influence, the fear of being a victim of crime, the conflictive nature of society, the way in which society handles conflict resolution, citizens' confidence in the justice system, police efficiency, etc. It is not possible to detail all these variables because it would exceed the limits of this paper. The idea is to base this analysis on two concepts: serious crime and visibility.

Accordingly, before getting to the core of the matter, it is necessary to examine two issues that should serve as a framework for analysis. First, whether there is a consensus in society on what is to be understood by serious crime, given that national and international strategic documents make use of this concept, under the premise of sustained agreements on criminal intervention in these cases. Second, whether the visibility of crimes is a determining factor in recognizing their seriousness and how this affects citizens' demands for criminal policy, stressing the punitive bias. In short, whether punitive populism, the profile of the criminal law of security that has been developed in recent years, is generalized or, as I try to show, it is strong for the weak and weak for the strong.

2 Serious Crime and Social Perception

The legal definitions do not indicate what should be understood by serious crime from a criminological perspective and from a comparative law perspective,[1] that is, what is considered serious crime from the social reality (material consideration), a

[1] El art. 13 del código penal considera delito grave al que se le impone pena grave, en una tautología difícil de dar contenido material a *qué conductas deberían entenderse como delincuencia grave*. Evidentemente la ley penal contiene otras variables para denotar la gravedad: agravantes, atenuantes, eximentes, habitualidad, reincidencia, etc. Un código penal que contiene más agravantes que atenuantes, es más punitivista. Art. 13 of the Criminal Code considers a serious crime to be one for which a serious penalty is imposed, in a tautology that is difficult to give material content to what behaviors should be understood as serious crime. Evidently, the criminal law has other variables to denote seriousness: aggravating factors, mitigating factors, exonerating factors, habituality, recurrence, etc. A penal code that contains more aggravating than mitigating factors is more punitive.

fundamental question, given that according to the principles of proportionality and subsidiarity, punishment in these cases (deservedness and necessity of punishment) would be legitimized.

International organizations, both the United Nations (UN) and the European Union (EU), have been focusing on serious crime, especially organized and transnational crime, since after the Cold War they were the main threats to world peace. Kofi Annan, in his report: *A broader concept of freedom: development, security, and human rights for all,*[2] proposes that *before global problems, global solutions must be found*. The barriers between states at least two decades ago have been overcome by transnational criminal organizations. Their scale is often measured by their ability to open up to new international markets. As a result, the boundaries between internal and external security are blurring. The supposed enemies of the states are not external agents that threaten the citizens enclosed within their borders. International criminal organizations are becoming *non-state actors* on the world stage. Other global threats such as global warming indicate the need to advance in common, coordinated, global responses, trying to harmonize the legislation of countries to achieve common criminal policies.

In this effort to reach international agreements, the United Nations Convention against Transnational Organized Crime, which represents the largest multilateral agreement to address this international problem, in addition to dealing with the common definition of the crime of participation in an organized criminal group, by referring to those offenses punishable by *severe penalties*, provides a definition of serious crimes (Art. 2 b). This is the seriousness parameter that has been followed internationally, according to this definition it is considered serious crimes those that contemplate prison sentences of at least four years. However, in practice, its interpretation hides a great difference in value, since there is nothing more diverse than the range of penalties, especially if we compare it from one country to another. As Militello states: "The reference to a certain level of punishment is, therefore, common only in absolute value, but keeps a relative differentiated value according to the ceilings or upper limits on the punishment that the jurisdiction itself internally establishes."[3]

Thus, to give an example, between two close EU countries, such as Spain and Italy, and a criminal characteristic of organized crime, such as illicit drug trafficking, one can observe large differences regarding the penalties in the basic type: Art. 368 of the Spanish Criminal Code (CP) establishes penalties ranging from 3–6 years

[2] NN UU (2005) En el punto 78 sostiene: "Entre las amenazas a la paz y la seguridad en el siglo XXI se cuentan no sólo la guerra y los conflictos internacionales, sino los disturbios civiles, la delincuencia organizada, el terrorismo y las armas de destrucción en masa ... Todas ellas pueden socavar a los Estados como unidades básicas del sistema internacional," NN UU (2005). UN (2005) In section 78 it states: "Threats to peace and security in the 21st century include not only war and international conflict, but civil unrest, organized crime, terrorism and weapons of mass destruction ... All of these have the potential to undermine states as the basic units of the international system," UN (2005).

[3] Militello (2014), pp. 103–104.

if the drugs *cause serious damage to health* and 1–3 years for other minor cases; while the Italian law against drug trafficking, in its Art. 73, establishes penalties of 8–20 years for hard drugs and 2–6 years for light drugs.

Broad sectors of society generally tend to attribute high levels of seriousness to crimes against persons and to those related to drugs.[4] Homicides, injuries, sexual assaults, thefts, as well as those related to drug trafficking, tend to be on the highest scales of social valuation as the most serious infractions, intolerable for society, especially if criminal organizations are involved. In criminological reality and judicial interpretation, the seriousness of the crimes goes together with *the complexity of the criminal* organization. Indeed, since the purpose is to punish the structure prepared to commit crimes, according to the seriousness of crimes in the criminal program, the structure will be more or less developed and this will denote a greater capacity to perpetrate its criminal intentions. We are dealing with structures suitable for carrying out immediate and secondary crimes that it will only be able to perpetrate when it has the material and personal means suitable for carrying them out. Thus, the greater the complexity of the organization, the greater its injurious capacity. However, this complexity aspect is also related to the distribution of tasks, the professionalism of its members, the capacity to infiltrate in legal business, in political power, etc.).[5]

In this sense, Art. 83 of the EU Treaty establishes:

> The European Parliament and the Council may, by means of directives adopted in accordance with the ordinary legislative procedure, *establish minimum rules concerning the definition of criminal offenses and sanctions in the areas of criminal offenses which are of particular gravity and have a cross-border dimension* resulting from the nature or impact of such offenses or from a particular need to combat them on a common basis... These areas of criminal offenses are the following: *terrorism, human trafficking and sexual exploitation of women and children, illicit drug trafficking, illicit arms trafficking, money laundering, corruption, counterfeiting of means of payment, computer crime and organized crime* ...[.]

Similarly, national anti-crime documents such as the *National Strategy against Organized Crime and Serious Crime 2019-2023*, which reviews and updates the previous Spanish Strategy against Organized Crime 2011–2014, has an impact on the seriousness of offenses. This one states:

> serious crime is considered to be that which affects the major rights or superior goods of the individual (life, liberty, etc.), that which has an intense impact on the values that sustain coexistence (property, ethics, beliefs, etc.) or that which attacks the most socially sensitive areas or aspects (sexual freedom, sensitive or vulnerable victims, such as minors, etc.). When serious crime is perpetrated by a plurality of individuals who expressly agree to commit their criminal activities in large territories, it becomes Organized Crime. Due to its characteristics of transnationality, flexibility, adaptability and resilience, it is also capable of interacting

[4]Torrente (2001), pp. 146–147.

[5]Zúñiga Rodríguez (2015), pp. 121 y ss Conviene diferenciar entre la propia gravedad de los delitos programados y la idoneidad de la organización criminal para realizarlos. Son dos aspectos relacionados, pero distinguibles. It is important to make a distinction between the seriousness of the programmed offenses and the suitability of the criminal organization to carry them out. These are two related but distinguishable aspects.

> with other risk-generating threats, such as armed conflicts, terrorism, proliferation of weapons of mass destruction, espionage, cybercrime and threats to critical infrastructures. (National Security Council 2019, p. 9).

In fact, the different forms of serious crime feed back into other forms of criminality such as terrorism, corruption (public and private) and corporate crime, increasing the vulnerability of societies and their political and economic structures. The international examples of Mexico and Colombia show that, if these challenges are not met decisively and professionally, criminal organizations can eventually put the state itself at risk and become a threat to national security.

International terrorism is unquestionably one of the forms of serious crime of greatest concern to countries. Therefore, also Directive (EU) 2016/681 of the Parliament and of the Council on the use of Passenger Name Record (PNR) data for the prevention, detection, investigation and prosecution of terrorist offenses and serious crime deals with these two connected phenomena, insofar as terrorism needs illegal markets and these provide good supplies and weapons for the perpetration of its crimes. In Spain, this issue has vital importance if we consider that we are a target of Jihadi terrorism, together with France, especially, with complex cultural and religious problems, and adaptation of subjects in Western societies.

However, all these international papers leave a great gap in the conception of *what is to be considered serious crime*, or what material content we give to this concept.

If crime is not only a legal construct but also a social construct, it is appropriate to investigate *how each society assesses the seriousness of its crimes*. It is true that, in plural societies such as Spain's, there may be differences between the evaluations of social groups, by gender, age, race, social position, etc. But it is appropriate to make an exercise of abstraction and try to establish certain consensuses.

In both the community of criminal lawyers and criminologists, serious crime is generally understood as that which causes *great social harm*. However, one issue is the real social harm and other is the perception of social harm, as this depends on many factors, among them, the tolerance of the social group towards deviant behaviors (for example, society usually has more tolerance towards white-collar crime than to violent street crime), the visibility of crimes (some crimes are practically invisible such as human trafficking, others are more visible depending on the *mass* media), the measurement of crimes (crime statistics are usually made from at least four perspectives: detainees/prisoners, victimization, state apparatus, social perception). As Torrente points out: "intolerance towards certain deviant acts is associated with the perception of their seriousness." Therefore, the seriousness of crimes is an assessment that depends a lot on the social perception and the tolerance of society towards these types of crimes and offenders.[6]

The social perception of the seriousness of crime, which is normally linked to the media's handling of information on crime, therefore influences *the fear of crime* (a subjective perception that does not always coincide with the objective reality of

---

[6]Torrente (2001), p. 146.

criminality) and the social demands for greater security, which can lead Criminal Policy to fall into an unsustainable vicious circle of greater punitivism unsupported by a criminal reality. In a classic article Soto Navarro notes:[7]

> [. . .] the media offer a distorted vision of the criminal reality of a country. They can start the coverage of an alleged crime wave, regardless of the rates provided by official data, and also put an end to it.

There are no studies available concerning media coverage of crime in a comparative manner by type of crime, but in general it is easy to see that there is greater coverage of blood crimes, of a violent nature, than those related to white-collar crime. Despite the fact that corruption is a topic that has been in the media nowadays, it tends to be a scandalous matter, too serious to be published in the newspapers. The media treatment of white-collar crime is a thorny issue because it generally involves subjects with economic and/or political power, where public visibility can have consequences and even significant reprisals for those who make the facts public).[8] As this author states:

> [. . .] news related to white-collar crime is presented in a trivial way or virtually ignored. In the story, the person with power or influence, who commits a white-collar crime, is usually perceived as someone who caused a scandal, who committed a slip-up. The problem is usually addressed as an anecdote. From the news narrative, the perpetrator of this type of crime is not even potentially dangerous to society.[9]

From a criminological point of view, the seriousness of the crime is also associated with *the dangerousness* of the perpetrator. Predictions of dangerousness are linked to the possibility that the person will reoffend and that he or she is likely to reoffend in a crime considered serious. A serious crime makes its perpetrator—in many cases—*dangerous* if there is a possibility of repetition. The recidivism of an offense may also result in greater dangerousness and greater severity. Formally and materially, the recidivism and habitual offending, even in the case of minor offenses, is usually considered serious. In the absence of certainty regarding the content of such vague notions as seriousness and dangerousness, there is a risk of falling into an

[7] Soto Navarro (2005), p. 3.

[8] Ojeda Segovia (2013), p. 35.

[9] El autor se fundamenta en un estudio de campo realizado en Ecuador, siguiendo la cobertura de los delitos de cuello blanco en el diario El Comercio, entre los años 2010 y 2012. El estudio destaca "que cuando se trata de fenómenos vinculados con delitos de cuello blanco, la información es de carácter descriptivo, e incluso anecdótico, que el tratamiento de esos hechos, considerados supuestamente como delitos de cuello blanco, ocupa espacios de noticias breves, concretas, con seguimiento precario" (2013, 37). Los resultados hallados, aunque se trate de otra realidad, se pueden reconocer fácilmente en nuestro medio. (The author based his work on a field study conducted in Ecuador, following the coverage of white-collar offenses in the newspaper El Comercio, between 2010 and 2012. The study highlights "that when it is a matter of phenomena linked to white-collar offenses, the information has a descriptive and even anecdotal nature, that the treatment of these facts, supposedly considered as white-collar offenses, occupies spaces of brief, concrete news, with poor follow-up" (2013, 37). The results found, even if it is a different reality, can be easily recognized in our environment.)

Author's Criminal Law, that is, in the negative evaluation of a person or groups of persons because of their way of life, ideology or race. Once again, we can see a bias in the dangerousness of the perpetrator, as it depends on the type of crime committed, social tolerance, the fear of citizens and the perception of insecurity towards them. It is traditional to consider crimes against life, health, sexual aggression, typical of violent street crime, as more dangerous than those considered socioeconomic crimes, committed by white-collar criminals, i.e., those affecting individual legal assets than those affecting collective interests. And this is in many cases due, once again, to the media's handling of information.[10] They do not usually provide homogeneous coverage of crime, but rather focus on street crime, those who produce the *mediatized citizen insecurity*.[11] Therefore, potential victims tend to feel more insecure in relation to street crimes than to those carried out in other contexts, such as business or power. Seriousness seems to have a greater scale when it refers to crimes that cause *social alarm*, whose content is again usually associated with the same kind of crimes and with the expansion of information not always with reference to real data. White-collar crime is not usually considered in the collective imagination as a real threat to the security of citizens, but rather those of a violent nature, those that cause *citizen insecurity*.

Corruption (both public and private) also causes great social damage to society and can even undermine the political and social stability of a country. The Odebrecht case, the *giant that corrupted an entire continent,* provides a good example of this. The case, exposed in December 2016 thanks to the rewarded collaboration of one of its managers in the United States, in compliance with the *Foreign Corrupt Practice Act,* is a clear example of economic transnational organized crime, capable of producing social damage similar to a political and economic earthquake in several states and on several continents.

The 2017 Report prepared by the European Police Office (EUROPOL), *Serious and organised crime threat assessment. Crime in the age of technology* (SOCTA 2017), which analyzes the most important threats of organized and serious crime in the EU, focuses on the (*drivers of crime*), highlighting three aspects: *the geopolitical context,* the *new technologies* and *business structures*. Certainly, wars, natural disasters (often caused by climate change) and the instability of countries are the factors that trigger large-scale migration, a breeding ground for trafficking, sexual exploitation, labor exploitation, human trafficking, crimes in which the most

[10]Como apuntan Parra y Domínguez (2004), p. 50: "La prensa sensacionalista explota el fenómeno delictivo y lo convierte en un producto de entretenimiento y lucro. Los medios, desde su lógica comercial, convierten la violencia en un producto de alto consumo para la opinión pública." En suma, lo que alimenta el consumo de los medios es la violencia y no la delincuencia de cuello blanco, salvo que se trate de personajes VIP. (As stated by Parra and Domínguez (2004), p. 50: "The tabloid press magnifies the criminal phenomenon and turns it into a product for entertainment and profit. The media, from their commercial perspective, turn violence into a product of high consumption for public opinion." In short, what feeds media consumption is violence and not white-collar offenses, except in the case of VIPs.).

[11]Varona Gómez (2011), p. 14.

vulnerable sectors are often the victims: children, women and other marginalized people. On the other hand, new technologies have brought us great advances in communication and information, but at the same time a free space for the development of multiple criminal activities.

Cybercrime is opening up as a new, unexplored field of study for the academy, requiring a multidisciplinary approach.[12] Once again, the lack of visibility and the invisibility of the perpetrators facilitates the commission of crimes and reinforces impunity. The prevention of these behaviors breaks paradigms due to the transnational character, the rapid spread of these behaviors and the consequent impossibility of stopping the social harm they cause. For example, a *fake news* that is not criminal in itself, can cause great social commotion thanks to its expansion.

The use of legal business structures, i.e., the use of shell companies and legal partnerships, has emerged as one of the most important challenges for criminal law, given the fact that it is a crime that takes place in normalized contexts, camouflaging itself in legal activities, it is difficult to detect, very sophisticated, and requires the collaboration of professionals (in many cases very prestigious) such as lawyers, accountants, financial agents, civil servants, police officers, etc. In these cases, the visibility of criminal behavior is also clouded or, at least, altered by the appearance of legality.

All these crimes, which constitute an interweaving of organized crime, private corruption, cybercrime and public corruption, take us to an economic criminal law in which the profit motive, the search for large illicit profits drives this conspiracy between different types of criminality that cause great social damage and, however, have little or at least unrealistic visibility.

3 The Visibility of Crime

It is indisputable that there are new types of crime, new instruments for crime, new social actors with great capacity to cause significant social harm, new legal assets to be protected by criminal law. *Old crimes* are also being modified with respect to their criminal activity by new instruments such as the use of technology or by new social actors such as criminal organizations and legal entities. Therefore, a first starting point for rationalizing penal intervention is to recognize these criminological realities, i.e., political, economic and social relations, which scientific knowledge cannot ignore.

If the criminalization process of behaviors is a complex social and political issue, involving different interests, actors, groups, etc., which has historically shown itself to be unequal or ambiguous, selectively affecting certain groups (usually marginal) and, therefore, affecting less or not affecting others (those who have the defining

[12] Posada Maya (2017).

power)[13], it seems clear that the issue of the *visibility of the crime* is fundamental. As Muncie points out, the core of the crime problem lies in the power to make certain harmful acts visible and define them as crime, while keeping others invisible. The issue of visibility is important because it highlights this process of social construction, how citizens become conscious of the harmfulness of certain behaviors. Visibility affects the perception of behaviors as socially harmful and, consequently, in need of criminalization.[14]

Therefore, *there is a bias in the demands for security,* determined by social perceptions of which behaviors are harmful to society and which are considered less so, which persons should go to jail, which should not or for less time, which victims are especially protected, etc. Social perceptions of criminality are selective, unequal, ambiguous, and produce security demands focused on certain behaviors, on specific sectors, on a certain class of individuals, under the protection of particular interests (legal assets). Of course, this is more evident in unequal societies, where there is greater social conflict, and less so in societies where there are no major class differences, such as in Europe. However, the fact that it is not less evident does not mean that it is non-existent in these societies. In prosperous societies, the prominence of financial crime and profit, socioeconomic crime and corruption are also a constant feature of criminal reality, but their vision as crime is not shared by society as a whole.

This social perception bias, based on the visibility (or visions) of criminality, feeds back into a punitive Criminal Policy focused on the social control of street crime, of the marginalized (poor, immigrants, small-scale dealers), to the detriment

---

[13] Algo que la criminología crítica puso en evidencia hace mucho tiempo. Desde la primera edición del libro de Baratta (1982) *Criminologia critica e critica del diritto penale: introduzione alla sociologia giuridico-penale*, este autor aunando las tesis del etiquetamiento y la sociología del conflicto, sus aportes han señalado este proceso desigual del Derecho Penal. Señala: "Desde la perspectiva de la criminología crítica la criminalidad no es más una cualidad ontológica de determinados comportamientos y de determinados individuos, es sobre todo un estatus asignado a determinados individuos a través de una doble selección: en primer lugar la selección de los bienes protegidos penalmente y de los comportamientos ofensivos de estos bienes recogidos en el tipo penal; en segundo lugar de los individuos estigmatizados entre todos los individuos que cometen infracciones de las normas penalmente sancionadoras. La criminalidad es pues, un 'bien negativo' distribuido desigualmente según la jerarquía d los intereses fijados en el sistema socio-económico y según las desigualdades sociales de los individuos" Baratta (2019), pp. 219–220. Something that critical criminology brought to light a long time ago. Since the first edition of Baratta's book (1982) Criminologia critica e critica del diritto penale: introduzione alla sociologia giuridico-penale, this author, combining the theories of classification and the conflict sociology, his contributions have pointed out this unequal process of criminal law. He states: "From the critical criminology perspective, criminality is no longer an ontological quality of certain behaviors and of particular individuals, it is above all a status assigned to specific individuals through a double selection: firstly the selection of the criminally protected assets and of the offending behaviors of these assets included in the criminal type; secondly the selection of the stigmatized individuals among all individuals who commit infractions of the criminally punishable rules. Criminality is thus a 'negative asset' distributed unequally according to the hierarchy of interests established in the socio-economic system and according to the social differences of individuals."

[14] Rodríguez Mesa (2017), p. 109.

of the visibility of other types of harmful socioeconomic behaviors, typical of the business world, carried out by socially well-placed individuals, which usually take place in normalized contexts, within an ambiguous legality, therefore camouflaged in legal activities. These include the major organized crime bosses who, with financial liberalization, have laundered their money and own *legal enterprises*. In some countries, they live like any *good citizen* thanks to the complicity of police and judicial corruption.

The criminal policies of *zero tolerance*, *broken windows* and *punitive populism* have been modeled on the (supposed) insecurity of the streets, focused on a certain type of violent crime, against people or heritage, often linked to the world of drugs (micro-trafficking and consumption). This selection of behaviors considered harmful to society focuses its attention on certain groups, especially regarding police action (secondary criminalization). The police usually operate with a set of standards: the lower classes are seen as groups susceptible to illegal behaviors and the middle classes enjoy greater sympathy as they are considered "honest people who do not need to commit crimes to make a living."[15]

Knowledge has also been selective. As Días dos Santos points out:[16]

> The old etiological criminology - in a line followed today by the mass media - focused its attention on serious crimes against life and sexual integrity, overlooking the fact that the vast majority of prisoners have always been imprisoned for crimes against property. The criminology of 'social reaction' focuses its attention on the latter -or on forms of subsistence crime-, revealing that the massification of the exercise of punitive power is a response to labeling. By focusing the attention on such disparate facts, the old criminology concealed labeling, the main conditioning factor of imprisonment and, by highlighting only serious – "natural" so to speak - criminality, it legitimized the arbitrary selective exercise of punitive power over the vulnerable ones.

Indeed, in almost all countries, prisons are full of people, mostly young people, linked to crimes against heritage and drugs (micro-traffickers, consumers).

If in the *information society* the social construction of criminality is linked to social visions of the most harmful reality for society, the one that supposedly causes insecurity, the orientation towards a certain sector of crime is clear. The most modern neuroscience studies support the selective consideration of the brain according to what it is capable of seeing (and not seeing). Obviously, the brain cannot detect all the sensory stimuli that exist in reality. According to its function of adaptation and evolution, it selects images, facts and events based on its particular previous experience and the need to adapt to the new circumstances it is presented with. In this specific neurophysiological process, vision plays a central role.[17] On the other hand, this particular consciousness of what we consider *criminality* is conditioned by

---

[15] Torrente (2001), pp. 245–246.

[16] Díaz dos Santos (2021), pp. 91–92

[17] Pellicer Graham (2011).

language, since it is the channel of interaction of and in the world of the human being. In the words of Rodríguez Ortiz:[18]

> [. . .] there are several elements that emerge from neurophysiology, but others that include the interaction with the social and cultural environment, an interaction with the world given in the pragmatic use of language. Language is an element without which it is not possible to speak about consciousness, nor to understand its nature. On the other hand, accepting the biopragmatic nature of consciousness does not imply stating that consciousness is reduced to language, but rather that biology and language make the existence of such a mental state possible. This not only overcomes Cartesian dualism, but also natural/social dualism.

The crime visibility has an impact on the perception of social harm, on the citizens' perception of insecurity, on the fear of crime and finally on the social construction of the collective imaginary concerning the content of criminality, at least, of what can be considered serious crime, with the consequent effects on Criminal Policy.

4 Reasons for an Unequal View of Crime

The cause/effect reasons[19] for this bias are multiple and complex, as is the criminal phenomenon itself. I will try to summarize the most important ones:

First, society generally tends to define as less serious those behaviors in which there is no direct confrontation with the victim (such as white-collar crime), the victim is difficult to identify (prostitution, drug trafficking) or society does not identify itself with the victim (hate crimes, xenophobia, racism).[20] This category also includes so-called consensual crimes, where the alleged victim collaborates with the perpetrator in perfecting the crime, as in the case of corruption or drug trafficking. These are, undoubtedly, crimes in which there is less consensus on the unlawfulness of the act or, at least, they are ambiguous.

Second, tolerance for deviant behaviors committed by socially well-placed individuals tends to be greater than tolerance for marginalized individuals. As Torrente states: "Society tends to tolerate a person who steals wallets less than a businessman who defrauds millions from the Treasury."[21] This happens, among other reasons, because of the complexity of the deviant behavior of white-collar criminals, whose understanding by the public is often beyond their capabilities and interests, and because it is difficult to represent the social harm of their behavior (*they are crimes committed by the rich*). On other occasions, it is the media, thanks to those who have

[18] Rodríguez Ortiz (2017), p. 255.

[19] Resulta difícil distinguir cuáles son causas y cuáles efectos. Lo cierto que entre ellas se retroalimentan y potencian. It is difficult to determine between causes and effects. What is certain is that they feed back on each other and enhance each other.

[20] Rodríguez Mesa (2017), p. 108.

[21] Torrente (2001), p. 76.

media power, who are in charge of emphasizing other crimes (street crimes, violent crimes), to the detriment of those committed by socially well-placed individuals.[22]

Third, in many of the new socioeconomic crimes underrepresented in criminal punishment, the value ambivalence is resolved with moral ambivalence: "the deviation is allowed as long as it is not too visible."[23] The common phrase regarding corruption, *"he steals, but he does work,"* is a good example of the bias with which citizens value the behavior of their governments, with a certain indulgence, as long as it is not *serious*. This double standard is solved with cognitive biases of justification of deviant behavior, as will be seen below.

Fourth, little is known regarding the volume and scope of white-collar crime, because these are behaviors that are complicated to detect, investigate, prosecute and regulate. As mentioned above, they are not usually represented in official crime statistics. Translating human behavior into figures is a complicated[24] analysis in itself, and it is even more complicated when it comes to crimes committed within organizations that serve as a cover for their misdeeds. Breaking down complex events into numerical units is a process that is likely to result in a gap between legal definitions of crime and criminal reality.

Fifth, in addition, these crimes are usually committed by *reputable criminals*—sometimes in complicity with *men of honor*—whose activities are usually subject to the control of their own profession, occupation or guild. Sometimes they act with the support or tolerance of certain sectors within their profession. As they are part of professional actions, they are difficult to identify and, although disciplinary control mechanisms exist within each profession, they function little or not at all.

[22] Es fácil percibir en los medios una noticia sobre delitos de cuello blanco una vez, pero luego no hay seguimiento del caso. Por ejemplo, la noticia de *El País*, 30 de Octubre de 2019, "La multinacional española FCC, imputada por corrupción por pagar sobornos en Panamá" Segoviano (2019). La investigación se centra en el pago de 82 millones de euros para la adjudicación de la construcción de líneas del metro y de la Ciudad de la Salud en dicho país, ha tenido poco seguimiento con posterioridad. En cambio, los delitos de sangre, violentos, suelen tener un seguimiento más incisivo, seguramente porque concita más interés de la opinión pública. It is easy to notice some news about white-collar offenses in the media once, but then there is no follow up on the case. For example, the news in El Pais, October 30, 2019, "Spanish multinational FCC, charged with corruption for paying bribes in Panama" Segoviano (2019). The research focuses on the payment of 82 million euros for the award of the construction of subway lines and the Health City in that country, has had little follow-up subsequently. On the other hand, blood crimes, violent crimes, usually have a more intense follow-up, probably because they generate more interest from the public opinion.

[23] Torrente (2001), p. 82.

[24] Como apunta Torrente (2001), p. 95: "Las estadísticas son armas de varios filos: sirven para mostrar un trabajo realizado, justificar necesidades y legitimar demandas, como instrumento para la gestión, como elemento de control, sirven de base para la investigación o para presentar imágenes favorables al exterior." As Torrente (2001), p. 95, states: "Statistics are multi-edged weapons: they are used to show the work done, to justify needs and legitimize demands, as a management tool, as an element of control, as a basis for research or to present favorable images to the outside world."

Sixth, white-collar criminals, individuals who use their profession or occupation to illegally obtain illicit benefits, do not consider themselves criminals[25]—sometimes the legal operators themselves do not consider them either—and are capable of rationalizing these behaviors, by developing a philosophy that makes them see their behavior as reasonable, whose reasoning turns around the idea that *almost everyone is dishonest*, or *everyone has committed some act of corruption*.[26] This is the *presentation bias*, the tendency to evaluate events according to a more or less personal way of presenting the facts, at one's own convenience.[27]

From all that has been explained up to this point, it can be inferred that in terms of the criminalization of behaviors, *not all of them are all that they are, nor are they all that they are.* Punitive populism and the criminal law of security, which is its correlate, have focused on one type of crime: street crime, marginal crime, mostly violent, towards which the criminal reforms of new criminalization and increased penalties have been fundamentally directed. Another type of crime is thus overlooked, that linked to business and power,[28] under-represented in the statistics, not very visible in the media and prosecuted with difficulty by legal operators, which in recent times have shown great social harm. Therefore, criminal intervention in these cases may be legitimate under certain conditions of proportionality (necessity and deserved punishment).

5 Crime Statistics (What We See and What We Do Not See)

It is difficult to translate into numbers those complex events considered crimes that affect people's lives and feelings, even more so those considered socioeconomic. The paradox is that Criminology needs statistical data to elaborate studies and design proposals, but these are extremely difficult to develop scientifically. The need to establish political-criminal proposals based on empirical evidence, that is, on figures obtained regarding crime, is a demand of broad academic sectors, especially as an antidote to a punitive populism that is based simply on diffuse fear and symbolic

---

[25] Por ese motivo la posibilidad de reincidencia es alta. For this reason, the possibility of recurrence is high.

[26] Torrente (2001), pp. 82–83. También *para qué pago impuestos, si todos son corruptos*, dice el corrupto. En suma, todo depende del propio relato que el delincuente se hace a sí mismo y a los suyos. Torrente (2001), pp. 82–83. Also why do I pay taxes, if everyone is corrupt, says the corrupt. In short, everything depends on the story that the offender tells himself and his own.

[27] Vilarroya (2019), p. 171.

[28] Sin contar con la cantidad de personalidades aforadas, con inmunidades personales para ser procesadas, los indultos, plazos de prescripción más cortos, etc. Without considering the number of personalities with personal immunities to be prosecuted, pardons, shorter statute of limitations, etc.

responses.[29] Undoubtedly, to prevent criminal phenomena, it is essential to know them well, using empirical data collected in a rational way.

However, with regard to socioeconomic crimes, there is an under-representation of their actual figures. Even assuming that in all types of crime there is a black figure of crime, the fact is that these crimes are practically not included in the statistics.

If we refer to police statistics, considered the most reliable data on crime reporting in Spain,[30] we can see the breakdown of criminal typologies highly represented by street crime. The *Statistical Yearbook of the Ministry of the Interior*, which publishes quarterly reports (Ministry of the Interior 2020a), states:

1. Intentional homicides and completed murders
2. Intentional homicides and attempted murders
3. Serious and less serious crimes of assault and rioting
4. Kidnappings
5. Crimes against sexual freedom and indemnity
6. Robberies with violence and intimidation
    6.1. Sexual assault with penetration
    6.2. Other offenses against sexual freedom and indemnity
7. Burglary in homes, establishments and other facilities
8. Theft
9. Vehicle theft
10. Drug Trafficking
11. Other criminal offenses

As can be seen, there is not a single reference to crimes related to corruption, power or business, those considered socioeconomic crimes. Obviously, this selection obviously denotes a vision focused on a certain type of crime and, consequently, an oversight or at least a distraction regarding other types of crime. Apparently, the only forms of crime are those that show signs of violence, something that

[29] Benito Sánchez (2020) La autora desarrolla la necesidad de contar en España con cifras sobre la criminalidad, con el fin de elaborar propuestas basadas en la evidencia empírica y poder evaluar con posterioridad dichas propuestas, siguiendo recomendaciones de la UE. Benito Sánchez (2020) The author develops the need to have figures regarding criminality in Spain to elaborate proposals based on empirical evidence and to be able to subsequently evaluate such proposals, following EU recommendations.

[30] A falta de encuestas de victimización, o de informes de autodenuncias. Cfr. Benito Sánchez (2020), pp. 52 y ss. También Serrano Tárraga (2017), p. 159: "son las más fiables de las estadísticas oficiales, frente a las estadísticas judiciales realizadas por el Consejo General del Poder Judicial y la Fiscalía General del Estado, que por la metodología utilizada en la recogida de datos, no son un instrumento válido para medir el volumen de criminalidad en nuestro país." In the absence of victimization surveys, or self-reporting reports. Cfr. Benito Sánchez (2020), pp. 52 et seq. Also, Serrano Tárraga (2017), p. 159: "they are the most reliable of the official statistics, as opposed to the judicial statistics carried out by the General Council of the Judiciary and the State Attorney General's Office, which, due to the methodology used in data collection, are not a valid instrument for measuring criminality volume in our country."

criminological reality has far surpassed. It seems that our penal code has remained in the classic crimes, natural crimes,[31] without considering that society has been modified and has elevated to the category of serious crime a series of behaviors carried out from the profession, power or organizations, which are of a collective nature.

The classification of crimes offered by the *Annual Report of the State Attorney General's Office* introduces greater visibility to socioeconomic crimes, given that the report is made according to the Titles of the CP.[32]

1. Crimes against life and physical integrity
2. Domestic violence crimes
3. Torture crimes
4. Crimes against freedom
5. Crimes against sexual freedom and indemnity
6. Crimes against family relationships
7. Crimes against heritage and socioeconomic order
8. Misrepresentation offenses
9. Crimes against Public Administration
10. Crimes against the Administration of Justice
11. Crimes against public order

[31] Sobre la naturaleza de los delitos existe bastante discusión, especialmente si existen *delitos naturales*, esto es, distinguibles de otro tipo de infracciones. Como recuerda Berdugo (2018), pp. 25–26, al comentar la primera obra sobre el derecho de castigar, que es de Alfonso de Castro (1550): "Bastantes de las tesis que defendía Alfonso de Castro, aunque formuladas en el contexto político y religioso de aquel entonces, marcan líneas de razonamiento trasladables al momento actual. En aquella época, la justificación del carácter delictivo de una conducta se plasmaba en el *quia pecatum est*... Alfonso de Castro tomó como punto de partida una triple clasificación de leyes: las morales, las puramente penales y las mixtas. Las morales no establecían pena, quedaban fuera del Derecho Penal, tan sólo tenían el reproche derivado de la religión, no así las meramente penales y las mixtas. Éstas últimas, en aquel momento histórico la mayoría, tenían el doble reproche, el moral y la pena, mientras que las denominadas 'leyes meramente penales', sólo eran acreedoras del castigo de la pena." Éstas últimas sólo suponían una desobediencia a la ley, a un mandato real y no divino. Hoy en día la discusión se traslada a la diferenciación con otras infracciones, como las administrativas y disciplinarias. There is considerable discussion regarding the nature of offenses, especially if there are natural crimes, in other words, distinct from other types of infractions. As Berdugo (2018), pp. 25–26, points out when referring to the first work on the right to punish, by Alfonso de Castro (1550): "Many of the ideas defended by Alfonso de Castro, although formulated in the political and religious context of that time, mark lines of reasoning that can be transferred to the current time. At that time, the criminal nature of a conduct was justified by the quia pecatum est.... Alfonso de Castro adopted as a starting point a triple classification of laws: the moral, the mixed and the purely penal. Moral laws did not establish penalties, they were outside Criminal Law, they only had the punishment derived from religion, but not the purely penal and mixed laws. The latter, in that historical moment the most part, had the double punishment, the moral and the penalty, while the so-called 'merely penal laws', were only deserving of the punishment of the penalty." The latter only involved disobedience to the law, to a real and not divine mandate. Today, the discussion moves to the differentiation with other infractions, such as administrative and disciplinary ones.

[32] Benito Sánchez (2020), p. 70. (Tabla 10).

The data provided by the Special Prosecutor's Office against Corruption and Organized Crime are more specific regarding these crimes, as could not be otherwise.[33]

1. Tax, Social Security and smuggling offenses
2. Prevarication
3. Abuse or inappropriate use of insider information
4. Embezzlement of public funds
5. Fraud and illegal exactions
6. Influence peddling
7. Bribery
8. Negotiations prohibited to officials
9. Frauds
10. Punishable insolvencies
11. Corporate crimes
12. Money laundering
13. Corruption in international business transactions
14. Private sector corruption
15. Related crimes
16. Organized crime

The data provided by the Ministry of the Interior regarding prison statistics by type of crime are based on this consideration (Ministry of the Interior 2020b):

1. Homicide and its forms
2. Injuries
3. Against freedom
4. Against sexual freedom
5. Against honor
6. Crimes and offenses of gender violence
7. Against family relationships
8. Against heritage and socioeconomic order
9. Against public health
10. Against traffic safety
11. Falsehoods
12. Against the administration and Treasury
13. Against the Administration of Justice
14. Against Public Order
15. Other Crimes

Once again, the visibility of socioeconomic crimes is in question, and this is even more understandable in the penitentiary environment, since the perpetrators who reach prison are not usually white-collar criminals. These are only now being

[33] Benito Sánchez (2020), p. 71. (Tabla 12).

represented in the prison figures in recent years in which custodial sentences are being applied to perpetrators of socioeconomic crimes.

It is worth considering, why is it difficult to translate socio-economic crime into figures? And the answer we will see that is connected to their visibility and complexity. Beyond the reasons for which some crimes are more visible than others previously mentioned, the fact is that socioeconomic crimes tend to be of a complexity that makes them difficult to detect and to translate into figures.

Plurality of intervening subjects: organized schemes, criminal organizations, legal entities, multiple persons intervening over time.

Plurality of victims: there are usually groups affected, but collective interests that are difficult to delimit. Some crimes produce an indefinite number of victims. In some cases, as we have seen, the victim cooperates with the crime, therefore, he/she will not denounce or collaborate with the justice system.

Collective legal assets: the determination of harmfulness in many cases is extremely difficult given the immateriality of some legal interests. For example, damage to the environment.

Complex causation: the determination of the agents causing the injury to legal assets is usually one of the most pressing problems, because many people, organizations and causal factors may be involved over time.

Plurality of criminal types: many of the socioeconomic crimes are presented as organized plots that perpetrate several crimes, not to mention that some of them are complex in themselves, as is the case of money laundering (laundering money derived from another crime).

All these elements mean that socioeconomic crime statistics, which are static records, are unable to reflect such dynamic events.

If criminal statistics are in themselves the result of a certain degree of discretion, the issue becomes more complicated when it comes to such complex criminal events as socio-economic crime, which in many cases uses financial engineering, corporate networks, tax havens, front men, etc.

As Torrente states, in any statistical count there are decisions to be made regarding which situations to include and which to exclude, regarding the measurement unit (victims, offenders, crimes), as well as the decomposition of complex events into units (which units to take?). In Spain, crimes are usually taken as the unit of measurement, but what happens with repeat offenses? When we are in front of behaviors that are complex in themselves, the discretion of these decisions becomes a matter of particular magnitude, even more so when dealing with events that are carried out covertly under the cloak of business, public contracts, private contracts, which show a legal face.[34]

The above-mentioned classifications of statistics by type of crime are a good example of this discretional nature in which some crimes tend to be highlighted in the sights of social demands for punishment, normally linked to violent crimes, to

[34] Torrente (2001), p. 94.

the detriment of other types of crimes that are less visible in the social reality and in many cases have a great criminogenic capacity (social harm).

Undoubtedly, this representation of crimes in statistical graphs reveals a great deal about the social construction of crime, its seriousness (social perception of the harmfulness of behaviors) and its subsequent criminal prosecution.

6 Conclusions

1. There is a correlate in the social consideration of serious delinquency, visibility, social tolerance towards deviant behaviors and demands for punishment. Thus, punitivism is selective; it tends to have a bias in favor of the criminal prosecution of street crimes, violent crimes against individuals, to the detriment of socioeconomic crimes, against collective legal assets that are more difficult to identify.
2. If crime is a social construct, it is necessary to focus attention on the mechanisms by which certain crimes are made visible and others, mostly associated with power and business, such as corruption, non-violent organized crime and white-collar crime in general, are made invisible or at least less visible.
3. For some time now, the media have been denouncing the bias in their treatment of crime, focusing on expanding certain crimes and giving little coverage to other forms of crime associated with de facto, economic or political powers. This unequal coverage is usually relevant for the visibility of crime and for the social construction of criminality, with the subsequent social demands for greater or lesser punishment.
4. Statistics, the media and the prosecution services have made certain forms of crime visible, while making invisible other forms of crime that can be extremely serious, such as public and private corruption, organized crime, crimes committed in the sphere of business and power, which often take place in normalized contexts, camouflaged under the law.
5. Particularly graphic of the greater or lesser visibility of certain crimes is the criminal typology of criminal statistics in Spain. Both police and prison statistics, especially, under-represent socioeconomic crimes, clearly tipping the balance in favor of violent, street crime, the so-called classic crimes such as homicides, injuries, thefts, sexual aggressions, etc.
6. The main reasons why it is difficult to translate dynamic events such as crimes occurring in the area of business and power into static figures are linked to their complexity and lower real visibility: plurality of perpetrators, plurality of victims, collective legal assets, complex causality, plurality of criminal types. It is not surprising, therefore, that this type of crime is difficult to quantify.
7. Therefore, the recognized expansion of criminal law based on social demands for public safety tends to emphasize greater punishment of classic crimes, those that are more visible and pose a greater direct threat to people. Socioeconomic crimes, on the other hand, given the complexity of these behaviors, which makes their

visibility more difficult and the social harm less perceptible, tend to be less represented in official crime figures and are less likely to be prosecuted.

References

Baratta A (2019) Criminologia critica e critica del diritto penale. Introduzione alla sociología giuridico-penale. Meltemi, Milán

Benito Sánchez D (2020) Evidencia empírica y populismo punitivo. El diseño de la Política Criminal. Bosch, Barcelona

Berdugo G d l TI (2018) Reflexiones penales desde Salamanca. "Decían ayer, decimos hoy, dirán mañana.". Iustel, Madrid

Consejo de Seguridad Nacional (2019) Estrategia Nacional contra el Crimen Organizado y la Delincuencia Grave 2019-2023, La Seguridad es un Proyecto Común. Gobierno de España, Ministerio de la Presidencia, Relaciones con las Corte e Igualdad, Madrid

Díaz dos Santos I (2021) La perenne expansión del poder punitivo: una selectividad jurídico-penal abisal. BdeF, Buenos Aires

Militello V (2014) L'identità della scienza giuridica penale nell'ordinamento multilivello. Rivista italiana de Diritto e procedura penale 1:106–132

Ministerio del Interior (2020a) Base de datos: Anuario estadístico del Ministerio del Interior, Ministerio del Interior, Gobierno de España, http://www.interior.gob.es/web/archivos-y-documentacion/documentacion-y-publicaciones/anuarios-y-estadisticas Acceso 15 de noviembre de 2020

Ministerio del Interior (2020b) Base de datos: Fondos documental, Estadísticas Penitenciarias, Ministerio del Interior, Gobierno de España, https://www.institucionpenitenciaria.es/es/web/home/fondo-documental/estadistica-penitenciaria Acceso 15 de noviembre de 2020

Naciones Unidas (2005) Informe del Secretario General A/59/2005, de 21 de marzo de 2005, Un concepto más amplio de la libertad: desarrollo, seguridad y derechos humanos para todos, correspondiente al Quincuagésimo noveno período de sesiones, Temas 45 y 55 del programa, Aplicación y seguimiento integrados y coordinados de los resultados de las grandes conferencias y cumbres de las Naciones Unidas en las esferas económica y social y esferas conexas. Seguimiento de los resultados de la Cumbre del Milenio

Ojeda Segovia L (2013) Tratamiento mediático de los delitos de cuello blanco y del poder. Chasqui. Revista Latinoamericana de Comunicación 122:31–38.

Parra González AV, Domínguez Torre M (2004) Los medios de comunicación desde la perspectiva del delincuente. Opción, Revista de Ciencias Humanas y Sociales 20(44):28–54 http://ve.scielo.org/scielo.php?script=sci_arttext&pid=S1012-15872004000200003&lng=es&tlng=es Acceso 15 de noviembre de 2020

Pellicer Graham F (2011) Conciencia y visión. La mirada dentro del ojo. Ciencia, octubre-diciembre 4(62):40–47. https://www.revistaciencia.amc.edu.mx/images/revista/62_4/PDF/ConcienciaVision.pdf Acceso 15 de noviembre de 2020

Posada Maya R (2017) Los cibercrímenes: Un nuevo paradigma de criminalidad. Universidad de los Andes, Bogotá

Rodríguez Mesa MJ (2017) La redefinición del crimen como propuesta de una Criminología global. Archivos de Criminología, seguridad privada y Criminalística 18:97–114

Rodríguez Ortiz A (2017) Hacia una visión biopragmática de la conciencia humana. Cuadernos de Filosofia Latinoamericana 116:237–258

Segoviano EG (2019) La multinacional española FCC, imputada por corrupción por pagar sobornos en Panamá. El País, 30 de octubre, Sección de Actualidad. https://elpais.com/economia/2019/10/30/actualidad/1572438853_383908.html Acceso 15 de noviembre de 2020

Serrano Tárraga D (2017) La medición del delito y la importancia de sus aportaciones para la Criminología contemporánea. Revista de Derecho UNED 20:127–160. http://revistas.uned.es/index.php/RDUNED/article/view/19473 Acceso 15 de noviembre de 2020

Soto Navarro S (2005) La influencia de los medios en la percepción social de la delincuencia, Revista Electrónica de Ciencia Penal y Criminología (7–9):1–46 http://criminet.ugr.es/recpc/07/recpc07-09.pdf Acceso 15 de noviembre de 2020

Torrente D (2001) Desviación y delito. Alianza, Madrid

Varona Gómez D (2011) Medios de comunicación y punitivismo. InDret (1):1–34 https://indret.com/wp-content/themes/indret/pdf/791_1.pdf Acceso 15 de noviembre de 2020

Vilarroya O (2019) Somos lo que nos contamos. Ariel, Barcelona

Zúñiga Rodríguez L (2015) Problemas de interpretación de los tipos de organización criminal y grupo criminal. Estudio a la luz de la realidad criminológica y de la jurisprudencia. En Pérez F. y Zúñiga L (eds) Instrumentos jurídicos y operativos en la lucha contra el tráfico internacional de drogas. Thomson Reuter, Pamplona, pp 91–138

The manufacturer's authorised representative in the EU is Springer Nature Customer Service Centre GmbH, Europaplatz 3, 69115 Heidelberg, Germany. If you have any concerns regarding our products, please contact ProductSafety@springernature.com

Printed and bound by CPI Group (UK) Ltd, Croydon, CR0 4YY
28/09/2026
02224070-0010